# Hidden Shakespeare

## A BIOGRAPHY

## NICHOLAS FOGG

AMBERLEY

# About the Author

Nicholas Fogg is an expert on Shakespeare's life and works and has lectured widely on the subject. He is a Fellow of Queen's University, Ontario. His other books include *Stratford-upon-Avon: Portrait of a Town*, and he is currently writing a new history of the Globe theatre, also for Amberley. He lives in Marlborough.

*For Edwina*

*To my fair friend you never can be old*

This edition first published 2013

Amberley Publishing
The Hill, Stroud
Gloucestershire, GL5 4EP

www.amberley-books.com

British Library Cataloguing in Publication Data.
A catalogue record for this book is available from the British Library.

ISBN 978 1 4456 1436 6

Typesetting and Origination by Amberley Publishing.
Printed in the UK.

# Contents

# Preface

'My Loveinge good ffrend & contryman'
— Letter from Richard Quiney to
William Shakespeare, 1598

## 'Between Heaven and Woolworth's'

The Liverpool poet Brian Patten describes his birth as taking place 'somewhere between Heaven and Woolworth's'. If I were to make the same claim, the store in question would be as unique as Heaven, because the branch of that chain store in Stratford-upon-Avon was the only one whose façade was painted in gold. Perhaps it was considered to stand on sacred ground, reflecting the feelings about the place expressed by James Boswell during David Garrick's famous Stratford Jubilee of 1769. Delighted with the occasion, he dashed off celebratory verses and rushed them round to one Fulke Weale, who advertised printing at one hour's notice. 'I suppose taking it for granted that Stratford would produce a general poetic inspiration that would exert itself every hour.'

Boswell's view of the literary prowess of the Stratfordians was not shared by other Jubilites. One remarked on their 'wonderful vacancy of Phiz', a sentiment shared a century later by the music publisher Vincent Novello. 'In most places the Almighty spreads His Genius through the population, but in His inscrutable Wisdom, in Stratford-upon-Avon he poured it all into one man, which has left all the other inhabitants bereft of wit for generations to come.'

As an old Stratfordian, I'm proud to have given my share of genius to William Shakespeare – and there were compensations in so doing. One of my companions on the school bus was a rose-cheeked lass called Sue Hathaway. When I came to man's estate, the barmaid in my local was called Judith Quiney – the married surname of Shakespeare's younger daughter. Most impressive of all was Sid Shakespeare, the first local to appear in the gear of the 50s youth cult, the Teddy boys. His bootlace tie, crepe soles, winkle pickers and fluorescent socks earned him the title 'King of the Teds'.

I must mention also that my sister-in-law is a descendent of Shakespeare's Aunt Kate and that therefore my genes must mingle with his through my brother's children. Even when I became the Mayor of my adopted town of Marlborough, I couldn't escape the Bard. One of my predecessors, John Walford, was sued by the poet's father for debt.

A final bonding with the Bard comes from the fact that we share the same birthday. Tradition says that he was born on 23 April by the reckoning of the Julian Calendar, which miscalculated the length of the year by 11 minutes. When Shakespeare was seventeen, the Pope introduced the Gregorian Calendar, which corrected this error. At the time of the reform the accumulated error was ten days, so 23 April is in fact 3 May. My birthday!

I can't remember how old I was when I realised that every place in the kingdom did not possess a theatre of international fame. I suppose there must have been a time when Prince Charles realised that he was not quite like every other boy! When I was a kid, older folk in Stratford used to compare the performances of actors like Peggy Ashcroft, Paul Scofield and Lawrence Olivier to those of a lost golden age: Ellen Terry, Basil Rathbone, Robert Donat and Sir Herbert Beerbohm Tree. It was Tree who, on being met at Stratford station before performing on Shakespeare's birthday, when the town was *en fête* with buntings and flags, murmured, 'Is this kind thought for my arrival?'

The most dominant name of all was that of Sir Frank Benson, who was often referred to as 'Pa'. He effectively began the artistic life of the theatre after its foundation by a local brewer, Charles Flower. Thus what is now the Royal Shakespeare Theatre was founded by local effort – as was its counterpart in Stratford, Ontario. This the two Stratfords have in common, and it must have contributed much to their mutual fame and success.

Benson's company was as much remembered for its prowess on the sporting field as on the stage. 'Send me a good fast bowler to play Laertes,' Pa is reputed to have once telegraphed his agent. He was an exponent of what we would now call community theatre. The old touring companies would recruit locals to play the extras wherever they visited. In Stratford these were known as 'supers'. Benson liked to think he'd picked them from Shakespeare's relations. 'Of course, they'll be bastards. Bound to be.'

Another fortune of my childhood was that a theatrical legend was in digs just a few doors away: one with bushy eyebrows and a subterranean voice. My first visit to the theatre was to see Donald Wolfit's *Tamberlaine*. I saw Albert Finney's version at the opening of the National Theatre a few years ago and was amazed that my mum could have unleashed such a trail of blood, torture and rapine on my young mind. Of Wolfit's performance I remember nothing, except that, at the end, a hand appeared and then the figure of our neighbour swung on the curtain in superbly played exhaustion.

Wolfit began every rehearsal with the words, 'There are very few of us left.' I suppose that there are now none of them left, but the phrase may be taken as a theatrical motto in any age. It could have been said by William Shakespeare during the period between 1592 and 1594 when the infant theatre was shut by plague and the actors' companies were literally decimated. The year of 1592 is a significant date in Shakespearean biography. The poet is then first mentioned as being in London, not as an obscure actor, but as a hugely successful playwright. He had come a long way since the previous extant mention of his name seven years before as the father in the baptismal record of his twin children, Hamnet and Judith. What happened to him in these years is the subject of much speculation and represents a formidable hurdle for his biographers. Yet we can be certain that Stratford-upon-Avon must have contributed greatly to the formative years of the child who was father to the man Shakespeare.

Imagine that we are the gods on Mount Olympus. It is our task to create the greatest writer who ever lived. That he would be a genius goes without saying, but that does not get us very far. The theme of Gray's *Elegy* is that the village is full of farm labourers whose lives, under other circumstances, might have been entirely different. If William Shakespeare were alive today he may have become a mute inglorious computer programmer, so we must bear in mind that the time, culture and place that we select are essential to the project.

# Acknowledgements

I would like to thank Brian Ashley, Dr Tom Axworthy, Mavis Cheek, Antoni Cimolino, Dr Robert Bearman, Dom Aidan Bellenger, Richard Demarco, Andrew Douglas, Kathy Hamilton, Prof. John Haldane, Mary and Lawrence James, Ernest Thorp, Catherine Maxwell-Stuart, Mairi Macdonald, Sylvia Morris, Dr Richard Ough, Dr Patrick Spottiswoode, Alan Sutton, Helen Redfern and Prof. Wilhelm Vossenkuhl.

This work is largely the product of invitations to speak at the following places, for which I am grateful: Bath University, Ludwig Maximillion University, Edinburgh Festival at Traquair House, Marlborough Literary Festival, Redlands University, Shakespeare's Globe Theatre, the Royal College of General Practitioners, Marlborough College Summer School, St Leonard's School, Eton College, Downside School, and the Shakespeare Festival, Stratford, Ontario.

# 1

# The Background, 1550–69

'The first of all the swains'

– David Garrick, 1759

In the eighteenth century, Shakespeare's works didn't fit into the classical models that were imposed on literature. To get round this, two things happened. The works were rewritten by virtually anyone who chose to have a crack at them, while the poet himself was recycled as an untutored genius: a kind of Warwickshire version of Man Friday. He was Rousseau's 'Natural Man', unsullied by the tainting force of corrupt civilisation, a thought expressed in the songs David Garrick wrote for his Jubilee in 1759.

> The pride of Nature was sweet Willy O,
> The first of all the swains,
> He gladden'd the plains,
> None ever was like to Sweet Willy O.

Yet William Shakespeare was neither from a humble background, nor was he ill-educated. He came from the same class of skilled artisans that begat Christopher Marlowe, a shoemaker's son, and Ben Jonson, whose stepfather was a bricklayer. As a young man, John Shakespeare, his father, left his father's farm in the village of Snitterfield, 3 miles from Stratford, to serve a craft apprenticeship before becoming a member of the 'Mystery, Craft or Occupation of the Glovers, Whittawers and Collarmakers'. In this he prospered. By the early 1550s, he was living and working in his now-famous house in Henley Street. He had become a member of that class of tradesmen who would constitute Stratford's elite for the next four centuries.

Because of its monastic foundation Stratford did not send two members to Parliament, as did most boroughs of similar importance, but its population of around 1,600 was comparable to that of such places as Warwick and Banbury. Indeed it was around half that of Edinburgh, Scotland's major city, but not yet its capital.

John Shakespeare made his first inauspicious entry into the records when he was fined 12 pence for keeping an unauthorised muckheap outside his front door. This was no disgrace. Among others fined for the same offence was the current Bailiff. Tudor Stratford was an Augean Stable, where the stench of animal dung mingling with the refuse of trade and markets was exacerbated by ill-paved streets and open ditches.

Henley Street was a thoroughfare of many trades. Other glovers and 'whittawers' resided there and must have used the water from the stream which ran across the street and into Merepool Lane for dampening skins. The Shakespeares' immediate neighbour was William Wedgwood, a tailor of dubious reputation who was expelled from his native Warwick after behaviour so scandalous that it even attracted the attention of the mighty Earl in his castle. The *Black Book of Warwick* recorded that

> leaving his wief he went to Stratford and divers other places and there married another wief, his first wief yet living; besides that he is a man very contentious, prowde and slanderous, oft busieing himself with naughty matters and quarrelling with his honest neighbours, which condicions forcing him to leave the place of good government first went from hence and afterward was compellid to goo from Stratford.

In 1573, John Shakespeare witnessed a land sale between Wedgwood and his other neighbour, Richard Hornby, a blacksmith whose shop was also an alehouse. William Shakespeare sued Hornby's son for a debt in 1609. In *King John* there is an apparent memory of these childhood neighbours.

> I saw a smith stand with his hammer, thus,
> The while his iron did on anvil cool,
> With open mouth swallowing a tailor's news,
> Who with his shears and measure in his hand,
> Standing on slippers, which his nimble haste,
> Had falsely thrust on contrary feet.

Like most Elizabethan tradesmen, John Shakespeare speculated in commodities. Nicholas Rowe, an early biographer, accurately described him as 'a considerable dealer in wool'. The extant records confirmed that he was a freelance wooldealer, or 'brogger'. A price would be agreed with farmers in the spring and the wool acquired after shearing in May or June. In 1571, he spent £210 on wool, mainly from Westminster, then a village near London, and from his own village of Snitterfield. The wool would then be sold at a large profit in regional markets.

When the parlour floor of the Birthplace was re-laid in the Regency era, 'remnants of wool, and the refuse of wool-combing' were found embedded in the foundations. A more recent discovery showed that, in 1599, John Shakespeare sued John Walford, who was three times Mayor of Marlborough, for a debt of £21 incurred thirty years before. This was for 21 tods (i.e. 588 lb), so John was indeed 'a considerable dealer'. Walford, a clothier, must have been a long-time customer of John Shakespeare. He had fallen on hard times, so the action may have been a friendly one to establish the right over long-standing credit.

Wool was to England what oil is to Texas. The most important official in the land, the Lord Chancellor, sits not on a golden throne in his role as Speaker of the House of Lords, but on a Woolsack. As Richard Hakluyt expressed it:

> But Flemings if yee bee not wroth,
> The great substance of your cloth at the full
> Yee wot ye make it of our English woll.

The vital trade was highly regulated and 'brogging' was technically illegal. In 1572, John Shakespeare was accused of illegal dealing under a Statute of the Merchants of the Staple designed to prevent the buying of wool by private individuals.

John Shakespeare made an excellent marriage with Mary Arden, the daughter of his father's landlord. His business acumen must have been observed by her father, for when Robert Arden of Wilmcote died he made him effectively his chief heir, dividing his property between his eight daughters but leaving the largest portion to his 'youngste daughter Marye'. For those who would like Will Shakespeare to have an appropriate genealogy, no better forebears can be found than the Ardens, whose very name is synonymous with the ancient Warwickshire forest and whose Saxon ancestry can be traced beyond the Norman Conquest. The Ardens of Wilmcote appear to have been connected to the aristocratic Arden family of Park Hall at Castle Bromwich, although the exact relationship is unclear.

In 1568, John Shakespeare applied to the College of Heralds for the right to bear a coat of arms. He was Bailiff (Mayor) of Stratford and this was his entitlement. For some reason, perhaps the cost, he did not proceed with the application. It was revived in 1596 and the plea was granted. Doubtless the social standing of William as a familiar of the royal court and the wealth he had acquired as a prominent man-of-the-theatre was influential in the decision to apply again. The Heralds sketched out the coat of arms that flies today over the Shakespearean properties in Stratford: a gold and silver spear, an obvious pun on the family name. Three years later, John Shakespeare applied for the right to quarter his newly gained coat of arms with that of the Park Hall Ardens. Later a design with the arms of a more obscure family of the same name from Cheshire was substituted. The implication is that the Shakespeares could not prove a connection with the Park Hall Ardens to the satisfaction of the Heralds. In fact, in a revision of the second application they downgraded Robert Arden from the coveted status of 'Gent' to the lesser one of 'Esquire'.

It is not uncommon for people to claim vague connections with the upper crust, but this does not mean there was no consanguinity in this instance. It's likely that it was so far in the past that it was a tradition without detail: something recounted by Mary Shakespeare to her children. In a subsequent explanatory note after the award of arms was queried, the Heralds added that John Shakespeare had 'maryed a daughter and heyre of Arden', but they are unspecific about the claim.

If indeed, as appears likely, William Shakespeare could claim some unspecified relationship with the noble family of Arden, he could also claim descent from Turchillus de Aerdine – Turhill de Arden – who is recorded as possessing lands in Warwickshire that filled four columns of the Domesday Book. His wife was Leverunia, granddaughter of the Earl Leofric of Mercia. This is the route to the putative descent from Alfred the Great. If it is to be followed, there stands an even more romantic figure in the line: none other than Lady Godiva, the wife of Earl Leofric, she of the nude ride of legend.

The Heralds also state that John Shakespeare's grandfather had done service for King Henry VII. There is no reason to doubt this. The King's reign was much troubled by revolts, so tenants of Midland farms under the lordship of the Earl of Warwick may well have been enlisted.

John Shakespeare's father, Richard, held his lands from Robert Arden. He was quite well off. On his death in 1560, his goods were valued at £35 17s 0d and he possessed a team of four oxen. He appears to have moved to Snitterfield before 1535 from the parish of Wroxall 6 miles away, where his family had lived for generations.

The Heralds state that John Shakespeare had been a 'justice of the peace and Bailiff[1], and a Queen's officer'. This was true. Since he had joined the oligarchy of families that dominated Stratford life, he was obliged to play his part in civic affairs. An Elizabethan borough was no democracy. Power was in the hands of the Capital Burgesses – those who were wealthy enough to pay the Poor Rate. An elaborate system of fines made it difficult to refuse service.

John Shakespeare's rise in the corporate hierarchy was rapid. In 1556, he achieved the enviable role of ale-taster to the Leet Court with a right to sample in the town's thirty alehouses. One of his responsibilities would have been to guard the people's brew against the introduction of hops 'and other subtle things'. Two years later, he was appointed one of the four Borough Constables and in this role encountered many of the social problems that bedevilled Elizabethan England. Recessions were frequent, part-engendered by seemingly interminable wars. Stratford's poor were always with their Corporation and frequent levies were imposed upon the Capital Burgesses for their relief.

There was little room at Stratford's metaphorical inn for abandoned pregnant women. Their offspring became a charge on the Borough and the Leet Court developed a regular obsession that 'no inhabitant of Stratford hereafter receive any woman to be brought to bed of child in his or their houses' on pain of a fine. In John Shakespeare's time as constable, Edmund Barrett of the Crown Inn in Fore Bridge Street was fined 20s 'for evell revell keepynge in hys hous and mayntayninge and recevenge of a strumpet woman'.

A means of dealing with such offenders against the moral code was contained in the Vicar's Consistory Court. In the Middle Ages, a local boy, John Hatton de Stratford, had risen through the hierarchy of the Church to hold the highest ecclesiastical, political and legal offices in the land: Archbishop of Canterbury and Chancellor of England. He never forgot his native place. He erected a wooden bell tower, which still surmounted the church in Shakespeare's day. He made Stratford into an ecclesiastical peculiar. He gave the endowment of Holy Trinity church to the chantry which he had founded. Two years out of three, the *custos*, or Warden, could exercise many of the powers of the Bishop, including the prosecution of offenders against Canon Law in his own court. At the Reformation, the powers of this court passed to the Vicar. Its propensity to try offenders against the sexual codes led to its nickname of 'The Bawdy Court'.

As a constable, John Shakespeare would have shared Dogberry's duty to 'comprehend all vagram men'. To him would have fallen the arduous task of enforcing the resolution passed in 1557 after a riot at the September fair.

> No sengle man dwellynge in Stratford … do weyre about hym wtin the burrowe or lybertyes of Stratford eny bill, sword, wood knyf or dagger, or anie such lyke wepon under payn of forfeyture of the same, and their bodies to prison, there to remain at the Bailey's pleasure.

Stratford was a violent town in a violent age. In 1553, Thomas Holtam was arrested for drawing his dagger 'and making a fray' on Richard Harrington, one of the constables. In the next year, Thomas Powell of Shottery was fined 3s 4d for 'revelynge as well against othere the quenes magestyez'. To maintain order, the constables carried bills and were supported by a robust team of Stratfordians who could be called out to deal with troublemakers.

In 1559 and 1561, John Shakespeare assessed fines at the Leet Court, signifying assent with his mark of a glover's compass. This does not denote illiteracy. A fellow burgess, Adrian Quiney, also made a mark, although he could write a fine hand. Had John Shakespeare been illiterate, the burgesses would not have made him Borough Chamberlain in 1561 and in the two years following: the only person to be honoured with this consecutive burden. John Shakespeare had a gift with figures. The Corporation called on him in two subsequent years to rescue lesser men from the ignominy of failing to present a coherent account.

When John Shakespeare was made a constable, the Borough of Stratford was only five years old. The town had been governed for centuries by the Guild of the Holy Cross, a tertiary order of the Augustinian Friars. This was dissolved together with the monasteries in 1547. Its properties were dispersed, chiefly to the Lord of the Manor, John Dudley, Earl of Warwick. For six years the town was without any form of administration and its life dissolves into a historical void. In 1553, a plea from the inhabitants gained a positive response on behalf of the dying boy king Edward VI and a Royal Charter was granted. The propitious fall of John Dudley in the next reign ensured that most of the corporate property was returned into the hands of the townspeople. The officers and functions of the new Corporation were much the same as those of the old Guild. Its spirit was reflected in the Corporation's orders. It was decreed that 'none of the aldermen nor none of the capital burgesses, neither in the council chamber nor elsewhere, do revile each other, but brother-like live together'. The compilers were cautious enough to add a pecuniary inducement to fraternal accord – those disruptive of harmony were to pay 6s 8d for every default. One such contentious type was Alderman William Bott, a wealthy merchant of dubious character, who lived at New Place. His son-in-law said, during a Star Chamber suit of 1564, that he had been 'openly detected of divers great and notorious crimes, as namely felony, adultery, whoredom, falsehood and forging'. 'Let every man beware of him,' warned another witness, 'for he is counted the craftieste merchant in all our countery ... and it is said that if Botte had made his righte he had been hanged long ago.' Bott, who had been accused of fraudulent conversion and forgery, was expelled from the Corporation in 1565 after speaking evil words about his colleagues. 'Ther was,' he declared, 'never an honest man of the Councell or the body of the corporacyon of Stratford.' John Shakespeare was elected an alderman in his place.

Bott's *confrère* in duplicity was Sir Lodovick Greville of Milcote. Imperious, cruel and well connected, he achieved the capital dispatch reckoned as Bott's desert. He was no respecter of persons, assaulting his cousin, Sir John Conway of Luddington, and threatening the mighty Earl of Leicester. When his son, Edward, shot an arrow in the air that killed his elder brother, his father jested about it, telling him 'it was the best arrow he ever shot'. Lodovick coveted the land of one of his tenants, Thomas Webb, who was strangled by two servants during a visit to Mount Greville. One of them, Thomas Brock, was placed in bed, impersonating Webb, 'dolefully groaning' and making a will in Greville's favour before feigning death: a plot worthy of the revenge tragedies of the age. The foul deed done, the horror escalated. Brock, 'in his cups at Stratford', let slip dark hints that he had it in his power to hang his master, who had him killed by the other servant, Thomas Smith. Smith was arrested and confessed all. Both were tried at Warwick. Greville refused to plead and stood mute. According to contemporary law it was impossible to convict, although a course of torture to any extremity was permitted and Greville was pressed to death on 14 November 1589. His estates, which would have passed to the Crown if he had confessed, were bequeathed intact to his villainous son, Edward: a courageous end to a dishonourable career that had terrorised the region.

Others found themselves in conflict with the Corporation. Alderman Robert Perrott, a cantankerous old alderman who kept the King's Hall Tavern in the Rother Market, was Bailiff in 1558, but subsequently refused to serve on the Corporation. The maintenance of the oligarchic system depended on the co-operation of all men of means. The quarrel was discussed by three Warwickshire dignitaries, Sir Thomas Lucy, Clement Throckmorton and Sir Henry Goodere at the Bear Inn in Bridge Street. The worthies made very merry at the public expense for the bill came to 37s 8d. The burgesses must have felt that the outlay was worthwhile when the three gentlemen suggested that Perrott, of his 'free goodwill', pay £53 6s 8d he owed in back fines and that all should 'henceforth be Lovers and ffrendes'. Unfortunately, Perrott's goodwill did not extend to paying this enormous sum. The Corporation tried to force his hand by electing him Bailiff in 1567, but he declared he would never serve again. The choice fell on John Shakespeare, who had stood unsuccessfully the year before, perhaps indulging in the ploy of associating his name with the office. Alderman Perrott bore the council no lasting animosity. He endowed an annual sermon to be preached at Holy Trinity, with provision for the Corporation 'to make merye withall after the sermon is ended'.

The election was held on the Wednesday before the Feast of the Nativity of the Blessed Virgin (8 September). Afterwards the Corporation retired to the home of the new Bailiff to drink wine, so the household in Henley Street would have been the scene of bustling activity rather like the preparations in the Capulet house for Juliet's wedding feast.

> Come, stir, stir, stir. The second cock hath crowed.
> The curfew bell hath rung. 'Tis three o'clock.
> Look to the baked meats, good Angelica.
> Spare not the cost.

On Friday week after the election, the Corporation held its annual 'Buck Feast' at the Bear at the bottom of Bridge Street, or at the Swan opposite. This was a grand occasion when the Corporation entertained local dignitaries. The Corporation surveyed its property on the Friday in Easter week. At Rogationtide, the Bailiff and the Burgesses perambulated the Borough boundaries.

An account from nearby Banbury instructed that the Bailiff was to be 'a lanthorn in good usage and order as well as to all the rest of his brethren as to the whole commonality'. He was to

> wel and decently behave himself in all degrees and indifferently and rightly judge and deal with all men … According to the right of the cause and so like-wise shall be comely attired in apparel and also at all such times as he shall be occasioned to go into the said town or the perambulation of the same wheth-er on Fair days, market days or any other times and about the execution of his office, or together with his brethren touching any affairs or business of the said Borough, he shall have the Sergeant-at-Mace to be attendant upon him.

From 15 December until twenty days after Christmas Day, he was obliged to hang a lantern outside his front door to 'give light in the streets'.

It is appropriate that companies of actors are first recorded in the town during John Shakespeare's bailiwick. The acting companies were under the patronage of the leading noblemen and wore their liveries. This ensured that they received money from their patrons, often for performing in their great houses. It also meant that they could invoke the name of their great masters in their dealings with petty officials as they toured the country.

Many years later, Robert Willis of Gloucester, born in the same year as William Shakespeare, wrote an account that reveals what must have happened at Stratford.

> When players of interludes come to town they first attend the Mayor to inform him what nobleman's servants they are and so to get a license for their public playing and if the Mayor likes the actors or would show respect to their Lord and master, he appoints them to play their first play before himself and the Aldermen and common council and that is called 'the Mayor's Play' where everyone that will goes in without money, the Mayor giving the players a reward as thinks fit to show respect unto them.

In the summer of 1569, no less a troupe than the Queen's Players was paid 9s for performing in the Guildhall. Later that year, the Earl of Worcester's Men gave less satisfaction and were paid a mere shilling. Perhaps John's eldest son, then aged five, accompanied his father to these shows. Roger Willis certainly did.

> At such a play my father took me with him and made me sit between his legs, as he sat on one of the benches, where we saw and heard very well. The play was called 'The Cradle of Security'. The sight of it made such an impression on me that when I came to man's estate it was as fresh in my memory as if I had seen it newly acted.

An indicator of the family's social status comes through Thomas Greene, Steward (Clerk) to the Corporation from 1603 to 1617, who described himself as Shakespeare's cousin. The family connection may come through the Thomas Green, *alias* Shakper, who was buried at Stratford's parish church of Holy Trinity on 6 March 1589/90. The *alias* indicates that his mother's maiden name was Shakespeare. It is possible that this is the father of Thomas Greene and his brother John and that the wife in question was a sister of John Shakespeare, but there is no conclusive proof of this.

The word 'cousin' was a vaguer one to the Elizabethans than it is to us today, but there can be little doubt about the consanguinity. Thomas Greene must have been at least a decade younger than his cousin. He was admitted to the Middle Temple on 20 November 1595 and is described as 'son and heir of Thomas Greene of Warwick, gent.' The father was dead, which makes identification with the other Thomas Green a possibility, particularly if 'Warwick' is taken to mean the county rather than the town.

Thomas Greene was called to the bar on 29 October 1600. In the following year he was acting as solicitor for the Stratford Corporation, which implies that he had influence in that body and that he had legal briefs in the area. His brother, John, was a lawyer of Clement's Inn. The Greenes' strong connection with Stratford is demonstrated by the fact that Thomas's wife, Margaret Lane, came from Alveston, across the river from the town.

The relationship with the Greenes further cements the position of the Shakespeare family in what we would now call 'Middle England', amidst the class of confident professionals and skilled artisans. As an early editor of Shakespeare's works put it, 'His family … were of good Figure and Fashion there, and are mention'd as Gentlemen.'

Does Shakespeare's background matter? In one sense, obviously not: yet in another way it does. As the gods on Mount Olympus, given the task of creating the greatest writer the world has ever known, obviously the time and the background into which we chose to set him is of vital importance. Where better than the aspirant and rising class of skilled artisans? At the same time, William Shakespeare had family links to the professional classes through the Greenes. The traditions of aristocratic connections in his family may also have enabled him to move easily in the courtly circles he would encounter in the future.

## 2

# Childhood and Schooldays, 1564–82

'Unwillingly to school'

– *As You Like It*

Early in the eighteenth century, the distinguished actor Thomas Betterton journeyed to Stratford 'on purpose to gather up what remains he could, of a name for which he had so great a veneration'. Although he examined the parish registers, most of what he discovered were gleanings about William Shakespeare and his family from the local inhabitants. The information he obtained was used by Nicholas Rowe as the biographical note in his edition of the Complete Works published in 1709.

Betterton's researches reveal a rich and flourishing seam of oral tradition about this notable local family. He states that William Shakespeare was the oldest of ten children. This may have been the case. Although the parish records show that the Shakespeares had eight children, five of whom survived infancy, it should be remembered that these are baptismal records. Children who died before they could be baptised would have been buried in unconsecrated ground. Baptisms of Mary's babies are recorded in 1558, 1562, 1564, 1566, 1569, 1571, 1574 and 1580. 'Two year breeders never cease' is an old country saying and Mary Shakespeare may well have been such a one.

The first recorded child was christened Joan, but did not survive, for another daughter was baptised with the same name in 1569. A second daughter was christened Margaret in 1562. In the following year John and Mary saw her little form lowered into the earth at Holy Trinity. William, the first son, was brought to baptism on 26 April 1564. Another son, Gilbert, was born in 1566 and a daughter, Anna, in 1571. She died at the age of seven and 'Mr Shaxper' paid 8*d* for the funereal pall and bell. Her elder brother, William, then aged fourteen, must have attended the burial. Another son, Richard, was born in 1574 and there were, perhaps, miscarriages and stillbirths before Mary bore her last child, Edmund, in 1580. Five of her children survived to adulthood, not a low proportion for the age. In the year Edmund was born, the chapel bell tolled its funeral knell twelve times for Stratford children.

England's greatest genius narrowly escaped a little winding sheet in the first few weeks of his life. On 11 July 1564, an apprentice weaver died at premises (now the Garrick Inn) in the High Street. In the burial entry the vicar, John Bretchgirdle, wrote the ominous words *Hic incipit pestis* – 'here begins the plague'. It had been carried into Warwickshire by soldiers returning from the Earl of Warwick's expedition against Le Havre. Before the year was out, 238 of the town's inhabitants had died: around an eighth of the population. It was by far the worst epidemic in Stratford's history. Mary Shakespeare may have fled back to Wilmcote with her baby. Her husband remained, attending the meeting of the Corporation on 30 August, which was held in the Guild garden rather than in the stuffy atmosphere of the Hall.

Death was an everyday matter in Elizabethan society. The phrase in the Book of Common Prayer – 'In the midst of life we are in death' – was a statement of fact. Infant mortality was high, plagues and pestilences frequent. There was an overwhelming belief that death was not the end. The body was a mere container of the immortal spirit, which would eventually shake it off. Shakespeare was to use this theme in Sonnet 146: 'Poor Soul, the Centre of my Sinful Earth'. An obsession with death is rarely far away in his plays.

John Shakespeare's civic status would have ensured his son's place at the free school over the Guildhall. The school had a tendency to overflow into the neighbouring Guild Chapel, necessitating occasional strictures from the Corporation to return whence it belonged. In *Twelfth Night*, Malvolio is likened to 'a pedant that keeps a school i' the church'. No record survives of Stratford School in this period, but the curriculum must have been as unvaried as that in other Elizabethan grammar schools. Education began at five years old. Learning was a mechanical pattern of repetition and the schoolroom echoes to chanting from the 'Absey' or ABC book.

> And then comes Answer like an Absey book

says the Bastard in *King John*. This was a wooden-framed primer which was covered with a thin sheet of transparent horn. On it was inscribed the alphabet in lower and upper case. It was preceded by the symbol of the Cross: hence the 'cross-row' mentioned in *Richard III*.

'They must read English before they can learne Latin' was the stricture of one school benefactor. Young William's earliest literary efforts would have consisted of letters copied into a horn book. These first essays in learning would have taken place under the instruction of an under-master or his wife. The vicar, John Bretchgirdle, in 1564 bequeathed 'to the common use of the scholars of the free scole', a copy of Thomas Ellyot's *Latin Dictionary*. If the book survived the ravages of schoolboy usage, it would have been used by the young Shakespeare. Rhetorical learning prevailed, hopefully not as incompetently as that used by the schoolmaster in *Merry Wives*.

| | |
|---|---|
| **Sir Hugh Evans:** | What is he, William, that doth lend articles? |
| **William Page:** | Articles are borrowed of the pronoun and be thus declined: *singularitor, nominativo, hic, haec, hoc*. |

| Sir Hugh Evans: | *Nominativo, Hig, hag, hog*; pray you, mark: *geni* |
| | *tive, hujus*: Well, what is your accusative case? |
| William Page: | Accusative, *hinc*. |
| Sir Hugh Evans: | I pray you, have your remembrance, child, accusa |
| | tive, *hung, hang, hog*. |

Sir Hugh is alluding to the prescribed exercises in William Lily's *Rudimenta Grammatices*: the obligatory means of instruction in the contemporary education system. Like all other grammar school boys, William Shakespeare would have been highly familiar with it. 'The relatiue agreeth with his antecedent in gendre, numbre and persone,' instructed Lily, as '*Vir sapit, qui pauca loquitor*, That manne is wyse, that speaketh fewe.' This very Latin adage is quoted by Holofernes, the pedantic schoolmaster, in *Love's Labour's Lost*.

A further reference to Lily's work comes in *Titus Andonicus*, where Demetrius quotes from Horace's First Ode.

'*Integer vitae, scelerisque purus, Non eget Mauri jaculis, nec arcu.*'

'O, 'tis a verse in Horace,' replies Chiron. 'I know it well: I read it in the grammar long ago.'

'Ay just,' responds Aaron the Moor, 'a verse in Horace; right, you have it.'

Shakespeare must have reckoned that there would be enough people in his audience who could pick up the meaning of the Latin tag to make it worth including – 'The man who is upright in life has no need of Moorish spears.'

Stratford School was an academy of distinction whose origins went back at least as far as the early fourteenth century. Its masters were men of academic standing. William Shakespeare was too young to have benefited from the learning of John Brownsword, described by Francis Meres as a prominent poet in the 'Latin Empire', who left Stratford in 1567.

The most interesting of Shakespeare's likely schoolmasters was Simon Hunt, who came to the little academy in 1571 – the year William would have transferred to the senior school. It was probably this Hunt who joined the Society of Jesus in Rome on 20 April 1578, although a namesake died at Stratford before 1598. In 1584, a request to send him into the dangerous rigours of the English Mission was rejected because 'Father Simon lacks sufficient learning'. Is this the source of the 'smalle Latin and less Greek' that Ben Jonson ascribed to his friend? The standard of comparison was high. Ben was tutored at Westminster by the great schoolmaster William Camden, while Hunt was being assessed under the stringent academic standards of the Society of Jesus. John Aubrey was probably nearer the mark when he said that Shakespeare 'understood Latine pretty well'. The works demonstrate considerable classical knowledge. Two-thirds of his classical allusions are from his favourite book: Ovid's *Metamorphoses*. 'As the soul of Euphorbies,' eulogised the Revd Francis Meres in 1598, 'so the sweet witty soul of

Ovid lies in the mellifluous and honey-tongued Shakespeare.' The fluent Latin of Stratford schoolboys is demonstrated in a letter from Richard Quiney, aged eleven, to his father and namesake, the Bailiff, who was about Borough business in London.

> I give you thanks that from the tenderest age ... you have instructed me in studies of sacred doctrine. Nothing could be further from my mind than mere adulation, for not one of my friends is dearer and more loving to me than you are and I pray sincerely that my special love may remain as it is.

It is likely that William Shakespeare's first exercises in acting would have occurred at school. There are records of plays being performed at St Paul's, Merchant Taylors', Eton and Westminster schools and it is unlikely that the same would not have happened at Stratford. Ben Jonson mentioned the vogue of the school play in the context of the Latin-dominated curriculum in *The Staple of News*.

> They make all their scholars play-boys. Is't not a fine sight to see all our children made interluders? Do we pay our money for this? We send them to learn their grammar and their Terence and they learn their playbooks.
>
> (III. Intermean, 46–50)

One of Shakespeare's earliest plays is *The Comedy of Errors*. It is based on Plautus' *The Menaechmi*. Since no translation into English appeared until the one published by William Warner in 1595, it may be surmised that this was a Latin play in which William appeared while at school.

William must have been taught by Thomas Jenkins, who arrived in 1575 and whom some have identified as the model for the Welsh schoolmaster Sir Hugh Evans. The common Welshness does not extend beyond their surnames. Jenkins was a Londoner, educated at St John's College, Oxford. When he left Stratford in 1579, he found his own replacement in an Oxford colleague, John Cottam, who paid £6 commission to the canny Jenkins.

Whatever debts William Shakespeare owed to his schooldays, he recalled them with the same lack of enthusiasm as his

> ... whining schoolboy, with his satchel
> And shining morning face, creeping like snail
> Unwillingly to school ...

'Love goes towards love,' Romeo tells Juliet, 'as schoolboys from their books, / But love from love, towards school, with heavy looks.' Shakespeare's schoolboy eagerly awaits the moment when school breaks up and 'each hurries to his home and sporting place', or his mind wanders beyond the school door to playing with tops, push pin, 'hide fox and all after', pursuing summer butterflies, birds nesting, or wantonly killing flies for sport.

When William Shakespeare drew heavily on the Classical tradition in his works, he would have been sure in the knowledge that the allusions would be understood by much of his audience, but he also called upon a native folklore which is now virtually lost. 'O, then, I see Queen Mab hath been with you,' Mercutio tells Romeo.

> She is the fairies' midwife, and she comes
> In shape no bigger than an agate-stone
> On the fore-finger of an alderman,
> Drawn with a team of little atomies
> Over men's noses as they lie asleep ...

The Shakespeares may have travelled to see the festivities at Kenilworth in 1575 when Robert Dudley entertained the Queen to a fourteen-day extravaganza, during which the clocks were stopped at the hour of feasting. A water pageant, *The Delivery of the Lady of the Lake*, was presented on the mere below the castle's walls. A huge mechanical dolphin, 'that from head to tail was four and twenty feet long', propelled by fin-shaped oars, containing musicians and bearing the figure of Arion, singing 'a delectable ditty', skimmed across the water.[1] If the eleven-year-old William Shakespeare was among the crowd who watched the spectacle, he may well have remembered it two decades later in *Twelfth Night*, 'Where, like Arion on the dolphin's back / I saw him hold aquaintance with the waves.'

John Shakespeare ran into financial difficulties soon after buying a property in Stratford in 1575. While he was previously a regular attendee at Corporation meetings, his presence is recorded only once after 1576. In 1578 he raised a loan of £40 from his brother-in-law, Edmund Lambert, offering part of his wife's inheritance, a house and 56 acres of land at Wilmcote as surety. On the same day, Alderman Roger Sadler, a High Street baker, made his will and recorded debts owed to him by John Shakespeare and Richard Hathaway, father of William's future bride. More of Mary Shakespeare's dowry was lost in 1579 when her share in two houses and 100 acres at Snitterfield was sold to her nephew, Alexander Webbe, for £10. It was likely that John Shakespeare considered that raising money from his wife's relations would make it easier to recover the collateral if prosperity returned. It is also possible that Robert Arden had stipulated a gentlemen's agreement ensuring that the husbands of Mary's sisters should have first refusal if her legacy were to be sold.

Impecuniousness was the likely cause of a petition by John Shakespeare to the Court of Queen's Bench in 1582, for sureties of the peace against Ralph Caudrey, Thomas Logginge and Robert Young, 'for fear of death and mutilation of his limbs'. The exaggerated phrase suggests that Alderman Caudrey, a volatile and violent man, would not be a sympathetic creditor. The matter must have been resolved by 5 November, when both men attended the election of the new Bailiff.

John Shakespeare's precarious financial position was well understood by the Commissioners for Recusancy in Warwickshire, who investigated those recalcitrant in their attendance at the services of the Established Church. His name appears among a group of nine considered to 'absent themselves for fear of processes'. Church services offered an opportunity to serve writs and William Burbage was trying to recover £7 owed to him from a decade before, obtaining an order for payment in the following month.

The nine debtors named by the Commissioners were all in bad financial shape. The intriguingly named William Fluellen and George Bardell (or Bardolph) left widows to the care of the parish. William Baynton fled to Ireland to escape his creditors. John Wheeler had his goods distrained and his son's barn was 'readi to fall for rottenness' in 1599. These were hard times in Stratford. Some 700 people, about a third of the population, were on the poor roll. The vital wool trade had been decimated by the Spanish sacking of Antwerp – England's main egress into Flanders – in 1576. This was the year in which John Shakespeare's difficulties first manifested themselves. His troubles look less severe in this context. Although property was mortgaged, the house in Henley Street remained. Even in his most pressing moments, he could stand credit for others, although his judgement was not always good. In 1586, he stood bail at Coventry for Michael Pryce, a local tinker charged with a felony. The money was forfeited when the defendant failed to appear. A month earlier he had guaranteed the debts of his unreliable farmer brother. When Henry Shakespeare defaulted, John only escaped gaol through the intervention of a kindly fellow alderman, Richard Hill.

John's troubles increased in June 1580 when he was bound over to keep the peace by the Court of the Queen's Bench. He was fined £20 for failing to appear and £20 for not bringing John Audley, a Nottinghamshire hatmaker, into court. On the same day, Audley was fined £70, which included £20 for not bringing John Shakespeare into court. Thomas Codey of Stoke-on-Trent, yeoman, was fined £30: £10 as surety for John Shakespeare, while two Worcestershire farmers were each fined £10 as sureties for Audley and Codey. One hundred and forty people from all over England were dealt with in a similar way. Their offence is unknown. It may be connected to the religious turmoil of the period. More likely, it represents a crackdown on broggers.

These difficulties underwrite Nicholas Rowe's assertion in 1709 that John Shakespeare's need for William's assistance at home forced his withdrawal from school. Doubtless he accompanied his father on wool-purchasing journeys through the 'high wild hills and rough uneven ways' of the Cotswolds. Two plays, *The Taming of the Shrew* and *Henry IV, Part II*, show an intimate knowledge of the region, even to naming specific inhabitants.

He was familiar with the tools of his father's trade. 'Does he not wear a great round beard,' asks Mistress Quickly, 'like a glover's paring-knife?' He was also aware of the ancillary trades on which the white tanners' business depended. The keech was a product of the slaughterhouse: a cake of consolidated fat which was rolled up to provide tallow. In *King Henry*

*VIII*, Shakepeare uses the product as a metaphor for Thomas Wolsey, the butcher's son.

> ... I wonder
> That such a keech can with his very bulk
> Take up the rays of the beneficial sun,
> And keep it from the earth.

We recall the project of the gods. Education is clearly a vital factor in the creation of our genius. Too little won't serve, but too much could equally mar him. He could become donnish and bookish. If he left school at the age of twelve when his father's financial troubles first manifested themselves, he would have had a sufficient knowledge of Latin for his later purposes.

We must also remember that experience of financial humiliation in childhood can create a determination to restore the family name and fortune. The circumstances are not so very different from those of Charles Dickens, whose father's bankruptcy forced him from school at the age of twelve to go to work in a blacking factory.

That his fellow councillors maintained John Shakespeare's name on their roll through his years of trouble indicates their esteem and their belief in his power of recovery. Had they vindictively desired to persecute him, they could have done so, for fines for non-attendance were high. Instead they mitigated his burden by lowering his tax assessments: a considerable gesture in an oligarchic structure where much of the financial burden fell on themselves. Finally in 1586 the councillors replaced John Shakespeare and another impecunious alderman, adding the sad note that 'Mr Wheeler dothe desire to be put out of the Companye and Mr. Shakespeare dothe not come to the halles when they be warned nor hathe done of longe tyme'. If they had decided, after the longest period of non-attendance ever permitted, that the Shakespeare fortunes were irretrievable, they were wrong. The lost wealth was amply recovered by William Shakespeare in the next decade, but it is not the function of a Borough Corporation to assess the potential of literary genius.

Certain it is, although not proven, that William Shakespeare would have been honing his literary skills from an early age. His Sonnet 145 stands out for its style, which, in comparison to the rest of the sequence, is immature and appears to be juvenilia.

> Those lips that Love's own hand did make
> Breath'd forth the sound that said 'I hate'
> To me that languish'd for her sake,
> But when she saw my woeful state,
> Straight in her heart did mercy come,
> Chiding that tongue that ever sweet
> Was us'd in giving gentle doom

> And taught it thus anew to greet:
> 'I hate', she alter'd with an end
> That follow'd it as gentle day
> Doth follow night, who, like a fiend
> From heaven to hell is thrown away:
> 'I hate', from hate away she threw
> And sav'd my life, saying 'not you'.

It was Professor Andrew Gurr who pointed out in 1971 that the 'hate away' in the penultimate line might be a pun on the surname of William Shakespeare's future wife. The final line could be interpreted as 'Anne saved my life ...' We may be in the presence of an incident from the poet's days of courting.[2]

As gods we choose a time for his birth when the English language was attaining its apotheosis. The literary vigour of his fellow townspeople is revealed in a series of scurrilous poems written after the easygoing Vicar was replaced by a Puritan in 1617. A lament of some merit is put into the mouth of the departing cleric by a local sonneteer.

> Who will relieve my woe? My heart doth burn
> To see man's state wane as the wind doth turn.
> He wars and wins and winnings lost by strife.
> War is another death, a sure uncertain life.
> Try then and trust, give credit for delay.
> The feigned friends with feigned looks betray ...

The fortuitous combination of environment, epoch and genius would ensure an early blossoming of talent. In 1587, Anthony Underhill was buried in the church at nearby Ettington. His family knew Shakespeare and his valedictory verses have been preserved.

> As dreams do fade and bubbles rise and fall
> As flowers do fade and flourish in an hower.
> As smoke doth rise and vapours rain shall pour
> Beyond the witt or reach of human power.
> As somers heat doth perish in the grass.
> Such is our stay. So lyfe of man doth pass.

By 1587, William Shakespeare was probably in London. Yet even if he did not write the verses, it is clear that Warwickshire was fertile in the potential imagination to produce a great poet.

William Shakespeare is arguably the most articulate man who ever lived. The *Harvard Concordance to Shakespeare* calculates that he uses, in the Works, 29,066 different words. Many of these were word variants like different participles of verbs, so his practical working vocabulary has been estimated at around 17,000 words – and it was almost certainly more.

He would have been familiar with the rich (and now virtually extinct) South Warwickshire argot. Since both his grandfathers were farmers, it is not surprising that he was familiar with the speech of the rural South Midlands.

When he wrote for a wider public, he did not drop often into the language of his hometown. There would have been no point in confusing London audiences with Warwickshire words and terms, but inevitably there were lapses. On occasions he uses the Midlands dialect pronoun 'a', which can mean 'he', 'she', 'they' or 'it'. My own grandmother, who was born in Derbyshire in 1877, not only said it, but wrote it in letters. Juliet's nurse uses it to recall her husband: 'God rest his soul. / A was a merry man.'

If the eighteenth-century critic Theobald's brilliant reading of a confused text in the First Folio is correct, Shakespeare also used the pronoun in Mistress Quickly's description of the death of Falstaff.

> 'He died like any Christian child … He said "God, God, God" as he pinched the sheet and then a babbled o' green fields.'

Was the fat knight trying to recite the twenty-third Psalm? 'He maketh me to lie down in green pastures.'

Falstaff lapses into Cotswold usage when addressing Justice Shallow's muster, adding a 'y' in front of a vowel. 'Hear ye Yedward: if I tarry at home and go not, I'll hang thee for going.' Even today, the Gloucestershire village of Ebrington, some 16 miles from Stratford, is known almost universally to the locals as 'Yubberton'.

The poet was familiar with the flora and fauna of the Warwickshire countryside – and the local words to describe them. He uses the local term – 'urchin' – for a hedgehog. He uses the old Warwickshire name 'tailor' for the goldfinch. 'I will not sing,' says Lady Percy. ''Tis the next way to turn tailor, or be redbreast teacher,' replies Hotspur.

Shakespeare is aware that red clover is a danger to cattle. In *Titus Andronicus*, he uses the Warwickshire term 'honey-stalks'.

> Than baits to fish, or honey-stalks to sheep.

In *Henry V*, the Duke of Burgundy refers to 'hateful docks, rough thistles, kecksies, burs'. Having grown up in Shottery, I still call the plant 'keck'. The prevailing names are 'cow parsley' or 'Queen Anne's Lace'.

A horse in the shafts is to Shakespeare a 'till-horse'. 'Thou hast got more hair on thy chin,' says Launcelot Gobbo in *The Merchant of Venice*, 'than Dobbin my till-horse has on his tail.' In *Henry VI, Part II*, it is appropriately the Earl of Warwick who uses the word 'lodge' in a distinctively local way, meaning 'to beat down'.

Shakespeare uses the word 'wench' in the Warwickshire way. It is never derogatory, as when Queen Katherine commands: 'Take thy lute, wench: my soul grows sad with troubles' (*Henry VIII*, III.1.1).

To 'shog off' in Shakespearean language is to make or clear off. It is often used pejoratively, as when Nym says, 'Will you shog off? I would have you solus.' In my Shottery playground in the 50s, the term had been modified to 'Shag off'.

There are Shakespearean echoes in the Stratford records. In 1628, Elizabeth or 'Goody' Bromley was presented before the Consistory Court for abusing the wife of Adrian Holder in terms redolent of the black arts. She threatened to 'overlook her and hern' (to put the evil eye on them). 'Aroint thee witch!' retorted Mistress Holder with an anathema used in both *Macbeth* and *King Lear*.

At the Stratford Consistory Court in 1633 a man was presented for 'putting hands in plackets', the opening in a woman's dress: one of the peccadilloes against which Lear's Fool admonishes.

Although as gods, we may have decided to endow William Shakespeare with this extraordinary quality of word-power, its source remains a mystery. One thing is certain. He was obsessed with words. Something like 17 per cent of the words he uses in the Works represent their first attested usage, including such everyday words as 'critical', 'obscene', 'submerged', 'hurry', 'housekeeping' and 'lonely'.

William Shakespeare must have been honing his talents as an actor during his formative years. There is circumstantial evidence of his youthful dramatic activity. Most of the leading companies of actors passed through Stratford during this period and doubtless he was an entranced spectator. The golden year was 1587 when five companies played there, including the celebrated Queen's Players who received the highest fee the Corporation ever dispensed to an acting company. Such was the crush to see these famous actors that a bench was broken. The Stratfordians were not always spectators. In 1583, 13s 4d was paid to 'Davi Jones and companye for his pastyme at Whitsontyde'. David Jones was a saddler whose second wife was a cousin of Anne Hathaway. Did William Shakespeare, then aged nineteen, take part in this performance at the Corporation's annual feast? His daughter Susanna was born in the same month, so it is likely that he was in Stratford

> ... at Pentecost,
> When all our pageants of delight were played.
> Our youth got me to play the woman's part,
> And I was trimm'd in Madam Julia's gown,
> Which served me as fit, by all men's judgements.
> ... I did play an honourable part,
> Madam. 'Twas Ariadne passioning
> For Theseus' perjury and unjust flight,
> Which I so acted with my tears,
> That my poor mistress, moved there withal,
> Wept bitterly ...

John Aubrey gives a further hint of the poet's youthful dramatic activity. He makes the dubious claim that the young William was apprenticed to a butcher and adds that when he killed a calf 'he would doe it in high style and make a speech'. This curious story gains credence with the knowledge that 'killing the calfe' was a popular charade, played behind a door or curtain, in which the performer acted the parts of both butcher and animal.

# 3

# Courtship and Marriage, 1582–85

'These pretty country folks'

*– As You Like It*, Act V

To many English men and women, the Protestant Reformation was a cataclysm. They were being ordered to put behind them a thousand years of faith and history. Change had been rapid and inconstant. Henry VIII's split with Rome had been followed by a Protestant Reformation under the Regents of Edward VI. A brief restoration of Catholicism followed under Mary. Elizabeth I was crowned as a Catholic, but rapidly reverted to that idiosyncratic sect which became known as Anglicanism. Two Acts of Parliament were passed in 1559 which made it virtually impossible to be both a loyal Catholic and a loyal subject of the Queen. The Act of Supremacy imposed an oath obliging any person taking public or church office to swear allegiance to the monarch as 'the only supreme governor of this realm'. Most Catholics would have had no difficulty in accepting this as an expression of the Queen's secular authority, but the next phrase defined this authority as being 'as well in all spiritual or ecclesiastical things or clauses'.

Another Act in the same year made the Mass an illegal form of worship and reissued the Book of Common Prayer as the prescribed liturgy. A century-long orgy of destruction was taking place which makes Mao Tse Tung's 'Cultural Revolution' appear innocuous. The 'Elizabethan Settlement' sought to revive the work that had been begun in the reign of Edward VI: to abolish all trace of Catholicism from the fabric of English life. The stone altars that expressed the Sacrifice of the Mass were broken up and replaced by Communion tables that represented the new theology. Rood screens and reredoses were demolished, altarpieces and vestments burnt, wall-paintings whitewashed, stained glass smashed and chalices melted. The great processions on the Feast of Corpus Christi, with their Exposition of the Blessed Sacrament, were banned – as were the many festivals in honour of the local patronal saint. An entire culture almost disappeared. Whereas Catholic Europe has a rich heritage of medieval art, in Britain it is all but lost.

This must have been felt particularly strongly in Stratford, where Catholicism was at the peak of its cultural vibrancy at the time of the Reformation. Holy Trinity church housed a College of Priests. The

Collegiate Dean, Thomas Balsall, rebuilt the choir with the kind of delicate tracery associated with the great cathedrals. Feast days made their impact. Every year, the townspeople disported themselves in the pageant of St George. The saint rode through the town on horseback, clad in armour, leading a dragon which belched flames and smoke from its nostrils. This was followed by a traditional Vice or buffoon in costume and warriors armed with pikes.

Other, pre-Christian customs survived and were to die hard. By the 1620s, the town was dominated by Puritans who sought to eradicate the ancient May Day revels. Something of the historic tradition is revealed in the attempts at its suppression by the Consistory Court. In 1621 Thomas Clarke was presented for 'playing with his tabor and pype upon the First daie of mai in evening prayer tyme at Bishopton'. In 1622, a number of May Day revellers appeared before the Court. George Quiney, the Curate, presented 'Mr. Birch's man for dauncing the morris in eveninge prayer tyme'. John Allen, William Plymmer and Humphrey Brown were presented for the same offence which took place 'on the feast day of Phillip and Jacob', which was May Day. Allen admitted his offence and 'saith that he will never committ the lyke'. The three were ordered to perform public penance on the following Sunday. Further insight into the Maying festival in the village is provided by Francis Palmer, servant to John Hobbins, who was presented 'for being the Maid Marrion' – presumably in the pageant called Robin Hood or Robin Goodfellow.

Historically, the Church had provided an educational system of surprising universality: the surest path into the echelons of society for young men from poorer backgrounds was through her hierarchy. Monasticism had provided sustenance to the poor and the destitute. Now the resources of these philanthropic communities were plundered for the avarice of the rich and powerful. The number of people living in abject poverty was increasing. It became necessary to enact no less than five Poor Laws between 1563 and 1601, detailing the treatment of the impoverished.

Rural depopulation caused a drift into the towns, which were overburdened by the influx. Stratford Corporation made regular appeals to the outlying parishes to contribute to the Poor Rates. 'No inhabitant,' it was ordered in the year John Shakespeare became a constable, 'to harbour strange beggars who if refractory are to be punished with the stocks.' In the following year, Richard Mekyns was employed at 20s a year, 'so long as he shall do his duties in drivinge out of beggars and vagabondes out of the towne and also shall whyppe such persons as shall be commanded hym to whyp'.

Faced with such a situation, every Englishman had to decide where he stood in relation to the new laws. Some – the Puritans – considered that the Protestant revolution had not gone far enough. Others remained deeply loyal to the Catholic faith, but most went along with the changes, whatever they thought of them. Some Catholics sought to equivocate on the oath in various ways like declaring that it could not be a sin to swear an invalid oath, but for men of conscience the situation was impossible. Although in one sense it was a political issue, it was also a religious and moral one. Indeed, for people of the time, the three were indivisible.

So where did the Shakespeare family stand on these vital matters? They must have had a collective or an individual view, but we have no direct indication as to what this was. Yet there is considerable circumstantial evidence of their faith.

It must be said that religious and political pluralism were concepts that were dimly perceived if perceived at all. To adhere to a religious persuasion that was not that of the monarch was considered treasonous. The situation was not helped by the complicated dynastic issues stemming from Henry VIII's domestic arrangements. The prevailing issue of the Tudor dynasty was that of childlessness. Henry's annulment of his first marriage to Catherine of Aragon was a product of a failure to produce a male heir. Crucially, it was not recognised by the Papacy. In fact the annulment made Mary, his daughter by that marriage, illegitimate. If the annulment was not recognised, then Elizabeth, his daughter by his second marriage, was illegitimate. Indeed both princesses had been officially declared illegitimate during the reign of Henry VIII, although he was to reinstate them in the line of succession before his death. Under Henry's son, Edward VI, who succeeded to the throne at the age of nine, a Protestant reformation was set in being. Nor was he to produce an heir, dying of tuberculosis when he was fifteen. Among his last acts was an attempt to bar his half-sisters, Mary and Elizabeth, from the throne, substituting his firmly Protestant cousin, the ill-fated Lady Jane Grey. After a nine-day interregnum, Mary gained the throne and restored England to the Catholic faith. Partly on dynastic grounds, partly to ensure a Catholic succession, Mary married the Spanish Prince Philip at the age of thirty-seven. Part of the terms of the marriage treaty was that he be styled 'King of England'. On the abdication of his father, Charles V, in 1556, Mary became Queen of Spain. Had she produced the heir for whom she hoped, England would have become an integral part of the Hapsburg Empire. How Englishmen would have reacted to that is a matter of speculation. Her marriage to Philip had already led to armed rebellions. On the death of Mary at the age of forty-two, Philip sought the hand of Elizabeth, who had succeeded to the throne under her father's will. Although she possessed the approbation of much of the nation, the uncertainty of her position was to dominate many of her policies.

The Catholics of the North rose in rebellion in 1569. Much was made by her opponents of the claim that the Queen was illegitimate. There were those who would have liked to place Mary, Queen of Scots, on the throne as the legitimate monarch. Elizabeth's failure to marry and produce an heir led to uncertainty about the succession and worry about the lack of continuity that might ensue with disastrous consequences. Her policy of supporting the Protestant rebels in the Netherlands led inevitably to a clash with the mighty power of Spain. Her reign may seem more heroic with hindsight than it seemed at the time.

Elizabeth's own religious views appear equivocal, perhaps inevitably so. While she appears to have possessed a personal tolerance that was untypical of the age, she undoubtedly favoured a State Church as the best solution to the religious question. Given the mores of the time, it was inevitable that those who chose to remain outside the Church should be regarded as disloyal.

As part of the effort to impose the Church of England on the people, attendance at its services was made compulsory. A Commission for Recusancy was established to root out persistent non-attenders. The Commissioners were active in the Stratford area, producing lists of those who did not attend church and giving the reason. It is on the list compiled in March 1592 that the name of John Shakespeare appears among those not attending church for fear of process for debt. The principal signatory on the document was Sir Thomas Lucy. Where there were militant recusants locally, they were named as such, including the influential William Clopton; Mrs Frances Jeffreys, wife of the Town Clerk; Joan, wife of Alderman George Caudrey, and their son George, suspected to be 'a semynerie preeste or Jesuite'; Edward Bromley, the town carrier; and William Underhill of New Place.

Several of the Catholics, regarding a peaceful existence worth a litany, paid lip service to conformity and attended services. In September, the Commissioners produced a second report naming those who had conformed and listing

> sutch dangerous and seditious Papistes and Recusantes as have bene presented to us or found out by our endevoire to [have] bene att any tyme heretofore of or in this countye ... and [are] now either beyonde the seas or vagrante within this Realme.

One name on the list was that of Richard Dibdale, a farmer of Shottery, where he was a near-neighbour of the Hathaway family. He 'hath not bene at church this yere'. His brother Robert trained for the Catholic priesthood in the seminary that had been established by exiled Catholics at Douai in Flanders and sent a letter from there to his family. The bearer was Thomas Cottam, a priest from Lancashire, whose brother John was Stratford schoolmaster. In the letter Dibdale told his 'right wellbeloved parents' that the 'cause of my wryting unto you ys to lett understand that I am in healthe, commending unto you my especiall friend Mr Cottame, who hath beene unto me the t[wo] halfe of my life'. Neither the letter nor the small gifts were delivered. Cottam was arrested at Dover in June 1580 and was ferociously tortured.

Undaunted by his friend's arrest, Robert Dibdale followed him into the hazards of the English Province. He was arrested and imprisoned, but did not suffer the torture endured with such valour by many of his fellows. On 5 November 1580, William Greenaway, the carrier from Bridge Street, brought a letter, a loaf, two cheeses and 5s from Dibdale's father to his son in Newgate Prison. The prisoner was released on 30 September 1582 and fled to France, but soon returned, establishing a reputation as an exorcist, casting out devils from a servant girl in Hertfordshire shortly before his recapture. This time he did not escape the fate of his friend and 'with constancy suffered martyrdom' at Tyburn on 8 October 1586.

The systematic persecution of his co-religionists produced an obsession to the level of derangement in a local Catholic, John Somerville of Edstone Hall, son-in-law of Sir Edward Arden of Park Hall. Arden was protecting a priest called Hugh Hall, who was disguised as one of his gardeners. On 25 October 1583, despair triumphed over reason in Somerville's troubled mind and he set off for London, after announcing, 'I will go up to the Court and shoot the Queen with a pistol.' He was arrested near Banbury. His crazed imagination provided the opportunity to settle old scores. Sir Thomas Lucy of Charlecote, whose sympathies were entirely with the new age, arrested Edward Arden, his wife and most of the rest of his family, together with Hall and various others on the orders of the Privy Council. Hall died in prison: Lady Mary was reprieved, but her husband, a former High Sheriff of Warwickshire, was hanged, drawn and quartered. John Somerville, who had precipitated the tragedy, was found strangled in his cell. Perhaps the authorities felt that the public execution of this demented youth would reveal the sparseness of the case against Arden.

Sir Thomas Lucy prosecuted his campaign against local Catholics with vigorous enthusiasm. With the assiduous assistance of Thomas Wilkes, Clerk to the Privy Council, he searched a number of houses in the district with little success. Since no plot existed there was little to find. Wilkes wrote to London in evident frustration.

> Unless you can make Somerville, Arden, Hall the priest, Somerville's wife and his sister speak directly to these things which you have discovered, it will not be possible for us here to find out more than is to be found out already, for the papists in this country greatly do work upon the advantage of clearing their houses of all shows of suspicion.

One who apparently so acted was John Shakespeare. In 1757, an extraordinary testament – six leaves of aged parchment stitched together – was discovered in the eaves of the Birthplace by tilers employed by Thomas Hart, his sixth-generation descendant. It passed to John Payton, owner of the nearby White Lion. When the scholar Edmund Malone heard of it in 1785, he borrowed it. By then the first sheet was lost, but John Jordan, a local wheelwright and self-appointed Shakespeare scholar, obligingly forged a replacement. Fortunately Malone made a copy of the document, which was subsequently lost, probably by the great critic himself. He later expressed doubts about its authenticity, but in 1923 one which was virtually identical was discovered in the British Museum. This had been published in Spanish in Mexico City in 1661. In 1966, the Folger Shakespeare Library acquired a printed English version of the same text published in 1635.[1]

The document is an English translation of a triumphant affirmation of the Catholic faith written by the saintly Archbishop of Milan, Carlo Borromeo.

> I John Shakespeare do protest that I will pass out of this life armed with the last Sacrament of Supreme Unction, the which, if through any let or hindrance I should not be able to have, I do also for that time demand and crave the same, beseeching his Divine Majesty that He will be pleased to anoint my senses both internal and external with the sacred oil of his infinite mercy ...

The 'glorious and ever Virgin Mary' and John Shakespeare's 'patroness', St Winifred – perhaps he was born on 3 November, her feast day – are invoked to intercede for him.

The testaments were brought into England with the illicit Jesuit mission of 1580 led by Edmund Campion and Robert Persons. It was *de rigueur* for the Jesuits bound for the mission field to call on the Archbishop in Milan and the party of Jesuits had done so on their way northwards from Rome. They may have collected the testament then and translated it for printing at Douai. The testaments were a great success in reviving the faith of wavering Catholics. In the following year, William Allen, Head of the English College, which had moved to Rheims, reported to Rome that 'Father Robert wants three or four thousand more of the testaments.' This shortage necessitated the painstaking business for those in England of copying the limited supply. The supplicant would then enter his or her name on the standardised text. Both Campion and Persons were in the Midlands during 1580. 'I ride about some piece of country every day,' wrote Campion. 'On horseback I meditate my sermon. When I come to the house, I polish it. Then I talk with such as come to speak with me, or hear their confessions. In the morning after mass, I preach. They hear with exceeding greediness and very often receive the sacrament.'

Edmund Campion was arrested through treachery at Lyford Grange near Wantage on 17 July 1581. He was executed at Tyburn on 1 December.

In 1581, Sir William Catesby, a former High Sheriff, was imprisoned for refusing to say whether Campion had stayed with him at Bushwood House, an enclave of the Stratford parish situated 10 miles beyond the Borough boundary at Lapworth. Perhaps John Shakespeare and his family encountered the doomed priest, whom William Cecil, the Queen's Secretary, had once described as 'one of the diamonds of England'. That the Shakespeares' last child was christened Edmund on 3 May 1580 may be a mere coincidence – or it may reflect admiration for the fugitive priest.

One of Campion's twelve co-accused at his trial was Thomas Cottam. He was hanged, drawn and quartered at Tyburn six months later, shouting 'God bless you all' to the onlookers. His brother John, the schoolmaster, would have been known by William Shakespeare. Although it is unlikely that he ever taught him, his younger brother Gilbert would have attended the school in his time. It has been suggested that, through the good offices of Cottam, the young William found employment in a great Catholic house in Lancashire. The evidence for this is entirely circumstantial. It is probable that John Cottam was not himself a Catholic. The brothers had been brought up as Protestants and Thomas had been converted to Catholicism and decided to become a priest while working as a schoolmaster in London.

In his short biography of Shakespeare, John Aubrey records that 'he had been in his younger yeares a Schoolmaster in the Countrey'. His informant was William Beeston, whose father, Christopher, had been a member of Shakespeare's company of actors. The 'country' can mean anywhere outside London, but if the story has any credence it may have been that had the schoolmaster Cottam obtained a position for him, it was likely to have been in his native Lancashire. In his will – executed on 3 August 1583 – Alexander Hoghton of Hoghton Tower leaves his musical instruments and 'playe clothes' to his half-brother, Thomas Hoghton. He was aware that his bequest might involve unlooked-for expense, for he adds that if Alexander was not prepared 'to keppe and manteyne players', then the artefacts should pass to another neighbour, Sir Thomas Hesketh. Most significantly, the will requests Sir Thomas 'to be ffrendlye unto ffoke Gyllome and William Shakeshafte nowe dwellynge with me, and eyther take theym into his Servyce or els helpe theym to some good master, as my tryste ys he wyll'.

Private tutors could be utilised to teach their charges music and poetry. Indeed Shakespeare tells us as much in *The Taming of the Shrew*.

> And for I know she taketh most delight
> In Musicke, Instruments, and Poetry,
> Schoolemasters will I keep within my house ...

Hesketh was a patron of the players who performed in his mansion at Rufford Hall. If he took on the player Shakeshafte, it is possible but unlikely that he was taking on the future Bard. The name 'Shakeshaft' is specific. A search on the internet reveals over 31,000 examples of its usage. In any case, at the time the will was executed William Shakespeare was certainly in Stratford. In the summer of 1582, he was engaged in impregnating a lass from nearby Shottery called Anne Hathaway.

## To Have and to Hold

To agree with Sir Hugh Evans, 'it were a goot notion to leave our pribbles and prabbles and desire a marriage'. 27 November 1582 is the first date after William Shakespeare's baptism that can be recorded with certainty. On that day, the diocesan clerk in Worcester noted an application for a marriage licence *inter Willelmum Shaxpere et Annam Whateley de Temple Grafton* to secure the right to marry during the prohibited season between 2 December and 13 January. The complexity increased next day. William

was joined by two husbandmen of Shottery, Fulke Sandells and John
Richardson, who guaranteed a bond of £40 for the marriage of 'William
Shagspere and Anne Hathaway of Stratford'.

Did William leave Anne Whateley standing at the church door? Some
have thought so. The double marriage entry, William's youth – he was
eighteen – and the huge bond imply strange goings-on. Frank Harris
suggested that Shakespeare was enamoured of the lass from Temple
Grafton and intended to do the right thing by her. Meanwhile he dabbled
with Anne Hathaway and the bun was in the proverbial oven. In a bold
move, he fled to Worcester to make Mistress Whateley his own, only to be
thwarted by the burley husbandmen from Shottery, who pledged him to
the shrewish and aging Anne, seven years his senior. He endured her until
he could stand it no longer and fled to London. Thus Anne Whateley's
loss is our gain. Had he settled in solid, rural, connubial bliss, this literary
genius would have flowered unseen in rural Warwickshire.

Whateleys are not uncommon in South Warwickshire: an Alderman
Whateley was a near neighbour of the Shakespeares in Henley Street. Yet
none of that name resided in Temple Grafton, a village 5 miles west of
Stratford. Good as the story is, it is likely that William's other Anne never
existed. Bishop Whitgift's strict ecclesiastical regime at Worcester would
not have connived at youthful duplicity and philandering. The clerk must
have made an error in his first entry, as he did in the same year when he
wrote down the same person as 'Bradley' in one entry, 'Darby' in another.
William Whateley, Vicar of Crowle, had been in the Consistory Court on
that very day in a long wrangle over tithes. Perhaps he distracted the clerk
while he was dealing with the young man from Stratford – and telling
him that he could not issue a licence to an eighteen-year-old without
appropriate sureties.

In fact the only evidence for Anne being seven years older than William
is the figure of 67 on her grave in Holy Trinity which is given as her age
at her death in 1623. The lettering on the tombstones of Shakespeare's
family was re-cut in the 1730s when it was in a 'lamentable state'. The two
numbers that are most likely to be confused are '1' and '7', particularly if
the former is carved with a continental-style loop. Nevertheless, the lack of
a baptismal record for Anne – the register in the parish church dates from
1558 – implies that she was born before that date.

Still there was plenty on William's mind as he rode out from Stratford.
Anne Hathaway was three months pregnant – a fact open to many
interpretations but only one cause. Had the young man seduced the
older woman during the Warwickshire summer? Opportunity for such
consummation was not lacking amid the woods and fields of Arden.

> Between the acres of the rye,
> With a hey and a ho and a hey nonino,
> These pretty country folks would lie ...

Spinster Anne, eldest sister among a large family from her father's two marriages, might have been carried away by the young man that John Aubrey heard was 'handsome' and 'well shap'd'. 'I would there was no other age twixt ten and twenty, or that youth would sleep out the rest,' observes the shepherd in *A Winter's Tale*; '... there is nothing in between but getting wenches with child, wronging the ancientry, stealing and fighting.'

Or was the boot, to use an inappropriate metaphor, on the other foot? James Joyce (via Stephen Dedalus) suggested so.

> He was chosen, it seems to me. If others have their will Ann hath a way. By cock, she was to blame. She put the comether on him, sweet and twenty-six. The grey-eyed goddess who bends over the boy Adonis, stooping to conquer, as prelude to the swelling act, is a bold-faced Stratford wench who tumbles in a cornfield a lover younger than herself.

Courtship and marriage customs vary according to society and epoch. In rural communities, couples have jumped the broomstick, considering the approbation of God and their neighbours sufficient. Shakespeare's Aunt Agnes was recorded as the wife of Thomas Stringer several months before their marriage. There is a record of a couple from a nearby village exchanging vows before witnesses. 'I do confess that I am your wife and have forsaken all my friends for your sake and I hope you will use me well.' Some went too far. A rascally carpenter, William Slatter, confessed that he 'married himself in his chamber, nobody else being by and hopeth that marriage be lawful'. He hoped in vain. His homespun liturgy was declared invalid and he had to undergo a church ceremony.

It was the words 'nobody else being by' which ensured the invalidity of Slatter's marriage. Marriage and the circumstances of its validity were in something of a confused state at the time. In 1598, even the Attorney-General, Sir Edward Cocke, was summoned before the Consistory Court on an allegation that he had married a young widow, Lady Elizabeth Hatton, without a proper ceremony. Amazingly, until the Marriage Duty Act was passed in 1696, there was little formalisation of marriage procedures.

To set out regulations to cover the nuances of human relationships is no easy task. Indeed not much has changed. To define the status of common-law relationships and pre-nuptial contracts is a problem for the modern jurist. Men and women marry each other. The clergyman or registrar is a mere witness to the exchange of vows.

The self-organised marriages of contemporary Warwickshire have their echoes in the drama. On the issue of her exchange of vows in private before a witness, the Duchess of Malfi, in John Webster's eponymous play, expresses a view not dissimilar to that of the Stratford carpenter.

> I have heard lawyers say a contract in a chamber
> *Per verba de presenti*, is absolute marriage.

> Bless heaven, this sacred Guardian, which let violence
> Never untwine.

*Per verba de presenti* – words of proper consent which come from the hugely influential doctrine of marriage propounded by the twelfth-century scholastic theologian Peter Lombard and later endorsed by Pope Alexander III. In his view, a simple agreement was sufficient to create a binding and indissoluble sacramental union, regardless of consummation, but only if the agreement was mutually spoken in the present tense (*consensus de praesenti*) and only if it was entered into freely by both parties rather than being coerced. It is worth noting that when, years later, William Shakespeare was the broker of an arranged marriage between the daughter and apprentice of his landlord in London, the match is described as having been consummated and solemnised in that order. Thus it was possible to marry spontaneously with no preparation or previous agreement: a custom known to the Elizabethans as 'handfasting'. Such ceremonies occur on a number of occasions in Shakespeare's plays. In *The Tempest* (III.1.81–97), Ferdinand and Miranda exchange such vows.

| | |
|---|---|
| Miranda: | I am your wife, if you will marry me; |
| | If not, I'll die your maid. To be your fellow |
| | You may deny me; but I'll be your servant, |
| | Whether you will or no. |
| Ferdinand: | My mistress, dearest; |
| | And I thus humble ever. |
| Miranda: | My husband then? |
| Ferdinand: | Ay, with a heart as willing |
| | As bondage e'er of freedom. Here's my hand. |
| Miranda: | And mine, with my heart in 't. |

In *Measure for Measure*, Mariana baulks at the Duke's suggestion that she has sexual intercourse with the duped Angelo, but he reassures her that the arrangement is valid.

> Nor, gentle daughter, fear you not at all
> He is your husband on a pre-contract
> To bring you thus together is no sin.

It is to such a pre-contract that Claudio appeals in the same play, in terms that might fit a version of the Shakespeare marriage, although, fortunately for the couple, Antonio's stringent views on ante-nuptial fornication did not prevail in contemporary Warwickshire.

> Thus stands it with me: upon a true contract
> I got possession of Juliet's bed.
> You know the lady. She is fast my wife,

Save that we do the denunciation lack
Only for propagation of a dow'r
Remaining in the coffer of her friends.[2]

Although such exchanges may be doctrinally sound, it is clear that without a degree of regulation, legal and administrative chaos ensues. Such was the state of affairs at the time of Shakespeare's wedlock. Self-contracted marriages had some legal standing, but the inheritance and titular rights of children born of such liaisons were disputable, as was the validity of the marriages themselves. Pregnancy was a reason to regularise the situation. If the expected child were a boy, he would be the heir to the Shakespeare dynasty: the eldest son of the eldest son.

Extraordinary conjugal relations were not smiled upon in the Stratford peculiar. In 1584, two men were presented before the Consistory Court for not living with their wives and William Shepherd for cohabiting with Elinor Philips while reportedly having another wife. An undated entry upbrades 'Mr. Holder, curate at Bishopton' for marrying 'wandering persons without license or banes asking'. If William and Anne were regarded as sexual transgressors, they too would have appeared before the 'Bawdy Court', but 1582 was one of the triennial years when its jurisdiction reverted to the diocesan authorities in Worcester. Anne was only three months pregnant, so her condition may not yet have become a matter of concern to the ecclesiastical authorities. The prohibited season for marriage was approaching so the couple may have been urged to act by those close to them. Without the licence the couple could not marry between Advent Sunday, which fell on 2 December 1582 and the octave of the Epiphany, which fell on 15 January 1582/83. The banns would have to be called three times so the couple would not be able to marry until after Sunday 24 January, by which time the condition of the bride would be obvious. The fact that there was opportunity for the thrice-calling in November implies that the request for the special licence was as a result of external pressures. By the time the baby was born, the jurisdiction of the Bawdy Court would have reverted to the Vicar of Stratford. There was every likelihood that the couple would be obliged to make a public confession that they had committed the sin of fornication. Such a confession was made in Holy Trinity on 30 March 1716. by a local weaver, who stood through Divine Service clad in a white sheet and after the Nicene Creed repeated after the minister in 'a distinct and audible voice'.

I Thomas Hudson do here in the presence of God and this Congregation humbly confess and acknowledge that not having the word of God before mine eyes, but being seduced by the Devil and my own sinful lusts I have committed the foul sin of Adultery and have two bastard children unlawfully begotten ... Whereby I have greatly offended Almighty God, endangered my own soul and gave an evil example and scandal to all good Christians, for which offence I am heartily sorry and do humbly beg pardon of God and this congregation for the same hereby promising (God assisting me with his Grace) never to offend in the like again, but to live more chastely hereafter, asking this congregation to pray for me and with me to say, 'Our Father ...'

So William travelled to Worcester and appeared before the Consistory Court, which was situated in the south aisle of the cathedral. Maybe Anne was with him. It is highly likely that his father would have been. His son was a minor so his consent would have been required, although his name would not appear on the marriage certificate. Indeed the presence of a former Bailiff of an important town in the diocese may have reassured the Court. We may be sure that the Chancellor of the Court, Richard Cosin, would have embarked on a close questioning into the circumstances that required the special licence. It is possible that Anne's condition was not revealed. The huge size of the bond – double the schoolmaster's annual salary – indicates that the Court was extremely uneasy about this marriage, although the precise reason is unclear. It may have been because of a combination of issues rather than a single factor. The Court's immediate issuing of the licence was based on its assessment of the integrity of the applicants. If there was indeed a seven-year age difference, it would have raised eyebrows on the bench. Was there a possibility that Anne had a husband yet living? The Court may have been seeking to indemnify itself against any action against it for permitting bigamy. Presumably the Shottery farmers were brought in as guarantors because neither the Hathaways nor the Shakespeares could raise that kind of money. Whatever the causes for the contract, it must surely demonstrate that the guarantors held the parties to it in a considerable degree of trust.

The marriage could have been a means to alleviate the monetary difficulties of the Shakespeares, with the legal prose masking a financial arrangement. It would also have provided an extra pair of skilled feminine hands in the beleaguered business. Contracted marriages were the norm. They abound in Shakespeare's plays. When there was a legal dispute about the terms of the marriage settlement that he himself was to help arrange in 1604, he appeared as a witness in the Court of Requests. The Stratford records contain a number of similar suits. In 1593, Henry Wagstaffe was sued by Charles Wheeler for breaching an undertaking to give him on his marriage with Rose Cawdry, daughter of Joan Cawdry, widow, ten bushels of rye and ten bushels of barley, 'which defendant had promised the said Rose, being his kinswoman'. William Slatter claimed that George Croftes had promised him money 'whenever he should celebrate a marriage with his daughter Anne'. The words of the banns – 'A marriage has been arranged' – meant what they said.

The marriage of an eligible daughter against her father's wishes could provoke fury. In Armada year, Shakespeare's friend, Richard Tyler, married Susanna, eldest daughter of Richard Woodward of Shottery Manor. The bride's grandfather, Robert Perrott, that same cantankerous old alderman who had fallen out with the Corporation, cut her out of his will and issued stern warnings to her sisters against following her example.

The Hathaways were a family of local standing. Their prosperity may be seen in Hewland's Farm, their substantial farmhouse. John Hathaway, who was probably Anne's grandfather, appeared on a muster of 1536, where he is described as an archer. He later became one of Stratford's constables. Anne's brother, Bartholomew, was twice a churchwarden at Holy Trinity. His son, Richard, became Bailiff in 1626. Anne's father left holdings of over 120 acres in 1581. To his daughter 'Agnes' – the name was interchangeable with Anne, the 'g' being silent in the French fashion – he left 10 marks for a dowry and expressed the hope that his chief heir, Bartholomew, would be 'a comforte unto his Bretherene and Sisters to his powers'. Fraternal largesse was expected. With the death of her father and the growth to maturity of his many children, Anne's domestic services were less essential. It was important to find her a husband. Her dowry was worth having. The 10 marks were what a skilled artisan might hope to earn in a year.

If one of the aims of the marriage contract was to cement a bond between two prominent local families, it amply succeeded. The links between the families endured as long as William's descent. His granddaughter left bequests to the five daughters of 'my kinsman Thomas Hathaway, late of Stratford'. Four of them bore the Shakespeare family names of Judith, Joan, Elizabeth and Susanna.

Anne may not have been living at home when she married. Temple Grafton is the village mentioned in the Clerk's first marriage entry and it is there that she may have been living. The vicar was the Revd John Frith, an old Romish priest, who received a poor assessment in a furious Puritan survey of local ministers of religion in 1586. It described him with inadvertent charm as 'unsound in religion, he can neither preach nor read well; his chiefest trade is to cure hawks that are hurt or diseased for which purpose many do usually repair to him'.

There is another possibility why Temple Grafton is mentioned. St Andrew's church there may have been the location for any act of penance undertaken by Anne and William for their antenatal fornication. This was generally conducted in full view of the congregation at morning service, but, if the Court agreed, it could be conducted in private before a clergyman. Given that these were local families of some prominence, there would have been a desire to avoid public scandal. Temple Grafton is some 4 miles beyond Shottery, so perhaps William and Anne elected to make their private confession before Mr Frith and this is why his parish got into the record. Perhaps he also married the couple. Where the wedding took place is a matter of speculation. It is certain that it was not in Stratford's parish church of Holy Trinity.

It could have taken place in the private chapel at Shottery Manor. This was the nearest consecrated ground to Hewlands Farm and William was familiar with the Woodward family. When this author was a boy in

Shottery, the story told locally, for what it is worth, was that the couple held their wedding breakfast there. The manor house is now part of the Stratford Grammar School for Girls. Its website repeats a legend that Shakespeare's betrothal took place in the chapel. To complete the picture, there is even a priest's 'hidey-hole' on the premises.

Another potential nuptial setting is the tiny All Saints church at Billesley, situated just off the road between Shottery and Alcester. It is but a mile from Temple Grafton in which parish it was. The nearby manor house was the seat of the Trussell family, who had been lords of the manor for over 400 years. The current lord was Thomas Trussell. His uncle and namesake was an attorney who did legal work for Stratford Corporation, so the Shakespeares would have been familiar with the family. That the couple's granddaughter was married in this church in 1649, to Sir John Bernard, may be an indicator that the place had a nostalgic family connection for her. If the younger Thomas Trussell attended the ceremony it was among his last public acts for some time. In the following year, he was involved in sensational happenings. He was accused of participating in a highway robbery at Bromley in Kent and was tried and sentenced to death in 1588. What he was up to is a mystery, but it appears that he was not executed. Billesley Manor was sequestrated by the Crown.

The little church of All Souls at Luddington is another candidate for the nuptial rites. Someone standing on Bordon Hill which rises behind Hewlands Farm could see it, so it is just a step across the fields from Shottery. This is another place with something of a tradition that it was here that the wedding took place. Around 1860, the Shakespearean biographer S. W. Fullom visited the village and picked up the curious tale that could be traced back 150 years through Mrs Dyke, who lived in the old parsonage. She had heard it from Martha Casebrooke, who lived all her ninety years in the village, who not only declared that she was told in her childhood that the marriage was solemnised in Luddington, but claimed to have seen the ancient tome in which it was registered.

> This, indeed, we found, on visiting the neighbouring cottages, was remembered by persons still living, when it was in the possession of a Mrs Pickering, who had been housekeeper to Mr Coles, the last curate, and one day burnt the register to boil her kettle.

The couple need not have been married in church at all. The special licence enabled the ceremony to be conducted elsewhere. Thomas Gardner was married in the alehouse at Haselor by 'Sir Roger of Preston [-on-Stour]. Upper-crust Catholics obtained the licence to give a private ceremony secular standing, but it is unlikely that William and Anne could have been married by the old rite even if they desired it. Such was the effectiveness of the government's campaign to suppress Catholicism that it is unlikely that a priest would be available.

In any case, if the bride and groom were indeed Catholic, a rite of their church would not have been necessary to validate the marriage. Throughout his works, William Shakespeare demonstrates familiarity with Catholic doctrine. He would have been aware that marriage is a bond between a man and a woman. The priest is both a witness and a validator of the legality of the rite. An Anglican marriage, properly conducted, is valid to Catholics.

The awaited child was christened Susanna on 26 May 1583. Twins followed. Hamnet and Judith were baptised on 24 February 1584/85. The godparents were evidently the Sadlers, a couple who gave the twins their Christian names. They kept a baker's shop on the corner of High Street and Sheep Street and named a son William in 1597. Hamnet Sadler travelled frequently on business – sometimes as far away as East Anglia. He was a loved and potent husband. His neighbour, Abraham Sturley, noted that 'Judith Sadler waxeth very heavy for the burden of her childing and the want of her husband'.

There were to be no more children for Anne. This could imply estrangement, but the women of her line were not distinguished by their fecundity.

# 4

# The Warwickshire Poacher, c. 1586

'By the keeper's nose'

*– Titus Andronicus*

The lack of documentary information about William Shakespeare during the nine years following his marriage has enabled his biographers to wander as freely and extravagantly as they will. Some have noted his extensive use of legal terminology and articled him to a lawyer. The Elizabethans were highly litigious, although the Shakespeares indulged less than most. William Shakespeare, like a number of other notable writers, appears not to have held lawyers in great esteem. If he were so engaged, he cannot have found the experience edifying. Further speculation has put him in the military. Many Elizabethans had such an experience, if only through the kind of muster organised by Falstaff. 'Care I for the limb, the hewes, the stature, bulk and big assemblance of a man? Give me the spirit, Master Shallow.' William Shakespeare's name, however, is not among those Stratfordians summoned for duty in the Armada year of 1588. On 4 August, the gentlemen of Warwickshire sent their levies to the great army assembled at Tilbury. At Stratford the town armoury was replenished and a little band of eight recruits was sent off to war. They marched off, spent some time at Warwick, reached Banbury and then returned, presumably having heard of the Spanish fleet's dispersal.

It is significant that William Shakespeare was not a member of this gallant troupe. As a fit twenty-four-year-old, he would certainly have been conscripted had he been in Stratford, so he was almost certainly elsewhere. But where?

If the most colourful legend of Shakespeare's youth is credited, his departure from Stratford was precipitate. Some half-century after his death, the Revd Richard Davies, Chaplain of Corpus Christi College, Oxford, dined at High Table. The talk of the Fellows turned to the life of the great poet. Afterwards he wrote down what he recalled of the conversation.

> Much given to all unluckiness in stealing venison and Rabbits, particularly from Sr Lucy who had him oft whipt & sometimes imprisoned & at last made him fly his native country to his great Advancemt, but his reveng was so

good that he is his Justice Clodpate and calls him a great man yt in allusion to his name bore three lowses rampant for his Arms ...

This curious story is repeated independently by Nicholas Rowe.

He had, by a Misfortune common enough to young fellows, fallen into ill Company: and amongst them, some that made a frequent practice of Deer-stealing, engag'd him with them in robbing a Park that belong'd to Sir *Thomas Lucy* of *Charlcot*, near *Stratford*. For this he was prosecuted by that Gentleman, as he thought somewhat too severely; and in order to revenge that ill Usage, he made a Ballad upon him. And tho' this, probably the first Essay of his Poetry, be lost, yet it is said to have been so very bitter, that it redoubled the Prosecution against him to that degree, that he was oblig'd to leave his Business and Family in *Warwickshire*, for some time and shelter himself in *London*.

Unlike Davies, Rowe gets the name of Justice Shallow and the play in which he appears correct.

Amongst other Extravaganzas, in *The Merry Wives of Windsor*, he has made him a Dear-stealer, that he might at the same time remember his *Warwickshire* Prosecutor, under the name of Justice *Shallow*: he has given him very near the same Coat of Arms which *Dugdale*, in his antiquities of that County, describes for a Family there ...

So what are we to make of this curious business? We have seen the power of oral tradition, yet the story is one that the earliest biographer, John Aubrey, would have loved. Yet he fails to mention it.

Nor is the stern Sir Thomas Lucy a likely model for Justice Shallow. He was a strong Protestant, as befits a man whose private tutor was John Foxe, the author of *The Book of Martyrs*. In the words of Alice Fairfax-Lucy, he 'was a man at peace with his conscience and with the established Church'. It was he who rebuilt Charlecote House as the classic Elizabethan mansion we see today.

At least Sir Thomas fits one aspect of the legend. He is highly likely to have ordered that any poacher caught on his land should be whipped. The issue was one of more than local importance to him. In 1584, he became High Sheriff of Worcestershire and continued his relentless pursuit of recusants. Nor need the legend necessarily relate to Charlecote. In the year Lucy became a High Sheriff, a law was passed enabling the sequestration of the lands of Catholics who had fled abroad. Contiguous to this was a Private Bill which gave Sir Thomas the 'assurance' (but not the title) of certain undefined lands belonging to such Catholic proprietors. There was wealth in Protestantism as well as advancement.

The lands in question were close to the Charlecote estate and belonged to William Clopton and Sir Francis Englefield. Englefield had left the country on Elizabeth's accession, so his estate at Fulbrooke had remained untended for a quarter of a century. It may be significant that Rowe describes the scene of the poaching as a park that *belonged* to Sir Thomas Lucy of Charlecote, rather than as Charlecote Park. Doubtless Fulbrooke had provided fair game for the locals in both senses of the word. Sir Thomas restored the fences and clearly would take a dim view of interlopers with intent. It is not impossible that the young William Shakespeare was one of these. He is well aware of the vagaries of poaching, as he makes clear in *Titus Andonicus*, a play that would have been written within a few years of any such incident.

> What hast not thou full often struck a doe,
> And borne her cleanly by the keeper's nose?

The story of Shakespeare's deer-poaching is almost invariably presented as an episode of youthful high jinks, but the fruits of the countryside were an essential part of Stratford's domestic economy. Open country was a mere ten-minute walk from the town centre in any direction. Within modern living memory, men would go out with their dogs into the surrounding fields, to trap rabbits and gut them on the spot, or to put ferrets down the holes. Many poorer families depended on rabbits for their meat – and they would get a penny for the skin. Hares were highly prized. One would feed a family for two or three days.

> Edward and Richard like a brace of greyhounds,
> Having the fearful flying hare in sight.

says Queen Margaret in *Henry VI, Part III* and there is a fulsome description of Wat, the terrified hare, as well as other hunting scenes, in *Venus and Adonis*.

We recall the Shakespeares' shaky finances. Stealing what had been stolen would not have seemed immoral and the booty, well-salted, might feed their expansive household for several weeks. We recall the role of Sir Thomas as a hammer of the Catholics. The alarm that his name must have aroused in certain quarters in South Warwickshire is further revealed in his actions in Parliament in 1585. He sponsored a Bill that extended a potential death sentence to any 'Jesuits, seminary priests and other such-like disobedient persons' who had become Catholic priests since the Queen's accession if they had spent more than forty days in England. Just one member opposed the third reading. Dr William Parry, MP for Queenborough, denounced the measure as 'savouring of treasons, full of blood, danger and despair to English subjects, and pregnant with fines and forfeitures which would go to enrich not the Queen, but private individuals'. Parliamentary privilege was, to say the least, strictly circumscribed at the time. The Speaker ordered Parry to be taken into custody. He was released after apologising for his speech. It was this Bill that was to enable the execution of Mary, Queen of Scots.

Parry was a curious character who, like Somerville, was symptomatic of the schizoid state that the religious controversies of the age could produce – and also of the paranoia that the authorities had developed about Catholicism: a religion which most Englishmen had practised just two decades earlier. A Welshman by birth, he had come to London and entered the service of the Earl of Pembroke and then that of the Queen. He married a well-off widow, Mrs Powell, and on her death another widow, Catherine Heywood, who brought him several manors in Lincolnshire and Kent. Despite this affluence, he was a spendthrift who managed to run through both inheritances. Pursued by his creditors, he approached the Queen's minister, Lord Burghley, and asked to become a spy in her service. Like many others, he was sent to infiltrate the English Catholic exiles in France. It was a double game he was to play for the rest of his life. It was also one that fatally confused him. He became an *agent provocateur*, encouraging people into making inflammatory statements, which he then reported to Burghley. It would appear that Parry was strongly influenced by the Catholics on whom he was spying and developed a deep sympathy with them, but nevertheless he continued his nefarious activities. Following a severe assault on one of his creditors, he was sentenced to death, but eventually pardoned by the Queen. Worse was to follow. It may well have been a continuation of his role as an *agent provocateur* that he approached an associate, Sir William Neville, with a plot to kill the Queen. This is what he claimed when arrested, but this time it availed him nothing. Two days before his trial on 23 February 1584/85, Sir Thomas Lucy moved that some especially dreadful death be found for him. He was executed in Palace Yard, Westminster, on 2 March 1584/85, probably in the presence of Parliamentary colleagues, including Lucy. It is difficult to think of a more dreadful death than hanging, drawing and quartering, but Sir Thomas appears to have got his wish. The execution is described as being conducted 'with much delay'.

It takes little leap of the imagination to realise the terror that institutionalised psychopaths like Sir Thomas Lucy might strike – and intended to strike – into the hearts of those they regarded as their opponents. The case of Edward Arden shows that conclusive proof of complicity was not required – animosity was enough. Had the young William Shakespeare offended Sir Thomas for whatever reason, it might have seemed appropriate to disappear from the locality for a while. The contact with the players might have been recalled – or a company might have been passing through the town. Professor Mark Eccles discovered[1] that the Queen's Men were two actors short when they arrived at Stratford in 1587, for William Knell was killed by John Towne during a brawl at Thame. Since Towne had struck in self-defence, he was later pardoned, but, in the meantime, had his place been taken by a young man of theatrical enthusiasm from Stratford? Where better to seek refuge until the storm had passed than in the anonymity of being a factotum in an acting company?

So the deer-poaching legend is possible but not proven. What is less likely is that the poet should wait a dozen years or so before lampooning a man who, if the story is to be believed, was his inadvertent benefactor, ensuring that he went to London to make his fame and fortune. Sir Thomas Lucy probably never attended a London theatre in his life and his name would probably have been unknown to most of the audience. Nor is the stern Sir Thomas a likely model for Justice Shallow, who, in any case, was 'of Gloucestershire', not Warwickshire. Yet the satire points blatantly towards the Lucys. In *The Merry Wives of Windsor* Justice Shallow is 'armigero' – i.e. entitled to bear arms – and has twelve white luces, or pikes, as his coat of arms. Admittedly the Lucys generally displayed three rather than twelve, but in an illustration in Dugdale's *Antiquities* they are quartered, making the requisite number. Shallow's family had possessed this right 'these three hundred years'. One of the ancient line of Lucy's proudest possessions at Charlecote was the parchment Roll of Arms that traced the family's lineage back to the Norman Conquest.

So who might Shakespeare be satirising? To find a likely candidate we need look no further than down the Thames from the Globe Theatre. When the character of Shallow first appeared on the London stage, Thomas Lucy, only son of the Warwickshire squire, was living in Tower Ward. He would have been a familiar figure in London. Significantly, in the Ward returns he was styled as a 'Knight of Gloucestershire'. His first wife, Dorothea Arnold, brought to him her ancestral estate of Highnam in that county. Like Justice Shallow, this Sir Thomas might well be considered as 'lecherous as a monkey'. His will makes provision for two natural daughters.

Justice Shallow is 'of Clement's Inn', one of London's ten Inns of Court, where young men gained their articles to the legal profession. It ceased to be in 1868. Few records survive, so it is not possible to discern whether Sir Thomas Lucy II was associated with it. Certainly he was familiar with the luminaries of the legal profession, balancing friendship with the two leading lawyers of his day, Sir Edward Cocke and his bitter rival, Sir Francis Bacon.

Nor is there any record of Shallow's named companions at Clement's Inn. Yet, of all Shakespeare's plays, *Henry IV, Part II* is the one which most appears to bring into the text the names of actual living people. Whoever 'Black George Barnes, and Francis Pickbone, and Will Squele, a Cotswold man' may have been, they are almost certainly lost to us forever, apart from, that is, 'little John Doit of Staffordshire'. The Dyotts were a noted family in and around Lichfield. John Dyott, a barrister, was thrice Bailiff of the city. He was granted a coat of arms in 1563 and died in 1580. His grandson, another John, is the most likely original of Shallow's companion.

Like Justice Shallow, this Sir Thomas was an ardent litigator, which may be another indicator of his legal grounding. Like Shallow, he was conversant with the Star Chamber. He started litigation concerning his late wife's estates in Monmouthshire which dragged on for eighteen years: a kind of Elizabethan *Jarndyce and Jarndyce*. Even in that age of vexatious litigation, such a case must have aroused comment and interest. Like Shallow, he may well have boasted around town of his ancient lineage. It is difficult to disagree with the verdict of Alice Fairfax-Lucy, the family historian: 'Nothing that has survived about the second Sir Thomas shows him in a particularly good light.'

The opening lines of the *Merry Wives of Windsor* must have brought the house down, combining, as they did, a parody of Sir Thomas, the noted litigant, discussing taking legal action against the most famous fictional comic figure of the age.

**Shallow:**   Sir Hugh, persuade me not. I will make a Star Chamber matter of it. If he were twenty Sir John Falstaffs, he shall not abuse Robert Shallow, esquire.

Slender proceeds to confirm that his cousin, like the second Sir Thomas, is indeed of the County of Gloucester and a Justice of the Peace. Legalisms are used to confirm his grounding at the Inns of Court. He is a 'Coram', a justice whose presence was necessary to constitute a bench of magistrates. He is also variously a 'Custolorum' and a 'Ratulorum', the *Custos Rotulorum*, the chief of the justices of a county, having in his care the records of the sessions.

Thus it is possible that the story heard by Davies and Rowe has entangled two strands of oral tradition. There was some sort of clash between the Shakespeares and the first Sir Thomas: perhaps on the religious issue, or a poaching incident, or some mixture of the two. Years later, he lampoons the second Sir Thomas, a noted figure around London.

William Shakespeare's likely distaste for the first Sir Thomas, and his mockery of the second, did not extend into the next generation. The third Sir Thomas was a man of learning, wit and charm, an associate of George Herbert and John Donne and a devotee of the drama. In 1633, two itinerant actors, Bartholomew Jones and Richard Whitinge, appeared before the magistrates in Banbury for some petty breach of the peace. On being examined, Jones said 'that he hath gone with the Company these two years and that he hath acted his parts in divers places'. One of these was Sir Thomas Lucy's mansion at Charlecote. It was also revealed that Whitinge 'hath acted a part with this company of players lately at Leicester, Stratford, Meriden, Solihull, at Sir William Spencer's. Sir Thomas Lucy's, etc.'

Whether the young William Shakespeare's departure from Stratford was precipitate or no, the London Road was certainly familiar to Stratfordians. A number of them were articled as apprentices in the great city. In 1577, Roger Lock, another glover's son, began a ten-year apprenticeship to Richard Pickering, a London stationer. On 28 Septembe 1579, Richard

Field, son of Henry Field, the tanner in Back Bridge Street who was William Shakespeare's senior by two years, was apprenticed to George Bishop, a prominent London stationer, for the normal term of seven years. It was agreed that the first six of these be spent in the service of Thomas Vautrollier, a Protestant refugee from Catholic France, in St Paul's Churchyard. Vautrollier published a great variety of books. It must have been his faith that led him to publish a number of treatises of Calvinistic and anti-Catholic polemic, including *An Answer of a true Christian to the proude challenge of a counterfeit Catholicke* in 1577 and *The Institution of the Christian Religion,* 'wrytten in Latine by maister Iohn Caluin' in the following year.

Stratford girls entered service in the city. In 1594, Elizabeth Trowte, sister of a local butcher, sued Elizabeth Hancocks for alleging that after the death of her mistress in London she stole all her clothes

> and came down into the countrye and hyd head for the space of halfe a yeare and afterwards flourished abroade in the said clothes lyke a gentlewoman, but after that she was taken and carried to London where the same clothes were received agayne by her master without anye punishment.

Her airs and graces caught her Henry Prettie, another butcher, whom she bore five children before she and her husband perished during the plague year of 1606. More respectable advancement was secured by Katherine Rogers, daughter of a High Street butcher and alderman. Her considerable fortune from outliving three wealthy husbands enabled her only son, John Harvard, to endow the American university which bears his name.

A normal means of travel for those who could afford it, but were not sufficiently affluent to possess their own transport, was to accompany the carriers who made regular journeys between Stratford and London, carrying a variety of goods and passengers. 'If ther be any cloth for mee to bee sent downe, send it by Edward Bromley,' wrote Daniel Baker to Richard Quiney at The Bell in Carter Lane, who was in London on Stratford's business during 1598. Five days later, Quiney's wife sent him tobacco, cheeses and other articles by another carrier, William Greenway. 'She longeth to hear how he progresses with the town business,' noted his father, Adrian Quiney.

Around 1605, John Sadler, son of the tenant of Stratford Mill, fled from an arranged marriage.

> He joined himself to the carrier and came to London, where he had never been before and sold his horse in Smithfield and having no acquaintance … to recommend or assist him, he went from street to street and house to house, asking if they wanted an apprentice and though he met with many discouraging scorns and a thousand denials, he went on till he light upon Mr. Brooksbank, a grocer in Bucklersbury.

This enterprising young man prospered, becoming a shareholder in the Virginia Company. His partner and brother-in-law was Richard Quiney, brother of Shakespeare's son-in-law. The two grocers did not forget their home town. In 1632, they presented the Corporation with a mace 'to be borne before the Bailiffe and Chief Alderman ... for this time being for ever', which is still in use.

All these Stratfordians are eclipsed in memory by their fellow. On an unknown date in the 1580s, he crossed the great bridge over the Avon on the start of his momentous journey. Stratford was the source of his genius, but only in London could he find his destiny.

# 5

# The Rise of the Theatre, 1559–96

'This wooden O'

*– Henry V*, Act I, Scene 1

As the committee of the gods, it is surely our task to provide our playwright with a theatre. Fortuitously, such a building had been created some ten years before the time of William Shakespeare's probable arrival in London, but the roots of the Elizabethan drama go deeper than that – to the liturgy of the Catholic Church. Even today, the reading of the Passion of Christ on Palm Sunday is in a semi-dramatic form. This reflects the medieval liturgical form of the trope, which embellished existing texts used in worship without diminishing them through addition. One of the earliest, the *Quem Queaeritis* trope, was recorded in the *Regularis Concordia*, or Book of Rules, produced by Ethelwold, Bishop of Winchester, for his Benedictine brethren in the tenth century. On Easter Sunday, before the Gospel was chanted at Matins, three brethren entered, representing the women who came to anoint the body of Jesus. They wore copes and carried thuribles. They moved towards the sepulchre, where other brothers were concealed, representing angels. They were wearing albs and holding palms. One angel began to sing 'in a dulcet voice of medium pitch'. '*Quem Quearitis in sepulchre, O Christicolae?*' ('Who do you seek in the sepulchre, O Christian women?') '*Jesum Nazarenum Chrucifixum, O Caelicaeli.*' ('Jesus of Nazareth, the crucified, O heavenly beings.') '*Non est hic. Surrexit. Sicut praedicerat.*' ('He is not here. He is risen. Just as he foretold.')

It was not long, just a few centuries, before the dramatic setting represented by the tropes began to move out of the ecclesiastical building and into the wider world. The catalyst was Corpus Christi. Following the visions of an Augustinian nun, St Juliana of Liège, this Feast of the Eucharist was instituted by Bishop Robert of Liège in 1246. In 1264, the Pope made it a universal Feast.

It became a customary part of the Corpus Christi ritual to take the Blessed Sacrament in its monstrance through the streets for the veneration of the faithful: an acknowledgement that the sacrament was part of the Church's life in the community. This led to the development of elaborate forms of worship. In many places it became customary to present a dramatic cycle in the streets, recounting Salvation History from the

Creation to the Last Judgement. In Valencia in Spain, these *Entemeses* or *Misteris* are still performed in the local dialect of the fifteenth century. Huge decorated floats provide the platforms for the *Misteris* along the processional route. Like many such rites in Catholic countries, the sacred and the secular sit easily side by side. *Los Gigantes* (giants) and *Cabezudos* (carnival figures with enormous heads) dance along behind the religious procession.

Such pageants were familiar in many parts of medieval Europe, not least in England. The texts of the mystery cycles of Chester, 'N,Towne' (probably Northampton), Wakefield and York survive virtually complete, as do parts of the texts from Coventry, Norwich and Newcastle. Evidence of their widespread popularity is provided by the fact that three extant plays are in the Cornish language.

The word 'mystery' derives from the Latin *mysterium*, which means 'handicraft' and indicates that the plays were performed by various trade guilds, each with its own play. That the drama was indigenous to the people is reflected in the rough humour and in the transition of the dialogue from the Latin of the tropes to the vernacular. The Mystery Plays, although reverential, are anything but pietistic.

A noted figure in the Mysteries was that of King Herod, a *grand guignol* character whose ranting and raving must have provoked audience participation.

> For I am even he that made both heaven and hell,
> And of my might power holdeth up this world round,
> Magog and Mandrake, both them did I confound.

Another melodramatic character was Termagant: a word that has passed into the language. This was the god supposedly worshipped by Muslims. He usually appeared as a turbaned figure wearing long robes in the Eastern style. As a stage-villain, he ranted at the lesser villains who were his servants and worshippers.

A parallel process to the development of the Mysteries was that of the Miracle Plays. They represent what the title purports: an episode concerning the miraculous doings of a saint, usually, in the surviving texts, the Blessed Virgin Mary or St Nicholas. The earliest recorded such production in England was of a play of St Catherine in Dunstable in 1119.

The Morality Plays grew out of the Mysteries in the late fifteenth century. Again the name expresses the function. The human and divine characters of the Mysteries are replaced by ones representing abstract vices and virtues. In most the central figure represents 'Everyman' (the title of the best-known morality play) or 'Mankind' (the proponent in another well-known play, *The Castle of Perseverance*), who is confronted with a moral dilemma and has to make a choice between Good and Evil. There is clearly a prototype for Shakespearean tragedy here, although the choice for Shakespeare's tragic heroes is infinitely more complex.

The eccentric poet John Skelton (1460–1529) broke new ground for the Moralities with his play *Magnyfycence*. He extended the moral setting into the political arena. The central character, Magnificence, is tempted by such evils as Crafty Conveyaunce and Courtly Abusyon. He is supported by such virtues as Measure and Felicity. Other plays followed which adapted the Morality tradition.

Performances of the Mysteries could surely have survived into the present age – at least in some localities. They did so in Valencia. The reason they did not do so in England may be ascribed to the Protestant Reformation and the power of Puritanism. There was some attempt to integrate them into the new order. John Bales's *Kynge Johann* is an anti-Catholic polemic which features two figures from English history: King John and the Archbishop of Canterbury, Stephen Langton. The other characters are morality figures. Yet to many Protestants, the Mysteries reeked of the Catholic past. The Puritans loathed all forms of drama, regarding it as idolatry to create the false images that they considered acting roles to be. The assault on this form of drama was not co-ordinated, so the Mysteries disappeared one by one rather than collectively. In Coventry the last performance took place in 1589, when it was decided to commission a version that would be more acceptable to the new order. It was called *The Destruction of Jerusalem* and written by John Smythe of Oxford. It was a flop. The Guild of Smiths paid 20s not to participate in it.

It is probable that William Shakespeare went to see the Mysteries in Coventry. As a chronicler in the Middle Ages expressed it:

> The state and reverence and show,
> Were so attractive, folks would go
> From all parts, every year to see
> These pageant plays at Coventry.

William Shakespeare was twenty-five when the Mysteries ceased to be and by then almost certainly in London, but he shows a familiarity with them that must come from personal observation. When Hamlet gives his famous advice to the players, he refers to the famous *grand guignol* characters.

> O, it offends me to hear a robustious periwig-pated fellow tear a passion to tatters, to very rags, to split the ears of the groundlings, who for the most part are capable of nothing but inexplicable dumb shows and noise. I would have such a fellow whipped for o'erdoing Termagant. It out-Herods Herod.

It is significant that as late as 1601, when *Hamlet* was first presented, a London audience would understand references to the Mysteries, such had been their popular hold.

While the Puritans had a point of view, there is no doubt that, overall, Elizabethan drama represented a morality, a struggle between good and evil. The idea that life had no meaning or purpose would have seemed an ultimate blasphemy. This moral structure was part of William Shakespeare's dramatic inheritance. That this was well recognised by his contemporaries is revealed in the furious strictures of the Puritan John Northbrooke, who lamented that people 'shame not to say and affirm openly that playes are as good as sermons, and that they learn as much or more at a play than they do when God's word is preached'.[1]

The developing drama was dominated by respect for its classical predecessors. The concept of the 'classical unities' was based on a misinterpretation of a passage in Aristotle's *Poetics*. The three unities that those influenced by the classics believed to be essential to the drama were Unity of Action (a play should follow one action, with few or no subplots), Unity of Place (it should not feature more than one setting), and Unity of Time (the action should take place over no more than twenty-four hours).

The models were the Latin writers Seneca (for tragedy) and Plautus (for comedy). The first known production of a play by Plautus in England was at Oxford University in 1522/23. It was in these rather rigid modes that the first writers for the Elizabethan stage would set their works.

On 18 January 1562, a group of law students known as the Gentlemen of the Temple performed a play called *Gorboduc* before Queen Elizabeth. It was written by two aristocratic courtiers, Thomas Norton and Thomas Sackville. Its chain of slaughter and revenge draws on Senecan forms. It is a turgid piece – the Queen was to sit through much better stuff during her long reign – but it is significant because it introduces the form of blank verse to the English drama. The first known user of this means of literary expression was Henry Howard, Earl of Surrey, in his translation of the *Aeneid* around 1554. It is likely that he simply rendered the non-rhyming form of the Latin verse as closely as he could into the English language. In so doing he inadvertently established the vehicle that would be utilised by finer dramatists than Norton and Sackville later in the century.

It became customary for aristocratic houses to maintain troops of players, although whether they were part of a noblemen's retinue or just operating under his patronage is unclear, but from subsequent developments it is the latter form that prevailed. The earliest-known example of such a company bore the Earl of Oxford's name in 1492. In 1559, the Earl of Leicester's Men were formed from the members of his household. They can be traced as they move from place to place throughout the 1560s and 70s. When the Elizabethan Poor Laws were amended by an Act of Parliament of 1572, the status of the actors was potentially threatened. They could be classed as vagabonds and fined or imprisoned. Thus it became essential for the actors to seek the patronage of a great nobleman and be regarded as his servants.

Head of Leicester's Company by 1574 was James Burbage. He was probably a joiner before he became an actor: a skill that was to stand him in good stead. On 3 January 1572 he wrote a letter to Robert Dudley, Earl of Leicester, that reveals how the system of patronage worked. He requests that the actors be appointed not only as the Earl's liveried servants, but also as his 'household retainers', a distinction that would give them greater freedom of movement around the country. They would not expect 'any further stipend or benefit from the Earl'. What they wanted was the prestige and protection of his name while operating as an independent commercial entity. As John Stowe put it, 'Comedians and stage-players of former time were very poore and ignorant ... but now being grown very skilful in all matters, they were entertained into the service of great lords.'

As the Queen's favourite, Robert Dudley used his influence at court in 1574 to secure the first Royal Patent granted to any theatrical company. It authorised his company

> to use, exercise and occupy the art and faculty of playing comedies, trag-
> edies, interludes, stage plays and others such like ... as well within our City
> of London and liberties of the same, as also within the liberties and freedoms
> of any of cities, towns, boroughs, etc. whatsoever ... throughout our Realm
> of England.

Crucially, the warrant overrode earlier policies which enabled local officials to censure or ban plays. This power was now invested in the royal authority through the Lord Chamberlain and the Master of the Revels. It meant that, once the players had gained this approval, they could perform their plays anywhere without local interference. Even more importantly, it put the theatre on a fully professional basis and opened up the opportunity for the creation of great drama.

Leicester's Men performed at court during the Christmas festivities in both 1574 and 1575. The company also played a central part in the entertainments provided by Robert Dudley at Kenilworth Castle in 1566, 1572 and at the fourteen-day extravaganza in honour of the queen in 1575.

In the 1560s a development occurred which was to present a severe challenge to the professional companies. Richard Edwards was appointed a Gentleman of the Chapel Royal and Master of the Singing Boys. He was a poet, musician and playwright. In 1566, his play *Palaman and Arcite* was performed before the Queen at Oxford. The stage collapsed and three people were killed. In what was to become a noted tradition of the theatre, the show went on.

At least since the reign of Henry VII, the Children of the Chapel Royal had been presenting interludes at court. Richard Edwards was the ideal man to extend this output. The boys appeared frequently at court under the tutelage of his successor, William Hunnis. In the year in which Burbage built his theatre, Hunnis's deputy, Richard Farrant, rented space for public performances at the old Blackfriars Priory by the Thames. The Children of Paul's – the choir of the great cathedral – was another highly successful troupe which performed frequently at court – and at the Blackfriars Theatre.

Doubtless, the Children's Companies were a source of young actors for the adult ones. It was a theatrical tradition that the women's parts were played by boys. This is a reflection of the ecclesiastical origins of the drama and its roots in the trade guilds which were entirely masculine. The boys were apprenticed into the companies and would have learnt the ancillary crafts of their trade – fencing, dancing and music-making. The parts that were created for them demonstrate their skills as actors, but the dramatists were conscious of the need to create the appropriate atmosphere in which they could perform effectively – and the potential for ribaldry if they appeared too familiar with their co-stars. Kisses are few and far between in Shakespeare's works and generally represent a consummation of what has gone on before: 'Come kiss me Kate', 'Thus with a kiss I die', and the like. An exception comes when Cressida kisses five different Greeks: a scene that must have been shocking to the audience, representing her transition from virgin lover to wanton. Even then, the scene has to be interpreted by Ulysses.

> There's language in her eye, her cheek, her lip,
> Nay, her foot speaks; her wanton spirits look out
> At every joint and motive of her body.

At some point the drama moved into the courtyards of inns. This may have been a comparatively late development: a response to the increasing crackdown on the religious drama. The earliest record of such a performance in London is of a 'lewd play' called *A Sackful of News* at the 'Bore's Head without Aldgate' in 1557.

The shape of urban inns was dictated by the high cost of their frontages onto the streets. They tended to be narrow, with the premises going back a good way. Many were built around a courtyard and contained upper walkways and galleries. If a wagon was placed in the centre, the place became a natural 'theatre in the round'. Such performances became increasingly popular, so that, in 1574, the City Corporation began to regulate, and eventually constrain, these activities.

With hindsight it seems a logical step to progress the theatre from the inn courtyard to a system-built edifice. Buildings like the Boar's Head must have been more like theatres than inns by then, with resident companies attached to them. In 1567, Burbage's brother-in-law, John Brayne, built the first permanent theatre in England since Roman times: the 'Red Lion Theatre at Mile End'. It was not a success and closed soon after. It was probably too far beyond the City boundary. The lesson was not lost. In 1576, Burbage and Brayne acquired the lease of land at Spitalfields from Giles Allen. It has been stated frequently that Allen was a Puritan, hostile to the theatre, who had been given no idea of Burbage's intentions. This is belied by a clause in the contract which gave Allen and his family a free season ticket to the best part of the house.

> And further, that it shall or may [be] lawful for the said Gyles and for his wife and family, upon lawful request therefor made to the said James Burbage, his executors or assigns, to enter or come into the premises, and there in some one of the upper rooms to have such convenient place to sit or stand to see such plays as shall be there played, freely without anything therefor paying.

Inadvertently, or otherwise, but certainly serendipitously, Burbage and Brayne gave the Elizabethan theatre its shape, which was based on the inn courtyard. The projecting apron stage meant that the audience was at an intimate distance from the actors. The virtual absence of scenery meant that what was to be Shakespeare's 'wooden O' was a supreme theatre of the imagination: the action had to be envisaged in the mind. This thought is nowhere better expressed than in the prologue to *Henry V*. In the opening line the Chorus regrets that he does not possess

> ... a Muse of fire, that would ascend
> The brightest heaven of invention,
> A kingdom for a stage, princes to act
> And monarchs to behold the swelling scene!

In other words, Shakespeare desires the capacity of the modern newsreel to depict events as they happen, but that is not the case. He apologises for the fact that, to portray this mighty scene, all he has is a bunch of actors.

> ... can this Cockpit hold ...
> Within this wooden O, the very Caskes
> That did afright the air at Agincourt?
> O pardon, since a crooked figure may
> Attest in little place a million,
> And let us, ciphers to this great account
> On your imaginary forces work.
> Suppose within the girdle of these walls
> Are now confined two mighty monarchies,
> Whose high uprearèd and abutting fronts
> The perilous narrow ocean parts asunder.
> Piece out our imperfections with your thoughts.
> Into a thousand parts divide one man
> And make imaginary puissance.
> Think, when we talk of horses that you see them,
> Printing their proud hoofs i' th' receiving earth.
> For 'tis your thoughts now must deck our kings,
> Carry them here and there, jumping o'er times,

> turning th' accomplishment of many years
> into an hour-glass ...

During the season, performances were given almost every day. Paul Hentzner, a German visitor to one of the theatres in 1598, may not have understood a lot of the action, but he was impressed when the show concluded with 'excellent music, a variety of dances and the excessive applause'. He also noted the great clouds of smoke that rose from the clay pipes of the 'very numerous audiences ... along with plenty of phlegm and defluxion from the head'. Fruits in season – such as apples and pears – and nuts and ale and wine were carried about to be sold.

Being in the open air, the theatres were at the mercy of the weather. Many a performance must have been called off in the midst of torrential downpours or even snowstorms. They were also obliged to close during the Lenten season of fasting and penitence.[2]

Within a year of the opening of The Theatre (the name given to the new establishment – after all, it was the only one at the time), a second public playhouse, The Curtain, opened its doors in Finsbury Fields just 200 yards to the south. The new form of entertainment soon acquired quasi-respectability. It was given a huge boost in 1583 when the Queen's Men were formed under royal patronage. The Queen's Principal Secretary, Sir Francis Walsingham, was tasked with assembling the new company. He did it with aplomb, using his influence to recruit leading actors. His greatest coup was to secure the services of Richard Tarlton, the greatest comic actor of his day. John Stowe eulogised about his 'wondrous plentifull pleasant extemporal wit', adding that 'hee was the wonder of his time'.[3] 'Tarlton, so beloved that men use his picture for their signs,' wrote a contemporary.[4] Such was the charm that Tarlton exercised over the Queen that she made him a Groom of her Chamber: a precedent to be followed in the next reign. It is an engaging thought that he might have been with the Queen's Men when they visited Stratford in 1587.

Years later, Henry Peacham was to recall the effect that his first appearance had on an audience.

> Tarleton when his head was only seen,
> The tire-house door and tapestry between,
> Set all the multitude in such a laughter,
> They could not hold for scarce an hour after.

To Tarlton is attributed one of the most successful works of the day. The text of the two-part play *The Seven Deadly Sins*, first produced around 1585, is lost, but this take on the morality plays of the previous generation was clearly a vehicle for his comic genius. He died in 1588, but his play continued to attract audiences to The Theatre into the 1590s. In its original cast were a number of the future colleagues of William Shakespeare.

Not only did the aristocracy patronise the acting companies, but educated men – the 'University Wits' – wrote for them. They burst onto the scene shortly before the time that William Shakespeare became a man of the theatre. Among the most prominent were the Cambridge graduates Christopher Marlowe, Robert Greene and Thomas Nashe, and the Oxford graduates Thomas Lodge, John Lyly and George Peele.

Blank verse became an important means of dramatic expression. Its predominant form, the iambic pentameter, gave the impression of natural speech rhythms and a dramatic realism. Given the uncertainty of who wrote what and when, it is impossible to pinpoint how the form was generally adopted as the norm. The first play to certainly use it extensively was *Dido, Queen of Carthage*, ascribed to Christopher Marlowe and Thomas Nashe and probably written around 1585. It has been suggested that it was Marlowe who introduced the form into the popular theatre, but there is no conclusive evidence for this. It is more likely that its extensive use as a dramatic medium was part of a general process. It is certain, however, that 'Marlowe's mighty line' was hugely influential in making it into a vehicle of force and beauty. It burst onto the world in its fullest power yet in the two parts of *Tamburlaine the Great*, written around 1587. Yet these two plays demonstrate Marlowe's shortcomings as a dramatist. They are full of meaningless and gratuitous violence. They are lacking the essence of drama – tension. It's not unreasonable to suggest that they show the emotional limitations of their author.

Born in the same year as William Shakespeare, Christopher Marlowe came from a similar kind of artisan background as did a number of other prominent Elizabethan dramatists. His father was a member of the Guild of Shoemakers in Canterbury, where he attended the King's School. From thence he went up to Christ's College, Cambridge, in 1579. In December 1580, he was awarded a six-year scholarship that had been established by Matthew Parker, the Master of the College from 1544 to 1553 and later the Archbishop of Canterbury. It was implicit in the award that the recipient should study for Holy Orders. This may have been Marlowe's intention, but it was never pursued. At this point his career assumes an air of mystery. It appears that he was recruited into the extensive Elizabethan system of surveillance and espionage that had been built up by Sir Francis Walsingham – he may be said to have been the first of the Cambridge spies. Although what he did is uncertain – agents by definition live in a twilight world – it involved him leaving Cambridge for months on end. It was rumoured that he had gone abroad to join the English Catholic seminary at Rheims. Although probably untrue, this was entirely believable. Some of the finest scholars of his generation in England had done so. Whether it was because of his absence or the rumours or a combination of the two, Robert Norgate, the somewhat corrupt Master of the College, determined not to award him his MA degree. The importance of the secret work that Marlowe had been undertaking was revealed when members of the Privy Council, with the apparent approbation of the Queen, wrote to Cambridge demanding his reinstatement. The letter is lost, but its content was noted by the Clerk.

Whereas it was reported that Christopher Morley [*sic*] was determined to have gone beyond the seas to Reames and there to remaine, Their Lordships thought good to certifie that he had no such intent.

In all his accons he had behaued him selfe orderlie and discreetlie wherebie he had done her majestie good service, and deserued to be rewarded for his faithfull dealinge. Their Lordships' request was that the rumour thereof should be allaied by all possible meanes, and that he should be furthered in the degree he was to take at next commencement; Because it was not her Majestie's pleasure that anie one emploied as he had been in matters touching the benefit of his countrie should be defamed by those that are ignorant in th'affaires he went about.[6]

The letter was signed by the Rt Revd John Whitgift, the Archbishop of Canterbury; Lord Burghley, the Lord Treasurer; Sir Christopher Hatton, the Chancellor; Lord Blunsdon, the Lord Chamberlain and Sir William Knollys, Comptroller of the Royal Household. The Queen's ministers clearly considered that those who had done her service should be well regarded. Marlowe's scholarship certainly made him worthy of his degree. He was to translate the first book of Lucan's *Pharsalia* and Ovid's *Elegies* into English. In a letter to Lord Burghley written in 1592, the English Governor of Flushing describes Marlowe as 'by his profession a scholar'. Despite his great literary achievements, this, it appears, was how he preferred to be known.

Marlowe is arguably the most intriguing character in English literature. We know nothing of him that comes from his own pen. Much of our knowledge comes from the hostile statements of his enemies, or from those who disapproved of his attitudes and morals. Yet the fact that they were so numerous, consistent and disparate is a statement in itself. Three strands abound: that he was a governmental agent; that he was a homosexual; and that his religious opinions were distinctly unorthodox.

The most successful of the new wave of playwrights was Thomas Kyd. Little is known of his early life except that he was born in 1558 and attended Merchant Taylors' School in London. In the middle to late 1580s he created a sensation with his *Spanish Tragedy*, arguably the most popular play of the era. At a stroke, he perfected the revenge tragedy, based on Senecan models. Much of his work is lost, but he may have written the version of *Hamlet* on which Shakespeare was to base his own work.

Around 1591, Kyd seems to have retired, at least temporarily, from the theatre and become the secretary of a great nobleman, probably the Earl of Sussex. At the time, he was sharing lodgings with Christopher Marlowe, an arrangement that was to have disastrous consequences for both.

The theatre attracted serious opponents who would eventually bring it down. It has been suggested that the implacable opposition of the Corporation of London to the staging of plays was due to the fact that it was Puritan-dominated. There is no great evidence for this. Of the Lord Mayors between 1586 and 1613, only Sir Richard Martin, who was Lord Mayor in

1588 and 1594, is clearly identifiable as a Puritan, He and his wife, Dorcas, a translator of Calvinistic works and a bookseller, were active in such radical religious causes as the 'Admonition Controversy', concerning the wearing of vestments in worship. They were among those who sought to persuade the Queen to make the Protestant Reformation more thoroughgoing. In 1573, the remarkable Dorcas published *A replye to An answere made of M. doctor Whigift*: the response of the leading Puritan scholar, Thomas Cartwright, to the denunciation of Presbyterianism by the Vice-Chancellor of Cambridge University. Other Lord Mayors may have had Puritan leanings. Sir Richard Saltonstall, Lord Mayor in 1599, was the uncle of his namesake, a founder of the Puritan Massachusetts Colony. Several were men of intellectual and even literary pretensions. Sir Henry Billingsley was the first translator of Euclid into English. Sir Thomas Myddelton was a High Churchman who commissioned the translation of the Bible into Welsh. Others performed acts of philanthropy, particularly in the field of education. Sir Wolstan Dixie endowed scholarships and fellowships at Emanuel College, Cambridge, and founded the grammar school in Market Harborough that still bears his name. He was no friend to the theatre, remarking that 'to play in plague time increases the plague by infection: to play out of plague time calls down the plague from God'.[6]

Nevertheless, the tradition of the 'Lord Mayor's Show', every 8 November, when the new incumbent was sworn into office with much pomp and ceremony, was highly theatrical. The new Lord Mayor went to Westminster in his gilded barge. On his return, he was greeted with a series of pageants, which were often devised by noted poets and playwrights, including George Peele, Thomas Dekker, John Webster, Anthony Munday and Thomas Middleton. On this day at least there was intercourse between the City and the theatre.

At Sir Wolstan Dixie's inauguration, children, dressed in appropriate costumes, represented such subjects as London, the Thames, Magnanimity and Loyalty. One child, 'apparelled like a Moor', reminded the Lord Mayor of his duties towards his city.

> This now remains, right honourable lord,
> That carefully you do attend and keep
> This lovely lady, rich and beautiful,
> The jewel wherewithal your sovereign queen
> Hath put your honour lovingly in trust,
> That you may add to London's dignity,
> And London's dignity may add to yours.

Sir Wolstan's successor as Lord Mayor, Sir George Barne, shared the anti-Papal zeal of his brother-in-law, Sir Francis Walsingham, but he was no Puritan. As Sheriff in 1577, he had stormed the private residence of the Portuguese ambassador, where a mass was being celebrated. He was incarcerated briefly in the Fleet Prison after a diplomatic outcry.

The Show could celebrate contemporary themes. In 1605, Sir Leonard Mosley marked his investiture with his own pageant on the Union of the Crowns of England and Scotland, *The Triumph of Re-united Britannia*. One of the most elaborate shows was devised by Anthony Munday in 1616 for the installation of Sir John Leman of the Fishmongers Company. A series of tableaux, mounted on wheels, was drawn through the City. The first was a fishing boat, with the fishermen 'drawing up their nets, laden with living fish, and bestowing them bountifully upon the people'. The wheels were hidden under drapery painted to resemble waves. The ship was followed by a crowned dolphin: an allusion to the Lord Mayor's arms, and, 'because it is a fish much inclined by nature to musique, Arlon, a famous musician and poet, rideth on his backe'. There followed the King of the Moors, attended by six tributary kings on horseback. They were succeeded by 'a lemon tree richly laden with fruit and flowers', in punning allusion to the Lord Mayor's name. Then came a bower, adorned with the names and arms of all the members of the Fishmongers Company who had served as Lord Mayor. The Genius of London was represented by 'a crowned angel with golden wings'. Lastly, came the grand pageant, drawn by mermen and mermaids, 'memorizing London's great day of deliverance' when Wat Tyler was slain by the Lord Mayor and fishmonger Sir William Walworth. On top sat a victorious Angel. King Richard was represented beneath, surrounded by impersonations of royal and kingly virtues.[7]

There were reasons other than doctrinal to oppose the theatre. Those in authority had good reason to be wary of large gatherings. In 1593, the Lord Mayor banned the then (and now?) unruly pastime of football, which involved hundreds of men chasing a ball through the streets. On this issue, Shakespeare seems to have shared the Lord Mayor's distaste for England's future national sport. In Act I of *King Lear*, the worst epithet that Kent can hurl at Oswald is that he is a 'base football player'.

Disturbances among the disaffected were frequent in late Elizabethan London – Professor Ian Frederick Moulton estimates that there were thirty-five such outbreaks between 1581 and 1602.[8] Nor can it be said that those connected with the theatre were considered, rightly or wrongly, entirely respectable. We remember the fracas that led to the death of William Knell before the Queen's Men visited Stratford in 1587. Christopher Marlowe had a history of violence. On 18 September 1589, he engaged in a sword and dagger fight in Hog Lane with a man called William Bradley. Marlowe's friend and fellow poet Thomas Watson intervened and stabbed Bradley to death. The two men were arrested on suspicion of murder and jailed at Newgate. On 3 December, they appeared for trial at the Middlesex Sessions. It must have been decided that they struck in self-defence for they were discharged with a warning to keep the peace.[9] Further troubles followed. On 9 May 1592, Allen Nicholls, the constable and Nicholas Elliott, the sub-constable of Holywell Street in Shoreditch, formally appealed for protection from Christopher Marlowe. He was bound over to keep the peace in the sum of £20. On 15 September, he was in his native Canterbury, where he allegedly attacked a local tailor, William Corkine, with a stick and a dagger. Five days later, the tailor sued for damages of £5. The outcome is uncertain.[10] Ben Jonson killed the actor Gabriel Spenser in a duel in 1598. Two years earlier, Spencer himself had killed someone, probably under similar circumstances. On 6 June 1599, one of Philip Henslowe the theatre manager's dramatists, Henry Porter, described by Francis Meres as one of 'the best for comedy', was mortally stabbed through the left breast by his fellow dramatist John Daye, who also worked for Henslowe. Next day, at the Southwark Assizes, the extraneous information was provided that the rapier with which the fatal blow was struck had 'the value of two shillings'. Daye, whom Ben Jonson described as a 'rogue' and a 'base fellow', was charged with murder, but entered the customary plea of self-defence, stating that he had fled beyond 'a certain wall'. The verdict is lost, but it appears that Daye obtained a Royal Pardon.

In 1602, Margaret White, the widow of a cloth worker, was charged with giving birth to an illegitimate child. In her defence she claimed that she had been raped on the previous Midsummer's Eve by the actor Christopher Beeston, of the Lord Chamberlain's Men. 'Hee did it forciblie,' she claimed, 'for said hee, I have lyen with a hundred wenches in my tyme.' On 13 November, Beeston was brought before the court. He brought his colleagues with him.

> The said Beeston and others his confederates plaiers did very undecentlie demeane themselves to certen governors and much abused the place and yett upon some reports made known to this court [Beeston was] greatlie suspected to have committed the crime.[11]

The outcome is unknown. Beeston's career does not seem to have been affected by the incident, although he may well have been obliged to perform public penance and contribute to the support of the child.

On at least one occasion, the players ignored attempts to ban them from the City. On 6 November 1589, Sir John Harte, the Lord Mayor, sent a report to Lord Burghley, the Secretary of State, on an abortive attempt he had made to restrain the acting companies.

> There appered before me yesterday the L. Admeralles and the L. Straunges Players, to whom I specially gave in Charge and required them in her Maiesties name to forbere playing … Whereupon the L. Admeralles Players very dutifullie obeyed, but the others in very contemptuous manner departing from me, went to the Cross Keys and played that afternoon, to the greate offense of the better sorte.

It is possible that William Shakespeare, who was associated with Lord Strange's Men, was among those who appeared before the Lord Mayor and subsequently defied his authority. If so, he may have received his comeuppance. 'I coulde do no lesse,' added his Worship, 'but this evening comitt some of them to one of the compters.'[12]

A goodly selection of clerics, not all of them Puritan, was also implacably opposed to the theatre. The most celebrated and effective of the Puritan assaults on the theatre was contained in the *Anatomie of Abuses* by Philip Stubbes. He lambasted the stage in the chapter graphically entitled 'Of Stage-Playes and Enterluds, with their wickedness'.

> Who will call him a wise man that playeth the part of a fool and a vice? Who can call him a Christian that playeth the part of a devil, the sworn enemy of Christ? Who can call him a just man that playeth the part of a dissembling hypocrite? And, to be brief, who can call him a straight dealing man, who playeth a cozener's trick? And so of all the rest. Away therefore with this so infamous an art.

The playwright Thomas Nashe made a spirited defence of the drama in his *Piers Penniless* in 1592. Although his pleading that it kept various types of roué from vices in which they might otherwise have indulged is less than convincing, it gives an insight into at least some of those constituting the audience.

> For whereas the afternoon being the idlest time of day, wherein men that are their own masters (as gentlemen of the court, the Inns of Court and the numbers of captains and soldiers about London) do wholly bestow themselves upon pleasure, and that pleasure they divide (how virtuously, it skills not) either into gaming, following of harlots, drinking or seeing a play; is it not then better (since of four extremes all the world cannot keep them but they will choose one) that they should betake them to the least, which is plays?

The contemporary satirist Samuel Rowland narrowed the choice to two.

> Speak gentlemen, what shall we do today?
> Or shall we to the Globe to see a play?
> Or visit Southwark for a bawdy-house?

This theme was further developed by another satirist, William Goddard.

> Go to your play-house you shall actors have
> Your bawd, your gull, your whore, your pander knave.
> Go to your bawdy-house, y'ave actors too
> As bawds, and whores, and gulls: panders also.
> Besides, in either house (if you enquire)
> A place there is for men themselves to tire.
> Since th'are so alike, to choose there's not a pin
> Whether bawdy-house or play-house you go in.

According to Thomas Decker, prostitutes were so often in the theatres that they got to know the plays word for word – 'every punk and her squire, like the interpreter and her puppet, can rant out by heart'.[13] Thomas Platter, a twenty-five-year-old Swiss visitor noted the 'great swarms' of prostitutes frequenting the taverns and playhouses. Special commissions were established in attempt to control this trade.

> When they meet with a case, they punish the man with imprisonment and a fine. The woman is taken to Bridewell, the King's palace, situated near the river, where the executioner scourges her naked before the populace.

Shakespeare recalled such scenes in *King Lear*.

> Thou rascal Beadle, hold thy bloody hand!
> Why dost thou lash that whore? Strip thine own back;
> Thou hotly lusts to use her in that kind
> For which thou whipp'st her.

# 6

# In London, 1587–92

*'Johannes Factotum'*
– Robert Greene, *Groats-worth of Witte*, 1592

William Shakespeare was almost certainly in London by 1587. In that year, John Shakespeare began legal proceedings at the Court of the Queen's Bench to recover the property that had been mortgaged to his brother-in-law, Edmund Lambert. This was part of a series of actions. None appears to have been successful. William Shakespeare's name is on the attainder. It was probably he who had launched the action on behalf of his father. He would have briefed the lawyers on his father's behalf. Deductions can be drawn from this simple reference. The first is that William had prospered sufficiently to be able to employ lawyers in a lengthy and expensive action – something his father could not have done. It is also clear that he was in touch with his family in Stratford. Had he abandoned his wife and children to their care, it is unlikely that they would have been involved with him in the intricacies of a lawsuit. It is likely, however, that the affair had led to the severing of relations between the Shakespeares and at least two of Mary's sisters and their husbands.

By the mid-1590s, William Shakespeare was living in the parish of St Helen's in Bishopsgate, within the City walls. Nearby was the impressive Crosby Hall. Built in 1466, as the home of a wealthy merchant, it was the largest house in London. It had been home to the Duke of Gloucester, the later King Richard III, and featured in the play of that name. To reach The Theatre, he would pass through the Bishop's Gate in the City Walls, after which the area took its name – a bishop's mitre was carved in stone high above the portico. Beyond was the street called Bishopsgate. Along its breadth were numerous coaching inns – the White Hart, the Dolphin, the Flower Pot, the Green Dragon, the Wrestlers, the Angel, the Catherine Wheel and the Black Bull, which was a theatrical venue, notably for the Queen's Players. On his way to The Theatre, Shakespeare would have passed the hospital known as Bedlam, where those declared insane were incarcerated. The stink from its drains was noxious and the noise made by the inmates 'so hideous, so great, that they are more able to drive a man that hath his wits rather out of them'. Beyond were 'base tenements and houses of disorderly resort ... as namely poor cottages, and habitations of beggars and people without trade, stables, inns, alehouses, taverns, garden-houses converted to dwellings, ordinaries, dicing houses, bowling alleys and brothel houses'. Needless to say, 'these noisome and disorderly houses' harboured a 'great number of dissolute, loose and insolent people'.[1]

It is not until 1592 that the first extant reference to Shakespeare the actor and playwright comes in a furious attack made on him by the playwright Robert Greene. It confirms that Shakespeare was an actor before he became a playwright. It also establishes that, by then, he was a successful dramatist.

Robert Greene was born around 1558, the son of a Norwich sadler. He was proud to be a graduate of St John's College, Cambridge. After doing the Elizabethan equivalent of the 'Grand Tour' in Italy, he got married around 1585. His wife bore him a son, but he left her as soon as her marriage portion was spent. He was one of the first men in England to make his living as a professional writer. He produced a prolific array of pamphlets, plays and prose works. He was also a libertine, irresistibly attracted to the low life, which provided him with a rich source of literary material.

According to his Puritan adversary Gabriel Harvey, Greene's death was precipitate. On 3 September 1592, he overindulged in pickled herring and wine at dinner at his lodgings in the house of a poor shoemaker in Dowgate Ward. He was tended by the shoemaker's compassionate wife, Mrs Isam, and two other women, one of whom was the mother of his illegitimate son, Fortunatus Greene. The other was the sister of a notorious cutpurse known as 'Cutting Ball'. Shortly before his death, he wrote a note to his misused wife about a bond for £10 he had given to the shoemaker. 'Doll, I charge thee by the love of our youth and by my soul's rest that thou wilt see this man paid, for if he and his wife had not succoured me I had died in the streets.'

Shortly after Greene's death, Henry Chettle, a writer and printer, published a pamphlet entitled *Greenes Groats-worth of Witte, bought with a million of Repentance*. The title gives the clue to the work. It is a somewhat rambling cautionary tale describing the low life encountered by the author during his exotic career. It counsels the reader to take heed of his unfortunate example and avoid mixing with bad characters. Actors come into this category. He warns three of his 'fellow Schollers about this Citie' of their ingratitude. 'Is it not like that you, to whome they all have bene beholding, shall (were ye in that case as I am now) bee both at once of them forsaken?' He scathingly dismisses them as 'Puppets ... that spoke from our mouths ... Anticks garnisht in our colours'. One actor is picked out for special vitriol.

> Yes, trust them not, for there is an Upstart Crow beautified with our feath-ers, that with his *Tyger's Hart wrapt in a players hyde*, supposes he is as well able to bombast out a blanke verse as the best of you, and being an absolute *Johannes Factotum*, is in his owne conceit the only Shakes-scene in a coun-trey.

The reference to William Shakespeare is unmistakeable. As happens so often, the attack falls tantalisingly short of the full story, but provides enough information to enable the conclusion that Shakespeare's writing is popularly admired. The misquotation from *Henry VI, Part III* – the line should read 'Tiger's heart wrapped in a woman's hide' – shows that his lines could be quoted without reference to the source. Since Greene and the playwrights to whom he addresses his diatribe were university men, the phrase 'supposes he is as well able to bombast out a blank verse as the best of you' may refer to Shakespeare's lack of such an education. 'And thou hadst small Latin and less Greek' was to be a matter of regret expressed by Ben Jonson in his valedictory poem to him.

An 'Upstart Crow beautified with our feathers' – the implication is that Shakespeare was a plagiarist. Although the context is unclear, there is an amount of truth in this. Like Montaigne, Shakespeare believed the function of the poet was to gather 'other men's flowers'. Few of his plots are original.

'*Johannes Factotum*' – the implication is clear. We are told that Shakespeare is an actor and that he has been writing plays. In other words, he will turn his hand to anything. The passage gives a clue as to where he must have been for most of the seven missing years. He must have been learning the actor's trade before making the transition to the playwriting that so disturbed the author of the *Groats-worth*.

Nor do two of Greene's previously esteemed fellow writers escape his onslaught. He attacks the 'famous gracer of Tragedians' (almost certainly Marlowe) for his atheism and his devotion to the works of Machiavelli. The other, probably Thomas Nashe, this 'young Juvenal, that byting Satyrist', he reproaches for 'too much liberty of reproofe'.

It is sad that Robert Greene, a powerful and innovative literary figure, should be best remembered for this intemperate attack, but it is possible that he never wrote it. Even when the *Groats-worth* was published, this was rumoured. Amazingly, the name of Thomas Nashe was put forward. He reacted with fury. Within a month of the attack his pamphlet *Piers Penniless* vehemently denied the suggestion.

> Other news I am advertised of, that a scald trivial lying pamphlet, cald Greens groatsworth of wit, is given out to be my doing. God never have care of my soule, but utterly renounce me, if the least word or sillible in it proceed from my pen, or if I were any way privie to the writing or printing of it.

Marlowe also appears to have reacted angrily. The public charge of atheism was serious and could have grave consequences. Shakespeare made no public reply, but sensibly enlisted others in his support. Henry Chettle was constrained to make amends. His pamphlet *Kind-Hartes Dreame* is ostensibly a reply to *Piers Penniless*. He is pained by the furore he has caused. 'About three months since,' he writes in the preface, died *M. Robert Greene*, leauing many papers in sundry Booke sellers hands, among others his Groats-worth of wit, in which a letter written to diuers play-makers is offensiuely by one or two of them taken, and because on the dead they cannot be auenged, they wilfully forge in their conceits a living Author; and after tossing it to and fro, no remedy, but it must light on me.

He must have made his peace with Nashe, for he escapes mention. He had never met either of the other two recipients of the diatribe. He adds insult to injury concerning Marlowe. 'With one of them I care not if I never be,' he says scathingly. Doubtless Marlowe's violent reputation went before him. The other playwright was a different matter. Chettle had met him since the attack. 'Because my selfe haue seene his demeanor no lesse civill than he exelent in the qualitie he professes.' 'Divers of Worship' had taken up Shakespeare's case with Chettle and reported 'his uprightnes of dealing, which argues his honesty, and his facetious grace in writing, that approoues his Art'.

Rumours were circulating that Chettle himself was the author of *Groats-worth* – a charge he indignantly denied. 'I protest it was all Greenes, not mine nor Maister Nashes, as some most vnjustly haue affirmed.'

In fact modern textual analysis tends to uphold this charge. Chettle was frequently in debt and the temptation to add a sensational dimension to Greene's pamphlet may have proved irresistible. Indeed, he had greater grounds for jealousy than Greene, who died a highly successful writer. Although highly prolific, Chettle never achieved such success and little survives of his work. Nevertheless, if the attack was indeed his, he calculated well. *Groats-worth* must not only have sold well; such was the stir it caused that it gave him the opportunity to launch another widely circulated pamphlet.

That some of the mud flung by *Groats-worth* stuck is demonstrated by the appearance of a pamphlet entitled *Greene's Funeralls*. The author is identified only by his initials, 'R. B.' Only twelve pages of the original survive in the Bodleian Library, but they contain a short verse that indicates continuing controversy.

> Greene is the ground of everie painter's die:
> Greene gave the ground to all that write on him,
> Nay, more, the men that so Eclipst his fame,
> Purloynde his Plumes, can they deny the same?

Clearly it was not only Shakespeare who was accused of plagiarising Greene's work. The charge had little effect. He was to find in Greene's *The Scottish History of James IV* ample material to use in *A Midsummer Night's Dream* and his sources for *The Winter's Tale* in the same author's hugely popular novel *Pandosto*.

Chettle's apology makes it clear that William Shakespeare was already in with people of influence in the city – 'divers of worship'. We can only speculate on who they were. They may well have been members of the 'Essex Circle', the group of noblemen and gentry that surrounded Robert Devereux, Earl of Essex. *Love's Labour's Lost*, one of the two plays written by Shakespeare with no known sources, may be some kind of satire on this group. It presents difficulties to the modern reader who is unable to grasp its 'in-jokes'. It was almost traditional to regard the piece as a very early play of Shakespeare's, if not the earliest. Modern scholarship tends to place it on stylistic grounds to around 1595, but there is direct evidence that the play was revised by the author himself around that period.[2]

We do not know the process by which William Shakespeare was transformed from an actor to an actor/playwright, any more than we know what made him an actor in the first place. Perhaps he made such inspired suggestions for improving the lines he had to say as an actor that he found himself rewriting entire plays before becoming a dramatist in his own right. It is certain that his writing abilities would have been soon recognised. It is equally true that he would have possessed a passion to write that thrust him forward. His earliest individual efforts were almost certainly in the classical mould as befitted the fashion of the time. *Titus Andronicus* is a Senecan tragedy full of blood and gore. To the modern theatregoer it is little more than a ghastly period piece, rarely performed, mainly of interest because of its authorship. Yet it was of the style of its time and it is an indication of Shakespeare's genius that he realised that such writing was not for him. Ben Jonson gives an indication of its date in the Induction to *Bartholomew Fair*.

> Hee that will sweare *Ieronimo* or *Andronicus* are the best plays yet, shall pass unexcepted at, here, as a man whose Iudgement shewes it is constant, and hath stood still, these five and twentie, or thirtie yeares.

*Bartholomew Fair* was written in 1614, so if Ben Jonson's twenty-five or thirty years is taken literally, it means that *Titus* was written some time between 1584 and 1589, which fits on both biographical and stylistic grounds. It was certainly in existence in 1592 when an allusion is made to it in a play called *A Knack to Know a Knave*.

> As Titus was unto the Roman Senators,
> When he made a conquest on the Goths ...

The Induction tells us more of the era: that *grand guignol* was hugely popular in the late 1580s, but is now regarded, by Jonson at least, as passé. *Titus Andronicus* clearly shared this popularity. The '*Ieronimo*' to which he speaks is an alternative name for Thomas Kyd's *Spanish Tragedy*, which brought the 'revenge tragedy' into vogue. Marlowe's *Tamburlaine*, written in the same period, whilst not a revenge tragedy, is fashionably gore-strewn.

*Titus* clearly retained its popularity for some time before becoming a period piece. It is the first play of Shakespeare's to be published. On 6 February 1594, the printer John Danter entered 'A Noble Roman Historye of Tytus Andonicus' onto the Stationers' Register.

To the modern audience, Shakespeare's touch is surer in *The Comedy of Errors*, another early play. It is closely modelled on Plautus' comedy *Menaechmi* and, with the much later *Tempest*, is his only play to observe the classical unities. It is his shortest play – a mere 1,777 lines. It contains a topical reference to the wars of succession in France, which would fit any date between 1589 and 1594, but this may be a later accretion providing suitable topicality. On the title page of his first quarto edition, Danter records that *Titus Andronicus* had been 'plaide by the Right Honourable the Earle of Darbie, Earle of Pembrooke, and the Earl of Sussex their servants'. This raises speculation about Shakespeare's relationship with these acting companies. It is possible that, at this stage in his career, he moved between companies like a modern actor. The Earl of Derby in question was Ferdinando Stanley. In the absence of a direct heir to Queen Elizabeth, he had a strong claim to the throne. Under the Third Act of Succession of 1543, his mother, the Countess of Derby, was heiress presumptive as the granddaughter of Henry VIII's sister, Mary.

The company's name had changed with Stanley's accession to the title in 1594. It had previously born the name of his courtesy title as heir apparent to the earldom: Lord Strange's Men. They had performed in Stratford as early as 1578, but it is likely that they were then a troupe of jugglers and tumblers rather than actors. On the death of the Earl of Leicester in 1588, a number of his leading actors transferred to them. Since William Shakespeare's name appears as a playwright whose works Derby's servants performed, it is not unreasonable to speculate that he might have been involved with them as an actor. The company included a number of those with whom he would be closely associated. The world of the contemporary theatre was pretty volatile, with actors and playwrights moving between companies. In 1590, Lord Strange's Men became directly associated with the Admiral's Men. This brought together, briefly, the two greatest actors of the age: Richard Burbage, the son of the James Burbage who had founded The Theatre, and Edward Alleyn (always known as 'Ned'), the son of a Bishopsgate innkeeper. In 1583, at the age of sixteen, Alleyn was with 'Worcester's Men', one of the earliest acting companies. Under the patronage of William Somerset, the 3rd Earl of Worcester, the company had toured as early as the mid-sixteenth century. Alleyn could have joined them as a boy actor. As the leading actor of the Admiral's Men, he created Marlowe's great title roles of Tamburlaine, Dr Faustus and the Jew of Malta. 'Not Roscius nor Aesope,' wrote Thomas Nashe, 'those admired tragedians that have lived ever since Christ was born, could ever perform more in action than the famous Ned Allen.' On 22 October 1592, he married Joan Woodward, Philip Henslowe's stepdaughter. Henslowe was one of the great impresarios of the age. He built the Rose Theatre on

Bankside in 1587, on similar lines to The Theatre. He was proprietor of the nearby Bear Garden. In February 1592, he entered into his diary that Lord Strange's Men were performing there. On 3 March, they produced a new play which he recorded as 'harey the vj' – probably the play to which the author of *Groats-worth* refers.

The three parts of *Henry VI* represent a turning for the dramatist from the classical tradition into the realm of the history play. The earliest known example of the genre is *The Famous Victories of Henry V*, written by an anonymous author around 1585. The publication of Raphael Holinshed's *Chronicles of the Historie of England* in 1580 had created great interest in the country's past. Textual research has shown that William had access to the three folio volumes of the second edition, published in 1587. He was a voracious reader. As well as Holinshed, he draws on at least five other documentary sources in writing *Henry VI, Part II*.[3]

That the historical play was perceived as a call to the nation in dangerous times was indicated by Thomas Nashe.

> What if I prove plays to be no extreme, but a rare exercise of virtue? First, for the subject of them, (for the most part) it is borrowed out of our English chronicles, wherein our forefathers valiant acts (that have long been buried in rusty brass and worm-eaten books) are revived and they themselves raised from the grave of oblivion, and brought to plead their honours in open presence; than which, what can be a sharper reproof to these degenerate effeminate days of ours?

He saw the genre as possessing a moral prerogative.

> In plays, all cozenages, all cunning drifts over-gilded with outward holiness, all stratagems of war, all the cankerworms that breed upon the rust of peace, are most lively anatomized; they show the ill success of treason, the fall of hasty climbers, the wretched end of usurpers, the misery of civil dissention, and how just God is evermore in punishing of murther. Whereas some petitioners of the counsel against them object.[4]

The last sentence is a swipe at the City Corporation – or 'the citizens' as Nashe calls them – who were incessantly petitioning the Privy Council to close the playhouses.

Shakespeare's three *Henry VI* plays constitute the first fruits of a saga of the history of England that stretches from the tragic reign of Richard II to the rise of the House of Tudor. This great work was not written in chronological order. The *Henry IV* plays were written in the mid-1590s. *Henry V*, the last play in the cycle, dates from 1599. It is unlikely that William Shakespeare had conceived the entire history at the time he wrote the parts of *Henry VI*. Yet, the themes which dominate the cycle are present in the earliest plays. The heroine is England herself. The theme is expressed in the final lines of a history play that is not part of it, *King John*.

> Naught shall make us rue,
> If England to herself do rest but true.

In *Henry VI*, Parts I and II, the English Crown loses its French possessions. The land becomes divided against itself through the rival Houses of York and Lancaster. The divisions are revealed in the highly stylised fourth scene of Part I. York and Lancaster cement their divisions by plucking red and white roses as respective emblems of their cause in the garden of the Inner Temple. The Earl of Warwick, a major protagonist in the quarrel, foresees impending disaster.

> And here I prophesy: this brawl to-day,
> Grown to this faction in the Temple-garden,
> Shall send between the red rose and the white
> A thousand souls to death and deadly night.

Civil war is the greatest evil that can befall a nation. It sets brother against brother, father against son. Yet the history plays represent something more than a plea for national unity. They are a contemplation of the nature of monarchy. In the series, Shakespeare goes some way towards espousing the doctrine of the divine right of kings. At his coronation, the King has been anointed which confers upon him a priesthood. To usurp the royal prerogative is a crime against God. Regicide is a heinous offence. The theme of the histories is a biblical one: that the sins of the fathers will be visited on the sons, even to the third and fourth generation. This is the fate of the House of Lancaster. In *Richard II*, the pieces of this historical jigsaw are added to Shakespeare's huge work around 1595. The Bishop of Carlisle urges the King to remember his divinely ordained role:

> Fear not, my Lord: that Power that made you king
> Hath power to keep you king in spite of all.
> That means that Heaven yields must be embraced,
> And not neglected; else, if heaven would,
> And we will not, heaven's offer we refuse,
> The proffer'd means of succour and redress.

Society, the history plays tell us, is hierarchical and pyramidical. Each man is born into his place and there is a place for every man. The 'privileges' of the governing classes bring with them huge responsibilities. No onus is greater than that of the monarch. He must bear the moral burden of the welfare of his nation. His subjects, in comparison, bear no such responsibilities. Following classical tradition, the shepherd is the exemplar of this order. This perspective is demonstrated in the highly stylised and hugely effective scene which takes place around the Battle of Towton in *Henry VI, Part III*. The King is alone on stage and takes his seat upon a molehill:

Oh God! methinks it were a happy life,
To be no better than a homely swain;
To sit upon a hill, as I do now,
To carve out dials quaintly, point by point,
Thereby to see the minutes how they run,
How many make the hour full complete;
How many hours bring about the day;
How many days will finish up the year;
How many years a mortal man may live.
When this is known, then to divide the times:
So many hours must I tend my flock;
So many hours must I take my rest,
So many hours must I contemplate;
So many hours must I sport myself;
So many days my ewes have been with young;
So many weeks ere the poor fools will ean:
So many years ere I shall shear the fleece:
So minutes, hours, days, months, and years,
Pass'd over to the end they were created,
Would bring white hairs unto a quiet grave.
Ah, what a life were this! how sweet! how lovely!
Gives not the hawthorn-bush a sweeter shade
To shepherds looking on their silly sheep,
Than doth a rich embroider'd canopy
To kings that fear their subjects' treachery?
O, yes, it doth; a thousand-fold it doth.
And to conclude, the shepherd's homely curds,
His cold thin drink out of his leather bottle,
His wonted sleep under a fresh tree's shade,
All which secure and sweetly he enjoys,
Is far beyond a prince's delicates,
His viands sparkling in a golden cup,
His body couched in a curious bed,
When care, mistrust, and treason waits on him.

Shakespeare was to return to this theme of the idyllic pastoral life in *As You Like It*, although the vision of Arcadia is brought into perspective by the acerbic views of Jacques.

The molehill scene moves on to express the deep horror of civil war, which divides families. The stage direction reads: *Alarum. Enter a son that has killed his father, dragging in the dead body.*

Son:    Ill blows the wind that profits nobody.
        This man, whom hand to hand I slew in fight,
        May be possessed with some store of crowns;
        And I, that haply take them from him now,

> May yet ere night yield both my life and them
> To some man else, as this dead man doth me.
> Who's this? O God! it is my father's face,
> Whom in this conflict I unwares have kill'd.
> O heavy times, begetting such events!
> From London by the king was I press'd forth;
> My father, being the Earl of Warwick's man,
> Came on the part of York, press'd by his master;
> And I, who at his hands received my life, him
> Have by my hands of life bereaved him.
> Pardon me, God, I knew not what I did!
> And pardon, father, for I knew not thee!
> My tears shall wipe away these bloody marks;
> And no more words till they have flow'd their fill.

The scene is paralleled on the other side of the stage: '*Enter a Father that has killed his son, bringing in the body.*'

**Father:**    Thou that so stoutly hast resisted me,
Give me thy gold, if thou hast any gold:
For I have bought it with an hundred blows.
But let me see: is this our foeman's face?
Ah, no, no, no, it is mine only son!
Ah, boy, if any life be left in thee,
Throw up thine eye! see, see what showers arise,
Blown with the windy tempest of my heart,
Upon thy words, that kill mine eye and heart!
O, pity, God, this miserable age!
What stratagems, how fell, how butcherly,
Erroneous, mutinous and unnatural,
This deadly quarrel daily doth beget!
O boy, thy father gave thee life too soon,
And hath bereft thee of thy life too late!

The distress of the King at the divisions in his nation is expressed in a further symbolic scene:

**King:**    Woe above woe! grief more than common grief!
O that my death would stay these ruthful deeds!
O pity, pity, gentle heaven, pity!
The red rose and the white are on his face,
The fatal colours of our striving houses:
The one his purple blood right well resembles;
The other his pale cheeks, methinks, presenteth:
Wither one rose, and let the other flourish;
If you contend, a thousand lives must wither.

| Son: | How will my mother for a father's death |
| | Take on with me and ne'er be satisfied! |
| Father: | How will my wife for slaughter of my son |
| | Shed seas of tears and ne'er be satisfied! |
| King: | How will the country for these woful chances |
| | Misthink the king and not be satisfied! |
| Son: | Was ever son so rued a father's death? |
| Father: | Was ever father so bemoan'd his son? |
| King: | Was ever king so grieved for subjects' woe? |
| | Much is your sorrow; mine ten times so much. |

Shakespeare would write fewer and fewer such scenes as his dramatic skills developed. Even so, the theme of the chaos ensuing when the natural order falls apart remained with him. In *Troilus and Cressida*, Ulysses thoroughly endorses the social order which he describes as 'degree'. Its collapse is epitomised by patricide.

> O, when degree is shak'd,
> Which is the ladder of all high designs,
> The enterprise is sick! How could communities,
> Degrees in schools, and brotherhoods in cities,
> Peaceful commerce from dividable shores,
> The primogenity and due of birth,
> Prerogative of age, crowns, sceptres, laurels,
> But by degree, stand in authentic place?
> Take but degree away, untune that string,
> And hark what discord follows! Each thing melts
> In mere oppugnancy: the bounded waters
> Should lift their bosoms higher than the shores,
> And make a sop of all this solid globe;
> Strength should be lord of imbecility,
> And the rude son should strike his father dead;
> Force should be right; or, rather, right and wrong,
> Between whose endless jar justice resides,
> Should lose their names, and so should justice too.
> Then everything includes itself in power,
> Power into will, will into appetite;
> And appetite, an universal wolf,
> So doubly seconded with will and power,
> Must make perforce an universal prey,
> And last eat up himself.

This highly conservative social view is not one that accords with the tempo of Shakespeare's times. As Shakespeare's own career demonstrates, there was a great deal of social mobility. Whether he held the view that a society should be hierarchically hidebound is debatable, but he certainly expresses it consistently, although we should not forget that the words are contributory to creating the character portrayed rather than necessarily representing his own views.

Another persistent theme is the fear of mob rule, which occurs when the normal constraints of society are shattered and 'strength should be the lord of imbecility'. Throughout his canon, Shakespeare shows contempt, not for the humbler classes as such, but the chaos that ensues when they overstep their designated social roles. Such is the case with Cade's rebellion in *Henry VI, Part II*. Then, as now, the familiar line must have been received with ironic cheers from the audience.

Dick:        The first thing we do, let's kill all the lawyers.

Despite the crudity of the characterisation of Cade and his followers, a reflection on history shows that Shakespeare had a point. The examples of the French and Russian revolutions show that such manifestations can, if they can turn wrong, become in themselves instruments of irrational oppression. The pogroms that such revolutions can unleash are noted by Jack Cade.

> And you that love the commons, follow me.
> Now show yourselves men; 'tis for liberty.
> We will not leave one lord, one gentleman:
> Spare none but such as go in clouted shoon;
> For they are thrifty honest men, and such
> As would, but that they dare not, take our parts.

Although the dating of Shakespeare's plays is an imprecise business, it is likely that he followed up the huge success of the *Henry VI* trilogy with a play that takes further the story of England. *Richard III* almost certainly set the seal on a dramatic partnership that was to be crucial to Shakespeare's development as a playwright. It is the first title role associated with the name of Richard Burbage. The company with which the twenty-three-year-old actor was most closely associated at this time was Lord Strange's Men and it is highly likely that it was for that company that Shakespeare wrote this play. 'And Crookback, as befits, shall cease to live,' states a valedictory verse to Burbage in 1619. A humorous anecdote of 1602 in the diary of the law student John Manningham asserts that Burbage provoked the attention of an early example of a 'groupie' when a lady fan 'grew so far in liking with him' that she

appointed him to come that night unto her by the name of Richard the 3. Shakespeare overhearing their conclusion went before, was entertained and at his game ere Burbage came. The message being brought that Rich. the 3d was at the door, Shakespeare caused return to be made that William the Conqueror was before Rich. the 3.

We are in the presence of a contemporary joke rather than an actual event!

In *Richard III* Shakespeare explores further the theme of the disasters ensuing when place is usurped. In the background is a clear awareness of the political philosophy of Niccolo Machiavelli. Although *The Prince* was a banned book – it was not translated into English until 1636 – it had a huge influence on Elizabethan thought, not least on the writings of Christopher Marlowe. In the *Jew of Malta*, it is Machiavelli, or Machiavel, as Marlowe calls him, who acts as the Chorus. The characteristic Marlovian hero is the antithesis of the world view expressed in Shakespeare's histories: he is more like today's 'anti-hero'. Tamburlaine, Barabas the Jew and Faustus are characters outside the moral norms, who prey on the society that they blame for their condition. Their moral sense is, to put it mildly, underdeveloped. This was a criticism made of Marlowe himself, by those who had reason to dislike and mistrust him. Even his Edward II is an outsider. In terms of the times, his blatant homosexuality makes him another anti-hero who is trying to impose his will on the world.

In *Richard III*, Shakespeare presents the opposite view. He had already presented Richard, Duke of Gloucester, as a ruthless psychopath who has his own designs on the throne in *Henry VI, Part III*. Richard is a party to the murder of Edward, Prince of Wales, and is the murderer himself of King Henry VI. In Marlovian style, Richard exults in these deeds in the second scene of *Richard III* after he has wooed the Lady Anne.

Gloucester:    Was ever woman in this humour woo'd?
Was ever woman in this humour won?
I'll have her; but I will not keep her long.
What! I, that kill'd her husband and his father,
To take her in her heart's extremest hate,
With curses in her mouth, tears in her eyes,
The bleeding witness of her hatred by;
Having God, her conscience, and these bars against me,
And I nothing to back my suit at all,
But the plain devil and dissembling looks,
And yet to win her, all the world to nothing!

According to Machiavelli's incontestable analysis, the government of states takes various forms. Power can be hereditary or elective. It can also be acquired, either by conquest or by skilful and ruthless manipulation. The audience is left in no doubt that it is the latter that Richard represents from his very first speech.

Gloucester:    I am determined to prove a villain
And hate the idle pleasures of these days.
Plots have I laid, inductions dangerous,

> By drunken prophecies, libels and dreams,
> To set my brother Clarence and the king
> In deadly hate the one against the other:
> And if King Edward be as true and just
> As I am subtle, false and treacherous,
> This day should Clarence closely be mew'd up,
> About a prophecy, which says that 'G'
> Of Edward's heirs the murderer shall be.

The theme of *Richard III* is that of Chapter 8 of *The Prince*: 'Concerning Those Who Have Obtained a Principality by Wickedness'. 'These methods are,' writes Machiavelli, 'when, either by some wicked or nefarious ways, one ascends to the principality, or when by the favour of his fellow-citizens a private person becomes the prince of his country.' In Richard's case, both strategies are pursued. The wickedness is self-evident. When the Lord Mayor and citizens appear to request him to take the crown, he appears between two bishops. 'See where he stands between two clergymen!' exclaims the Lord Mayor. The ensuing scene is all that Machiavelli required of a prince as Richard is propelled towards the throne by the voices of the citizens.

We do not know how easy it was for William Shakespeare to progress from actor to playwright. Certainly it was a rapid process in a period when to rise in the new medium of the theatre was in the grasp of every man of talent. It is likely that at least some of the 'University Wits' resented his success. Greene's supposed attack says as much, but Shakespeare was finding his own voice. In contrast to Marlowe's attitude towards his 'anti-heroes', Shakespeare does not admire his Richard. 'From forth the kennel of thy womb,' Queen Margaret tells Queen Elizabeth, his mother, 'hath crept / A hellhound that doth hunt us all to death.'

Yet Shakespeare is not a historian, but a dramatist. He is happy to distort history for the sake of drama. In *Richard III*, he uses Queen Margaret as a commentator on the evil of Richard of York and a counterweight to it. Yet this is the same Margaret who stabs to death Richard of York in *Henry VI, Part III*. Before she does so, he berates her in no uncertain terms.

> She-wolf of France, but worse than wolves of France,
> Whose tongue more poisons than the adder's tooth –
> How ill-becoming is it in thy sex
> To triumph like an Amazonian trull
> Upon their woes whom fortune captivates!

Historically it never happened. It is inconceivable that a leading protagonist of the Lancastrian cause should find a home – let alone full reign for her acerbic tongue – in the Yorkist court. In fact, Queen Margaret, after the final defeat of the Lancastrians at Tewkesbury in 1471, was imprisoned by the Yorkists until 1475, when she was ransomed by the King of France.

She lived in France as a royal pensioner until she died in 1482 – the year of Richard III's accession to the throne.

Nor is Shakespeare's portrayal of Henry Richmond as a kind of Arthurian deliverer accurate. His treatment of his wife's cousin, the simple-minded Earl of Warwick, who had a better dynastic claim to the throne than he did, is not unlike that ascribed to Richard III towards the Princes in the Tower by Shakespeare. He imprisoned him in the Tower when he was ten years old and had him executed on trumped-up charges of treason in 1499, when he was twenty-eight.

Whether Shakespeare was aware of the inaccuracy of much of his historical writing is immaterial. Not only was it subordinate to his dramatic purpose, it was also as a means of propaganda for the ruling House of Tudor, which represents legitimacy, the rule of justice and the unity of England – concepts expressed in the last Act of *Richard III*.

> Proclaim a pardon to the soldiers fled
> That in submission will return to us:
> And then, as we have ta'en the sacrament,
> We will unite the white rose and the red;
> Smile heaven upon this fair conjunction,
> That long have frown'd upon their enmity!
> What traitor hears me and says not amen?
> England hath long been mad, and scarr'd herself;
> The brother blindly shed the brother's blood,
> The father rashly slaughter'd his own son,
> The son, compell'd, been butcher to the sire:
> All this divided York and Lancaster,
> Divided in their dire division,
> O, now, let Richmond and Elizabeth,
> The true succeeders of each royal house,
> By God's fair ordnance conjoin together!
> And let their heirs, God, if thy will be so.
> Enrich the time to come with smooth-faced peace,
> With smiling plenty and fair prosperous days!

'The father rashly slaughter'd his own son' – that stylised scene in *Henry VI, Part III* of fratricide and filicide must have so impressed the audience that Shakespeare can refer to it in the knowledge that they will pick up the allusion.

The scene closes with a dire warning against those who would create such desperate divisions in England again.

> Abate the edge of traitors, gracious Lord,
> That would reduce these bloody days again,
> And make poor England weep in streams of blood!
> Let them not live to taste this land's increase,

That would with treason wound this fair land's peace!
Now civil wounds are stopp'd, peace lives again:
That she may long live here, God say amen!

While the sentiment expressed is a clear rallying call of support for the Tudor monarchy, it possesses another dimension. The Battle of Bosworth and the triumph of the Tudors had not brought an end to civil strife, which broke out periodically over the next century. Contrary to Shakespeare's view, it was not Bosworth that brought an end to the sporadic Wars of the Roses, but the Battle of Stoke two years later. Uprisings and insurrections occurred at regular intervals over the next century.

Within Shakespeare's lifetime, much of the North of England had been in rebellion. The growing force of Puritanism was to be an increasing threat to the stability of the nation. *Twelfth Night* is the last play to offer a belly laugh at these narrow-minded iconoclasts, but there are dark overtones. 'I'll be revenged on the whole pack of you!' swears Malvolio. Had Shakespeare lived till his seventy-eighth year, he would have seen Malvolio's prophesy fulfilled in the Puritan revolution.

Yet, despite such anxieties about the state of the nation, it is clear that by the early 1590s, William Shakespeare was a celebrated man-of-the-theatre, but a cataclysm was about to strike.

# 7

# An Aspiring Poet, 1593–95

'My untutored lines'
– Preface to *The Rape of Lucrece*

## Sundry Great Disorders

The Elizabethan age has passed into popular mythology as one of the most triumphant in English history. This view is only tenuously founded on fact. The defeat of the Spanish Armada did not represent the end of the war with Spain, but its beginning. The threat of invasion was ever-present. Foreign adventures took their toll. There were continuing and hugely expensive conflicts in Ireland, France and the Netherlands. The 1590s in particular were an exceptionally volatile period, characterised by high prices, food shortages, religious conflicts, heavy taxation and plague. The period saw the most sustained and severe inflation in English history: the price of flour nearly tripled between 1593 and 1597. The resultant effects were palpable. Shakespeare's noted fear of mob rule is perhaps made explicable by a proclamation that was issued in London in 1590.

> Whereas the Queen's most excellent Majesty, being given to understand of a very great outrage lately committed by some apprentices and others being masterless men and vagrant persons in and about the suburbs of the city of London, in assaulting of the house of Lincoln's Inn and the breaking and spoiling of divers chambers in the said house hath therefore thought good for the better avoiding of such outrages hereafter (by advice of her majesty's Privy Council) straightly to charge and command all such as be any householders … that they and every of them do cause all their apprentices, journeymen, servants, and family in their several houses … to tarry and abide within … and not to be suffoed to go abroad after nine of the clock at night upon pain of imprisonment.

The proclamation had little effect. In the following year there were 'sundry great disorders' propagated by 'unlawful great assemblies of multitudes of a popular sort of base condition'. This invoked even more extreme measures. Unlawful assemblies were prohibited under martial law. Offenders were to be 'execute upon the gallows'.

The riots were frequently directed against immigrants, who were accused of undercutting the market and taking away the livelihoods of native workers. Folk memory recalled the 'Ill' or 'Evil' May Day riots of 1517 when apprentices launched attacks on the much-resented foreigners. On 11 June 1592, a particularly virulent outbreak confirmed the worst fears of the City Fathers. A mob of apprentices rioted outside the playhouses in Southwark. Eleven days later 'for avoidinge of theis unlawfull assemblies in those quarters', the Privy Council ordered 'that there be noe playes used in anye place neere thereabouts, as the Theater, Curtayne, or other usuall places'.

## The Purple Whip of Vengeance

To add to London's woe, one of the worst plague epidemics occurred in 1593. No one knew the cause, although various theories were propounded.[1] It was actually spread by the fleas (*Xenopsylla cheopis*) that dwelt parasitically on the black rat (*Rattus rattus*). Unlike the brown rat, which lived at ground level, the black rat inhabited roof areas such as thatch. Once the infected rat died, its fleas would move on to another one. The time that elapsed between the death of the first rat to the death of the second was just five days. As the rat population diminished, the fleas transfered their attention to other mammals, including humans. The time that elapsed from the death of the host rat to the death of the human was between eight and fourteen days. The poorer areas, where the houses were built of lath and straw, were particularly vulnerable to this transference. In the wealthier, brick-built areas it was less frequent.

The bubonic plague was in essence a sub-tropical disease. For the fleas to multiply in sufficient quantities for the epidemic to spread, sustained temperatures of 70 °F (21 °C) were necessary, although less sustained temperatures could produce minor outbreaks.

Puritan preachers and polemicists identified the outbreak of the plague as a punishment for sin. Others saw it as resulting from a malignant alignment of the planets that created 'miasma', or 'bad air', a poisonous vapour or mist filled with particles from decomposed matter.[2] In *Timon of Athens*, Shakespeare alludes to all three of these supposed causes.

> A planetary plague, when Jove
> Will o'er some high-vied City, long hang his poison
> In the sick air.

Others rightly saw the connection between poverty, lack of hygiene and the plague. In 1593, the Stationers' Register recorded that

> Mr Simon Kellway hath written *A Defensative against the Plague*, containing two parts, the first how to preserve from the Plague, the second how to cure those that are infected, with a short treatise on the smallpox, is entered, being dedicated to the Earl of Essex.

Kellway's treatise proposed ways to make the city more hygienic and provided a regimen for fighting the plague among those infected.

The symptoms of the plague were horrendous. They were described by Thomas Lodge in his *Treatise of the Plague* as giving rise to 'alienation and frenzie'.

> Blewnesse and blacknesse appearing about the sores and carbuncles, and after their appearances the sodaine vanishings of the same, cold in extreame partes, and intollerable heate in the inwarde, vnquenchable thirst, continually soundings, urines white, and crude, or red, troubled and blacke. Colde swet about the forehead and face; crampes, blacknesse in the excrement of the body, stench, and blewnes, the flux of the belly, with weaknesse of the heart, shortnes of breath, and great stench of the same, lacke of sleepe, and appetite to eate, profound sleepe, changing of colour in the face, exchanged to palenesse, blacknesse or blewnesse, cogitation of great vnquietnes.

Something of the paroxysms of terror into which the advent of the plague sent the populace was caught by Thomas Dekker.

> The purple whip of vengeance, the plague, having beaten many thousands of men, women and children to death, and still making the people of the city every week by the hundreds for the grave, is the only cause that all her inhabitants walk up and down like mourners at some great silent funeral.

We begin to understand the force of Mercutio's 'A plague on both your houses'.

The first parish to show an increase in mortality during the pandemic of 1593 was St Botolph's without Bishopsgate on 15 April. It was one of London's poorest parishes. Less than 1 per cent of the dwellings were substantially built. It had been the first parish to be afflicted during the last great outbreak in 1563 and it would be the first during the next in 1603. It was a feature of the disease that it spread slowly but apparently inexorably. Only one other parish – St Mary Somerset by the Thames – showed a rise in mortality before the end of the month.

St Botolph's was just a few hundred yards from The Theatre, situated in the adjoining parish. Many of the theatrical fraternity lived in the area, including William Shakespeare. Our first knowledge of where he dwelt in London is dated to 15 November 1597, when he is recorded as failing to pay the second payment of 5s on goods rated at £5 in St Helens parish, in Bishopsgate Within.

An immediate reaction of the authorities to the outbreak was to close all public places of entertainment, including the theatres. Rosemary – believed to be a disinfectant – was scattered in the streets. For the same purpose, people saturated their clothing with vinegar. Those afflicted with the plague were obliged to carry a yard-long white rod if they ventured abroad: those tending them, a red one. Physicians wore bizarre masks with long beaks filled with bergamot oil as a disinfectant. A red cross and the words 'Lord have mercy on us' were painted on the door of infected houses, as the accounts of the parish of St Mary Woolnoth for 1593–94 reveal.

> Item for setting a crosse upon one Allen's doore in the sicknesse time     ijd
> Item paid for setting two red crosses upon Anthony Sound his dore  iiijd[3]

'Searchers of the Dead' were appointed. These were mainly destitute elderly women who had enough practical medical knowledge to examine corpses and identify those who had died of the plague. Given the virulence of the contagion, the job may not have appeared to have had much future, but it is likely that many would have developed some immunity. They were paid 4d per corpse, but the levels of infection meant that the authorities were hard-pushed even to find this comparatively small sum. According to John Gaunt's *Bills of Mortality*, more than 22,000 people perished in London during the epidemic. Once the searchers had done their diagnosis, the house was boarded up and the inhabitants forbidden to go abroad until there had been no further outbreak there for forty days.

Shakespeare was familiar with the function of the searchers. In *Romeo and Juliet*, which he probably wrote in the aftermath of the great outbreak, Romeo does not receive the message about Juliet's feigned death because Father John, the priest who is supposed to convey it, is confined to a house he has visited because an outbreak of plague has been identified by the searchers.

> Going to find a barefoot brother out
> One of our order to associate me
> Here in this city visiting the sick
> And finding him, the searchers of the town,
> Suspecting that we both were in a house
> Where the infectious pestilence did reign,
> Seal'd up the doors and would not let us forth,
> So that my speed to Mantua there was stayed.

Those who could flee the city did so. Perhaps William Shakespeare was among them. He could have gone back to Stratford, to the country estate of one of the theatrical patrons – or elsewhere. There were plenty of reasons why he should leave and perhaps just two why he should stay. The first was that refugees from London were not welcome in the provinces during times of plague. Checkpoints were established on the main roads and travellers questioned about from whence they had come. If it was a place afflicted by the plague, they were turned back. The Queen took more extreme measures, threatening to execute any Londoner arriving in Windsor, whence the court had fled.

Wherever William Shakespeare may have been, we have knowledge of an important task he undertook. On 18 April 1593, a lengthy poem, *Venus and Adonis*, was entered on the Stationers' Register. The printer was an obvious choice, Shakespeare's fellow Stratfordian, Richard Field, whom he had known since boyhood.

Field had prospered in the city. After his six-year apprenticeship to Thomas Vautrollier, he received his articles as a Freeman of the Stationers' Company on 2 February 1587. It appears that much of his apprenticeship was conducted under the supervision of his mistress rather than that of his master. Vautrollier had established himself as a printer in Edinburgh by 1584. He may have seen commercial opportunities there or he fled thence because he was fearful of the charge of 'Separatism' – i.e. adhesion to a sect other than the Church of England. This may have led to his expulsion from the Stationers' Company. He did return to London, however, where he died in July 1587. His widow attempted to continue the business, but soon ran into trouble. 'Mrs Vautrollier, late wife of Thomas Vautrollier deceased,' read an order issued by the Court of Assistants on 4 March 1588, 'shall not hereafter print any manner of book or books whatsoever as well by reason that her husband was no printer at the time of his decease, as also by the decrees set down in the Star Chamber she is debarred from the same.'

A way was found around the problem. On 12 January 1589, Richard Field was married to 'Jacklin Vautrolier'. If this was the widow of Thomas Vautrollier rather than his daughter, she would have been at least twenty years older than the bridegroom. Either way, there was an element of a *mariage de convenance* about the affair. Field could officially run the existing business. Whichever woman it was, she could not.

Field did not forget his family in Stratford, taking on his brother Jasper as an apprentice after his father's death in 1592. If the books he produced are indicative, he adopted the extreme Protestant faith of the family into which he had married. He published a number of Calvinistic tracts in the Spanish language, but he also printed many other notable works.

*Venus and Adonis* was the first printed work to bear Shakespeare's name. This may be why he described it as 'the first heir of my invention'. It provides the second reason why he might have stayed – to work with Field in preparing the poem for publication. It is dedicated 'To the Right Honourable Henry Wriothesly, Earl of Southampton, and Baron of Tichfield' in what seem to the modern reader to be extravagant terms.

RIGHT HONORABLE,

I know not how I shall offend in dedicating my unpolished lines to your lordship, nor how the world will censure me for choosing so strong a prop to support so weak a burden: only, if your honour seem but pleased, I account myself highly praised, and vow to take advantage of all idle hours, till I have honoured you with some graver labour. But if the first heir of my invention prove deformed, I shall be sorry it had so noble a god-father, and never after ear so barren a land, for fear it yield me still so bad a harvest. I leave it to your honourable survey, and your honour to your heart's content; which I wish may always answer your own wish and the world's hopeful expectation.

Your honour's in all duty,
WILLIAM SHAKESPEARE

Patronage was a vital ingredient in the Elizabethan literary scene. We have seen how great noblemen extended it over their companies of players, but largesse extended in other directions. Poets clamoured for the patronage of great nobles.

The process by which one noted poet acquired an equally noted patron was described by John Aubrey. Edmund Spenser sought to deposit a copy of his soon-to-be-celebrated *Fairie Queene* with Sir Philip Sidney, who was known to be a patron of literature as well as being a fine poet himself.

Sir Philip was busy at his study, and his servant delivered Mr Spencer's booke to his master, who layd it by, thinking it might be such kind of stuffe as he was frequently troubled with. Mr Spencer stayed so long that his patience was wearied, and he went on his way discontented and never intended to come again. When Sir Philip perused it, he was so exceedingly delighted with it that he was extremely sorry that he was gonne, and where to send for him he knew not. After much enquiry he learned his lodgeing, and sent for him, mightily caressed [him] and ordered his servant to give him ... pounds in gold.

The role of the Elizabethan patron was very different from that of the modern sponsor. He was seen as a vital part of the creative process. Patronage crossed the barriers of social class. It enabled the glover's son from Stratford to mix with the most powerful figures in the land.

The tone of the dedication of *Venus and Adonis* is one of hope rather than certainty. Like Spenser, Shakespeare may have been seeking patronage from a nobleman whose acquaintance he had already made rather than producing his work as a result of the patronage. He may have already arranged for the work to be printed before casting around for a dedicatee. The young aristocrat, noted for his munificence towards writers, was an obvious choice.

*Venus and Adonis* was the most successful printed work of the era. It went through at least ten editions in the next decade. Richard Field printed the first four. Its huge popularity made its author a cult figure. In *The Second Part of the Return from Parnassus, or The Scourge of Simony*, a play that was part of a series of Christmas performances by the undergraduates of St John's College, Cambridge, around 1600, Gullio, one of the characters, is unequivocal in his admiration. 'Let this duncified world esteem of Spenser and Chaucer, I'll worship sweet Mr. Shakespeare, and to honour him will lay his *Venus and Adonis* under my pillow.'

## The Priest in Surplice White

It is likely that William Shakespeare became acquainted with the Jesuit priest and future martyr and saint Robert Southwell in the early 1590s. Southwell came from a family of Catholic gentry in Norfolk. He was born around 1561. In 1576, he was sent to the Douai seminary. A year later, he set off for Rome with the intention of joining the Society of Jesus. His application was rebuffed, possibly on grounds of his youth. He was obliged to spend a two-year novitiate in Tournai before his admission to the Society in 1580. He was ordained priest in 1584: the year in which Thomas Lucy's draconian anti-Catholic Bill was passed. Southwell, despite his youth, became Prefect of Studies at the English College in Rome. In 1586, at his own request, he was sent to England as a missionary together with a fellow Jesuit, Henry Garnett. Thus began his remarkable six-year mission as he moved between safe Catholic houses, often disguised as a servant. He not only administered the sacraments to the faithful, he realised the influence that the written word could exercise, producing a steady outpouring of poetry and tracts which were widely circulated in manuscript and had a strong influence on other writers. Ben Jonson declared that he would have willingly sacrificed many of his own poems to have written Southwell's *The Burning Babe*. His longest poem, *St Peter's Complaint*, describes the distress of St Peter at his rejection of Christ.

Southwell was finally apprehended in 1592 by the notorious spy and sadist Richard Topcliffe. He suffered three years of incarceration and torture in appalling circumstances. He was finally tried before the Queen's Bench on 10 February 1595 and hung drawn and quartered at Tyburn next day. *St Peter's Complaint* was published later that year, with the dedication 'The Author to his Loving Cosin'. A further edition was published in 1616. The dedication now reads 'The Author to his Loving Cosin Master WS'. The probability is that this is William Shakespeare. But cousin? As we saw with Thomas Greene's usage of the word to describe his relationship with Shakespeare, it was used by the Elizabethans to denote any consanguinity, however distant. Shakespeare uses the word in this way frequently, particularly in terms of royal relationships. 'Yet leave our cousin Katherine here with us,' says Henry V concerning the French princess.

Research has shown that Robert Southwell had no close relatives with the initials 'W. S.' He was probably distantly related to William Shakespeare through the Arden lineage, although the precise detail is lacking. The two men may have compared notes on their distant relationship.

According to the dedication, it is the dedicatee who has encouraged Southwell to write poetry.

> Blame me not (good Cosin) though I send you a blame-worthy present; in
> which the most that can commend it is the good will of the Writer; neither
> arte nor invention giuing it any credite. If in me this be a fault, you cannot be
> faultlesse that did importune me to commit it, and therefore you must beare
> part of the penance when it shall please sharp censures to impose it. In the

> meane time, with many good wishes, I send you these fewe ditties; adde you
> the tunes, and let the Meane, I pray you, be still a part in all your musicke.

So was Southwell addressing a musician? Not necessarily: he is not
sending the addressee a 'fewe ditties', but a poem, so he is using the term
figuratively. That he is given to using the kind of elaborate conceit beloved
by Shakespeare is revealed by his punning on the word 'mean'. He uses it
as 'meantime', a word whose meaning was much the same as it is today.
He also refers to the 'Meane', in contemporary usage, the middle part of
a three-voice polyphonic texture. Southwell's conceit is an invocation of
the Trinity: the Father, the Son and the Holy Spirit. The second person
– or 'meane' of the Trinity is Jesus Christ. It is He who should inspire the
dedicatee's creativity.

In *St Peter's Complaint*, Southwell upbraids contemporary poets for
'abusing their talent, and making the lollies and faynings of loue the
customarie subiect of their base cndeuours.' By so doing, they 'haue so
discredited this facultie, that a poet, a louer, and a Iyer [liar], are by many
reckoned but three words of one signification.' Shakespeare may have
echoed the latter phrase in *The Merchant of Venice* when he wrote of 'the
lunatic, the lover and the poet'.

In the letter to the reader that is appended to the poem, Southwell
continues to chide his fellow poets.

> This makes my mourning muse dissolve in tears,
> This themes my heavy pen, — too plain in prose;
> Christ's thorn is sharp, no head his garland wears;
> Still finest wits are stilling Venus' rose:
> In paynim [heathen] toys the sweetest veins are spent;
> To Christian works few have their talents lent.

'Venus' rose'? Although Southwell is referring to a collectivity of poets, we
may deduce a reference to *Venus and Adonis*. Some have seen Southwell
and other Catholic martyrs as the subject of Shakespeare's poem *The
Phoenix and the Turtle*, part of a collection published by Robert Chester in
1601. It is a fine poem but a highly enigmatic one: another puzzle to which
the key has been lost, although it is certain that the pagan phoenix and the
turtle (dove) of the title represent two people's obsequies. The narrative
features a number of other birds. The swan represents a priest.

> Let the priest in surplice white,
> That defunctive music can,
> Be the death-divining swan,
> Lest the requiem lack his right.

Both the white surplice and the term 'priest' had been retained in the
Anglican Church of the Elizabethan Settlement, but the word 'requiem'

and the pun on 'right' (rite) indicate that this is a Catholic priest. The Church of England's *Homily on Prayer* specifically condemned the practice of praying for the dead.

> Neither let us dreame any more that the soules of the dead are any thing at all holpen by our prayers: But as the Scripture teacheth us, let us thinke that the soule of man passing out of the body, goeth straight wayes either to heaven, or else to hell, whereof the one needeth no prayer, and the other is without redemption.

## A Superfluous Moiety

Richard Field also printed the first edition of Shakespeare's second narrative poem *The Rape of Lucrece*, which was entered into the Stationers' Register on 9 May 1594 and published later that year. This is the 'graver labor' promised in the preface to *Venus and Adonis*. Although this was not as popular as the former work, it was, nevertheless, a great success, running through six editions by 1616. It was dedicated to the Earl of Southampton in more extravagant and intimate terms than its predecessor.

> To the
> Right Honorable Henry Wriothesly
> Earl of Southampton, and Baron of Tichfield.

> The love I dedicate to your lordship is without end, whereof this pamphlet, without beginning, is but a superfluous moiety. The warrant I have of your honourable disposition, not the worth of my untutored lines, makes it assured of acceptance. What I have done is yours; what I have to do is yours; being part in all I have, devoted yours. Were my worth greater, my duty would show greater; meantime, as it is, it is bound to your lordship, to whom I wish long life, still lengthened with all happiness.

> Your lordship's in all duty,<br>WILLIAM SHAKESPEARE

The choice of subject is a curious sequel to the lush eroticism of *Venus and Adonis*. It may give some indication of the political interests of the patron. Although the theme is ostensibly the outrage implicit in the title, that is not the entire point of the narrative. Southampton was a member of the 'Essex Circle'. It was a group with which poets, including Shakespeare, must have been familiar. Edmund Spenser wrote of Essex House, the Earl's mansion in The Strand, in his *Prothalamion*.

> Next whereunto there stands a stately place,
> Where oft I gained gifts and goodly grace
> Of that great Lord which therein wont to dwell,
> Whose want too well now feeds my friendless case.

Essex paid Spenser's funeral expenses in 1599.

Given that the Queen had no direct heir, the succession was bound to be a live topic. In the same year that *Lucrece* was published, a pamphlet was printed in Antwerp entitled *A Conference about the next Succession to the Crown of England*. The name of the author was given as R. Doleman, undoubtedly a pseudonym for an exiled Catholic. It is not only the place of publication that suggests this. The second half of the pamphlet delineated exhaustively all those who had even the remotest claim to the succession. Most controversially, it revived the claims of the House of Lancaster, descendants of John of Gaunt, thereby negating the legitimacy of the House of Tudor. The claims of the Infanta Isabella Clara Eugenia, daughter of Philip II of Spain, are strongly pressed, although the author must have realised that the chances of a Catholic princess, particularly a Spanish one, succeeding were slim indeed.

The most likely author of the tract was the Jesuit controversialist Robert Persons, who was in the process of establishing a school (later to become Stonyhurst College) at St Omer, which, like Antwerp, was part of Spanish Flanders. It is most likely that it was a composite work, however, and that Richard Rowlands, an English exile from a Flemish background, who had reverted to his ancestral name of Versteagan, was the publisher and co-author.[4]

The tract begins by defending the thesis that it is within the power of 'the commonwealth' to depose its monarch or to decline the accession of an heir who met with disapproval. This extends the Catholic belief that a monarch who falls short of the requirements of the Faith may be deposed by the will of the Church. It vests such authority in the will of the people.

> Propinquity of blood or blood alone, without other circumstances, is not sufficient to be preferred to a crowne ... A body ciuil may have diuers heades, by accession, and is not bound euer to one, as a body natural is.

*A Conference* stands in revolutionary contrast to the developing Anglican doctrine of non-resistance, expressed in the *Homily Against Disobedience and Wilful Rebellion* of 1570. Its provisos are those of 'A Church by Law Established'. The rebellion of subjects against their prince was in every circumstance a grievous sin.

> Kings and Princes, as well the evil as the good, doe reigne by God's ordinance, and ... subjects are bounden to obey them.

Passive obedience was the attitude to be adopted by the subject towards the unlawful commands of his prince. He was not bound to assist in their execution, but he must not resist them by force. This is expressed in the homily, where the authority of King David ('good David') is invoked.

*The demande* What shall we then doe to an euill, to an unkinde Prince, an
enemy to vs, hated of God, hurtful to the common wealth, &c.

*The answer* Lay no violent hand vpon him, saith good David, but let him liue
vntill God appoint and worke his end, either by naturall death, or in warre by
lawfull enemies, not by traiterous subjects.

The tract caused a sensation, as doubtless intended. Like many actions of
Catholics abroad, it did not help the cause of those at home. In August,
1596, the Scottish Jesuit, William Crichton, wrote a letter of protest to
'Persons in Flanders': 'There is a French proverb, you don't catch a hare
by a drum. Ministers are now beating it in the pulpits both of England
and Scotland.'

*A Conference* was dedicated to the Earl of Essex. He, probably correctly,
interpreted this as a devious plot to imply that he lacked loyalty to the
Crown. When a copy of the book came into the hands of the Queen, she
showed it to him. Using his noted charm, he turned the difficult situation
to his advantage. On 12 November, a courtier noted that

my Lord of Essex had put off the melancholy he fell into by a printed book
delivered to the Queen: wherein the harm that was meant to him, by her
Majesty's gracious favour and wisdom is turned to his good, and strengthens
her love unto him.

Nevertheless the dedication was a canny choice. That the Earl may well
have been highly receptive to the radical ideas therein propounded is
amply borne out by subsequent events.

Robert Devereux, the 2nd Earl of Essex, was an attractive, brave,
unreliable and impetuous figure. A second cousin of the Queen, he was
the stepson of her previous favourite, Robert Dudley, Earl of Leicester
and a nephew of the future patron of Shakespeare's company, George
Carey, Lord Hunsdon. After coming to court in 1584, he rapidly became
a favourite of the Queen. After Leicester's death in 1588, she granted him
the monopoly for collecting the excise on the import of sweet wines. Given
that many Englishmen shared Falstaff's penchant for such beverages, this
was a highly lucrative concession.

If I had a thousand sons, the first humane principle I would teach them should
be, to forswear thin potations and to addict themselves to sack.

*(Henry IV, Part 2, IV.3.133)*

Essex fought with great gallantry against the Spanish in the Netherlands
in 1586, and distinguished himself at the Battle of Zutphen, where
his cousin, Sir Philip Sidney, was mortally wounded. This may have
influenced the Queen's decision to appoint him as Master of the Horse
in succession to his stepfather. As well as giving him a military command,

this brought him into the higher echelons of her government – at the age of twenty-one.

Essex consistently thwarted the Queen's declared wishes, relying on his considerable charm and her genuine affection for him to restore her favour whenever his impetuosity and insensitivity caused a temporary fall from grace. In 1589, a 'counter armada', commanded by Sir Francis Drake, was launched to take advantage of the Spanish naval defeat in the previous year. It was partly organised in support of the Portuguese pretender, Dom Antonio, who promised a popular uprising if the expedition landed in Portugal. The enterprise proved a disaster. Essex demonstrated his usual gallantry at the siege of Lisbon, but his request for artillery and siege engines was refused. Elizabeth had more sense than to be pressurised into a continental land war that she had no chance of winning. On his return, Essex was again in trouble with her. He married secretly Sir Philip Sidney's widow. When the Queen discovered this, she was furious, but, once again, the Devereux charm won her round.

Essex's military reputation saw him appointed as the commander of an expeditionary force into France in 1591. The Protestant Henri IV had succeeded to the French throne in 1589 and Elizabeth was pledged to support him to prevent the Catholic League gaining control of France. To this effect, two previous expeditions had been sent. Both lacked vital supplies. One, under Peregrine Bertie, Lord Willoughby, had roamed through Northern France to little effect and half his force was lost. The other, under the most celebrated English commander of the day, Sir John Norreys, fared little better.

Devereux's task was to support Henri IV in the siege of Rouen. He was to join the remnants of Norreys' force to his own. Yet he was faced with a difficult, if not impossible task. The parsimony of the Queen ensured that the troops had not been paid. Initially they were quartered in Dieppe, where 'they were given to all manner of evils, as blasphemy, burning of houses and whole villages, robbing of churches, disobedience to their officers'.

Essex's communications with the court were chaotic (in fairness that applied to the other English commanders). 'Where he is, or what he doth,' wrote Elizabeth, 'or what he is to do, we are ignorant.' In despair, she ordered the recall of the force on 24 October, only for her spirits to revive when Henri sent a communiqué, saying that he'd joined forces with Essex. She countermanded the order. The siege of Rouen achieved little, however, although Essex demonstrated 'true valour and discretion'. The force was finally recalled in January 1592. This time the Queen did not change her mind.

It would be four years before Essex embarked on another military adventure. He felt strongly that his absence from court enabled others to gain the Queen's ear. He threw himself into the business of securing influence and became a regular attendee at the House of Lords. He was appointed a Privy Councillor in 1593, at the age of twenty-six. This was a position of great influence. The Privy Council was effectively the government of England. It could issue proclamations and orders in the monarch's name. There were two issues on which the Queen forbade discussion: foreign policy and the succession.

Essex's palpable ambition in terms of place-seeking for his known supporters did not help his prospects. In 1594, he tried, unsuccessfully, to secure the attorney generalship for his friend, Francis Bacon. He became paranoiac about the influence exercised on Elizabeth by her Secretary of State, William Cecil, 1st Lord Burleigh, and later by his son, Robert. Their characters stood in complete contrast to his. The Cecils exuded an air of reliability, loyalty and trustworthiness. The flamboyant Essex exuded none of these. They had a conspicuous ability to be unscrupulous and ruthless in what would always appear to be in the best interests of their monarch. 'This judgment I have of you,' Elizabeth murmured to the elder Cecil, 'that you will not be corrupted with any manner of gifts and that you will always be faithful to the state.'

With the death of Sir Francis Walsingham, the Principal Secretary, in 1590, Robert Cecil came more and more into prominence in matters of statecraft. It was not only in his qualities that he was the converse of Essex, the handsome man of action: the type who, together with the likes of Drake, Hawkins and Raleigh, would epitomise the spirit of the age. The younger Cecil was slight, hunch-backed and dwarfish in stature: the Queen referred to him as 'my elf' or 'my pigmy'. Unlike the aforementioned bullish heroes, to whom Spain was the natural and even permanent enemy, he realised that England was fighting a war she could not win – he had been sent on a mission to the Spanish court to put out peace feelers as early as 1590. His view that ultimately peace with Spain was a necessity may have been another reason for the aggressive Essex to scorn and underrate him.

By the early 1590s, as the author of *A Conference* fully realised, the question of the succession was a live one. Elizabeth uttered no view on the matter. This was wise, since it prevented parties coalescing around rival claimants. Nevertheless, it ensured continued speculation about England's dynastic future. The Jesuits possessed a considerable collective knowledge of the nuances of English political life, so the author may have had knowledge of Essex's interest in the issue. It is inconceivable that it was not a matter of discussion within the 'Essex Circle'. It is in this context that the *Rape of Lucrece* might be seen. The ravishing of Lucrece by Tarquin, the King's son, leads to the banishment of the royal house from Rome and the institution of the republic. Although, it would not have been the intention of Essex to abolish the monarchy, there is no doubt that he would seek to influence events surrounding the succession to his political enhancement.

Although the poem had potentially explosive political connotations, Shakespeare had already developed a notable skill in handling themes that could land him in trouble. He was exceptional among Elizabethan dramatists in that he appears never to have had a brush with the authorities. Among those who did for various reasons were Thomas Nashe, Ben Jonson, Thomas Kyd, John Marston, Christopher Marlowe, George Chapman, Thomas Dekker, John Daye and William Haughton.

In other contexts, Shakespeare might have made much of the overthrow of the Tarquins, but here he reduces the historic event to just two lines.

> The Romans plausibly did give consent
> To Tarquin's everlasting banishment.

Part of Shakespeare's talent lay in setting his plays in distant times and/or in distant parts, thus enabling him to claim that they bore no relation to contemporary England. He reveals the technique in *Hamlet*, where the Prince pretends to reassure the King, who is becoming disturbed about where the play within a play may be leading.

| **Claudius:** | What do you call the play? |
|---|---|
| **Hamlet:** | The Mouse-trap. Marry, how? Tropically. This play is the image of a murder done in Vienna: Gonzago is the duke's name; his wife, Baptista, you shall see anon; 'tis a knavish piece of work: but what o' that? Your majesty and we that have free souls, it touches us not. |

This skill served Shakespeare well when he turned to the delicate subject of the reign of King Richard II. As with a number of his plays, there was an earlier work on the same subject, although it only survives as an untitled and incomplete manuscript. This older play, which has been putatively titled both *Richard II* and *Thomas of Woodstock*, culminates in the events surrounding the murder of the King's uncle, Thomas of Woodstock, Duke of Gloucester, in 1397. Shakespeare's play begins where the older play left off, so there appears to be an assumption that the audience would be familiar with it, or, at least, its background. Like Elizabeth, Richard had no direct heir. He was overthrown by a powerful subject who made himself king in his stead. As we shall see, the political message of the play was to be interpreted by those hostile to the reigning monarch – and by that monarch herself – as a call for cathartic change. Why should Shakespeare venture into such contentious territory? The influence of the 'Essex Circle' must be regarded as a possibility.

In fact, Shakespeare steered a careful course between the views expressed in *A Conference* and those expressed in the *Homily Against Disobedience and Wilful Rebellion*. In the opening scene, Henry Bolingbroke accuses Thomas Mowbray of the murder of the King's uncle. Henry's father, John of Gaunt, Duke of Lancaster, believes that it was the King who ordered the murder. Nevertheless, he adheres to the principles expressed in the *Homily*.

> God's is the quarrel; for God's substitute,
> His deputy anointed in His sight,
> Hath caused his death: the which if wrongfully,
> Let heaven revenge; for I may never lift
> An angry arm against His minister.

On his deathbed, however, Gaunt espouses the principles of *A Conference* that heirs can be deposed if they prove unworthy of the throne, even before they inherit it.

> O, had thy grandsire with a prophet's eye
> Seen how his son's son should destroy his sons,
> From forth thy reach he would have laid thy shame,
> Deposing thee before thou wert possess'd,
> Which art possess'd now to depose thyself.

Richard has exiled Bolingbroke. After Gaunt's death, the King sequesters his property (and Bolingbroke's inheritance) to finance his war in Ireland. Taking advantage of Richard's absence, Bolingbroke invades England and rapidly gathers a powerful force of the disaffected to seize power. When his uncle York describes him as a traitor, he justifies his actions on the grounds of the natural law that *A Confession* saw as limiting the prerogative of monarchs.

> My father's goods are all distrain'd and sold,
> And these and all are all amiss employ'd.
> What would you have me do? I am a subject,
> And I challenge law: attorneys are denied me;
> And therefore, personally I lay my claim
> To my inheritance of free descent.

As an inadvertent response, the King cites his divine right in terms redolent of the *Homily*.

> Not all the water in the rough rude sea
> Can wash the balm off from an anointed king;
> The breath of worldly men cannot depose
> The deputy elected by the Lord.

He foretells the horrors that will ensue if the sacred person of the Lord's anointed is violated.

> Yet know, my master, God omnipotent,
> Is mustering in his clouds on our behalf
> Armies of pestilence; and they shall strike
> Your children yet unborn and unbegot,

> That lift your vassal hands against my head
> And threat the glory of my precious crown.

The deposition scene follows. The Earl of Northumberland embraces the argument contained in *A Conference* that a monarch who has proved unworthy may be deposed by the will of the people.

> These accusations and these grievous crimes
> Committed by your person and your followers
> Against the state and profit of this land;
> That, by confessing them, the souls of men
> May deem that you are worthily deposed.

After Richard is taken off to the Tower, his loyal supporter, the Bishop of Carlisle, prophesies the woes that his deposition will bring upon the land.

> My Lord of Hereford here, whom you call king,
> Is a foul traitor to proud Hereford's king:
> And if you crown him, let me prophesy:
> The blood of English shall manure the ground,
> And future ages groan for this foul act;
> Peace shall go sleep with Turks and infidels,
> And in this seat of peace tumultuous wars
> Shall kin with kin and kind with kind confound;
> Disorder, horror, fear and mutiny
> Shall here inhabit, and this land be call'd
> The field of Golgotha and dead men's skulls.
> O, if you raise this house against this house,
> It will the woefullest division prove
> That ever fell upon this cursed earth.
> Prevent it, resist it, let it not be so,
> Lest child, child's children, cry against you woe!

This is very much an echo of the *Homily*.

> For he that nameth rebellion, nameth not a singular or one onely sinne, as is theft, robbery, murder, and such like, but he nameth the whole puddle and sinke of all sinnes against GOD and man, against his Prince, his country, his countrymen, his parents, his children, his kins folkes, his friends, and against all men vniuersally, all sinnes I say against GOD and all men heaped together nameth he, that nameth rebellion.

When Henry Bolingbroke hears that Exton has murdered Richard, he realises the doom that he has placed upon his family and vows to pay an elaborate penance in the hope of averting the due nemesis.

> Lords, I protest, my soul is full of woe,
> That blood should sprinkle me to make me grow:
> Come, mourn with me for that I do lament,
> And put on sullen black incontinent:
> I'll make a voyage to the Holy Land,
> To wash this blood off from my guilty hand:
> March sadly after; grace my mournings here;
> In weeping after this untimely bier.

On 7 December 1595, a well-connected courtier, Sir Edward Hoby, wrote to his cousin, the Privy Councillor Sir Robert Cecil, inviting him to his house in Canon Row.

> Sir, findinge that you wer not convenientlie to be at London to morrow night I am bold to send to know whether Teusdaie may be anie more in your grace to visit poore Channon rowe where as late as it shal please you a gate for your shal be open: K. Richard present himselfe to your view.[5]

The reference to King Richard is unclear. It is unlikely that the Lord Chamberlain's Men should be on standby awaiting Cecil's acceptance. The possibility that it is to a performance that Hoby is inviting Cecil is increased by the fact that his father-in-law was the Lord Chamberlain, Lord Hunsdon, who was ultimately responsible for vetting performances on the public stage. Since *Richard II* was to remain the most controversial of Shakespeare's plays in his own era, it is not impossible that a performance was arranged to vet its potential impact on the volatile politics of court and state. In fact, it appears that the controversial deposition scene was excised by the censor. It does not feature in the three quartos of the play that were published in Elizabeth I's lifetime. A fourth quarto, published in 1608, contains it, but in a shorter form than that which eventually appeared in the First Folio in 1623.

There is one other play that incorporates a scene of the deposition of a monarch that Shakespeare wrote around this time. *The Life and Death of King John* features the contemporary theme of a power struggle between the English monarchy and the Papacy. Yet again, the force of the argument is contained within the conflicting views of the *Homily* and *A Confession*. King John refuses to accept Stephen Langton, the Papal nominee, as Archbishop of Canterbury. He has already stated that the cost of his expedition to France will be borne by the nation's abbeys and priories. He rejects the resultant strictures of Cardinal Pandulph, the Papal legate, in terms that are redolent of the Protestant spirit.

> What earthy name to interrogatories
> Can task the free breath of a sacred king?
> Thou canst not, cardinal, devise a name
> So slight, unworthy and ridiculous,

> To charge me to an answer, as the pope.
> Tell him this tale; and from the mouth of England
> Add thus much more, that no Italian priest
> Shall tithe or toll in our dominions;
> But as we, under heaven, are supreme head,
> So under Him that great supremacy,
> Where we do reign, we will alone uphold,
> Without the assistance of a mortal hand:
> So tell the pope, all reverence set apart
> To him and his usurp'd authority.

This accords with the thirty-seventh of the Thirty-Nine Articles of the Church of England, formulated in 1563 – 'The Bishop of Rome hath no jurisdiction in this Realm of England.'

Because of his defiance of Rome and subsequent excommunication, King John had become something of a Protestant icon. The polemicist John Bale makes his *Kynge Johan* arguably the first English history play, an anti-Popish diatribe. A similar vein is followed in *The Troublesome Reign of King John*, an earlier play which was probably one of Shakespeare's major sources.

Yet in Shakespeare's play, John's bid for independence from the Papacy ends in failure. In a speech that recalls the excommunication of Queen Elizabeth by the Pope, Pandulph retorts:

> Then by the lawful power that I have
> Thou shalt stand curs'd and excommunicate;
> And blessed shall he be that doth revolt
> From his allegiance to a heretic.

It is Pandulph who triumphs. He calls on the French king, Philip, to take action against John. Philip is reluctant. He has just made an accord with John that Louis, the Dauphin, will marry the English king's niece, Blanche, as part of a territorial settlement. This strengthens John's hand against the rival claimant, the boy prince Arthur. Nevertheless, Pandulph points out to Louis that he now has as strong a claim to the English throne as John and persuades him to join forces with the Papacy in suppressing the rebellious monarch. Arthur is captured by the English and John instructs his henchman, Hubert de Burgh, to kill him. Hubert does not do so, but tells John that he has. When the English nobles learn that Arthur is supposedly dead, they are outraged and desert John's cause for that of Louis. Thus it is no surprise that John is delighted to learn from Hubert that Arthur is alive after all. The relief is brief. Arthur, while attempting to escape, falls from the castle walls and is killed. In the face of a French invasion, expediency demands that John is reconciled to the Papacy.

| King John: | Thus have I yielded up into your hand |
| | The circle of my glory. |
| Pandulph: | [*Gives back the crown*] Take again |
| | From this my hand, as holding of the Pope, |
| | Your sovereign greatness and authority. |

This is not quite the argument of *A Confession*, which sees the 'common wealth' as representing ultimately a higher political power than the monarchy, which rules by its consent. Here the spiritual power of the Papacy is seen as possessing a prerogative over secular monarchs, a view which runs contrary to the Elizabethan consensus, but if Shakespeare were upbraided for this, he would have had a simple reply. It happened in history.

# 8

# Sonnets and a Patron, 1592–94

'His sugred Sonnets'

– Francis Meres, 1598

It is likely but not certain that most, if not all, of Shakespeare's sonnets were written during the period when the theatres were closed by the plague. There was a huge cult of this verse form in the early 1590s. There are around 1,200 extant such poems from this period. Many more must have been lost, including, perhaps, some of Shakespeare's.

Perhaps the earliest record of William Shakespeare writing sonnets is to be found in the text of *Love's Labour's Lost*, which he probably wrote before plague closed the playhouses in 1592–93. The text contains three embedded sonnets. The one spoken by Longaville (IV.3.14) begins:

> Did not the heavenly rhetoric of thine eye
> 'Gainst whom the world cannot hold argument
> Persuade my heart to this false perjury?
> Vows for thee broke deserve not punishment.

In Act IV (3.228–70) there is a lengthy dialogue which appears to comprise three consecutive sonnets.

Shakespeare continued to espouse the sonnet form in *Romeo and Juliet*, which was probably written soon after the theatres reopened. The Chorus speaks of

> Two households, both alike in dignity.
> In fair Verona, where we lay our scene,
> From ancient grudge break to new mutiny,
> Where civil blood makes civil hands unclean.
> From forth the fatal loins of these two foes
> A pair of star-crossed lovers take their life
> Whose misadventured piteous overthrows
> Do with their death bury their parents strife.
> The fearful passage of their death-mark'd love,
> Which, but their children's end, naught could remove,
> Is now the two hours traffic of our stage;

The which if you with patient ears attend,
What here shall miss, our toil shall strive to mend.

The poet must have thrilled to his own dexterity in writing a sonnet in the form of stage dialogue, while at the same time revealing his knowledge of the Catholic practices of pilgrimage and evocation of the saints.

| | |
|---|---|
| **Romeo:** | If I profane with my unworthiest hand |
| | This holy shrine, the gentle sin is this: |
| | My lips, two blushing pilgrims, ready stand |
| | To smooth that rough touch with a tender kiss. |
| **Juliet:** | Good pilgrim, you do wrong your hand too much, |
| | Which mannerly devotion shows in this: |
| | For saints have hands that pilgrims hands do touch. |
| | And palm to palm is holy palmers' kiss. |
| **Romeo:** | Have not saints lips and holy palmers too? |
| **Juliet:** | Ay, pilgrim, lips they must use in prayer. |
| **Romeo:** | O, then, dear saint, let lips do what hands do: |
| | They pray – grant thou, lest faith turn to despair. |
| **Juliet:** | Saints do not move, thou grant for prayers' sake, |
| **Romeo:** | Then move not, while my prayers' effect I take. |

In 1598, the Revd Francis Meres published his *Palladis Tamia* or *Wit's Treasury*. He praises contemporary writers, including Marlowe, Chapman and Drayton, but his greatest admiration is for William Shakespeare. It is of great value that he lists Shakespeare's plays, thereby aiding our dating of them, but he gives precedence to the poetic works: 'witnes his *Venus* and *Adonis*, his *Lucrece*, his sugred Sonnets among his private friends, &c.'

'Private friends'? This indicates that Shakespeare was involved in a literary circle. It was the custom for members of such groups to circulate their poetry among each other. The verse was not intended primarily for publication, although sometimes it was published eventually. This is the case with some of the finest poets of the epoch. John Donne's poetry was circulated privately, but was published in 1635. Andrew Marvell's poetry was similarly circulated and not published until after his death.

The poems of such a noted author as William Shakespeare must have been copied many times during their circulation from hand to hand. That Meres writes of them reveals that their existence was widely known. Two were published by a London printer, William Jaggard, in 1599, as part of a collection of twenty-two poems entitled *The Passionate Pilgrim*. The author of the work is named as William Shakespeare, although at least seven poems are the work of others. Apart from the two sonnets, three of the poems are taken from *Love's Labour's Lost*. Of the remaining thirteen, some may be by Shakespeare, but there is no decisive proof and Jaggard's casualness in attribution does not inspire confidence.

That Jaggard was able to get his hands on the two sonnets demonstrates how widely they had circulated and that the collection must have become fragmented. The volume sold steadily, for Jaggard issued another edition in 1612, expanding it to include nine extra poems. Despite the fact that Shakespeare's name still appeared on the title page, these were by Thomas Heywood, who protested against this piracy in his *An Apology for Actors* and added that Shakespeare was 'much offended' that Jaggard had made 'so bold with his name'.

By the 1600s the cult of the sonnet had diminished, but the verse form remained popular and the magic name of Shakespeare guaranteed good sales. It must have been with this in mind that on 20 May 1609, a London stationer, Thomas Thorpe, obtained a licence to publish the sonnets of William Shakespeare. In June he published a collection of 154 of them. The name of one purchaser is known. The actor Edward Alleyne bought a copy that month for 5*d*.[1] The sonnets were probably published by Thorpe without the author's permission – or at least his collaboration. There are gaps in several of the poems which surely would not exist had the author had oversight of the production. On the other hand, Thomas Heywood, who as a fellow dramatist would be acquainted with Shakespeare, stated that 'hee to doe himself right, hath since published them in his owne name'. This may be interpreted as saying that Shakespeare had decided that his sonnets should be published as he had written them, rather than appearing in dribs and drabs through pirate printers. A further indication of Shakespeare's possible involvement in the project is that the theatres had been closed by plague, just as they had been at the time of the publication of *Venus and Adonis*.

Sir Philip Sidney introduced the concept of a sonnet sequence, each poem taking up the theme of its predecessor, in *Astrophel and Stella*, published in 1591. There is no such sequence throughout the 154 sonnets that Thorpe published under Shakespeare's name, although there are recurring and linking themes. The first twenty poems in Thorpe's edition do represent a sequence. They are addressed to a young person of great beauty. The poet examines ways in which this beauty might be preserved for posterity. The first is through progeny. Shakespeare was an early inadvertent subscriber to the knowledge that genes are immortal. Beauty can be preserved through increase, but the young person is showing no urgency in achieving this, or even in acknowledging its necessity. The theme is explored thoroughly in the very first sonnet in the sequence.

> From fairest creatures we desire increase,
> That thereby beauty's rose might never die
> But as the riper should by time decease,
> His tender heir might bear his memory:
> But thou contracted to thine own bright eyes,
> Feedst thy light's flame with self-substantial fuel,
> Making a famine where abundance lies,

> Thyself thy foe, to thine own self too cruel:
> Thou that art the world's fresh ornament,
> And only herald to the gaudy spring,
> Within thine own bud buriest thy content,
> And, tender churl, mak'st waste in niggarding:
> > Pity the world, or else this glutton be,
> > To eat the world's due, by the grave and thee.

The next thirteen sonnets pursue this theme in the context of the passing of time and the decay of all that is mortal – a common theme in Elizabethan poetry. It is succinctly expressed in Sonnet 10.

> Make thee another self, for love of me,
> That beauty still may live in thine or thee.

Sonnet 15 brings in a new theme:

> And, all in war with time, for love of you,
> As he takes from you, I engraft you new.

'I engraft you new.' The poet is extending the ways in which immortality can be achieved. Art can survive beyond the life of its creator. This theme is developed in Shakespeare's most famous sonnet.

> Shall I compare thee to a summer's day?
> Thou art more lovely and more temperate;
> Rough winds do shake the darling buds of May
> And summer's lease hath all too short a date;
> Sometimes too hot the eye of heaven shines,
> And often is his gold complexion dimm'd;
> And every fair from fair sometime declines,
> By chance, or nature's changing course, untrimm'd;
> But thy eternal summer shall not fade,
> Nor lose possession of that fair thou owest;
> Nor shall death brag thou wander'st in his shade,
> When in eternal lines to time thou growest:
> > So long as men can breathe, or eyes can see,
> > So long lives this, and this gives life to thee.

The poem reflects the poet's self-confidence. This is a man who in seven years has progressed from the son of a local worthy in a provincial town to becoming an esteemed playwright who mixes with the highest gentry in the land. He also considers, quite correctly, that his works will survive to future generations.

Others may have thought it, but it was the critic George Steevens who appears to have been the first to have publicly realised that the first 128 of

Shakespeare's sonnets were addressed to a man. This may explain why he regarded the poems 'with an equal admixture of disgust and indignation'. There is no doubt that he was correct in his analysis. Sonnet 9 states it unequivocally.

> Is it for fear to wet a widow's eye,
> That thou consum'st thyself in single life?

Soon after Steevens' revelation, Thomas Tyrwhittle claimed to have identified the young man through a supposed pun in Sonnet 20.

> A man in hue all hues in his controlling

This led Tyrwhittle to conclude that the poem was addressed to a young man called William Hughes – although how the hypothetical pun extends to the Christian name is unclear. Nor could he identify precisely the subject of the poems beyond his name, an omission remedied by Oscar Wilde, who claimed that the said 'Willie Hughes' was a boy actor with whom the poet was enamoured. The suggestion underlines the astonishing capacity that people have to identify themselves personally with Shakespeare's writing. Yet despite such cavils, the question remains. Was his relationship with the beautiful youth of a homosexual nature? There is no means of knowing categorically, but there can be no doubt that the cited poem, Sonnet 20, demonstrates that both the poet and the beautiful youth were heterosexuals.

> A woman's face, with nature's own hand painted,
> Hast thou, the master-mistress of my passion;
> A woman's gentle heart, but not acquainted
> With shifting change, as is false women's fashion;
> An eye more bright than theirs, less false in rolling,
> Gilding the object whereupon it gazeth;
> A man in hue all hues in his controlling,
> Which steals men's eyes, and women's souls amazeth.
> And for a woman wert thou first created;
> Till nature, as she wrought thee, fell a-doting,
> And by addition me of thee defeated,
> By adding one thing to my purpose nothing.
> > But since she prick'd thee out for women's pleasure;
> > Mine be thy love, and thy love's use their treasure.

The poem demonstrates Shakespeare's brilliant dexterity and his love of wordplay. It may be paraphrased as follows:

The beautiful youth to whom the poem is dedicated has the looks and qualities of a beautiful young woman, but, although he has the virtues of women, he has none of their faults, such as their flirtatiousness or their inconstancy. The beauty of the young man is such that he endows whatever he looks upon with beauty: 'A man in hue all hues in his controlling'. Such is the young man's beauty that it was nature's intention to create him as a woman, but she fell in love with her own creation and did not know when to stop, 'adding one thing to my purpose nothing' – i.e. a penis. By doing this, nature baulked any hope of a physical relationship between the poet and the young man, but there was a consolation. The young man, in an obvious double entendre, is 'prick'd out' for women's pleasure. The poet is happy with this. He can enjoy the young man's love, while women can enjoy 'love's use' with him – i.e. sexual intercourse.

It must also be said that active homosexual relations carried the death penalty following an Act against Sodomy passed in 1562. In practice, few prosecutions occurred.[2] It is difficult to define Shakespeare's attitude towards love between men, but Sonnet 20 implies that he saw such platonic friendships as a different and a higher calling than the carnality of relations with women. Such a view is expressed by Gratiano in the opening scene of *The Merchant of Venice*.

> I tell thee what Antonio –
> I love thee and it is my love that speaks –

In *Romeo and Juliet*, old Capulet tells Paris:

> This night I hold an old accustom'd feast,
> Whereto I have invited many a guest,
> Such as I love, and you, among the store,
> One more, most welcome, makes the number more.

It must also be said that urging the young man to marry and beget children hardly sounds like a homosexual addressing his catamite. In fact the sequence represents a further example of the kind of extravagant flattery that a contemporary artist might offer his patron. Consider Machiavelli's dedication of *The Prince* to Lorenzo de' Medici:

It is customary for such as seek a Prince's favour, to present themselves before him with those things of theirs which they most value, or in which they perceive him chiefly to delight. Desiring in like manner to approach your Magnificence with some token of my devotion, I have found among my possessions none that I so much prize and esteem as the knowledge of the actions of great men, acquired in the course of a long experience of modern affairs and a continual study of antiquity. Which knowledge, most carefully and patiently pondered over and sifted by me, and now reduced into this little book, I send to your Magnificence. And though I deem the work unworthy of your greatness, yet I am bold enough to hope that your courtesy will dispose you to accept it, considering that I can offer you no better gift than the means of mastering it in a very brief time, all that in the course of so many years, and at the cost of so many hardships and dangers, I have learned, and know…

The high-blown flattery is for a purpose – to gain the patronage of the great man. Machiavelli humbly conceded that he was looking for obvious collateral.

Let Your magnificence, then, accept this little gift in the spirit in which I offer it; wherein, if you diligently read and study it, you will recognise my extreme desire that you should attain to that eminence which Fortune and your own merits promise you. Should you from the height of your greatness some time turn your eyes to these humble regions, you will become aware how undeservedly I have to endure the keen and unremitting malignity of Fortune.

The first group of Shakespeare's sonnets contain similar elaborate flattery, with the clear unspoken hope of some sort of largesse on the part of the young man, whose identity generations have been intrigued to know. It is unlikely that we will ever be certain of it, but Thomas Thorp may or may not give a clue in his famous dedication to his edition of the sonnets:

TO THE ONLIE BEGETTER OF

THESE INSVING SONNETS

M<sup>r</sup>. W. H. ALL HAPPINESSE

AND THAT ETERNITIE

PROMISED

BY

OUR EVER-LIVING POET

WISHETH

THE WELL-WISHING

ADVENTURER IN

SETTING

FORTH.

T. T.

So who was this mysterious Mr W. H. to whom the sonnets are dedicated? It goes without saying that every possible candidate – and as with the case of the non-existent Willy Hughes, some impossible ones – has been suggested. The obvious is overlooked. The dedication is not by Shakespeare but by Thomas Thorp. Although he may have known the identity of the beautiful youth, it is probable that he did not. The phrase 'onlie begetter' presents more difficulties. The only begetter of the sonnets is the author, 'William Himself' – not surprisingly, this has been suggested as yet another unlikely candidate. Conversely, if the dedicatee is the young man, it stretches the term even further, interpreting 'begetter' as 'inspirer'. Thorp's tortuous dedication shows that he could use words confusingly.

It is likely that the Mr W. H. is not the young man at all, but whoever it was who procured the poems for Thorp. This also stretches the word 'begetter', but it is stretched in whichever direction it is pulled. There is a front-runner on this one. In 1606, three years before the publication of the sonnets, a 'W. H.' wrote a dedication to an edition of *A Fourefould Meditation*, a collection of sacred verse by the executed Jesuit Robert Southwell. The printer of the work was George Eld, who also printed the *Sonnets* for Thomas Thorp, so there is a strong link. The sentiments behind the dedication are not dissimilar to that of the sonnets:

> To the Right Wor hipful and
> *Vertuous Gentleman. Mathew*
> Saunders, E quire.
> W. H. wi heth, with long life, a pro perous
> achieuement of his good de ires.

A dedicatory epistle follows, in which W. H. describes the process which led to the publication. 'Long have they lien hidden in obscuritie,' he wrote of Southwell's verses,

> and happily had never seene the light, had not a meere accident conveyed them to my hands. But having seriously perused them, loath I was that any who are religiously affected, should be deprived of so great a comfort, as the due consideration thereof may bring unto them.

The 'W. H.' in question may well be William Hall, the only contemporary member of the Stationers' Company with those initials. In 1600, Thomas Thorp had dedicated an edition of Christopher Marlowe's previously unpublished translation of Lucan's *Bellum Civile* to a fellow Stationer, Edward Blount, who may well have performed the same service presumed of Hall in passing on the manuscript.

So, if Mr W. H. is William Hall, who is the young man to whom the sonnets are addressed? We have seen that the language of the opening sequence is redolent of an extravagant address from poet to patron. Obviously the dating of the poems may be crucial to narrowing the field. Certainly most of them were written before 1598 when Francis Meres revealed their existence, but they may have been revised before their ultimate publication. As we have seen, during the period 1592–93 Shakespeare the dramatist's pen was less active because of the closure of the theatres. This is the only time when he is known to have had a personal patron as against a collective one for his company. This may be a key to the dating, at least of the opening sequence. On stylistic grounds, the sonnets fit the period between the appearance of the form in *Love's Labour's Lost* and its continuation in *Romeo and Juliet*.

The front-runner for the beautiful youth must be Henry Wriothesly, the 3rd Earl of Southampton. He was in his twentieth year when Shakespeare dedicated *Venus and Adonis* to him. His father, the 2nd Earl, the leading Catholic nobleman in England, had died when he was eight and he was made a royal ward, under the particular care of Lord Burghley. He went up to St John's College, Cambridge, at the age of twelve and took his MA when he was sixteen. At the age of seventeen he was presented at court. He was a devotee of the theatre. 'My Lord Southampton and Lord Rutland,' wrote Rowland White to Sir Robert Sydney in 1599, 'come not to the court ... They pass away the time in London merely in going to plays every day.'[3]

Significantly, Southampton was unmarried in 1593, but he was a highly eligible bachelor. His guardian, Lord Burghley, planned to marry him to his granddaughter, Lady Elizabeth de Vere, eldest daughter of the Earl of Oxford. There was just one snag. The prospective bridegroom was not keen and pleaded both his youth and his need for time to consider it. His equivocation cost him dearly. The astute Burghley exploited his naivety in the ways of the world to his advantage, persuading the couple to enter into a form of pre-marital contract. The Jesuit Henry Garnet recorded the cost of Wriothesley's final rejection: 'The young Earl of Southampton refusing the Lady de Vere payeth £5000 of present payment.' Within months, Burghley had secured an alternative match to another highly eligible bachelor. On 26 June 1594, the Lady Elizabeth married William Stanley, the 6th Earl of Derby.

A further clue to the identity of the youth is contained in Sonnet 26, of which the dedication of *The Rape of Lucrece* to the Earl of Southampton is a clear paraphrase.

> Lord of my love, to whom in vassalage
> Thy merit hath my duty strongly knit;
> To thee I send this written embassage,
> To witness duty, not to show my wit;
> Duty so great, which wit so poor as mine
> May make seem bare, in wanting words to show it,
> But that I hope some good conceit of thine
> In thy soul's thought, all naked, will bestow it:
> Till whatever star that guides my moving,
> Points on me graciously with fair aspect,
> And puts apparel on my tatter'd loving,
> To show me worthy of thy sweet respect:
>   Then may I dare to boast how I do love thee;
>   Till then, not show my head where thou may'st prove me.

The sonnet may have been written to accompany the narrative poem when Shakespeare presented it to his patron. The tone, although affectionate, is deferential.

After the opening sequence, the sonnets which follow take on the more familiar and affectionate tone established in Sonnet 29.

> For thy sweet love remembered such wealth brings,
> That then I scorn to change my state with kings.

He chides him in a teasing manner, which betokens the more familiar relationship.

> Why didst thou promise such a beauteous day
> And make me travel forth without my cloak?
> (Sonnet 34)

Nevertheless, the subject has ceased to be a model of perfection.

> No more be grieved at that which thou hast done:
> Roses have thorns, and silver fountains mud,
> (Sonnet 35)

The cause of the disillusion is a woman to whom the poet has been attached, but whom his friend has taken from him. Sonnet 42 sets the scene.

> That thou hast her, it is not all my grief,
> And yet it may be said I lov'd her dear.

Typically, Shakespeare turns the ostensibly fraught situation into a means of paying an elaborate compliment to the young man.

> But here's the joy, my friend and I are one;
> Sweet flattery! – then she loves but me alone.

As if there are not sufficient complications, in a further development in the vague plot, a rival poet arrives on the scene in Sonnet 78. The young man now has two poets rather than one. Shakespeare takes advantage of the situation to pay him a further compliment in Sonnet 83.

> There lives more life in one of your fair eyes,
> Than both your poets can in praise devise.

He appears to regard the other man's poetry as superior to his own. Yet the tone is mocking. In Sonnet 86, he accuses him of necromancy, using dark forces to contact dead poets by night.

> Was it the proud full sail of his great verse,
> Bound for the prize of all-too-precious you,
> That did my ripe thoughts in my brain inhearse,
> Making their tomb the womb wherein they grew?

> Was it his spirit, by spirits taught to write
> Above a mortal pitch, that struck me dead?

It is probable that the dead poet who is supposedly dictating the rival poet's verse is Christopher Marlowe. 'The proud full sail of his great verse' echoes Ben Jonson's reference to 'Marlowe's mighty line'.

If we make this assumption it facilitates the dating of the sonnets – or at least Sonnet 86 – to after May 1592, when Marlowe was killed, but who was the rival poet? If we assume Southampton is the young man of the sonnets, it may be possible to hazard an enlightened guess by considering which other poets were pursuing his patronage at this time.

Like Sir Philip Sidney, Henry Wriothesly was a noted literary patron. Thomas Nashe dedicated his romance of *The Life of Jack Wilton* to him: 'a dear lover and cherisher as well of the lovers of poets as of the poets themselves'. Gervase Markham dedicated his *Most Honourable Tragedy of Sir Richard Grenville* to him. John Florio, the prominent Italian man of letters, was taken into his 'pay and patronage'. Another who sought his munificence was Barnabe Barnes. Outside academic circles, his name is virtually forgotten, but he was a considerable contemporary figure. The fourth of the nine sons of the Bishop of Durham, in 1591 he had participated in the Earl of Essex's expedition against Spain. On his return, he became involved in an imbroglio between rival poets: his friend Gabriel Harvey and Thomas Nashe. In a sonnet he wrote for Harvey's pamphlet, *Pierces Supererogation*, he labelled Nashe a confidence trickster, a liar, a viper, a laughing stock and mere 'worthless matter' who should be flattered that Harvey even deigned to insult him. Nashe took due note of the jibes and reserved his fire.

Barnes's reputation in May 1593 was high after the publication of his *Parthenophil and Parthenophe, Sonnettes, Madrigals, Elegies and Odes*. Nashe took his opportunity to pour scorn on its elaborate conceits, including one in which the poet expresses the desire to be transformed into the wine his mistress drinks, so that he may pass through her. 'Therein he was very ill-advised,' he sneered, 'for so the next time his mistress made water, he was in danger to be cast out of her favour.' Yet Barnes's work was impressive in its very scale, consisting of 104 sonnets, 26 madrigals, 5 sestinas, 21 elegies, a canzone, a translation of the first Idyll of Moschus, and 20 odes. One of the sonnets is a flattering verse written to Southampton, which implies that the wider body of Barnes's work is dedicated to the young earl.

> Receive, sweet Lord, with thy thrice sacred hand
> (which sacred Muses make their instrument)
> These worthless leaves, which I to thee present,
> (Sprung from a rude and unmanurèd land)
> That with your countenance graced, they may withstand
> Hundred-eyed Envy's rough encounterment,

> Whose patronage can give encouragement
> To scorn back-wounding Zoilus his band.
> Vouchsafe, right virtuous Lord, with gracious eyes –
> Those heavenly lamps which give the Muses light,
> Which give and take in course that holy fire –
> To view my Muse with your judicial sight:
> Whom, when time shall have taught, by flight, to rise
> Shall to thy virtues, of much worth, aspire.

Is this what provoked Shakespeare's reaction, jocular or otherwise?

Nashe's counterblast came in 1596, although his character assassination may have circulated previously. In *Have With You To Saffron-Walden* (the birthplace of Gabriel Harvey) he observed that Barnes was an awful poet. He was scathing about his dress sense. He wore 'a strange pair of Babylonian britches, with a codpiece as big as a Bolognian sausage'. He accused him of cowardice during the expedition to France, claiming, not entirely seriously, that he had gone to the general to complain war was dangerous and he wanted to go home at once. Despite six burly captains offering to be his bodyguards, 'home he would, nothing would stay him, to finish *Parthenophil and Parthenophe* and to write in praise of Gabriel Harvey'.

Like the rival poet, Barnes had an interest in necromancy. He contributed to the spate of plays on witchcraft that followed the accession of James I. *The Divil's Charter* was performed by Shakespeare's company at around the time that *Macbeth* was written. Like the 'Scottish Play', it must have been inspired by the King's presumed interest in witchcraft.

Whoever the 'rival poet' was, and whether Shakespeare's attack was serious or otherwise, he seems to have seen him off. In Sonnet 127 a fourth character appears in the drama. This is the famous 'dark lady' – his word for her is 'black'. While to the modern ear it has connotations of negroid, to the Elizabethans it simply meant dark. Short of her name, we learn quite a lot about her. She is not beautiful, but has a hypnotic quality that persuades people that she is. This is the essence of the first sonnet in the 'Dark Lady' series, although her existence has been hinted at previously.

> In the old age, black was not counted fair,
> Or, if it were, it bore not beauty's name,
> But now is black, beauty's successive heir,
> And beauty slandered with a bastard shame.
> For since each hand hath put on Nature's power,
> Fairing the foul with Art's false borrowed face,
> Sweet beauty hath no name, no holy bower,
> But is profaned, if not lives in disgrace.
> Therefore my mistress' eyes are raven black,
> Her eyes so suited and they mourners seem
> At such who, not born fair, no beauty lack.
> Sland'ring creation with a false esteem;

> Yet so they mourn becoming of their woe,
> That every tongue says beauty should look so.

The dark lady is wanton. That the relationship is one of mutual deceit is revealed in Sonnet 138 where he plays on two meanings of the word 'lie': to tell an untruth, or to have sexual intercourse.

> When my love swears that she is made of truth,
> I do believe her, though I know she lies,
> That she might think me some untutor'd youth,
> Unlearned in the world's false subtleties.
> Thus vainly thinking that she thinks me young,
> Although she knows my days are past the best,
> Simply I credit her false-speaking tongue;
> On both sides thus is simple truth suppressed:
> But wherefore says she not she is unjust?
> And wherefore say not I that I am old?
> O! love's best habit is in seeming trust,
> And age in love, loves not to have years told:
> > Therefore I lie with her, and she with me,
> > And in our faults by lies we flattered be.

'And wherefore say not I that I am old?' This is curious. If the estimate that most if not all the sonnets were written around 1592–93 is correct, then Shakespeare was still in his late twenties: hardly old. It is possible that he was old in comparison to the lady, who may have been several years younger, or we may be in the presence of another in-joke whose meaning is lost.

In Sonnet 128 Shakespeare reveals that the lady plays a keyboard instrument with some skill.

> How oft when thou, my music, music play'st,
> Upon that blessed wood whose motion sounds
> With thy sweet fingers when thou gently sway'st
> The wiry concord that mine ear confounds,
> Do I envy those jacks that nimble leap,
> To kiss the tender inward of thy hand,
> Whilst my poor lips which should that harvest reap,
> At the wood's boldness by thee blushing stand!
> To be so tickled, they would change their state
> And situation with those dancing chips,
> O'er whom thy fingers walk with gentle gait,
> Making dead wood more bless'd than living lips.

Yet he can temper his extravagant conceits with a mock realism which betokens genuine affection. In Sonnet 130, he brilliantly challenges the conceits of the day.

My mistress' eyes are nothing like the sun;
Coral is far more red, than her lips red:
If snow be white, why then her breasts are dun;
If hairs be wires, black wires grow on her head.
I have seen roses damasked, red and white,
But no such roses see I in her cheeks;
And in some perfumes is there more delight
Than in the breath that from my mistress reeks.
I love to hear her speak, yet well I know
That music hath a far more pleasing sound:
I grant I never saw a goddess go,
My mistress, when she walks, treads on the ground:
   And yet by heaven, I think my love as rare,
   As any she belied with false compare.

Unlike that with the Fair Youth, Shakespeare's relationship with the Dark Lady is brazenly sexual. He writes three sonnets in which he uses the word 'Will'. As well as being his own name, in contemporary argot the word also referred to the sexual organs, both male and female. That it is used in the same way today is shown by adding a 'y' to 'will', although the term now refers exclusively to the male sexual organ. He uses the pun to ribald and witty effect in Sonnet 135.

Whoever hath her wish, thou hast thy Will,
And Will to boot, and Will in over-plus;
More than enough am I that vexed thee still,
To thy sweet will making addition thus.
Wilt thou, whose will is large and spacious,
Not once vouchsafe to hide my will in thine?
Shall will in others seem right gracious,
And in my will no fair acceptance shine?
The sea, all water, yet receives rain still,
And in abundance addeth to his store;
So thou, being rich in Will, add to thy Will
One will of mine, to make thy large will more.
   Let no unkind, no fair beseechers kill;
   Think all but one, and me in that one Will.

So the Bard signs off with his own name. This must present difficulties to those eccentrics who consider that Shakespeare didn't write the works that bear his name. If there is any doubt, he is even more specific in the next sonnet, which concludes:

Make but my name thy love, and love that still,
And then thou lovest me for my name is 'Will.'

One must conclude that, if it wasn't Will Shakespeare, it can only have been another 'Will'.

The next development in this vague plot has a certain air of inevitability: the Dark Lady gets off with the Fair Youth, or at least Shakespeare thinks she does, but he is not completely sure. What may be described as a *ménage à trois* develops. There has been a previous hint of this in Sonnet 35, but now the poet becomes obsessed with it. In Sonnet 132, he sees the Fair Youth as a fellow victim who is ensnared by the Dark Lady.

> Beshrew that heart that makes my heart to groan
> For that deep wound it gives my friend and me!

He sums up the situation in Sonnet 144, where he uses the concept created by Christopher Marlowe in *Doctor Faustus* of a good angel and a bad competing for a soul.

> Two loves I have of comfort and despair,
> Which like two spirits do suggest me still:
> The better angel is a man right fair:
> The worser spirit a woman coloured ill.
> To win me soon to hell, my female evil,
> Tempteth my better angel from my side,
> And would corrupt my saint to be a devil,
> Wooing his purity with her foul pride.
> And whether that my angel be turned fiend,
> Suspect I may, yet not directly tell;
> But being both from me, both to each friend,
> I guess one angel in another's hell:
>     Yet this shall I ne'er know, but live in doubt,
>     Till my bad angel fire my good one out.

Yet, however wanton the lady, Shakespeare realises that he is more so.

> In loving thee thou know'st I am forsworn,
> But thou art twice forsworn, to me love swearing;
> In act thy bed-vow broke, and new faith torn,
> In vowing new hate after new love bearing;
> But why of two oaths breach do I accuse thee,
> When I break twenty; I am perjured most;
> For all my vows are oaths but to misuse thee …
>
>                                   (Sonnet 152)

The promise of which the poet is forsworn is presumably his marriage vow. The lady has broken her 'bed-vow' to him and reneged on her promise to love him. Yet for the two promises she has broken, he has broken twenty. The temptations for a man three days' ride from his family, who possessed star status, with all that implies, must have been considerable: the guilt even more so.

Naturally, every possible candidate and more than a few impossible ones have been suggested as the Dark Lady, including Queen Elizabeth herself. It is worth mentioning that there is only one woman other than Anne Hathaway whose name was linked romantically with Shakespeare's. Jane (or Jennet) Sheppard, the daughter of a minor court official, was baptised at St Margaret's, Westminster, on 1 November 1568. Around 1593, she married John Davenant, a widower three years her senior. He was a vintner, with premises on the waterfront at Queenhithe, close to where Southwark Bridge now stands. John Aubrey heard that she was very beautiful, 'of a very good witt and of conversation extremely agreable'. Posterity is silent on whether she was dark or musical. She clearly did the talking in their household. Her husband was of a melancholic disposition, never seen to laugh, but he was a great lover of the theatre. Perhaps he provided the company with its wines.

Jennet had at least six miscarriages in the 1590s, as well as giving birth to two daughters. Around 1600, the family moved to Oxford when Davenant became the tenant of New College of a tavern at No. 3 Cornmarket. We will hear more of them.

Whatever the cause, Shakespeare appears to have gone through a period of intense sexual disillusionment. This is most fully expressed in Sonnet 129, arguably the greatest sonnet ever written. It works in exact parallel. On one level it describes a spiritual journey: on another, it expresses disgust at carnality. The word 'expense' means both 'expenditure', but also 'to spend' was to have an orgasm. The effect of the sonnet is that of a tumultuous tirade. 'Spirit' may be interpreted as the divine spirit, but also as the semen that is 'spent' in the sex act.

> The expense of spirit in a waste of shame
> Is lust in action: and till action, lust
> Is perjured, murderous, bloody, full of blame,
> Savage, extreme, rude, cruel, not to trust;
> Enjoyed no sooner but despised straight;
> Past reason hunted; and no sooner had,
> Past reason hated, as a swallowed bait,
> On purpose laid to make the taker mad.
> Mad in pursuit and in possession so;
> Had, having, and in quest to have extreme;
> A bliss in proof, and proved, a very woe;
> Before, a joy proposed; behind a dream.
> All this the world well knows; yet none knows well
> To shun the heaven that leads men to this hell.

The poem's theme of sexual disillusion is implicit in Sonnet 144. It has been claimed that Shakespeare went through a period of disenchantment with sex at the time he wrote his great tragedies, which are permeated with vicious sexual images. The sonnets demonstrate that his great themes were always with him. It was in the tragedies that they were fined and universalised.

Is there any other way in which we can seek to crack these seemingly impenetrable mysteries? It is necessary to ask a simple question. What did the sonnet mean to the Elizabethans? The answer lies in the history of the poem.

The sonnet form was invented in Sicily in the thirteenth century by Giacomo da Lentini, a member of the Sicilian School of poets that gathered around the court of the Emperor Frederick II. From thence it passed rapidly to Tuscany, where its best-known exponents were Dante Alighieri and Francesco Petrarca (usually known in English as Petrarch). Dante dubbed the form *dolce stil nuovo* (sweet new style). The form was dominated by the concept of courtly love, although not inextricably so. Indeed the earliest extant example, written in 1264, is a song of praise to King Pedro III of Aragon by Paolo Lanfranchi da Pistioia.

Courtly love is a difficult issue for the modern mind to grasp. The term is not even of its period. It was coined as *amour courtois* by Gaston Paris in 1883. There appears to be no contemporary term that expresses the idea. In both its origins and its manifestations it is a complex issue. An important aspect of the concept, however, was the search for perfection through an ideal: a search epitomised in the line from St Paul's Epistle to the Corinthians.

> For we know in part, and we prophesy in part, but when that which is perfect
> is come, then that which is in part shall be done away.

Paul's eschatology is entirely compatible with the school of philosophical neo-Platonism of which Aristotle is the best-known proponent. In the Middle Ages interest in Aristotle's philosophy enjoyed a great revival. Although we cannot attain it in this life, we can grasp the nature of perfection from the limited glimpses we obtain of it. In this transitory existence, living things can only reach it briefly, if at all. This platonic theme hints at immortality and the existence of God: a glimpse of perfection entails that a true state of perfection must exist. The theme is encapsulated in Sonnet 15.

> When I consider everything that grows
> Holds in perfection but a little moment.

One of the themes of the courtly code was to explore this quest for perfection within a human relationship: that of a man and woman. The courtly lover selects a lady who represents his ideal of perfection. Because of this, the relationship cannot be carnal. Both Dante and Petrarch famously established their muses of courtly love. For Dante, it was

Beatrice; for Petrarch, Laura. It may shed light to recount briefly the tale of these loves.

Dante Alighieri first saw Beatrice Portinari when he was nine and she a year younger. Even at that young age, he confessed that she became a source of inspiration to him. Although he claimed he only saw her once more, that is unlikely to be so, as they lived in the same quarter of Florence. What he was probably saying was that there was only one other direct encounter. This occurred when he was eighteen. He met her in the street and she greeted him, which denotes that she had an idea who he was. He was so overwhelmed that, back in his room, he experienced an ecstatic vision. But it had been arranged that each should marry another. At the age of twelve, Dante was betrothed to a lady called Gemma Donati. They wed in 1285. Beatrice married Simone del Bardi, a prominent banker. Her death three years later at the age of twenty-three did not diminish Dante's devotion. His important work *La Vita Nuova*, written in 1295, expresses his continuing love.

As befitted his station, Dante became involved in Florentine factional politics. He fought for the Guelphs against the Ghibellines at the Battle of Campaldino. When his party split after this victory, he sided with the 'White' faction, which was in control of the city, against the 'Black Guelphs'. This was largely an internecine dispute between rival families, but the two parties were divided on the issue of Papal authority as it related to Florence. Dante became an important figure in civic affairs. In 1301, while he was in Rome on an embassy to the Pope, the Black Guelphs seized power with outside assistance. Dante was condemned to exile on pain of death. Like Coriolanus he was compelled to seek refuge among his former enemies, chiefly the leading Ghibelline, Bartolomeo I della Scala, in Verona. He never returned to Florence. In Verona, he began his major work, the *Commedia*.[4] He completed it in Ravenna shortly before his death in 1321.

Francesco Petrarch's story is not dissimilar. He was born in 1304 at Arezzo, a town in Tuscany. Like Dante, his father, a notary public who did legal work for the Papacy, had been driven into exile after the Black Guelph coup in Florence. These were restless times. In 1309, Pope Clement V, fearful for the safety of his court amid Rome's turbulence, moved the seat of the Papacy to Avignon, at that time a Papal enclave within France. The Petrarch family followed him there in 1312. Francesco and his younger brother, Gherado, were sent to study law, first at Montpelier, later at Bologna. In 1326, Francesco sought ordination, but did not progress beyond the minor orders, so he never took the diaconal vow of celibacy.

Good Friday – 6 April 1327 – was a fateful day for Petrarch. In the church of Sainte Claire d'Avignon, he saw a woman whose name he discovered was Laura. It is not possible to identify her precisely, but she may have been Laura de Noves, who had married the Comte Hugues de Sade two years before at the age of fifteen. She was to bear him eleven children.

In 1330 Petrarch entered the service of the powerful Cardinal Stefano Colonna, on whose behalf he undertook many embassies. He established a huge reputation as a scholar and a writer. Around 1340, he wrote his epic poem *Africa* in Latin, the language he regarded as the proper vehicle for literary expression. It tells the story of the Second Punic War. In 1341, he was crowned Poet Laureate in Rome.

Petrarch fathered two illegitimate children, whom he always acknowledged, by a woman whose name is unknown. Despite this, Laura was to him what Beatrice was to Dante – the ideal of his courtly love. He celebrated her in his *Il Canzoniere (Songbook)*, also known as the *Rima Sparsa (Scattered Rhymes)*. This work was written in the vernacular, possibly because he regarded it as personal, not possessing the lofty style of the classical tradition. In *Il Canzoniere*, he refines the sonnet form into a formalised structure. It is a fourteen-line poem. The first eight lines – the octave – follow the rhyming pattern of abbaabba. The next six lines generally follow the pattern of cddcdd, although there are variations. An issue is introduced in the first four lines – the quatrain. This is developed in the second quatrain. The sextet comments on the issue and can provide a conclusion.

Petrarch's fame spread to England. In 'The Clerk's Prologue' in *The Canterbury Tales*, written around 1380, Geoffrey Chaucer wrote:

> I woll yow telle of a tale which that I
> Lerned at Padow of a worthy clerk,
> As preved by his wordes and his werk,
> Fraunceys Petrak, the lauriat poete,
> Highte this clerk, whos rhethorike sweete,
> Enlumyned al Ytaille of poetrie.

It was a century and a half before the sonnet form passed into the English language through the court poets of Henry VIII's reign, namely Henry Howard, Earl of Surrey, and Sir Thomas Wyatt, a courtier of precocious talent. Born in 1503, at the age of seventeen Wyatt married Elizabeth Brooke, the daughter of Lord Cobham. She bore him a son, but he parted from her five years later because of her adultery. It was probably in the 1520s that he began to write sonnets, both his own compositions and translations of Petrarch. His muse was apparently the ill-fated Anne Boleyn. An account by George Wyatt of his grandfather's first encounter with the future queen bears a strong resemblance to the experiences of both Dante and Petrarch.

> The knight, in the beginning, coming to behold the sudden appearance of this new beauty, came to be holden and surprised somewhat with the sight thereof; after much more with her witty and graceful speech, his ear also had him chained unto her, so as finally his heart seemed to say, *I could gladly yield to be tied for ever with the knot of her love,* as somewhere in his verses hath been thought his meaning was to express.[5]

At the age of twenty-five Wyatt was appointed High Marshall of Calais, a post he held for two years. He received the King when he visited that port with Anne Boleyn shortly before their marriage. He attended on her at her subsequent coronation. That she fulfilled the courtly love necessity of being unobtainable is expressed in one of his finest sonnets, written unmistakably in the manner of Petrarch.

> Whoso list to hunt? I know where is on hand!
> But as for me, alas! I may no more,
> The vain travail hath wearied me so sore;
> I am of them that furthest come behind,
> Yet may I by no means my wearied mind
> Draw from the deer: but as she fleeth afore
> Fainting I follow; I leave off therefore.
> Since in a net I seek to hold the wind
> Who list her hunt, I put him out of doubt
> As well as I, may spend his time in vain!
> And graven with diamonds in letters plain
> There is written her fair neck round about;
> 'Noli me tangere; for Caesar's I am
> And wild to hold though I seem tame.'

The reference to Caesar is unmistakable. Others were to find that even a suspicion of involvement with a royal wife could be a deadly business, so Wyatt's platonic passion was either kept discreet or understood.

Wyatt was imprisoned in the Tower in 1536 as a result of a quarrel with Henry VIII's brother-in-law, the Duke of Suffolk. While there he witnessed the execution of Anne Boleyn's alleged lovers from his cell window – and possibly that of the Queen herself. Restored to freedom, he was made ambassador to the court of the Holy Roman Emperor. He was again imprisoned in the Tower in 1541, on the capital charge of treason. Bonner, the Bishop of London in Henry VIII's new religious order, had claimed three years before that Wyatt had been rude about the King while he was abroad as an ambassador and that he had had secret dealings with the exiled Cardinal Pole, whom Henry regarded as a mortal enemy. Few prisoners passed twice in each direction through the Watergate at the Tower of London, but Wyatt did so, possibly as a result of an intervention by Henry's fifth queen, Katherine Howard. He returned to the royal favour and was given various offices of state. He was taken ill after greeting the ambassador of the Emperor Charles V at Falmouth and died at Sherborne on 11 October 1542.

Henry Howard, Earl of Surrey, was born in 1517, the son of Thomas Howard, who later succeeded as the 3rd Duke of Norfolk. Like Wyatt, he married young – at the age of sixteen. As may be expected from the courtly tradition, his muse was not his wife, but the ten-year old Lady Elizabeth Fitzgerald, the daughter of Gerald Fitzgerald, the Earl of Kildare. He refers to her as 'Geraldine', the name of her patrimony. She too is unobtainable and he acknowledges that she is destined for another:

> Happy is he that may obtain her love.

The happy man in this instance was to be Sir Anthony Browne, a sixty-year-old widower, the Master of the King's Horse, one of the wealthiest men in England and father of eight children. Elizabeth bore him another two.

Henry Howard was the last victim of the psychopathic Henry VIII. He and his father were indicted for high treason in January 1547. He was charged with announcing that his father should be Protector to the young King Edward VI on the death of Henry VIII. It was likely that the dying king wished to deal with the powerful Howard faction, which was related to his discredited and executed fifth wife, Katherine. Henry Howard was executed on 19 January 1547, the day before the King died. His father was more fortunate. He was due to be executed next day, but was reprieved on the death of the King.

Howard's sonnets varied from the Petrarchan form in that they incorporated a final rhyming couplet which summarises the argument of the poem and gives its conclusion. Wyatt also used this form and, since he was senior to Howard by fourteen years, it is likely that it was he who devised it. It was the form used by many later sonneteers, including Shakespeare.

Neither Wyatt nor Surrey's sonnets were published in their lifetimes. They emerged to public view in an anthology published by Richard Tottel in 1557 entitled *Songes and Sonnettes* – it is usually referred to as *Tottel's Miscellany*. It includes poems by Wyatt, Surrey and a number of other authors. It was hugely popular, going through nine editions before 1587. It also had a huge influence on the development of English poetry. William Shakespeare possessed a copy. He refers to it in both *Merry Wives* and *Hamlet*.

The irrepressible Thomas Nashe reveals the extent of the cult in his *Anatomie of Absurditie*, published in 1588. Nor is he in any doubt about its prime source in *Tottel's Miscellany*. He rails against

> Our babling Ballets and our new found Songs and Sonets, which every redoose Fidler hath at his fingers end, and every ignorant Ale Knight wil breath forth over the potte, as soon as his braine waxeth.

He pursued this variant view of the effects of Henry Howard on English poets in *The Unfortunate Traveller*. He may not have been far off the mark with the comments voiced by his Jack Wilton:

> I persuade myself that he was more in love with his own curious-forming fancy than her face, and truth it is, many become passionate lovers only to win praise to their wits.

It is fascinating to consider that had Surrey, like his father, outlived Henry VIII by one day, he could have still been alive, in his mid-seventies, at the time Shakespeare was writing his sonnets. Yet his posthumous influence on the development of English poetry was huge. In his *Defence of Poesy*, Sir Philip Sidney described his lyrics as one of the four fundamental texts of English literature. Sidney was probably the poet most responsible for the cult of the sonnet in the early 1590s. As well as being an admired poet, he was regarded as an exemplar of chivalric virtues. His *Astrophel and Stella*, which was published in 1591, five years after his death, had a huge impact. Like Petrarch, Wyatt and Shakespeare, he is vague about the identity of his muse, although she has been closely identified with Penelope, Lady Rich. The narrative of the 108 sonnets in the sequence is equally vague. There are hints that Sidney's obligatory platonic passion for his muse may have been tempered by physical desires, but it is equally apparent that the affair remained unconsummated.

Sidney's younger sister Mary married in 1577, at the age of sixteen, Henry Herbert, the 2nd Earl of Pembroke, becoming his third wife. Around 1587, the poet Samuel Daniel became tutor to her son William. She became his muse under the name he gave her – Delia. When his sonnet cycle was published in 1592, he dedicated it to her in terms that were appropriately deferential and which make clear the platonic nature of the relationship.

> Yoe doe not onely possesse the honour of the present, but also do bind pos-
> terity to an euer gratefull memorie of your virtues, wherein you must survive
> yourself.

Another sonneteer following the Petrarchan tradition was Michael Drayton. He was born at Hartshill in Warwickshire in 1563. As a youth he entered the service of Sir Henry Goodere of nearby Polesworth on the River Anker. Anne, the younger of Sir Henry's two daughters, became Drayton's platonic muse. He refers to her as his 'Idea', a word that meant something subtly different then, approximating more to the modern word 'Ideal'. In so using the word Drayton unequivocally refers back to the Aristotelian traditions of courtly love. He follows the convention in not identifying his muse specifically, but there are a number of unmistakable references, including one to the river by which she dwells.

> Arden's sweet Ankar, let thy glory bee
> That faire Idea onely lives by thee.
> (Sonnet 32)

Drayton's cycle of sixty-four sonnets was published under the title 'Idea's Mirrour' in 1594. Like Beatrice, Laura, Anne Boleyn and Geraldine,[6] Anne Goodere was destined for another. In 1595/96, she married a Warwickshire squire, Sir Henry Rainsford of Clifford Manor, on the banks of the Stour, just two miles from Stratford-upon-Avon. The arrival of his muse on its banks led Drayton to celebrate another river.

> Which daily looks upon the lovely Stowre.
> New to that Vale, which of all vales is Queen.
>                                           (Eclogue VIII)

Like William Shakespeare, Drayton can address his muse with astonishing directness.

> Since there's no help, come let us kiss and part.
> Nay, I have done, you'll get no more of me.
>                                           (Sonnet 61)

As befits the genre, Drayton was on excellent terms with his muse's husband. He spent his summers at Clifford Manor, from whence he must have visited William Shakespeare. On Sir Henry's death in 1622, he wrote an elegy on 'his incomparable friend … Past all degrees that was so dear to me'.

One of William Shakespeare's great capacities was to take a literary convention and radically alter it without changing its basic format. It goes without saying that he would have been aware of the Aristotelian tradition of the sonnet form – that it is to be addressed to a muse who is not only sexually unobtainable but whose qualities engender inspiration beyond the carnal. Did he decide that, if the subject of the sequence was to be sexually unobtainable, then he might just as well address it to a man as a woman? We recall Francis Mere's statement that Shakespeare's 'sugred Sonnets' were circulated 'among his private friends'. Whoever these may have been, there can be no doubt that they would have constituted a highly sophisticated literary circle, who would have appreciated the poet's mild mockery of the convention while strictly adhering to its norms – and, as we have seen, the subtle change in focus would have presented a golden opportunity to flatter a potential or actual patron.

Although Shakespeare cannot enjoy a sexual relationship with the beautiful youth, his dramatic instincts lead him both to challenge and extend the convention. Rather than being destined for another, the youth defies the path that he should be destined to follow – to marry and have children. In chiding him for this failure, the poet seizes on another chance to flatter him extravagantly.

The poet introduces a new and dramatic innovation with the advent of the Dark Lady. With her he can indulge the sexual relationship that he is denied with his muse. His two poetic creations become prototypes – those of the good and the bad angel. Shakespeare is again both adhering to and redefining the convention. Through a glimpse of perfection, we may gain a vision of a wider perfection, but what of the imperfection that is implicit in the equation? The innocent perfection of the youth is challenged by the raunchy worldliness of the Dark Lady. This literary creation is so effective that the reader may be left wondering whether these represent real people at all or are products of that most fertile of imaginations. In this again, Shakespeare mirrors the convention. As early as 1336, Cardinal Colonna suggested to Petrarch that his Laura was not a real person but a product of his invention and that the very name was a symptom of his desire to achieve poetic *laurels*: an allegation which Petrarch hotly denied. Although Dante's Beatrice undoubtedly existed, he does acknowledge that there are aspects of her that are products of his imagination. He refers to her as *La gloriosa donna della mia mente* – 'The glorious lady of my mind'.

Shakespeare would be unique among Elizabethan sonneteers if the personalities he creates in his sonnets were mere products of his imagination. Yet he follows carefully the convention in shielding so carefully their identities as to engender intense frustration among his biographers. He provides clues, but not as liberally as his contemporary sonneteers. Nor does he reject the neo-Aristotelian thesis of perfection, which Thomas Aquinas set in a theological framework.

Now the maximum in any genus is the cause of that genus as fire, which is the maximum heat, is the cause of all hot things. Therefore there must be also to be something which is to all beings the cause of their being, goodness, and every other perfection; and this we call God.

Shakespeare would have found accord with John Donne's view that his love for his dead wife was a signpost towards the immortal.

Since she whom I lov'd hath paid her last debt,
To nature, and to hers, and my good is dead,
And her soul early into heaven ravished,
Wholly in heavenly things my mind is set.
Here the admiring of her my mind did whet
To seek thee God, so streams do show the head.
(Holy Sonnets)

Shakespeare's exploration of the negative and destructive aspects of the relationships he describes enables him to develop a metaphysical positive. Once again, he utilises and extends the convention, but refers back to its roots. Dante sees his earthly and platonic love for Beatrice as a signpost towards divine love. In *La Commedia*, Virgil is his guide around the *Inferno* and the *Purgatorio*, but it is Beatrice who guides him around nine celestial spheres of *Paradiso*.

In *Il Canzioniere* Petrarch's poems represent Laura as the ideal, or as Drayton would have put it, the 'idea' of earthly perfection. His final verse is a Hymn to the Virgin Mary, the epitome of heavenly perfection. In this poem, he repents of his earthly attachments and resolves to direct his energies towards the growth of his spirit. Shakespeare's Sonnet 146 expresses a similar resolution.

> Poor soul thou centre of my sinful earth,
> [Thrall to][7] these rebel powers that thee array.
> Why dost thou pine within and suffer dearth,
> Painting thy outward walls so costly gay.
> Why so large cost, having so short a lease,
> Dost thou upon thy fading mansion spend?
> Shall worms, inheritors of this excess,
> Eat up thy charge? Is this thy body's end?
> Then soul, live thou upon thy servant's loss,
> And let that pine to aggravate thy store;
> Buy terms divine in selling hours of dross;
> Within be fed, without be rich no more:
> So shalt thou feed on death that feeds on men,
> And death once dead, there's no more dying then.

It is not known whether Shakespeare intended his entire sonnet series to be read as a sequence. Many have tried to place them in a coherent order. Six sonnets follow number 146, which appear to be reproachful of the Dark Lady, but even more so of himself. The last two sonnets would appear to be juvenilia, or at least early essays in the art. If Shakespeare did intend there to be a final sonnet to the series, it is likely that he followed Petrarch's example. Sonnet 146 gives a third answer to the original conundrum of how man might defeat time – through his own immortal soul. It also makes the poet the central figure of the series. It is not only the perfection of the beautiful youth that has led him to a vision of eternity, but his own imperfections and those of the Dark Lady. He is at one with Dante and Petrarch in that a process of spiritual growth is innate in the series, but he comes to it by a different route. In this he shares the vision of his tragic heroes, who come to self-knowledge through the realisation of their imperfections.

If indeed William Shakespeare realised that his sophisticated audience would appreciate the carnal restrictions inherent in the courtly love code and recognise his purpose in dedicating many of his sonnets to a man, it was a humorous ploy that was not entirely appreciated by the wider world. No further edition of the sonnets appeared in his lifetime. It was to be another thirty-one years before a second edition appeared and then it was something of an oddity. In 1640, John Benson, another London stationer, published an edition of the sonnets entitled *Poems: written by Wil. Shake-speare, Gent.* It is probable that he had a source other than Thorpe's edition. He omits eight of the sonnets altogether and uses the versions of the two sonnets that had appeared in *The Passionate Pilgrim* rather than those of the 1609 edition. He places the poems in a different order and amalgamates five of them, whereby they cease to be sonnets – a clear indication that the form was no longer fashionable. Each of the new sections has its own heading: a number attempt to falsify the origin of the poems addressed to the beautiful youth. Such headings as 'Self-Flattery of her Beauty' and 'An Entreaty for her Acceptance' attempt to make it appear that the poems were addressed to a woman. In addition, Benson attempts to eradicate what some might have perceived as the homoerotic nature of the poems by changing certain pronouns.

Benson's edition of the sonnets appeared twenty-four years after the death of William Shakespeare. The Earl of Southampton had died in 1623. William Jaggard, publisher of *The Passionate Pilgrim* and of the First Folio of Shakespeare's works, died in the same year. Thomas Thorpe had eventually retired to an almshouse at Ewelme in Oxfordshire, where he died in 1635 – the same year that John Benson was received into the Stationers' Company. As a member of that closed body, he would have engaged in its professional and social intercourse. He must have learned of any controversy that had surrounded the publication of the sonnets and resolved to ensure that his own publication would receive no disapprobation: hence his attempt to excise the references to the beautiful boy and to send the reader along a different track. His wish not to arouse any controversy led him to pen a rejoinder in the preface, expressing the poet's views as he had heard of them. He describes his edition as 'Some excellent and swetely composed Poems, of Master *William Shakespeare*, which in themselves appeare of the same purity, the Author himselfe then living avouched.' We may assume that Benson was familiar with the true circumstances under which the sonnets were written, although he discreetly avoids any comment on Shakespeare's relations with the lady. Doubtless he felt moral censure would be, in that instance, irrelevant to his purpose.

This is a further indication that Shakespeare's sonnets were published without his connivance. It is unlikely that he would have wanted his relationship with the beautiful youth to be the feature of a publication. It was highly likely that the ill-informed reader might not grasp the subtleties of the literary genre. Still less would he wish his poems to the lady to be viewed by the world. In 1609, in his home town at least, he was a respectable married man with aspirations to gentility and whose daughter had recently made a good match. It is significant that John Aubrey, who readily picked up the scurrilous gossip of the previous generation – as his brief lives of Francis Bacon, Mary Herbert, Francis Beaumont, Sir Walter Raleigh and others show – makes no such references to Shakespeare in his short biography, other than the somewhat odd story of William Davenant's supposed begetting in Oxford. Whatever the poet may have done, it seems he did not establish a reputation as a philanderer.

# 9

# The Lord Chamberlain's Men, 1593–94

'A Bounty very great'

– Nicholas Rowe, 1709

Early in 1594, leave was given for the theatres to reopen. 24 January saw the first of three performances of *Titus Andronicus* by the Earl of Sussex's Men. The choice of play indicates that understandably the company had nothing new in its repertory. The long two-year closure of the theatres had taken a severe toll. The Burbages had to continue paying for the lease of The Theatre, with no hope of a return. A growing antagonism with their landlord may date from this time. There must have been those who doubted whether things would ever return to their former state, particularly in the light of other blows which had fallen. On 11 May 1593, what the Privy Council called 'divers lewd and mutinous libels', intended to inflame opinion against Protestant refugees from France and Holland, had been posted on the walls of the Dutch church at Austin Friars and elsewhere in the City. The rebukes that immigrants have received over the centuries were churned out in blank verse verging on doggerel. They were taking the bread from the mouths of honest English workers and 'twenty in one house will lurk'. Unfortunately for Christopher Marlowe, the 'libel' concluded 'Fly, Flye and never return', followed by the words '*per* Tamburlaine'.[1]

The play was invoked as a threat to the immigrant community that the vengeance to follow would be as ruthless and bloody as that meted out by Marlowe's eponymous character. Perhaps suspicion fell on Thomas Kyd because of his association with Marlowe, or perhaps the authorities were unaware that the two men were no longer sharing accommodation. It may have been what is now known as 'a routine enquiry' but, for whatever reason, Kyd's lodgings were searched. Nothing was found there to link him to the scurrilous posters, but what was discovered was potentially as bad for him. The investigator uncovered what he described as a 'vile heretical conceits denying the eternal deity of Jesus Christ found among the papers of Thomas Kydd prisoner'. Kyd was confined in the Bridewell. The Privy Council was determined to unravel the truth of the matter.

On 11 May, the Commissioners investigating the affair were authorised to put to the torture those who 'refuze to confess the truth ... and by th' extremity thereof to be used at such times and as often as you shal thinke fit, draw them to discover their knowledge concerning the said libells'. When interrogated,[2] Kyd claimed that the papers must have been 'shuffled with some of mine (unbeknown to me) by some occasion or writing two years since'. In other words, they belonged to Marlowe. A warrant was issued for his arrest on 18 May. He was not in London at the time. He was at Scadbury Manor in Kent, the residence of Sir Thomas Walsingham, who, like his late cousin, Sir Francis, had played a crucial role in the Queen's spy system. Marlowe appeared before the Privy Council two days later. The charge he might face was tantamount to treason. The Queen's authority derived from her being divinely ordained of Christ. To deny His divinity was to deny her authority.

It was not only Papists who felt the weight of the law against religious dissent. The Congregationalists John Perry, Henry Barrow and John Greenwood had been hanged on charges of 'devising and circulating seditious books', in the previous month. The books in question were written by Robert Browne, whose name was synonymous with Separatism.[3] Shakespeare was familiar with his persona. 'I had as lief be a Brownist as a politician,' Sir Andrew Aguecheek declares in *Twelfth Night*. All three condemned were Cambridge scholars. Marlowe may well have known them. Certainly he would have known of them and their fate. He was ordered to report every day to the officials of the Council. The authorities were clearly considering what to do with him. He must have realised the seriousness of his position. He told Kyd that he intended to flee to Scotland: a safe home for those who dissented from the doctrines of the Established Church. Kyd had heard that Marlowe's friend, the poet Matthew Roydon, had already fled there. He too was under suspicion for unorthodox views. He could have even been the author of the Dutch Church Libel.

Marlowe was killed in a mysterious brawl on 30 May 1593 in the home of a widow called Eleanor Bull on Deptford Strand. This was probably what would now be called a 'safe house'. Why Marlowe should have met Ingram Frizer, Nicholas Skeres and Robert Poley – all three described as 'gentlemen' – there that day is unclear. All four had been in the service of Sir Thomas Walsingham. Poley as a double agent had been instrumental in the uncovering of the Babington Plot, which led to the execution of Mary, Queen of Scots. This indicates what they had in common, but does not elucidate the purpose of the meeting. It is possible that the intention was to place Marlowe aboard a ship bound for Scotland and safety from the forces gathering against him. The meeting may have been a 'debriefing'. The four men had lunch, a walk in the garden and then dinner. Apparently there was then a dispute about the 'le recknynge'. In a state of fury Marlowe supposedly grabbed Frizer's dagger and inflicted two severe wounds on his head. Frizer had then grabbed back the knife. In the ensuing struggle Marlowe was stabbed to death through his temple, two inches above the eye. The two wounds inflicted were two inches long and a quarter of an inch deep. The ensuing Coroner's Jury was impressed that Frizer had stood his ground and did not flee. It is reasonable to accept their verdict delivered 'upon view of the body of Christopher Morley, there lying dead and slain' that Frizer had struck in self-defence: a decision which was accepted within a month in a royal pardon. Marlowe's reputation for violence must have gone before him. Yet the fact that he was in deep trouble with the authorities lends itself to conspiracy theories. There may well have been good reasons to want him out of the way, but there would surely have been easier ways of disposing of him than the brawl at Mrs Bull's house.

At the time of his death, Marlowe was following Shakespeare's example and turning his hand to the long narrative poem, probably also in the hope of finding a patron. *Hero and Leander* is a brilliant evocation, laden with the author's homoerotic themes. 'In his looks,' he writes of Leander, 'were all that men desire'. As he swims to visit Hero, he is captured by the sea god Neptune, whose lasciviousness he provokes.

> The lusty God embraced him, call'd him 'Love' ...
> He clamped his plump cheeks, with his tresses played

Marlowe's death was a sensation. Rumours and misinformation abounded in its wake. In the following September, Gabriel Harvey referred to him as 'dead of the plague'. According to Francis Meres, he was 'stabbed to death by a bawdy servingman, a rival of his in his lewd love'. The Puritan Thomas Beard, in his *Theatre of God's Judgements*, in 1597, sought to interpret, with no great regard for accuracy, the death of 'this barking dog' as a divine judgement.

> It so fell out that in London streets as he purposed to stab one whom he owed a grudge unto with his dagger, the other party perceiving so avoided the stroke, that withal catching hold of his wrist, he stabbed his own dagger into his own head, in such sort that notwithstanding all the means of surgery that could be wrought, he shortly after died thereof. The manner of his death being so terrible (for he even cursed and blasphemed to his last gasp, and together with his breath an oath flew out of his mouth) that it was not only a manifest sign of God's judgment, but also an horrible and fearful terror to all that beheld him. But herein did the justice of God most notably appear, in that he compelled his own hand which had written those blasphemies to be the instrument to punish him, and that in his brain, which had devised the same.

Shakespeare went along with the Coroner's verdict. In *As You Like It*, Touchstone voices the lines.

> When a man's verses cannot be understood, nor a man's good wit seconded with the forward child understanding, it strikes a man more dead than a great reckoning in a little room.

There is a reference here to Marlowe's much-admired line in *The Jew of Malta* – 'infinite treasures in a little room'. That the reckoning is described as 'great' gives a cause for the quarrel. Marlowe was not flush with cash and the bill for a day's eating and drinking may well have been steep. Since he was probably invited to the mysterious meeting, he may well have assumed that the tab was on Walsingham and reacted with fury when he found it was not. Such a reaction was in character with his previous record of violent behaviour.

Marlowe was much on Shakespeare's mind when he wrote *As You Like It*. He pays his own tribute to the dead poet when he refers to Marlowe's poem 'The Passionate Shepherd to His Love' and quotes from his *Hero and Leander*.

> Dead Shepherd, now I find thy saw of might,
> 'Who ever loved that loved not at first sight?'

A second great blow to the Admiral's Men came with the death of the company's other leading dramatist, Thomas Kyd, in August 1594. He had not written for them for some time, but with the revival of the playhouses, hopes must have been harboured that he would pick up his quill again. Had he lived, he may have been obliged to. His mother formally renounced the administration of his estate, probably because it contained only debts.

The pressing need for the theatre companies was to raise money. One way to do this was to get the plays whose copyright Derby's Men owned into print. On 6 February 1594, *Titus Andronicus* was registered with the Stationers' Company, which, in theory at least, would prevent anyone else publishing it. On 12 March 1594, *Henry VI, Part II* was registered.

Whether William Shakespeare had continued to write plays during the plague years in the expectation of the reopening of the theatres is unknown, but given the scale of his outpourings in the 1590s, it is likely. The first act of the revived company was to go on an extensive nationwide tour to places as far apart as Bristol, Shrewsbury, Chester and York. Later 'Rich Burbage' received payment for two comedies performed at court during the Christmas Revels on 26 and 28 December.

No sooner was the company back in business than another blow fell: one that was as awful for them as the deaths of Marlowe and Kyd were for the Admiral's Men. On 15 April 1594, the Earl of Derby died under circumstances which can only be described as 'suspicious'. He had succeeded to the title on the death of his father just seven months before. According to the antiquarian John Stowe, a man named Richard Hesketh attempted to persuade him to advance his claim to the throne through his descent from Mary, the younger sister of Henry VIII. He threatened him with a terrible death if he did not accede to this proposal. The Earl, 'fearing lest some trappe were layd for him', rejected the idea. He died under mysterious and painful circumstances a few months later. According to William Camden,

He expired in the floure of his youth, not without suspition of poyson, being tormented with cruell paynes, by frequent vomitings of a darke colour like rusty yron ... The matter vomited up stayned the silver Basons in such sort, that by no art they could possibly be brought up againe to their former brigtnesse ... No small suspicion lighted upon the Gentleman of his horse, who, as soone as the Earle tooke his bed, tooke his best horse, and fled.[4]

Derby's Men were still on tour in East Anglia at the time of his death. The loss of their patron and the influence he exerted on their behalf represented a severe crisis. By what process a new patron was found is uncertain, but there can have been no better choice than Henry Carey, the 1st Lord Hunsdon.

Henry Carey was born in 1526, the son of Mary Boleyn and a courtier, Sir William Carey. His mother had been the mistress of King Henry VIII. On her death, he became the ward of her sister, the fated future queen, Anne Boleyn. He was ten when she was executed. There were suggestions that he was the King's son, but this is unlikely – the affair appears to have been over at the time of his begetting. Even if he were not Queen Elizabeth's half-brother, he was certainly her cousin and had shared part of his childhood with her. She had raised him to the peerage soon after her accession. Such was her trust in him that she appointed him Captain of the Gentlemen at Arms – effectively her personal bodyguard – in 1564. He won her lasting gratitude for his part in the suppression of the Northern Rebellion of 1571. In 1574, she gave him a grand grace-and-favour home, making him Keeper of Somerset House, where she had lived during the reign of Queen Mary. It mattered greatly to the players that Hunsdon held the hugely influential office of Lord Chamberlain. As such, he was in charge of the Master of the Revels, Edmund Tilney, who would also prove a good friend to the company.

Tilney was himself an author of repute. In 1568, he published *The Flower of Friendship*, a treatise on marriage, which proved highly popular, going through five editions before the end of the century. In his role as Master of the Revels from 1578, his task, as his title implies, was to organise the court entertainments. Over the years his job evolved so that he became, in essence, the official censor of new plays. He was a force for tolerance, tending to exercise his authority only over material that might be deemed subversive. His support also protected the players from the hostile civic authorities. William Webbe, the Lord Mayor of London in 1592, named Tilney as an obstacle to ending public dramatic performances in the City. His importance to the company was further enhanced in 1594 when he was given the additional responsibility for licensing playhouses.

So, the Lord Chamberlain's Company was formed. Its backbone was the former Earl of Derby's Men, re-formed under a different name and patron. Many of the most prominent performers of the day joined its ranks. Crucial to its function was Richard Burbage's brother, Cuthbert. He never appears to have acted. His role, as the administrator of this complex enterprise, was, in its way, more important. To form such a company was a bold stroke, but in practice there was little choice. The Privy Council had taken advantage of the temporary disappearance of the acting companies on the London scene to restrict the number permitted to play in London to two: the Lord Chamberlain's Men and the Admiral's Men. Doubtless the injunction was ignored by many of the companies and the two leading companies might have expected to have been the ones to be accredited, but there those who wished to ban the players altogether, so Hunsdon's support was certainly helpful if not decisive.

We return for the last time to the project of the gods. What is a theatre without actors? This was the dilemma faced by William Shakespeare and his colleagues when it was decreed that the pandemic was over and the theatres could reopen. Although there are various lists of the actors associated with the company, it is not always easy to discern when they joined it and in what roles. There is ample record that Shakespeare continued his acting career, almost certainly as a player of small parts. Theatrical tradition decrees that he played the part of Adam in *As You Like It* and the Ghost in *Hamlet*.

It is Richard Burbage who dominates Shakespeare's stage. A piece of doggerel written on his death delineates some of the parts he played, including Hamlet, Lear and Othello. In the 1590s he probably created a succession of major roles – from Romeo to Henry V, from Theseus to Brutus. It is significant that the leading parts age with him: from Romeo to King Lear and Prospero.

Yet, as well as Shakespeare and Burbage, there are a number of actors who can be identified as being with the Lord Chamberlain's Men from its early days. A fellow sharer in the new company was Will Kempe. He was one of the most renowned and popular comedians of the day, so it was a considerable coup to have recruited him. No company could afford to be without its 'Clown', although the relationship had its moments of ambivalence. The popularity of the breed is revealed in a piece of contemporary doggerel.

> Why. I would have the fool in every act.
> Be 't comedy or tragedy, I've laugh'd
> Until I cried again, to see what faces
> The rogue will make. Oh it does me good
> To see him hold out 's chin, hang down his hands,
> And twirl his bauble. There is ne'er a part
> About him but breaks jests. I heard a fellow
> Once on this stage cry, *Doodle, Doodle, Dooe,*
> Beyond compare. I'd give the other shilling
> To see him act the *Changeling* once again.[5]

Kempe's position as a sharer may have been the price that had to be paid for his services. Nothing is known of his early life. He is known to have performed at Leicester House in 1585, so he may have been the jester to Robert Dudley, Earl of Leicester. He accompanied the Earl on his ruinous military expedition to the Netherlands in 1585. From thence, Sir Philip Sidney sent letters home with 'Will, my Lord of Leicester's jesting player'. In a subsequent letter, Sidney complained that Kempe had delivered the letters to Lady Leicester rather than Lady Sidney. After this brief return to England, he went on a great adventure with two other future Lord Chamberlain's Men, George Bryan and Thomas Pope. They played before King Frederick II of Denmark at Elsinore, a name redolent in Shakespeareana, and also played in Saxony on the same extensive tour.

Kempe fulfilled the role of the large and merry clown. A quarto records that he played Peter, the servant, in *Romeo and Juliet*. This is a small part, but one that would have given scope to his extemporising talents. The First Folio records that he played Dogberry in *Much Ado about Nothing* and that Richard Cowley played the part of Verges.

We do not know how and when the character sometimes described as 'the Clown' became an important part of the *dramatis personae*. It is a development likely to have been pioneered by William Shakespeare, or at least by the companies associated with the Burbages. That Kempe and his colleagues were regarded as being associated closely with the process is revealed in a quote from the undergraduate play *The Pilgrimage to Parnassus*.

> Clowns have bene thrust into plays by head and shoulders ever since Kempe could make a scurvey face.[6]

According to *Tarlton's Jests*, published in 1600, that famous clown recommended that Robert Armin take his place on his retirement. Armin was born in King's Lynn around 1568, the son of a tailor. One of his father's friends, John Lonyston, the Master of Works at the Royal Mint in London, took him on as an apprentice at the age of thirteen. Lonyston died in 1582 and the apprenticeship was transferred to another master. On one occasion, he was sent to collect money from a lodger at an inn which was apparently kept by Richard Tarlton. When the man defaulted, the young Armin wrote verses satirising him on the wall. Tarlton was impressed by their quality and took on the young man as his apprentice and natural successor. Armin may already have had something of a literary reputation by the time he finished his apprenticeship in 1592. In 1590 his name was affixed to a religious tract entitled *A Brief Resolution of the Right Religion*, although whether he wrote it is unclear. Both Thomas Nashe and Gabriel Harvey mention that Armin was a writer of ballads, but none has survived.

Armin was noted for his ability to extemporise doggerel on subjects suggested by the audience. Indeed, if it were not to the collectivity of clowns in general, it might well have been Armin to whom Shakespeare was referring in his advice to the players in *Hamlet*, rather than to Kempe, as some have suggested.

And let those who play your clowns speak no more than is set down for them.

Another anecdote from *Tarlton's Jests* gives some indication of the sort of intervention of which Shakespeare may have been thinking. In a performance by the Queen's Men of *The Famous Victories of Henry the Fifth* at the Bull Inn in Bishopsgate, the actor playing a judge was supposed to take a box on the ears from the King, but he failed to appear. Tarllton, 'ever forward to please', took on the part, in addition to his own clowning role as Derick, a French soldier. William Knell, playing Henry, smote him a sound blow, 'which made the people laugh the more because it was he'.

> But then, the judge goes in, and immediately Tarlton in his own clothes comes out, and asks the actors, 'What newes?' 'O' saith one, 'hadst thou been here, thou shouldst have seene Prince Henry hit the judge a terrible box on the ear.' 'What man!' said Tarlton, 'strike a judge!' 'It is true, yfaith,' said the other. 'No other like,' said Tarlton, 'and it could not be but terrible to the judge, when the report so terrifies me that methinkes the blow remains stil on my cheeke that it burnes againe!' The people laught at this mightily.[7]

It is not clear when Armin joined the Lord Chamberlain's Men. He seems to have been associated with the touring company of players under the patronage of William Brydges, the 4th Baron Chandos, at some point in the 1590s. He may speculatively be identified with the parts that Shakespeare wrote for a melancholy clown, Jacques, Feste and Lear's Fool among them.

Augustine Phillips was a key member of the company, although it is difficult to discern his precise role. He was certainly an actor. He had been a member of the Earl of Derby's Company and played the part of Sardanapalus in *The Seven Deadly Sins*. Later he would appear in Ben Jonson's *Every Man in His Humour* and *Sejanus*. In 1594, he was living in Paris Gardens on Bankside. He was a family man, whose wife Anne bore him at least five children. The Paris Gardens was a Royal Liberty – part of the estates of the Abbey of Bermondsey that had passed to the Crown following the Dissolution of the Monasteries. The manor was bought for £850 by Francis Langley, a wealthy goldsmith who held the office of 'Alnager and Searcher of Cloth' (i.e. one responsible for the trading standards of fabrics). Despite the almost inevitable opposition of the City Fathers, Langley built a theatre in Paris Gardens. It helped that he had connections in the right places. His brother-in-law was Clerk to the Privy Council. The Swan Theatre, the grandest built so far, was also outside the City's jurisdiction.

It appears that Phillips was also a musician. He may well have been in charge of the boy actors and musicians in the company. In his will he leaves his cittern, bandora and lute to James Sands, on the 'expiration of his term of years in his indenture of apprenticehood'. His bass viol he leaves to his 'late apprentice' Samuel Gilborne, and he leaves a 30s gold piece to his 'servants', the actors Christopher Beeston and Alexander Cooke, who were perhaps also former apprentices. He may have been the composer of a jig entitled 'Phillips His Slipper' which was entered on the Stationers' Register in 1595.

Phillips came from a theatrical family. He was the stepbrother of that Thomas Pope, who had accompanied Will Kempe to Elsinor. He also joined the Lord Chamberlain's Men. His sister married Robert Gough, who is also listed among the company's twenty-six principal actors in the First Folio. Such close family ties reflect a circle within which close relationships were formed, rather like modern fairground and circus folk, and may represent a continuity with the travelling entertainers of previous generations. It is not overly fanciful to suggest that many contemporary actors and musicians may have been following the trade of their forebears.

Another who married within the circle was John Heminges, who, in March 1588, espoused the widow of that William Knell who had been killed in the drunken brawl at Thame just a year before. She would bear him fourteen children. Knell was an actor of talent and prominence, praised by both Thomas Nashe and Thomas Heywood. A year before his death he had married the fifteen-year-old Rebecca Edwards at the church of St Mary Aldermanbury, which was the setting for her second marriage. Heminges, born in 1556, came to London at the age of twelve to serve an apprenticeship with the Grocers' Company. His route into the theatre is unknown, but he became another prominent member of the Lord Chamberlain's Men.

As well his theatrical interests, Hemminges capitalised on his status as a Freeman of the Grocers' Company to found a business as a wholesale grocer. He may well have established this to corner the lucrative trade in refreshments at the theatres where the company played.

Another prominent member of the company was Henry Condell. He may have been a Norfolk man: his will mentions family in the village of New Buckenham in that county. He too made a good match. In 1596, he married Elizabeth Smart, the daughter of a gentleman. She bore him nine children, but only three survived to adulthood. They lived in the parish of St Mary Aldermanbury, where, like John Hemminges, he became a churchwarden.

A number of the boy actors who played the women's parts would have graduated into the company, after serving their apprenticeships with an established actor. Since he played the part of Porrex in *The Seven Deadly Sins* in 1587, and the part of a young playgoer in the Induction to John Marston's play *The Malcontent* some sixteen years later, it is likely that William Sly was one of these. Alexander Cooke may have been another. In his last will and testament in 1614, he refers to John Hemminges as 'my master' and leaves his four children to the trust of Hemminges and Condell.

In June 1594, the company played a short season with the Admiral's Men at the Newington Butts Theatre, performing *Titus Andronicus* at least twice.[8] That month, they resumed their independent identities – an indication that the future was looking brighter. The value to the Lord Chamberlain's Men of their patron was further demonstrated on 8 October when Lord Hunsdon addressed a letter on their behalf to the Lord Mayor.

It would appear that the company was seeking a City inn – probably the Cross Keys – as a winter base, but the Corporation had turned down the application for licensing. The patron wrote in conciliatory style:

> My newe companie of Players have undertaken to me that, where heretofore they began not their Plaies til towardes fower a clock, they will now begin at two and haue don between fourer and fiue and will not vse anie Drumes or trumpettes att all for the callinge of peopell together.[9]

The outcome of Hunsdon's letter is uncertain but it confirms that the objections of the City Fathers to the theatre were not entirely theological, but were grounded in the disruption caused by theatrical performances.

Hunsdon's role as the man ultimately in charge of the Queen's Revels soon paid off for the company. During the twelve-day Christmas season, on St Stephen's Day and Holy Innocents' Day, they played 'two severall comedies or enterludes' at court for a fee of £13 6s 8d.[10] On 15 March 1595, the Queen's Chamberlain's accounts recorded payment of fees due 'to William Kempe, William Shakespeare and Richard Burbage'. Her Majesty was delighted with what she saw. The accounts record the payment of an additional £6 13s 4d – half as much again as the original sum, clearly a reward for an outstanding performance.

Given the circumstances of the anti-immigrant riots of 1592–93 and the Dutch Church Libel, it seems curious that a play which dealt with 'Ill May Day' should be presented to the Master of the Revels. The manuscript is a rare surviving Elizabethan play script. The principal hand in *Sir Thomas More* is that of Anthony Munday, who, as a dramatist, collaborated frequently with others. Other contributors have been identified as Henry Chettle, Thomas Heywood and Thomas Decker. Most intriguing are the three pages of the manuscript that scholarly opinion has long identified as being in the hand of William Shakespeare.

*Sir Thomas More* is conceived on a grand scale. There are no less than fifty-nine speaking parts, twenty-two of which appear in the first 500 lines of the play. Even with complex doubling, it would have taxed the ability of any company to present it. The part of More, at over 800 lines, is the fourth longest to have been written for the stage at that point.

Of course, topicality may have been a motive, but it was surely doubtful that the censor would look kindly on such a production. Sir Thomas More had been arraigned and executed on the orders of the Queen's father, Henry VIII. Already he was on the path to beatification. In 1579, the Papal bull *Quoniam Divinae Bonitati* proclaimed Thomas More and John Fisher, Bishop of Rochester, as Catholic martyrs.

The choice of subject is curious for another reason. Munday had attended the Catholic seminary at Rheims which had been established to train an English priesthood. Later he joined the English College in Rome. It is unclear whether he was employed by the government as a spy or whether he had used the knowledge he had gained to turn informer on his return home. Certainly he was a witness for the prosecution in various trials of Jesuit missionaries on his return. He wrote a number of anti-Catholic pamphlets, several of which described the trials and executions of priests. It seems he was employed to confront a number of them in an offensive way on the scaffold. While he was in Rome, the English College had commissioned a fresco from the painter Nicolo Pomarancio, depicting the martyrdoms of More, Fisher and Margaret Pole. This may have inspired Munday to recognise the dramatic qualities inherent in More's life.

Munday's play ran into trouble with the Master of the Revels, Edmund Tilney, who struck his pen through chunks of it. 'Leave out ye insurrection and ye causes thereof,' he wrote in the margin, but he does not seem to have discounted entirely the possibility of production.

It may have been Shakespeare's ability to work with Tilney that led whichever company that possessed the by now somewhat scored script to ask him to rewrite the 'Ill May Day' passages of the play. It may even have been Tilney who suggested he be so employed. The choice was a wise one. Shakespeare uses his familiar arguments against the fomenting of civil unrest and conceding power to mob rule. He also sympathises with the plight of the immigrants and condemns the cruelty of those who would expel them.

> Imagine that you see the wretched strangers
> Their babies at their backs, with their poor luggage,
> Plodding to the ports and coasts for transportation.
> ... What would you think
> To be thus used? This is the stranger's case
> And this your mountainish inhumanity.

There is no evidence that the play was ever performed. Presumably the many alterations and delays ensured that its hour had passed. Certainly the logistics of a production on such a grand scale may well have caused any company to baulk at the prospect. Apart from its immense value as a working document that almost certainly gives the intriguing sight of Shakespeare's handwriting, the manuscript demonstrates that, at least on this occasion, he was prepared to work with others. If this is so, what other collaborations might he have made?

The Chamberlain's account of 15 March is significant because it reveals that William Shakespeare had become a 'sharer' (or shareholder) in the company. Until now, the Burbages had controlled the finances, but they had little or no income for two years and many continuing outgoings. The new company must have been desperate for ready cash and yet, within a short time, it was thriving. An explanation for this dramatic change of circumstance may come in a curious note recorded by Nicholas Rowe. In his brief biography of William Shakespeare, he writes of the 3rd Earl of Southampton in terms he could hardly believe had he not trusted implicitly his sources.

There is one instance so singular in the magnificence of this Patron of Shakespear's, that if I had not been assur'd that the story was handed down by Sir William D'Avenant, who was probably very well acquainted with his Affairs, I should not have ventur'd to have inserted, that my Lord Southampton, at one time, gave him a thousand Pounds, to enable him to go through with a Purchase when he had a mind to. A Bounty very great and very rare at any time ...

Rowe is right. The story has a tenable pedigree. His informant was almost certainly the leading actor of the Restoration period, Thomas Betterton. Sir William Davenant was Shakespeare's godson. Although he was but a child when the poet died, his parents had known him well, so we are but three whispers from the poet himself. Elsewhere in the biography, Rowe makes claims that are justified by subsequent discoveries. He states that Shakespeare's 'wife was the daughter of one Hathaway'. It was to be another two decades before the marriage certificate was found in the diocesan archives by a Stratford schoolmaster, the Revd Joseph Greene.

Despite the losses due to his unfortunate involvement with William Cecil's granddaughter, Southampton remained a lavish patron of poets, a financier of colonial ventures and a considerable benefactor of his old Cambridge college. As a noted devotee of the theatre he might well have been amenable to a request to assist his favourite acting company restore its fortunes. He would also have had a debt of honour to William Shakespeare from the dedication to him of *Venus and Adonis* and *The Rape of Lucrece*. The expected collateral from patron to poet was financial largesse. As for so many, the plague years must have been lean ones for Shakespeare. The income he received from his plays dried up and opportunities for acting were few if any. It is inconceivable that Southampton did not respond to the poet's overtures for patronage in the expected manner. If so what might the 'Purchase' to which Rowe refers have been? To become a sharer in the company was an investment that was surely well beyond Shakespeare's previous means. No other playwright had ever achieved such a status and it may have been Southampton's largesse that enabled it.

There is clear evidence that Shakespeare had become affluent by the mid-1590s. The average payment given to a playwright for a play was £8: a considerable sum, but not enough to make a man wealthy. Yet in this period, Shakespeare bought into the company, bought and repaired the second biggest house in Stratford, embarked on the costly business of acquiring a family coat of arms and probably set up his brother in business in London.

It is significant that Shakespeare's relationship with the new company is different. Rather than being a journeyman actor and playwright, he is a force within it. Indeed it may well have been he who conceived the idea of a permanent company, geared to the production of his plays. This had never happened before. In future, all his plays would be written for the company. Each part would be drafted to a particular actor. It is not overly fanciful to detect a new confidence and a distinctive style in his work once he achieves this vital role. He can dictate his literary terms and metier and increasingly does so, breaking out of the classical straitjacket to develop his own style. While it is difficult to date most of the earlier plays precisely, there is a pre- and post-plague feel to his output.

If the proverbial plunge is taken, there is a strong case for making *Romeo and Juliet* an early example of Shakespeare's new confidence. The play was a huge success – probably his most successful work to date. The title page of the first quarto in 1597 states that it 'hath been often (with great applause) played publiquely'. While he may have worked on the play during the plague years, it is probable that the final draft and performance post-date them. The play has the ostensible hallmarks of a 'Revenge' tragedy – the feuding houses of Montague and Capulet are on the collision course that is central to the action. That Tybalt kills Romeo's friend, Mercutio, and is then killed by Romeo appears to set up the classic cycle of revenge, but it is not to be. The play moves beyond such nemesis to a Christian theme of growth and reconciliation through suffering. While the lovers are 'star-crossed', their fate expiates the fallen world of Verona and gives hope of a better future. The love between Romeo and Juliet leads to their destruction, but in the process it leads to the reconciliation of the warring houses. As the Prince expresses it:

> Where be these enemies? Capulet? Montague?
> See, what a scourge is laid upon your hate,
> That heaven finds means to kill your joys with love.
> And I for winking at your discords too
> Have lost a brace of kinsmen: all are punish'd.

**Capulet:** O brother Montague, give me thy hand:
> This is my daughter's jointure, for no more
> Can I demand.

**Montague:** But I can give thee more:
> For I will raise her statue in pure gold;
> That while Verona by that name is known,
> There shall be no figure at such rate be set
> As that of true and faithful Juliet.

**Capulet:** As rich shall Romeo by his lady lie;
> Poor sacrifices of our enmity.

This theme of expiation, to which Shakespeare will return in his great tragedies, is only partly explored here. Circumstance is the overriding theme. Romeo is 'fortune's fool' and the lovers are famously 'star-crossed'.

1. Engraving of Shakespeare's birthplace, by Richard Greene, based on the earliest-known picture of the building, *c.* 1762.

2. The old market house, Stratford-upon-Avon, by James Saunders, prior to its demolition in 1826. John Shakespeare would have traded here with the other glovers.

3. South-west view of Holy Trinity Church, 1762, showing the wooden spire built by Archbishop John de Stratford.

564

April 3  Edwardus filius Thome Chefole

6  Benedicta filia Thome ffleminng

22  Iohannes filius william Brookes

26  Gulielmus filius Iohannes Shakspere XX

4. William Shakespeare's baptismal entry, 26 April 1564.

5. Schoolroom at Stratford Grammar School.

6. An early nineteenth-century engraving of Anne Hathaway's Cottage, which shows the building when it was still a working farm.

7. Picture of Charlecote Park.

8. Richard Tarlton, depicted as part of a decorated initial: Harley 3885. f. 19. perm Br, Library. (© Jonathan Reeve JR149b3fp258 15501600)

*Above:* 9. Devastating outbreaks of plague. (© Jonathan Reeve JR1106b21p213 16001650)

*Opposite:* 10. The interior of the Swan Theatre by Johannes de Witt, 1596. (© Jonathan Reeve JR1080b3p299 16001650)

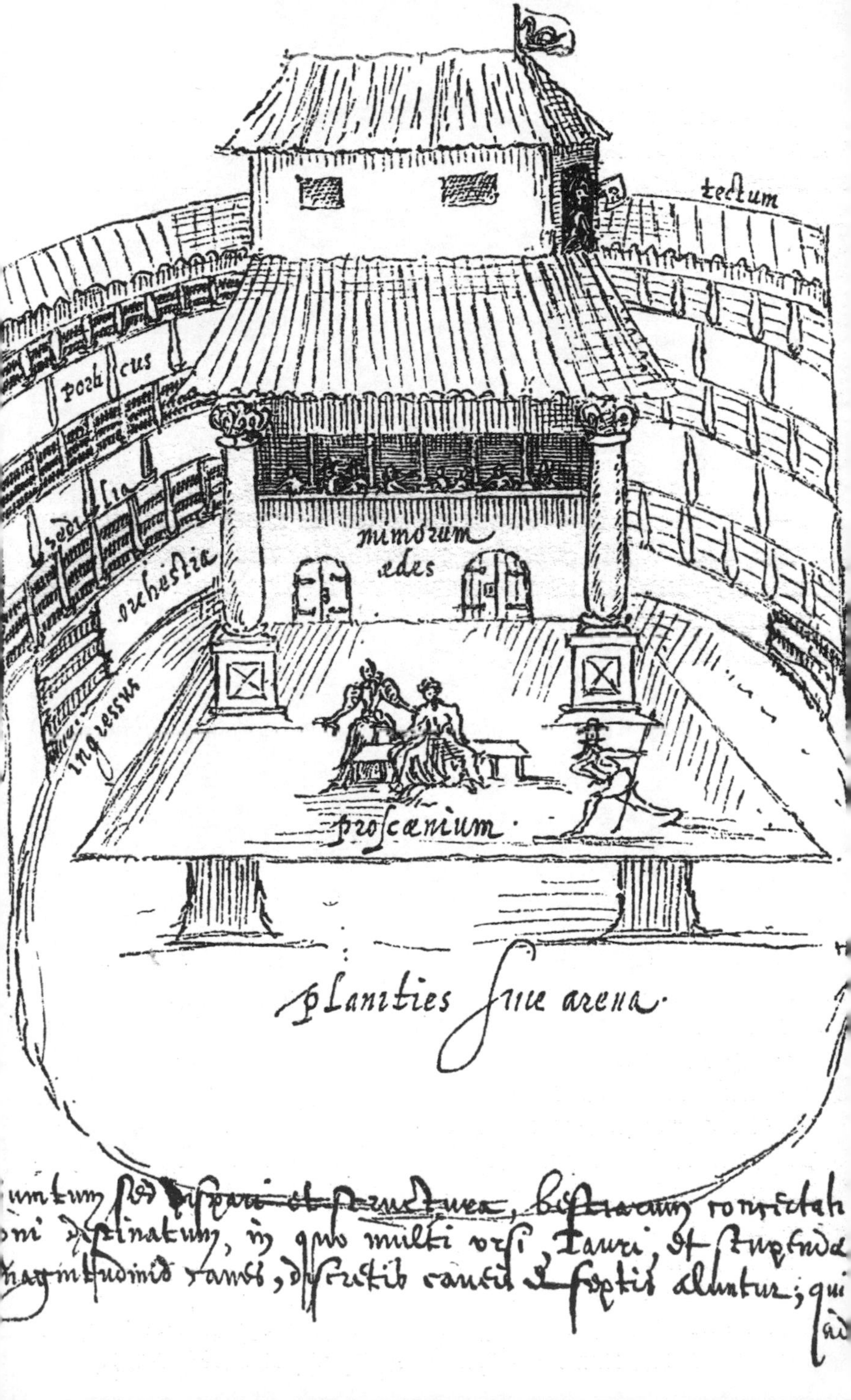

tectum

porticus

sedilia

orchestra

mimorum
ædes

ingressus

proscænium·

planities siue arena·

...um..... ... ...spare et ...uc..ure·, be......um conspectab-
oni destinatum·, in quo multi ursi·, tauri·, et stupenda
...magnitudinis canes·, distinctis ...n.is... septis aluntur; qui
...ai

11. Drawing of Middle Temple Hall, scene of a production of *Twelfth Night* seen by John Manningham in 1602. (© Jonathan Reeve JR1100b2p761 15501600)

12. Arms granted to John Shakespeare.

13. A drawing of New Place, done from memory by George Vertue in 1737 after the house's demolition in 1702.

14. Section of Claes van Visscher's 'Panorama of London' (1616) showing Globe Theatre and Bear Garden. (© Stephen Porter)

15. Tower of London from Claes Visscher's view, 1616. (© Stephen Porter)

16. Signature of John Hall.

Æ: SVÆ. 30.    A.D. 1599.

17. Portrait of Michael Drayton, friend and alleged drinking companion of William Shakespeare and a patient of John Hall.

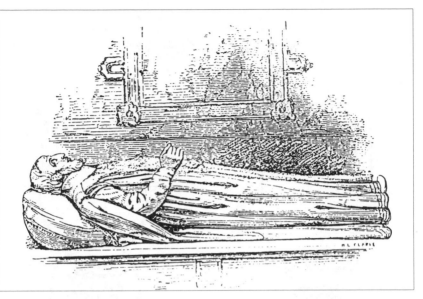

18. An early nineteenth-century engraving of the tomb of John Combe in Holy Trinity Church.

19. Thomas Quiney's signature, written in his capacity as Borough Chamberlain.

20. Various examples of Shakespeare's signature.

21. Shakespeare's portrait on First Folio. (© Stephen Porter)

*Above, left and right*: 22 & 23. Bust of Shakespeare – Holy Trinity Church.

# Troubled Times, 1593–96

'Such miserye as is lamentable'
– Thomas Deloney, 1595

## The Lopus Affair

Roderigo Lopus (or, in Spanish, 'Lopez') was the best-known doctor in England. A Portuguese Jew who had converted, as a *christiano nuevo*, a 'New Christian', he came to England in 1559 and became a physician at St Bartholomew's Hospital. His medical knowledge and reassuring manner inspired confidence. He soon assembled a circle of wealthy and influential patients, becoming the personal physician to the Queen's favourite, Robert Dudley, Earl of Leicester. Even then his name was smeared with unfortunate associations. A 1584 libelous pamphlet entitled *Leicester's Commonwealth* suggested that he distilled poisons for Dudley and other noblemen. Despite this, he reached the pinnacle of his profession in 1586, when he was appointed as the Queen's physician. She was pleased with his ministrations, for in 1589 she granted him a monopoly on the importation of aniseed and sumac.

In January 1593/94, Lopus was a prosperous elderly professional man, with a son at Winchester College and a house in the fashionable suburb of Holborn, but nemesis awaited. He became involved in the machinations of the Earl of Essex, which may have seemed sensible at the time, but ultimately proved as disastrous for him as for many others. After the death of the last king of Portugal, Henrique, a cardinal of the Catholic Church, in 1580, Dom Antonio, an illegitimate son of the Duke of Beja, claimed the throne. His reign lasted a mere thirty-three days before he was overthrown by Philip II of Spain, who had better claims to the succession. Antonio fled, but maintained his regal pretentions for three years from the Azores with the support of French and English privateers. After being ousted from the last remnant of his kingdom by the Spanish Admiral Santa Cruz, he fled, first to France and then to England, where the Queen established him in a court-in-exile at Eton College. The Earl of Essex became a firm advocate of the Pretender and employed Dr Lopus as his interpreter. Together with his brother-in-law, William Añes, also a *christiano nuevo*, Lopus took on the thankless task of being the permanently impecunious Dom Antonio's financial agent. What follows is unclear, but Lopus appears to have become intrigued by the world of statecraft and deception to which he had long been close and inadvertently became a victim of disparate and irreconcilable factions, most notably the intense rivalry between Essex and the Cecils.

In January, 1593/94, Essex convinced himself that two of Dom Antonio's henchmen, Esteban Ferreira and Emanuel Loisie, were double agents in the pay of the Spanish. He obtained an order for their arrest. Instructions were sent to the Channel ports that all correspondence in Portuguese was to be opened and read. When the two men were interrogated by Essex, it emerged that they had had dealings with Lopus, which was not surprising, since he was in charge of the Pretender's finances. Ferreira wrote to Dr Lopus, warning him to prevent the arrival from Flanders of an associate of his called Gonez d'Avila. Lopus replied that he had already written to d'Avila to that effect and that he would spare no expense to prevent his arrival. His messages did not get through, but the correspondence between Ferreira and Lopus was intercepted. D'Avila was found to be carrying a letter in Portuguese which was deemed to be possibly encoded, although no evidence ever emerged that this was so.

The subsequent interrogations, largely conducted by Essex, demonstrated the truth of Portia's wise words, which may, perhaps, be seen in the context of this affair.

> But I fear you speak upon the rack,
> Where men enforc'd do speak anything.

When d'Avila was shown the rack in the Tower, he immediately confessed that he had been employed to carry letters between Ferreira and another Portuguese called Manuel Luis Tineco, a Spanish agent based in Brussels. Two months later, Lord Burghley received a communication from Tineco, offering to come to London to reveal important secrets to the Queen, provided he was given a safe conduct. This was duly dispatched, but he was arrested on his arrival at Dover. In an astonishing piece of casuistry it was claimed that the safe conduct guaranteed him ingress but not egress. It was probably Essex who was responsible for this cynical act of betrayal. He interrogated Tineco twice and he avowed that he had been in contact with Ferreira on behalf of the Spanish government.

Essex was becoming increasingly convinced – on extremely flimsy evidence – that Dr Lopus was at the heart of a conspiracy. He persuaded the Queen that the matter should be investigated. On 1 January 1593/94, Lopus was arrested and conveyed to Essex House. His residence in Holborn was searched, but nothing incriminating was found. He was then questioned by the two Cecils, who were convinced that he was the victim of Essex's anti-Spanish obsessions. The Queen concurred and upbraided Essex for his persecution of her doctor. This made him even more determined to prove his point. Two of Lopus's servants were questioned in the Tower. Faced with the threat of torture, one said that Lopus had been corresponding with Spanish agents, promising to do 'all that their King required'. The other's testimony was even more damaging. He said that his master had agreed to poison the Queen in return for 50,000 crowns. When questioned under the usual threat of torture. Lopus agreed that this was the case, but said that said he had promised it 'in order to cozen the King of Spain'. He claimed that Sir Francis Walsingham was fully aware of his activities. It is quite likely that Lopus had been recruited into the spymaster's network, but Walsingham had died two years before and Essex was not likely to give him the benefit of the doubt. 'I have discovered a most dangerous and most desperate treason,' he wrote exultantly to a friend. In February, the three men were brought to trial, found guilty of treason and sentenced to hanging, disembowelling and quartering. The Queen was evidently not convinced by the verdict and delayed signing the death warrant for several weeks. She may never have signed it but Lopus's enemies succeeded in getting him transferred out of her direct jurisdiction at the Tower into the Fleet Prison. From thence the three condemned men were hauled through the streets to Tyburn. Tineco was obliged to stand by while the grisly process of hanging, castration and disemboweling was performed on his two companions. If ever a man had reason to be aggrieved at his treatment, it was he. He had been double-crossed over his guaranteed safe conduct and charged with treason in a country of which he was not a citizen. He went down fighting, felling the executioner with a blow before he was finally overpowered and the excruciating sentence carried out. Years later, the Spanish ambassador in London told King Philip III that he believed Lopus was innocent. This appears to have been Queen Elizabeth's view. Significantly, she did not enforce the sequestration of Lopus's estate, as was normal in cases of treason, but allowed his widow and heirs to retain the residue.

It has been suggested that the character of Shylock in *The Merchant of Venice* is based on Dr Lopus. This is highly unlikely. Even Jewishness was not something they had in common, for Lopus had twice aposticised from his ancestral faith, becoming first a Catholic and then an Anglican. He was a sophisticated physician, accepted by the highest circles in the land. Shylock is a usurer who is treated as a pariah by those with influence in the city. It is possible that Shakespeare had never encountered a practising Jew. They had been expelled from England as long before as the reign of Edward I and the ban on their presence continued until the Commonwealth era. Since 1516, Jews in Venice had been compelled to live in their own quarter, literally the 'Ghetto'. They were subject to a dusk-till-dawn curfew and the occupations they could follow were restricted. One of these was medicine, the chosen profession of Dr Lopus. Because the medieval Church proscribed usury, Jews had filled that gap by becoming money-lenders. Thus, if Shylock represents a Jewish stereotype, it was because Jews had been so categorised. They do not feature large in contemporary literature, but there are enough such portrayals to be significant. Shakespeare clearly had some knowledge of Judaism. He was aware, for example, that practising Jews would not eat with those who were not of their faith.

Yes, to smell pork; to eat of the habitation which your prophet the Nazarite conjured the devil into. I will buy with you, sell with you, talk with you, walk with you, and so following, but I will not eat with you, drink with you, nor pray with you.

Although Shylock negates his own principle by going to supper at Bassanio's, this is necessary to the plot. It gets him out of the house to enable Jessica's escape. Nor does Shakespeare appear to know of the Ghetto. Shylock comes and goes as he pleases.

A significant influence, given that few, if any, contemporary authors can ever have encountered a Jew, was likely to have been the character of Herod in the mystery plays, although there is frequently some confusion as to whether he is Jewish or a Muslim. 'Be gracious Mahound more myrth never I had,' he exclaims in the Coventry cycle when he hears of the Massacre of the Innocents.

One of the contemporary stereotypes of Jews was that they dabbled in poisons. We recall that Lopus was libelled with the accusation that he distilled toxins for Robert Dudley. 'As for myself,' says Marlowe's Jew of Malta, 'I walk abroad a-nights / And kill sick people groaning under walls. / Sometimes I go about and poison wells.' In Nashe's *Unfortunate Traveller*, Dr Zachary, who is the Pope's Jewish doctor, converts his own bodily fluids, 'snot and spittle', and the outpourings of his rheumatic eyes, into medicines and poisons. At least Shakespeare spares Shylock such fiendish tricks. He is a straightforward usurer who is upset because Antonio has undermined the market by lending money free of interest. He is not intended to be a sympathetic character. 'With the extreame crueltie of Shylock the Jewe towards the sayd Merchant,' reads the blurb to the first quarto of the play and yet Shakespeare, famously, humanises him. He gives him motives for his hatred with which the audience can find sympathy.

If you prick us, do we not bleed? If you tickle us, do we not laugh? If you poison us, do we not die? And if you wrong us, shall we not revenge?

There is a moment of unexpected tenderness in the same scene when Shylock, in the midst of ranting about his losses, bewails the loss of a ring with reference only to its emotional value.

Out upon her! Thou torturest me, Tubal: it was my turquoise; I had it of Leah when I was a bachelor: I would not have given it for a wilderness of monkeys.

Leah is presumably Jessica's dead mother. This is another example of Shakespeare's technique of creating lives for his characters beyond the action of the play.

The attitude towards Jews in contemporary Christendom was ambivalent. On one level, they were a people of the Book. The Old Testament was the story of God's Covenant with them. The Puritans were fond of drawing analogies between themselves and 'the Children of Israel' as God's chosen people. On the other hand, the Jews could be seen as deicides, who had rejected Christ. Yet this very rejection formed a vital part of the scheme of salvation: a paradox well expressed by the Anglican divine Thomas Draxe.

> It is a maruellous worke of God, and not without his mistery, that the Iewes (now soeuer wandring and dispersed in al countries almost) should stil continue such a distinct and vnconfounded nation, so innumerable in multitude, and so constant in the keeping and observing of (as much as they possible may) their ancient lawes, rites, and ceremonies ... the conuersion of the nation of them is dayly expected ... so great a number of them shalbe againe ingrafted into Christ and beleiue the gospel.[1]

In so saying, Draxe was drawing on the traditions of the Early Fathers of the Church and the medieval schoolmen. The overriding theme was that the Second Coming of Christ would be presaged by the conversion of those Jews prepared to believe in him. 'The blindness of the Jews will endure,' wrote Thomas Aquinas in his *Commentary on the Epistle to Romans*, 'until the fullness of the gentiles have accepted the faith.' The contemporary champion of the Counter Reformation, Cardinal Bellamine, wrote in *De Summo Pontifice*:

> The coming of Enoch and Elias, who liue euen now and shall liue until they come to oppose AntiChrist himself, and to preserve the elect in the faith of Christ, and in the end shall convert the Jews, and it is certain that this is not yet fulfilled.

Andrew Marvell was to express a similar thought in more jocular vein to his coy mistress.

> And you should, if you please, refuse
> Till the conversion of the Jews.

One of the problems in dealing with *The Merchant of Venice* in modern times is that the approach is understandably and inevitably influenced by the terrible history of anti-semitism in Nazi Germany. Shakespeare knew nothing of such matters. The failing of Shylock, as he presents it, is not that he is a Jew as such, but that he inherits the Pharisaic failing of demanding the letter of the Law. 'When I was with him,' Jessica says,

> I have heard him swear
> To Tubai and to Chus, his countrymen,
> That he would rather have Antonio's flesh
> Than twenty times the value of the sum
> That he did owe him.

Portia makes an eloquent plea that Shylock embrace the 'Christian' quality of mercy.

> It is an attribute of God himself;
> And earthly power doth then show like God's
> When mercy seasons justice.

But he rejects her urgings, opting for the legalism of revenge. In so doing he would have lost any spark of sympathy that an Elizabethan audience might have felt for him. In the face of such intransigence, the Christians equivocate: a quality he treats with contempt.

> These be the Christian husbands, I have a daughter.
> Would any of the stock of Barabas
> Had been her husband rather than a Christian.

The evocation of Marlowe's Jew of Malta, who was prepared to murder his own daughter after her conversion to Christianity, and to poison entire cities, would demonstrate to the contemporary audience the lengths that Shylock is prepared to go to gain revenge. This attitude is used by Jessica to justify her betrayal, not only of her father, but of her ancestral roots.

> Alack, what heinous sin is it in me
> To be ashamed to be my father's child!
> But though I am a daughter to his blood,
> I am not to his manners. O Lorenzo,
> If thou keep promise, I shall end this strife,
> Become a Christian and thy loving wife.

As his later evocation of his daughter and his ducats reveals, Jessica is, to Shylock, a material asset, the means by which a new generation of Jews will be engendered. To serve this end, he keeps her a virtual prisoner in his treasure house.

The conversion of the Jews is an important theme in *The Merchant of Venice*. Both Shylock and his daughter are made Christians before the end of the play. Shylock is compelled to be one by Antonio. Nor does Jessica become a Christian out of conviction, but through her love for Lorenzo. In this she realises the sanctity promised by St Paul in 1 Corinthians 7.14.

> For the unbelieving husband is sanctified by the believing wife; and the unbelieving wife is sanctified by the believing husband: otherwise your children should be unclean; but now they are holy.

Shylock's conversion is even less a product of conviction. It is comparable to the enforced apostasy of the *conversos* in Spain and Portugal. It evokes the desire of the authorities in England that all should confirm outwardly to the practices of the Church Established by Law. Conversion was often outward, not inward. Hence the sincerity of the conversion of the *conversos* was frequently questioned. Here at last is a parallel with Dr Lopus, who was accused of subscribing towards a synagogue in Antwerp. Who can doubt that Shylock would not have been much of a convert? Yet his acceptance of his defeat in court at the hands of Portia is strangely mute. The man who has so inveighed against Christians is reduced to saying 'I am content' once his fate is revealed. Had he had a life beyond the play, there can be little doubt that, in material terms, Antonio has done him a good turn. He is specifically reunited with 'his son Lorenzo and his daughter'. He is released from the Ghetto and he can play a full part in the life of the city as a Venetian citizen. Many of the *conversos* rose into the highest ranks of society. There can be little doubt that Shylock's acumen would have enabled him to do the same.

It is not impossible that Shakespeare visited Venice, but it is unlikely. Yet a great port like London would have been full of travellers' tales. The Gobbo was a grotesque statue of a hunchback which supported a column from which heralds made announcements. It was the custom to place there verses satirising important figures in the city. It was an important mouthpiece of Venetian opinion, as are the cryptic observations of Shylock's servant, Launcelot Gobbo.[2]

## Quite Undone

In 1595, the campaign against the theatre achieved another success when the Lord Mayor succeeded in banning plays at inns. At least in the City of London, the links between the theatre and its origins had been broken. There were other matters to trouble the actors. An economic crisis was striking at London's populace. Food shortages and the familiar resentment against immigrants were causing unrest. The grievances were articulated by a silk weaver called Thomas Deloney in a book entitled *The Complaint of the Yeoman Weavers Against the Imigrant Weavers*. It charged that foreigners broke the trade's regulations by having more looms than were permitted and by teaching new immigrants the trade without then undertaking a proper apprenticeship. They

> sett wooemen and maydes at work, where, when they are become perfect in the occupation doe marry men of contrary trade, and soe bringe that which should be our livings to be the mainteynance of those that never deserved for it, and theis likewise increase an infinite number ... Many of poore Englishmen is quite undone with his wife and poore children, and brought to such miserye as is lamentable to be rehearsed.[3]

In 1595, martial law was again proclaimed. During June, there were twelve days of disturbances. The autonomous reaction of the civic authorities confirms the acute observation of the Venetian ambassador in the next reign that 'London seemed to be governed without the interference of either the monarch or his ministers'.

Early in the month, a silk weaver was arrested and confined to the Bethlem Hospital after protesting outside Crosby Place, the house of Sir John Spencer, the Lord Mayor. This may have been because the Bridewell was full to overflowing. On 6 June, a mob of some 300 apprentices stormed into the hospital and rescued their colleague. In response the authorities decreed that apprentices and servants should be confined within their masters' houses on Sabbath and holy days (i.e. public holidays). 'Idle persons' (presumably the growing army of unemployed) causing trouble were to be committed to the Bridewell. Thomas Deloney and fourteen others were arrested for printing subversive literature.

Sir John Spencer bore the brunt of the blame for the deteriorating situation, but he was not inactive in attempting to alleviate the woes of the populace. He persuaded the City Livery Companies to buy corn abroad to dispense to the poor. As was customary, it was stored at Bridge House at the Southwark end of London Bridge. The Privy Council was also active, producing a 'Book of Orders' against hoarding. This authorised magistrates to order residents to compile a return of the commodities they were holding. The Earl of Essex, who was emerging as a kind of people's champion, was particularly vociferous in his demands that hoarders should be dealt with.

The protests against rising food prices took a practical form on 12 June when apprentices invaded Borough Market and forcibly bought fish and butter from the market women. Three pence a pound was proffered for butter rather than the asked-for five and 500 lb was forcibly taken. A number of the perpetrators were arrested. The decision of the Star Chamber to sentence them to be flogged and pilloried only served to escalate the violence. Three days later, the markets were invaded by the angry mob again. This developed into a riot of protest against the imprisonment of the apprentices. The pillories on Cheapside and Leadenhall Street were pulled down and a mock gallows set up outside the Lord Mayor's house. Next day, gangs of apprentices, discharged soldiers and vagrants congregated at St Paul's Cathedral to ferment an insurrection against the Lord Mayor. The mob yelled its intention to 'play the Irish trick on him' (remove his head). Such was the fear among the authorities that, in that same month, the Lord Mayor decreed that apprentices were 'to have open punishment for their lewd offences' – i.e. there would be no restriction on the level of punishment that offenders might expect to receive. Every householder was ordered 'to have a sufficient weapon at his dore for the preservation of her Maiesties peace'.

On 27 June, the authorities made an example of 'certaine young men apprentices and other' who had been arrested as a result of the incidents in Borough Market, punishing them by 'whipping, setting in the Pillory, &c.' This had no more effect than previous attempts to cower the unruly. On 29 June the worst riots of all occurred. A crowd of 'unrulie youthes' gathered on Tower Hill. The local wardens instructed them to return home, but they were driven back into Tower Street by a shower of stones. The situation was complicated by a territorial dispute. The Lord Mayor claimed that Tower Hill came within his jurisdiction. The Lieutenant of the Tower of London, Sir Michael Blount, claimed that it was in his. The Yeoman Warders of the Tower refused to assist the Lord Mayor and even launched an attack on his entourage. After a considerable riot, the crowd was dispersed. Several apprentices had been arrested and the Lord Mayor decided it was time to make an ultimate example of them. On 22 July, five were arraigned before him in the Guildhall. It was alleged that they planned 'to robbe, steale, pill and spoile the welthy and well disposed inhabitants ... and to take the sword of authorytye from the magistrats and governours lawfully authorised'. The Queen sent the Earl of Essex to observe the trial on her behalf. The prisoners were found guilty and sentenced to be hung, drawn and quartered. In his order of execution, issued next day, the Lord Mayor directed that the householders of Tower Street Ward

> Keep within their houses all their men servants and apprentices to morrow from three of the clock in the morning until eight at night, and the same householders be ... all that time ready at their door ... with a weapon in their hands.[4]

Two days later the prisoners were drawn from Newgate to the scene of their alleged offences on Tower Hill and there 'executed accordingly'.

The sentence was appropriate to the accused having been found guilty of treason rather than less severe impositions arising from charges of riotous behaviour. This was stretching the spirit of the law. The riots were leaderless and without a specific purpose. The Earl of Essex may have drawn his own conclusion. Power would be in the grasp of whoever could bring cohesion and direction to this unfocussed mob. He had actually appointed the executioner who would have dispatched the five apprentices. Thomas Derrick had been convicted of rape and would have been executed had not Essex offered him the job of public executioner in exchange for his life. This was not a job for which there were many takers: not because of moral scruples, but because the friends and relations of those executed had a record of murdering and maiming the executioner. Derrick proved adept at his work, even devising a pulley system that would enable the simultaneous hanging of over twenty people. It is from this that the modern lifting device takes its name.

Of course, the theatres were closed during the riots. This would have been an ideal time for the Lord Chamberlain's Men to go on tour, but it does not appear that they did so. As if the domestic situation were not sufficient cause for alarm, news would have arrived in London in the following month which must have made the very existence of the nation seem precarious. The defeat of the Spanish Armada was not the end of a war, but its beginning. The seemingly interminable conflict dragged on through the 1590s. On 23 July 1595, four Spanish galleys landed troops in Cornwall. They sacked Mousehole and Newlyn. At Penzance they set fire to more than 400 houses. England seemed extremely vulnerable again.

## Ducdame, Ducdame, Ducdame

The desperate disasters of the nation must have affected the now well-honed artistic judgements of William Shakespeare. Rather like the film-makers of the Hollywood years in the 1930s, with his great instinct for the moment, he realised that, in a time of economic and social depression, escapism is the order of the day. Just as Hollywood responded to the Great Depression with Busby Berkley's extravaganzas, so Shakespeare responded to the Great Dearth with a series of sparkling comedies. Amid the pains of scarcity, it is easier to stretch the imagination to 'A wood near Athens', than to the apprentices' riots of *Sir Thomas More*. Who would want to go to the theatre to see distressing sights from around the corner? Although the subject of history continued to be addressed, it is the comic muse which dominates, even in the most notable of the history plays written at this period. The two parts of *Henry IV* contain some of Shakespeare's most consummate comic creations in the characters of Sir John Falstaff and his companions of the Eastcheap Tavern.

Yet the comic flow is tempered by a melancholic strain. In 1586, Timothy Bright, a physician at St Bartholomew's Hospital, published his *A Treatise on Melancholy*. He later became a clergyman and devised a system of shorthand. His elaborate treatise, with its analysis of the melancholic humour, need not detain us. It is sufficient to quote his summary of the causes, which he saw as dietary and physiological.

> As all naturall humours rise of nourishment, so melancholie being a part of the bloud, from thence it springeth also.

Shakespeare may well have been familiar with Bright's work, but if he were, he does not incorporate it into his overall world-view to any great extent. Yet he is very much aware of the cult of melancholy that prevailed in sections of contemporary society and uses it to temper his comedies. 'It is a melancholy of mine own,' states Jacques in *As You Like It*, 'compounded of many simples, extracted from many objects, and indeed the sundry contemplation of my travels, which, by often rumination, wraps me in the most numerous sadness.'

It is a function of Shakespeare's 'melancholy' characters to inject a note of realism into the comic idyll. Jacques is a critic of the Arcadian ideal – the romanticised view of rural life. This is expressed in the play's famous song which begins 'Under the Greenwood Tree ...' Jacques requests the second verse and Amiens obliges.

> Who doth ambition shun
> And loves to live i' the sun,
> Seeking the food he eats
> And pleased with what he gets,
> Come hither, come hither, come hither;
> Here shall he see no enemy
> But winter and rough weather.

Jacques responds with a third verse which puts the pastoral life into perspective.

> If it do come to pass
> That any man turn ass,
> Leaving his wealth and ease,
> A stubborn will to please,
> Ducdame, ducdame, ducdame:
> He shall he see
> Gross fools as he,
> An if he will come to me.

'What's that "ducdame"?' asks Amiens.

''Tis a Greek invocation,' replies Jacques, 'to call fools into a circle.'

Similarly in *Twelfth Night*, the conventional but exquisite love lyric sung by the Clown is completed by a second verse expressing the urgency of the moment in terms of the finite.

> Oh mistress mine, where are you roaming?
> Oh, stay and hear, your true love's coming,
> That can sing both high and low.
> Trip no further pretty sweeting:
> Journeys end in lovers meeting,
> Every wise man's son doth know.

> What is love? 'tis not hereafter.
> Present mirth hath present laughter.
> What's to come is still unsure.
> In delay there lies no plenty:
> Then come kiss me sweet and twenty,
> Youth's a stuff will not endure.

Shakespeare, who expresses his dislike of the practice of comic ad-libbing in *Hamlet*, gives the Clown an enhanced role as a kind of contrary critic of the action. This is certainly the case in *As You Like It*, where Touchstone's recognition of his probable future cuckolding stands in contrast to Orlando's idealistic courtship.

As horns are odious, they are necessary. It is said, 'many a man knows no end of his goods:' right; many a man has good horns, and knows no end of them. Well, that is the dowry of his wife; 'tis none of his own getting.

Shakespeare has explored this theme before – in *Love's Labour's Lost*.

> The cuckoo then on every tree
> Mocks married men; for thus sings he,
> > 'Cuckoo
> Cuckoo, Cuckoo' – O word of fear,
> Unpleasing to a married ear!

Shakespeare's greatest comic creation also brings a pragmatic and earthy approach. Falstaff's famous speech on honour in *Henry IV, Part I* stands in sharp contrast to the chivalric values earlier expressed by Hotspur.

> By heaven, methinks it were an easy leap
> To pluck bright honour from the pale-faced moon,
> Or dive into the bottom of the deep,
> Where fathom line could never touch the ground,
> And pluck up drowned honour by the locks,
> So he that doth redeem her thence might wear
> Without corrival all her dignities;
>
> (Act I, Scene 3)

**Prince:** Why, thou owest God a death. *[Prince exits]*
**Falstaff:** 'Tis not due yet: I would be loath to pay him before his day. What need I be so forward with him that calls not on me? Well, 'tis no matter; honour pricks me on. Yea, but how if honour prick me off when I come on? How then? Can honour set to a leg? No. Or an arm? No. Or take away the grief of a wound? No. Honour hath no skill in surgery then? No. What is honour? A word. What is in that word honour? What is that honour? Air – a trim reckoning! Who hath it? He that died a Wednesday. Doth he feel it? No. Doth he hear it? No. 'Tis insensible then? Yea, to the dead. But will it not live with the living? No. Why? Detraction will not suffer it. Therefore I'll none of it. Honour s a mere scutcheon – and so ends my catechism.

> (Act V, Scene 1)

Shakespeare's revolutionary technique of providing an internal critique ensures that his comedies do not lapse into sentimentality but are always exposed to the cold light of reality. It was surely this quality of tingeing the comedies with melancholy and the tragedies with comedy that led to the later desire to rewrite the tragedies with happy endings. In the early scenes *Romeo and Juliet* could be shaping up as a comedy, with Mercutio providing the realistic contrast to the lovelorn Romeo. It is his death that turns the play. In *Much Ado*, a different sequel to Beatrices's words 'Kill Claudio' could have sent the play in a tragic direction.

It is impossible to date with any great precision most of the plays. Their first appearance in print is but a small marker. The list made by Francis Meres indicates that, by 1598, most of the great comedies had been written and performed. After *Romeo and Juliet* Shakespeare leaves the tragic muse alone for quite a while. Its hour will come again.

# 11

# Bankside, 1596–99

'The cockpit, galleries, boxes, all are full'
— Leonard Digges, 1640

The close proximity of Augustine Phillips's home to the Swan Theatre may indicate that the Lord Chamberlain's Men had some kind of arrangement with Francis Langley and his theatre. It is probable that William Shakespeare was also living in the area. 'From a paper now before me,' wrote the critic Edward Malone in 1796, 'our poet appears to have lived in Southwark near the Bear Garden, in 1596.' This surmise is given substance by the Pipe Roll for St Helen's parish, where Shakespeare had been residing. He is deemed to owe the sum of 13s 4d in back rates. A marginal note adds: 'on[retus] Ep[iscop]o Winton[ensi]'. In other words, he was living in that part of Southwark known as the Liberty of the Clink. This was the manor of the bishops of Winchester, whose fine palace was situated on the banks of the Thames, near London Bridge. The area might be described as an Elizabethan 'fun palace'. Three hundred inns and brothels serviced the varied needs of their clients. The Thames waterman and poet John Taylor noted that the whores were 'wont after they had good trading, or reasonable comings in, to take a boat and air themselves upon the water'. Those in search of the extensive range of entertainments available could cross the river by boat. The hazards of one propelled by a scull, swirling about on the tide, cost a halfpenny, while the sounder option of two oarsmen cost a penny. This was big business for the watermen. Several thousand people would attend the Bankside theatres in their heyday. Alternatively, they could take the longer route by foot across London Bridge, the 'beautiful structure' admired by a German visitor, Paul Hentzner. The houses on it gave it 'the appearance of a continued street, not at all of a bridge'. On the gatehouse at the Southwark end the heads of those who had been executed for treason were impaled. They remained there until they rotted away and fell. Hentzner and his companion counted thirty of them. When William Shakespeare used this route across the Thames, it is likely that he would have encountered the severed heads of his distant kinsmen Sir Edward Arden and John Somerville.

The Bear Garden, situated in the Paris Garden, was at the heart of this exotic district. It offered varied entertainments – interludes and fencing displays as well as the baiting of bulls and bears. The local air would be permeated with the whelping of dogs and the anguished cries of tortured animals. It was a substantial three-storey building that, externally at least, resembled the nearby theatres. The 'sport' therein enjoyed royal favour. In 1573 Ralph Bowes was appointed as the 'Master of Her Majesty's Game at Paris Garden'. The area was so dark at nights that it needed 'cat's eyes' to see one's way.[1]

Paul Hentzner recorded his impressions of the Bear Garden around 1598:

> There is still another place, built in the form of a theatre, which serves for the baiting of bulls and bears; they are fastened behind, and then worried by great English bull-dogs, but not without great risk to the dogs, from the horns of the one and the teeth of the other; and it sometimes happens that they are killed upon the spot; fresh ones are immediately supplied in the places of those that are wounded or tired. To this entertainment there often follows that of whipping a blinded bear, which is performed by five or six men, standing circularly with whips, which they exercise upon him without any mercy, as he cannot escape from them because of his chain; he defends himself with all his force and skill, throwing down all who come within his reach and are not active enough to get out of it, and tearing the whips out of their hands and breaking them.

The bears became celebrities in their own right, and were given such names as Harry Hunks, George Stone and Ned Whiting. The most famous one of all is alluded to by Slender in *The Merry Wives of Windsor*.

> I have seen Sackerson loose twenty times, and have taken him by the chain; but, I warrant you, the women have so cried and shrieked at it, that it passed.

Shakespeare seems to have had some sympathy for the bear. In *King Lear*, when Gloucester realises that he is to be tormented by Lear's daughters, he identifies himself with a bear: 'I am tied to th'stake, and I must stand the course' (III.7.56). A few lines later his eyes are put out, just like poor Harry Hunks, the blind bear.

Yet the 'sport', faced with the new craze of the theatre, was in decline. To support it, in 1591, the authorities decreed that no theatrical performances should take place on a Thursday to give the bear-pits a clear run. It was probably enacted through the influence of the proprietors of such establishments, who would have included the theatrical impresario Philip Henslowe.

By the beginning of 1596, the Lord Chamberlain's Men had probably decided that their position at The Theatre was tenuous. The landlord, Giles Allen, may have been already making noises about not renewing the lease. This is likely to have led to negotiations with other playhouses like the Curtain and the Swan about finding a new home. In a bold move, which must have seemed a masterstroke at the time, James Burbage bought the freehold of the *dorter* and a number of the surrounding rooms of the former Blackfriars Priory from the executors of the estate of a former Master of the Revels, Sir Thomas Cawarden, for the hefty sum of £600. The *dorter* was a large hall that had been the dormitory of the Dominican friars. It was situated in a different part of the extensive site from where the Children of the Chapel Royal had once performed. It seemed an ideal location. It retained its religious status as a Liberty, which put it outside the jurisdiction of the hostile City Fathers. It was on the north bank of the Thames, so there was no necessity for most of the audience to cross the river. Most of all, it was an indoor location, so performances were not dependent on the weather. It gave scope for special effects and for securing a better-heeled clientele who would pay more money than the groundlings at The Theatre. Burbage began the extensive work necessary to turn the building into a working theatre. Yet what had seemed a brilliant stroke produced a near catastrophe. It is an indication of the status of the theatre and the rowdy behaviour which was associated with it that the prospect that Blackfriars might be so utilised caused great alarm among the somewhat upmarket local residents. In November 1596, they petitioned the Privy Council to oppose the scheme. No argument against the project was spared.

> The said Burbage ... meaneth very shortly to convert and turn the same into a comon playhouse, which will grow to be a very great annoyance and trouble, not only to all the noblemen and gentlemen thereabout inhabiting but also a generall inconvenience to all the inhabitants of the same precinct, both by reason of the great resort and gathering togeather of all manner of vagrant and lewd persons that, under cover of resorting to the playes, will come thither and worke all manner of mischeefe, and allso to the great pestring and filling up of the same precinct, yf it should please God to send any visitation of sicknesse as heretofore hath been, for that same precinct is already grown very populous; and besides, that the same playhouse is so neare the Church that the noyse of the drummes and trumpets will greatly disturbe and hinder both the ministers and parishioners in tyme of divine service and sermons. In tender consideracion whereof, as allso for that there hath not at any tyme heretofore bean used any common playhouse within the same precinct, but now that all players being banished by the Lord Mayor from playing within the Citie by reason of the great inconveniences and misrule that followeth them, they now thinke to plant them selves in liberties.

The petition was signed by twenty-six local inhabitants. Among them was the formidable and influential Elizabeth, Lady Russell, a friend of the Queen and sister-in-law of Lord Burghley, her chief minister. Even more ominous was the presence of the 2nd Lord Hunsdon's name on the petition. Sadly for the players, their influential patron had died at his residence at Somerset House on 23 July 1596. He was succeeded as their patron by his son, George Carey, so the company became known as Lord Hunsdon's Men. His mansion, Hunsdon House, was close to Blackfriars, so we are in the presence of what is now known as 'Nimbyism'.

In response the 'owners and players' of the Blackfriars Theatre petitioned the Privy Council, 'for permission to finish the reparations and alterations begun at their own expense'. The Privy Council supported the residents. It must have betokened a potential financial disaster for Burbage, who had laid out large amounts of money with little prospect of a return.

The incident had no lasting effect on relations between the company and its patron. Like his father, George Carey had a deep enthusiasm for the theatre. It is highly probable that it was the father or the son who built a playhouse in Tonbridge, where they were successive lords of the manor.[2] Doubtless a performance was *de rigueur* for the company during their occasional touring forays into the proximate county of Kent.

Further evidence of a connection between William Shakespeare and Francis Langley comes with curious and unexplained legal proceedings. That same November, Langley issued a writ of attachment against William Wayte and William Gardiner. The court could order such a writ if the appellant demonstrated fraud on the part of the defendant, or if it was shown that he was attempting to hide assets from the court. In other words, a prejudgment writ of attachment preserved the status quo pending a final resolution. It also provided a means of financial recovery for the plaintiff, so the business was about material matters. Normally, a plaintiff seeking such a writ had to post a surety bond worth up to twice the damages claimed.

William Gardiner's name was a byword for corruption and avarice. A property dealer and money-lender, he had cheated many of his clients, including his wife's relations. As a result of his nefarious activities he had acquired great wealth, which enabled him to boost his social status. He had acquired the lay rectorship of Ewell in Surrey but had failed to pay an adequate stipend to the parson, so the place was clergy-less. His record included menacing and violent behaviour, for which he had been briefly imprisoned. Nevertheless, he had become a Justice of the Peace for Southwark. It was surely his money, rather than his reputation, that had enabled him to become the High Sheriff of Surrey and Sussex in 1594/95.

William Wayte was Gardiner's stepson and an equally dubious character. In one legal action he had been described as a 'loose person of no reckoning or value, being wholly under the rule and commandment of the said Gardiner'. Thus it may well have been Gardiner who put him up to petitioning for sureties of the peace against William Shakespeare, Francis Langley, Dorothy Soer and Anne Lee, 'for fear of death'.

The pairing of the names of Shakespeare and Langley further implies that Lord Hunsdon's Men were performing at the Swan. What other connection could there be between the two men? Nor does the inclusion of the other names mean that there is necessarily any connection between them. Nor need the fact that Gardiner and Wayte were conspicuously villains mean that their behaviour was necessarily villainous on this occasion. It may well have been that Gardiner, as a magistrate, felt it necessary to emulate his colleagues in the City and crack down on the various activities taking place on Bankside. It could be that Dorothy Soer and Anne Lee participated in an entirely different form of entertainment than the theatre.

A Dutch visitor, Johannes de Witt, wrote an invaluable account in Latin in his diary of the newly-built and enchanting theatre scene when he visited London around 1596:

> There are four ampitheatres in London so beautiful that they are worth a visit, which are given different names from their different signs. In these theatres, a different play is offered to the public every day. The two more excellent of these are situated on the other side of the Thames, towards the South, and they are called the Rose and the Swan from their signboards. There are two other theatres outside the City towards the North, on the road that leads through the Episcopal Gate, called Bishopsgate in the vernacular. There is also a fifth, but of a different structure, intended for fights of animals, in which many bears, bulls and dogs of stupendous size are held in different cages and behind fences, which are kept for the fight to provide a most pleasant spectacle to the people. The most outstanding of all the theatres, however, is that whose sign is the swan ... as it holds 3,000 people. It is built out of flint stones stacked on top of each other (of which there is a great store in Britain), supported by wooden pillars, which, by their painted marble colour, could deceive even the most acute observers.

'As its form seems to bear the appearance of a Roman work, I have made a drawing of it,' wrote de Witt of the Swan Theatre. In fact, he drew what is probably the most important sketch made in the entire history of the theatre. The original is lost, but his friend Arend van Buchell made a copy of it in his commonplace book. It is the only known depiction of the interior of an Elizabethan theatre. Whereas de Witt was a skilled draughtsman, van Buchell was not. His drawing lacks perspective. The doors that he places at the back of the stage could only be used if the actors crawled through them on their hands and knees. Yet he purveys a clear idea of the mechanics of the Elizabethan theatre: the projecting stage; the 'theatre-in-the-round' with its intimate contact with the audience; the inner stage under a projecting roof; the area above that can be occupied by spectators if not required for Juliet's balcony or the walls of Harfleur; and the two inner doors mentioned in the stage directions to *A Midsummer Night's Dream*:

> Enter a FAIRY at one door and ROBIN GOODFELLOW [PUCK] at another.

## My Old Lad of the Castle

With the death of the 1st Baron Hunsdon, not only had the players lost a deeply valued friend, but his successor as Lord Chancellor, William Brooke, the 10th Lord Cobham, was to prove ineffective in their support, possibly because he was less influential than his predecessor. In any case he was probably ailing – he died just seven months later. He was certainly no Puritan. At one time he had had his own troop of actors under his patronage.

Certainly Cobham's accession to the office gave the City Fathers new energy in their campaign against the theatre. Thomas Nashe, writing to a friend later that year, complained that the players were 'piteously persecuted by the Lord Mayor and Aldermen, and however in their old Lord's time they thought their estate settled, it is now so uncertain that they cannot build upon it'.[3]

Cobham may have had a personal grievance against William Shakespeare and his company. It has been claimed that he was a descendant of Sir John Oldcastle, the name under which Shakespeare's most celebrated comic character made his first appearance, but in fact the relationship was tenuous. Cobham was descended from Joan Braybroke and her first husband, his great-great-great-grandfather, Sir Thomas Brooke, the 5th Lord Cobham. She was four times widowed, and her third husband was Sir John Oldcastle, whose fourth wife she was. As a result of this alliance, Oldcastle could assume the courtesy title of Lord Cobham.

The historic Oldcastle was a courtier of Henry V who had served the Crown with distinction during the Owain Glyndwr rebellion on the Welsh Marches and in Prince Hal's campaigns in France. He became a Lollard, however, a member of a millennialist faith that denied certain Catholic doctrines on similar grounds to those espoused by Protestants a century later. Lollards avowed that contemporary society was corrupt and unjust. The Second Coming of Christ would see the establishment of the Kingdom of God on Earth. It was the duty of the adherents to work to bring this about. Thus, Lollardism was an active political movement whose aim was the destruction of the status quo.

Oldcastle's adhesion to Lollardism led to allegations of heresy against him, but the King, mindful of his past services, used his influence to protect him. Oldcastle's response was to formulate a plot to seize him while he was on a visit to Eltham Palace. The plot was discovered, so Oldcastle went into open rebellion, waging a kind of guerrilla warfare on the Welsh borders. Almost certainly he was a party to the plot to assassinate the King on the eve of his famous expedition to France, which Shakespeare dramatises in *Henry V*. He was eventually captured and hanged for treason at Smithfield before his body was burnt as that of a heretic.

In an extraordinary rewriting of history, Oldcastle was to become a Protestant hero. His treason against the King was wiped from the record by such polemicists as William Tyndale, John Bale and John Foxe. Instead he was presented as a victim of Catholic tyranny.

That Shakespeare's original name for Falstaff was Oldcastle is beyond doubt. Prince Hal refers to him as 'My old lad of the castle' in *Henry IV, Part I* (I.2.40–1). It persists through to Part II, where a speech prefix escapes alteration in I.2.114. By then Cobham was probably dead. We do not know what force whipped up the controversy that caused Shakespeare (or his company) to change the name of his character. It was a name he had inherited from his main source: *The Famous Victories of Henry V*. In that play, Oldcastle is one of a bunch of dissolute ne'er-do-wells who are the companions of the young Prince Hal. It is tempting to speculate that Shakespeare could not resist having a pop at this Protestant icon (if that is not a contradiction in terms). Given his clear interest in history and his noted caution about offending the powers that be, it is difficult to conceive that he would not realise the significance of the name of Oldcastle and the reverence bestowed on it by the militant wing of Protestantism.

Some clue as to the source of the complaints about Shakespeare's use of the name is given by an Anglican divine, Dr Richard James, in a letter to Sir Harry Bourchier in 1625. It is attached to a manuscript he wrote entitled 'The Legend and Defence of ye noble Knight and Martyr Sir Jhon Oldcastle'. He is shaky on his knowledge of the plays – Falstaff does not appear in *Henry V* – and he follows the prevailing view of Oldcastle as a heroic victim of Catholic persecution.

> That in Shakespeare's first shewe of Harrie ye fift, ye person with which he undertook to playe a buffone was not Falstaffe, but Sr Jhon Oldcastle, and that offence beings worthily taken by personages descended from his title, as peradventure by manie others allso whoe ought to have him in honourable memorie, the poet was putt to make an ignorant shifte of abusing Sr Jhon Fastolphe, a man not inferior of vertue though not so famous in pietie as the other, whoe gave witnesse vnto the truth of our reformation with a constant and resolute martyrdom, vnto which he was pursued by the Priests, Bishops, Moncks and Friers of those dayes.

We may ponder why Shakespeare's exploitation of that name should arouse such fury when it had been employed in *The Famous Victories* without any apparent comment. The answer may be that Falstaff is such a consummate comical creation that the slight upon Oldcastle's memory could no longer go unnoticed. It should also be noted that among those offended were 'personages descended from his title'. Dr James writes of these in the plural. This may refer to the old Lord Cobham's successor, William Brooke, the 11th Lord Cobham; his brother, the Revd Sir George Brooke, the Prebendary of York; and, significantly their brother-in-law, the hugely influential Robert Cecil, who had married Frances Brooke in 1588. The 'manie others' to whom Dr James refers are undoubtedly those who revered Oldcastle as a proto-Protestant martyr. As his exposition demonstrates, the slur on the name of their hero was long remembered.

The name had to go. In its place, the name 'Falstaff' was substituted – either by Shakespeare himself, or by a member of the company, which possessed the copyright. The name is taken from that of a cowardly knight called Sir John Fastolf, who flees from the battlefield in *Henry VI, Part I*. It is subtly changed, which was perhaps just as well. The real Sir John's descendents were still living in Suffolk, but perhaps they were not theatregoers and never heard about this slight on their ancestor. While they were at it, the company clearly decided that it would be judicious to change the names of Russell and Harvey, characters who were inherited as Oldcastle's rowdy companions, but who survived in a scene direction in *Henry IV, Part II*. Both surnames were those of prominent courtiers.

Whatever else, there can be no doubt of the popularity of Shakespeare's great comic creation. He features prominently in the blurb to the quarto of 1598.

> The History of Henrie the fourth; with the battell at Shrewsburie betweene the King and Lord Henry Percy, surnamed Henrie Hotspur of the North. With the humorous conceits of Sir John Falstaffe.

It is likely that the second part of *Henry IV* was written to follow up the huge success of the first part. In the blurb to the quarto of 1600, Sir John's henchman joins him in the star billing.

> The second part of Henrie the fourth, continuing to his death, and coronation of Harrie the fift. With the humours of Iohn Falstaffe and swaggering Pistol.

A theatrical tradition picked up by two sources in the early eighteenth century indicates that the part was popular in high places. 'I know very well that it hath pleased one of the greatest queens that ever was in the world,' wrote John Dennis in the preface to his adaptation of *The Merry Wives of Windsor* of 1702. Five years later, Nicholas Rowe elaborated the story.

> She was so well pleas'd with the admirable Character of *Falstaff*, in the two Parts of *Henry* the fourth, that he commanded him to continue it for one Play more and to hew him in love. This is aid to be the occasion of his writing *The Merry Wives of* Wind or.

Eleven days after the death of Lord Cobham on 6 March 1596/97, George Carey was appointed as Lord Chamberlain, so the company reverted to its previous title. He was appointed a Knight of the Garter in that same year, so the play may be linked to that occasion. Prince Frederick of Mompelgard, the heir to the Duke of Würtemberg, had also been elevated to the Order, but could not be present. There are a number of references to the absence of German visitors in the text. It makes a pleasing story, but it doesn't quite fit the known facts. The Queen attended the Garter Feast at Whitehall Palace on 23 April, but it was not her custom to attend the Garter ceremony, which took place at Windsor in June. Of course, *Merry Wives* could have been presented at the feast, but surely everything about the play pleads for a Windsor setting. There are references to the Order of the Garter and St George's Chapel and to such local topography as Frogmore and Eton. Indeed it must be reckoned that references like those to the legend of the ghost of Herne the Hunter and his oak tree would not be grasped by a London audience but would be familiar to a courtly one in Windsor. John Taylor, the ubiquitous water poet, records the existence of a Garter Inn in the town in 1636, so the Host in *Merry Wives* is likely to be based on a real person.

The thought that the play was in some way bound up with the Garter ceremony is supported in the final scene where, in a speech reminiscent of the fairies blessing the bridal beds in *A Midsummer Night's Dream*, the pseudo-fairies of the *Merry Wives* bless Windsor Castle, the stalls of the Knights of the Garter and their motto.

> About, about;
> Search Windsor Castle, elves, within and out:
> Strew good luck, ouphes, on every sacred room:
> That it may stand till the perpetual doom,
> In state as wholesome as in state 'tis fit,
> Worthy the owner, and the owner it.
> The several chairs of order look you scour
> With juice of balm and every precious flower:
> Each fair instalment, coat, and several crest,
> With loyal blazon, evermore be blest!
> And nightly, meadow-fairies, look you sing,
> Like to the Garter's compass, in a ring:
> The expressure that it bears, green let it be,
> More fertile-fresh than all the field to see;
> And 'Honi soit qui mal y pense' write
> In emerald tufts, flowers purple, blue and white …

If the tradition picked up by Dennis is to be trusted, the play was written with great rapidity. The Queen 'was so eager to see it acted that she commanded it to be written in fourteen days'.

Another indication of the cult of Falstaff came in the summer of 1599 when the young Countess of Southampton, wife of Shakespeare's former patron, wrote to her husband from Place House, Titchfield.

> All the news I can send you that I thinke will make you merry is that I reade in a letter from London that Sir John Falstaffe is by mrs. dame pintpot made father of a godly millers thumb, a boye that's all heade and litel body – but this is a secret.

Who 'Falstaff' was in this instance is unknown. The Countess may be referring to the actor who played him. Edmond Malone claimed to have seen a paper associating John Heminges' name with the part, but, like so many items associated with that critic, it has disappeared. Certainly Heminges was the father of many children with the former widow Knell. It is likely that he owned an alehouse on Bankside next to the Globe Theatre[4] – hence the 'pintpot'? Yet the fact that the matter is treated as a piece of gossip indicates an air of illegitimacy. Did Will Kempe, surely the most likely Falstaff, beget a child by a tapstress. Who knows?

The issue of Oldcastle/Falstaff never quite went away. In 1603/04, Robert Persons, the indefatigable and prolific Jesuit polemicist, by now Rector of the English College in Rome, revived the issue in *A Treatise of the Three Conversions of England*, in which he described Oldcastle as 'a ruffian knight, as all England knoweth, and commonly brought in by comedians on their stage'. In 1611, the Puritan and cartographer John Speed delivered a riposte to these remarks in his *History of Great Britain*. He denounced the accusations against Oldcastle as 'taken from the *stage-plaiers*'. He describes scathingly Persons and Shakespeare, as 'this Papist and his Poet ... of like conscience for lies, the one ever faining, and the other ever falsifying the truth'.

## Injurious Imposters

Having defined, at least in part, the company that acted Shakespeare's plays, it is time to ponder who wrote them. This is not to pursue the weird ideas of those who consider that the Stratford man was not the author of the works that bear his name. That is incontrovertible. The question is that, since specific parts were written with specific actors in mind, whether they had, over the course of a production, input into the script. Despite Hamlet's injunction to the contrary, it is likely that the ad-libbing of such noted clowns as Kempe and Armin would find its way into the script? The verdict may depend on the view taken of the various texts of Shakespeare that were published in his era. Twenty-one of his plays were published in quarto in over seventy editions before 1642. Six of these are classified as 'bad quartos' – i.e. published in pirate editions by stationers who wished to cash in on Shakespeare's popularity. It has been suggested that the bad quartos were reproduced from memory by small-part actors who had been bribed to recount their parts to the publisher. Heminges and Condell allude to this kind of practice in their preface to the First Folio of 1623.

> You were abus'd with diverse stoine [stolen] and surreptitious copies, maimed and deformed by the stealthes of injurious imposters, that expos'd them, euen those are now offered to your view cur'd, and perfect of their limbes, and all the rest, absolute in their number as he conceived the[m].

Undoubtedly the plays changed in performance. There is evidence that Shakespeare himself revised his plays. Indeed the variant texts of the quartos and the First Folio may be cited as indicators of this. When *Loves Labour's Lost* was first published in quarto in 1598 by the bookseller Cuthbert Burby, his title page states that the play was 'newly corrected and augmented by W. Shakespeare'.

Further evidence that the text changed in performance, sometimes by accretions from the actors, sometimes at the hand of the author himself, comes in Frances Meres' noted list of 1598. Among the plays that he accredits to Shakespeare is the mysterious *Love's Labour's Won*, in contrast to *Love's Labour's Lost*, which is also on the list. It may be a sequel to the latter play. It was long suggested that it was an alternative title for *The Taming of the Shrew*, but in 1953 Solomon Pottesman, an antiquarian book-dealer, discovered the stock list of Christopher Hunt, a stationer, for 1603. It had been used as part of the binding for a volume of sermons. The document lists copies of the quartos of *The Merchant of Venice*, *The Taming of a Shrew*, *Love's Labour's Lost* and *Love's Labour's Won* on his shelves. So the play existed.

This may well be an earlier version of a play that is in the canon, but which one? Meres' list is not comprehensive. He does not include the three parts of *Henry VI* or *The Taming of the Shrew*. Nor are *Twelfth Night* and *Much Ado About Nothing* on his list.

Since Leslie Hotson discovered in the papers of the Duke of Northumberland a record of the entertainment of the Muscovite ambassador and an Italian nobleman, Virginio Orsini, the Duke of Bracciano, at court on 6 January 1601/02 – Twelfth Night – there has been something of a consensus that it was on this occasion that the play was first performed. It is suggested that the name of an important character in the play – Orsino – was incorporated in honour of the Duke. If so, it was an odd gesture. Like most dukes, Orsini was well connected – his mother (who had been murdered by his father) was a member of the powerful Medici family, so he was related by marriage to the French royal house. The various branches of his father's family were among the most celebrated in Italy, but he was not particularly distinguished in his own right. Although as a lover of music, he shared one thing with his near namesake. He had been the patron of Luca Marenzio, the renowned composer of madrigals, who exercised much influence on contemporary English music.

The chief guest that evening was not Orsini, but the representative of Tsar Boris Gudenov, Grigory Ivanavich Milulin. The English government was keen to extend trade and so 'it was ordered that the Embassador for the mershants of Muscovia should in confirming the League dine or eate Bread and Salt [the traditional way of confirming a treaty] with the Queenes Maiestie'.[5]

The Queen had requested the Master of the Revels 'to make choyse of the play that shalbe best furnished with rich apparell, have greate variety and change of musicke and daunces, and of a subject that may be most pleasing to her majestie'.[6]

*Twelfth Night* does not feature dances within its text. Nor is it certain that the Lord Chamberlain's Men performed at court on that night. The earliest-known performance of the play took place at Middle Temple Hall, one of the Inns of Court, on Candlemas Night, 2 February 1602. John Manningham, a young lawyer, was present and recorded in his diary that

> At our feast we had a play called 'Twelfth Night. Or What You Will' much like 'The Comedy of Errors' or 'Maeaechmi' in Plautus, but most like and near to that in Italian called 'Ingami'. A good practice in it to make the steward believe that his lady-widow was in love with him, by counterfeiting a letter as from his lady, in general term telling him what she liked best in him and prescribing his gesture in smiling, his apparel, etc. and then, when he came to practice, making him believe they took him for mad.

Whether it was the Lord Chamberlain's Men or the students of the Middle Temple who presented the play is unclear from Manningham's remarks. We recall that it was the 'Gentlemen of the Temple' who first acted *Gorboduc* in 1562. There was a long and continuing tradition of such dramatic activity. In 1613, the Gentlemen presented an elaborate masque at court as part of the celebrations of the wedding of the King's daughter.

Whoever performed the play, Manningham enjoyed it immensely, which makes it curious that it never appeared in quarto. An explanation for this may be that the popular favourite, Will Kempe, was no longer with the company. The Burbages had included him as a sharer in the scheme to build the Globe Theatre early in 1599. At some point after that, he left the Lord Chamberlain's Men. The part of Sir Toby Belch is very much in the genre that Shakespeare wrote for Kempe.

Perhaps the most curious feature in the de Witt drawing of the Swan Theatre is the little cameo sketch of three actors on the stage. Two appear to be playing women's parts. The third is an affected figure making a low obeisance. The scene shouts out '*Twelfth* Night, Act III, Scene 4'. Olivia is seated as befits the mistress of the house: behind her stands Maria, as befits a maid. It is Malvolio who is making the exaggerated bow. His dress appears extravagant and he carries his steward's staff of office. If indeed the play was the one which de Witt saw, perhaps in a form that was subsequently revised, the departure of the company's leading comedian may have had an affect on its repertoire.

As well as Hotson's hypothesis, Maria's line in Act III has been cited in support of a later dating: 'He does smile his face into more lines than is the new map with the augmentation of the Indies.' The allusion is specific. It is generally thought that it refers to the map published in Richard Hakluyt's monumental work *The Principal Navigations, Voiages, Traffiques and Discoueries of the English Nation*, between 1599 and 1600, so the map was not exactly 'new' when Manningham saw the performance. Even then, it had been in existence for several years. It was based on the terrestrial globe created by Emery Molyneux of Lambeth in 1592. As the first globe to be produced in England, it created a sensation. Molyneux had sailed with Drake on his circumnavigation of the world. On his terrestrial globe he tracked that voyage and Thomas Cavendish's subsequent circumnavigation in red and blue lines respectively. Cavendish was the fifth sailor to achieve this feat, but the first to set out to do so. His voyage followed the same pattern as Drake's, plundering Spanish treasure ships and towns in the Americas before fleeing home across the Pacific. There can be little doubt that he discussed his voyage with Molyneux on his return. The blue line shows that he passed by the Philippines as he plotted his course through the East Indies.

Molyneux presented both his terrestrial globe and the celestial one he had created to the Queen at Greenwich in July 1592. In the words of the intriguingly named Italian artist and courtier Petruccio Ulbaldini, 'he gave her the globe so that she could see at a glance how much of the world she could control by means of her naval forces'.

The globes were expensive: the largest ones cost up to £20, but it was a price that those who could afford them were prepared to pay. Among those acquiring one were Sir Walter Raleigh; Thomas Bodley for his famed Oxford library; the Warden of All Souls, Oxford; Shrewsbury School library; and Robert Cecil. The one the Middle Temple acquired was presumably around when Manningham saw *Twelfth Night*. Smaller versions were available as navigational aids for ships at sea and Thomas Cavendish probably acquired one for his ill-fated second voyage in 1591.

Shakespeare was familiar with Molyneux's creations. In *The Comedy of Errors*, Dromio of Syracuse compares a kitchen maid to one of his globes.

No longer from head to foot than from hip to hip: she is spherical, like a globe; I could find countries in her.

Shakespeare was to return to 'country matters' in *Hamlet*.

Molyneux had his gores (the flat map segments which were attached to the globes) printed by the Flemish cartographer Jodacus Hauduis, who was based in London until 1593. Several works were published describing his globes and providing guides on their use. Molyneux himself wrote a treatise, now lost, *The Globes Celestial and Terrestrial Set Forth in Plano*, which his patron, William Sanderson, published in 1592. In the same year, Thomas Hood, a mathematician who had written a 1590 work on the use of celestial globes, published *The Vse of Both the Globes, Celestiall and Terrestriall*. In 1594, a description of the globes was included in *Blundeville His Exercises*, a book on astronomy and navigation by Thomas Blundeville. That year, a further commentary on the use of the globes by Robert Hues – *Tractatus de Globis et Eorum Ucu* – appeared. It went into at least thirteen printings and was translated from the Latin into Dutch, English and French. By the time of the appearance of the second edition of Hakluyt's *Voiages*, the map of the Indies was hardly 'new'.

A few lines of *Twelfth Night* appeared in print before the play was revealed to posterity in the First Folio of 1623. The words and music of the beautiful song 'O Mistress Mine' were included in a miscellany of settings by the composer Thomas Morley, which appeared in 1599, the only part of the play to appear in print in Shakespeare's lifetime. It is possible that the words of the song are by another author, but they are characteristically Shakespearean. If this is the case, it is another indication that *Twelfth Night* was written in the 1590s.

So, even if *Twelfth Night* is not *Love's Labour's Won* (and the activities of Viola certainly fit that title), it could be the play that de Witt saw at the Swan that afternoon. If so, it may have set a theatrical convention. Daniel Maclise's painting *Scene from 'Twelfth Night' ('Malvolio and the Countess')*, first exhibited in 1840, shows a very similar setting to de Witt's sketch. Olivia is seated with Maria behind her as Malvolio, staff of office in hand, performs a grotesque bow. If this was the play that de Witt saw, the gulling of Malvolio stuck in his memory so vividly that he sketched it. The play's popularity was enduring. In valedictory lines to Shakespeare, Leonard Digges was to link its success with that of *Much Ado*.

> ... let but Beatrice
> And Benedicke be scene, loe, in a trice
> The cockpit, galleries, boxes, all are full
> To hear Malvoglio, that crosse garter'd gull.

The play was certainly performed at court at Eastertide in 1618 and at Candlemass in 1623. At the Restoration, when the theatres reopened, Samuel Pepys deemed Sir William Davenant's adaptation, with the leading actor Thomas Betterton playing Sir Toby Belch, 'a silly play', but he saw it three times between September 1661 and January 1669.

It is a mystery why some plays appeared in quarto and others did not. If indeed it was a version of *Twelfth Night* that de Witt saw in 1596, we can only speculate why it did not make a bigger impact at the time. Maybe it did – and there was another reason it did not progress as it might have done. Around a year after de Witt made his sketch, the Earl of Pembroke's Men presented a new play at the Swan entitled *The Isle of Dogs*, which caused such outrage among influential circles that it led to the closing of the theatres.

Another candidate for both *Love's Labour's Won* and the Twelfth Night entertainment is *Much Ado About Nothing*. It is a play that bears clear evidence of revision. The Hero/Claudio passages are written in a blank verse that relates to the earlier works, while the Beatrice/Benedick passages are in a more sophisticated prose. There is a 'ghost character', who appears for no apparent purpose without saying a word. Innogen, wife of Leonato, makes brief appearances in Act I, Scene 1 and Act II, Scene 2. She may well have had a more significant role in an earlier setting.

# 12

# A Man of Wealth, 1594–99

According to John Aubrey, it was William Shakespeare's custom to go into 'his native country once a year'. It has to be conceded that his domestic arrangements were decidedly unusual. There is no evidence that his wife and children ever joined him in London. On the other hand, there is no reason to doubt Aubrey's statement. It was in Stratford that he made the investments of his newborn wealth and it was to Stratford and his family that he was ultimately to return. Perhaps it was on his visits to Stratford, away from the bustle of the great city, that he wrote the two plays that he regularly turned out each year for his company.

The summer was the obvious time for his sojourn. He may have been present at the wedding, in 1594, of the widower Alexander Aspinall to the widow Anne Shaw. Aspinall had been schoolmaster of the King's New School since 1582. He was described by Shakespeare's cousin, John Greene, as 'great Philip Macedon'. Anne Shaw was the widow of Ralph Shaw, the wool-driver in Henley Street, who had died two years before. We are back in a close-knit world. Shakespeare's father had compiled the inventory of Ralph Shaw's goods after his death. His son, Julian Shaw, would witness William Shakespeare's will. In 1629, Sir Francis Fane noted in his commonplace book:

> The gift is small
> The will is all,
> A shey ander Aspinall.
> Shaxpaire upon a peire of gloves that mas[t]er sent to his mistress,

As we have seen, the play on 'will' is one of Shakespeare's favourite double entendres. We may indulge the fancy that the gloves were bought in John Shakespeare's shop.

Stratford was sharing the nation's troubles. Shakespeare was probably in London at the time of the great fire which occurred in the town on 22 September 1594. It may have begun in one of the fifty or more malt-houses that constituted the town's most important economic activity. Elizabethan Stratford was an elaborate incendiary device of wattle and daub, open hearths, thatch and timber. The fire devastated Wood Street and the west sides of Chapel Street, High Street and Henley Street, where his wife, children and kinsfolk must have watched with great anxiety as the great hooks provided by the Corporation were used to pull down the blazing buildings opposite. Almost a year to the day later – on 21 September 1595 – another great fire destroyed an entire block in the middle of the town, bounded by Sheep Street, High Street and Bridge Street. The damage from the two great fires was estimated to have cost £12,000.[1] Puritan preachers made much of the fact that both fires broke out on a Sunday. 'That which is most strange,' wrote Thomas Beard in *The Theatre of God's Judgements*, 'a whole town hath bene twice burnt for the breach of the sabboth by the inhabitants.'

The Corporation was more concerned with temporal practicalities. In September 1594, eight emissaries were appointed to raise money around the shires for the relief and rebuilding of their town. They did well. Thomas Barber raised £21 8s 9d in Worcestershire. William Parsons collected £10 11s 2d in Gloucestershire, and Abraham Sturley £4 3s 8d in 'Darby' and 55s 8d in 'Abrington'. Most successful of all was Richard Quiney, who raised £22 5s 3d in Northamptonshire and, with Shakespeare's friend, Hamnet Sadler, the huge sum of £75 6s 0d in Norfolk and Suffolk.

Increasing penury and high inflation produced a rising crime rate and the diminution of respect for authority epitomised by Elizabeth Wheeler, *alias* Rundles, who was presented before the Bawdy Court in 1595 'for continually brawling and not attending church'. Her response was graphic. 'Goodes woundes,' she exploded. 'A plague a God on you all. A fart of ons ars for you.' 'Excommunicated,' the record notes tersely.

The fires were only part of Stratford's troubles. The same famine that had caused the great riots in London was having its effects. Shakespeare may have been there during the melancholy June of 1595. On 3 October, the Corporation forbade innkeepers to brew and bake and ordered them to use the public brewers and bakers. Milk was imported from 'the villadges about us ... to the relieving of our children and others'.

William Shakespeare's reputation in Stratford as a man of wealth is revealed in a note written by the Revd John Ward, the Vicar of Stratford after the Restoration. 'Hee spent att ye Rate of 1,000£ a year as I have heard.' Ward's informant was probably Shakespeare's daughter Judith. The sum seems absurdly high, but if it is reckoned to refer to the man's enterprises rather than his personal spending, it falls into perspective. Shakespeare was a major shareholder in the top theatrical company. There is no doubt that such a role could make a man as rich as Croesus.

In *The Return from Parnassus*, a play written and performed at St John's College, Cambridge, around 1600, an undergraduate is amazed by the way the actors have risen from near vagrancy to wealth and gentility.

> England affords those glorious vagabonds
> That carried earst their fardels on their backes.

Courses to ride on through the gazing streetes,
Sooping it in their glaring Satten sutes,
And pages to attend their Maisterships:
With mouthing words that better wits have framed,
They purchase lands, and now Esquiers are made.

Another indication of the aspirations of the actors to higher social status is given in an anonymous humorous work called *Ratseis Ghost*, published in 1605. A highwayman called Thomas Ratsey encounters a group of strolling players in the provinces and pays them to perform for him. He advises the leader to go to London to make his fortune, telling him, 'When thou feelest thy purse well-lined, buy thee some place of lordship in the country, that, growing weary of playing, thy money may bring thee dignity and reputation.' 'I have heard indeed of some that have gone to London very meanly,' the player replies, 'who have in time become exceedingly wealthy.' That Shakespeare was by no means the only actor to whom these words could apply shows the sagacity of the advice. James Burbage could survive the apparent failure of his huge investment in the Blackfriars scheme. As befits those moving upwards in the world, a number of actors acquired second homes upriver in what was then the country: Augustine Phillips and John Heminges bought properties at Mortlake and Henry Condell one at Fulham. Most successful of all was Edward Alleyn, who possessed the largest business empire of anyone associated with the theatre. He retired from the stage in 1597 at the age of thirty, probably to concentrate on his enterprises. In 1605 he bought the Manor of Dulwich for the huge sum of £35,000.

The handsome earnings of Shakespeare's prolific genius were, apart from necessary professional investments, ploughed back into the Stratford area. The humiliations of the austere years were to be wiped out and the family prestige restored. Thus John Shakespeare resurrected a twenty-year-old claim to a coat of arms, which was granted on 20 October 1596. The very high cost – 30 guineas – of the petition to the College of Heralds would have been well beyond his means. The account must have been settled by his affluent eldest son. The main device on the coat of arms, a spear of steeled argent, was a clear pun on the family name. The motto *Non Sanz Droit* – 'not without right' – seems defensive and was perhaps parodied by Ben Jonson as 'Not Without Mustard'. The message is clear. This is not an award to an upstart, but to a man who had held high office, married 'a daughter and heyre of Arden' and claimed an ancestor rewarded by Henry VII. In 1602, after a personality clash, the York Herald, Peter Brooke, accused the Garter King-at-Arms, Sir William Dethick, of elevating base-born persons, including John Shakespeare. A successful defence was made of the Shakespeare claim by Dethick and the Clarenceaux King-at-Arms, William Camden, who knew both the London and Stratford ends of William Shakespeare's life.

Subsequently, John Shakespeare applied to pair his crest with that of his wife's family. The heralds sketched the arms of the Ardens of Park Hall, but later substituted those of a junior branch of the family. The application was never pursued. The enthusiasm of the Shakespeares for the project was probably diminished by domestic grief. Hamnet Shakespeare, aged eleven, the only direct heir to the family name, was buried at Holy Trinity on 11 August 1596. Shakespeare's company was in Kent, but its chief dramatist was probably in Stratford, working on his adaptation of *The Troublesome Reign of King John*. Thus he may have been in the sad group that carried the little body to the church. If any speech in his plays reflects his own feelings, it is surely that in *King John* when the stricken Constance mourns the loss of her son.

> Grief fills the room up of my absent child,
> Lies in his bed, walks up and down with me,
> Puts on his pretty looks, repeats his words,
> Remembers me of all his gracious parts,
> Stuffs out his vacant garments with his form.
> Then I have reason to be fond of grief.

## 'A Praty House of Brick and Tymbre'

On 4 May 1597, Shakespeare bought New Place, 'a praty house of brick and tymbre' – whose elegance had been noted by John Leland – from William Underhill, a recusant, for £60 in silver. A few weeks later, this 'subtle, covetous and crafty man' was poisoned by his eldest son, Fulke. Although conspicuously crazy and a minor he was executed for the murder at Warwick. New Place was Stratford's first all-brick dwelling. It was entirely rebuilt before 1702 by Sir Hugh Clopton. George Vertue, the engraver and antiquary, visited Stratford in 1737 and talked with Shakespeare Hart, then sixty-seven, great-grandson of the poet's sister. He remembered the house well and Vertue made a sketch from his description which shows a fine three-storey, half-timbered building, with five gables and two entrances. Through the Chapel Street entrance, 'before the House itself', there was a little grass-covered courtyard.

Shakespeare secured this fine property cheaply because it was in a state of 'great ruyne and decay and unrepayred'. Extensive work was necessary and 'Mr Shaxpere' sold the Corporation 'a lod of ston' in 1598. His concerns creep into his current play, *Henry IV, Part II*.

> When we mean to build
> We first survey the plot, then draw the model
> And when we see the figure of the house,
> Then we must rate the cost of the erection.

The implications of buying the second-biggest house in Stratford were considerable. A household would have to be created that befitted a man of standing and wealth. Repairs and improvements were undertaken. The Great Garden of New Place was brought into order. A persistent local tradition maintained that the poet planted a mulberry tree which was cut down to the fury of the inhabitants in 1758. Probably like Angelo he had a 'garden circummured with brick, whose Western side is with a vineyard back'd'. In 1631 Sir Thomas Temple of Wolverton instructed a servant to ride to Stratford and 'desire Mr. Hall Phiscon[2] ... to suffer Harry Rose or any better in skill to gather ... 2 or 3 of the fairest of these budes or shutes of last yeares vines'.

A delightful picture of Shakespeare in the heart of his family is found in a note from Sir Hugh Clopton, who lived at New Place at the beginning of the eighteenth century.

> Several little epigrams on familiar subjects were found upon the glass of the house windows, some of which were written by Shakespeare and many of them the product of his own children's brain.[3]

Anne Shakespeare ran her own household for the first time at New Place, This anonymous woman emerges fleetingly from the shadows in the will of Thomas Whittington, the Hathaway shepherd at Shottery, who in 1601 left 'unto the poore people of Straford xls that is in the hand of Anne Shaxpere Wyf unto Mr William Shaxpere and is due debt to me'. Was the poet's spouse a scrounger from her brother's servants? More likely she was a trusted holder of savings.

Domestic chores would increase at New Place, although the retinue of servants living around the courtyard would diminish the burdens. Anne would be skilled in the arts of weaving and brewing. Inventories John Shakespeare made of the goods of two deceased neighbours show that equipment for these tasks was standard in Stratford households. Ralph Shaw's home contained barrels, a sieve, a spinning wheel, four pairs of wool cards, 20 quarters of malt, pails and looms. Henry Field possessed six beer barrels, five looms, four pails, two skips, one outing vat and three malt shovels. 'The chief trade here,' observed Daniel Defoe a century later, 'is in corn and malt of which last it makes in great abundance.'

This abundance was not apparent when Shakespeare bought New Place. In that year, the townsmen petitioned the local justices to impose the Privy Council's 'Book of Orders' against hoarding. A survey of barley held by the citizens was ordered. At New Place the Shakespeares held 18 quarters, a standard household quantity. A petition to the Queen stressed the hardship caused by the prohibition on household malting, 'in that oure town hath no other especiall trade havinge thereby onlye tyme beyonde mans memorye lyved by exersysing the same, our houses fitted to no other uses, manye servantes amonge us hyered only to that purpose.'[4] Alderman Abraham Sturley noted 'growing malcontent' against hoarders. 'God send my Earl of Essex down to see them hanged at their own doors,' he wrote vehemently: Elizabeth's ill-starred favourite had sealed his reputation as a national hero in the previous year when he commanded the English land forces in a spectacular and hugely successful raid on the Spanish port of

Cadiz. The Earl of Southampton was among the gallants who accompanied him. In 1597, he finally obeyed the poet's injunction when he impregnated Elizabeth Vernon, one of the Queen's ladies-in-waiting. The couple were married on 30 August but they encountered the Queen's wrath and were both briefly incarcerated in the Fleet Prison.

Characteristically, Essex threw away the huge credit he had obtained in the year after the Cadiz raid, in the 'Islands Voyage', an expedition to the Azores intended to capture the Spanish treasure fleet. It ended in disaster and acrimony in which he attempted to arraign his second-in-command, Sir Walter Raleigh, on capital charges. Philip II attempted to take advantage of England's lack of preparedness to send a second Armada. Fortunately for the nation, it shared the fate of the first, storms scattering it in the Channel. The Queen was again furious with the erratic behaviour of her errant favourite.

Sturley had tried to enlist the aid of the lord of the manor, that fratricidal heir, Sir Edward Greville, in his cause. On 24 January 1596/97, he wrote to Richard Quiney:

> Theare might bi Sir Ed. some meanes made to the knightes of the Parliament for an ease and discharge of such taxes and subsides wherewith our town is like to be charged and I assure u I am in great feare and doubte bi no means able to paie. Sir Ed. Grev. is gonne to Brestowe.

Relations between the Corporation and Greville were good at this time, exemplified by a dinner given for him at Richard Quiney's house in 1596/97. Lady Greville was entertained in 1597 and amity appeared compounded at a meeting on 3 November when Sir Edward agreed to support an application for a new charter. Sturley wrote to Quiney that Sir Edward 'saith we shall not be at any fault for money for procuring the cause, for himself will procure it and lay it down for the time'. Yet Sturley had his misgivings. In considering the financial gains to be expected from the new charter, he suggested that half should be offered to Sir Edward, 'lest he shall thinke it to good for us and procure it for himself, as he served us last time'.

The 'last time' had followed the death of the Earl of Warwick in 1590. The Corporation petitioned for the right to appoint the schoolmaster and vicar, but Greville moved faster and secured the lordship of the manor. A deep antagonism between Quiney and Greville perhaps dated from this incident. In 1592, Greville exercised his right of veto over the appointment of Quiney as Bailiff. The Corporation lobbied Sir Fulke Greville at Warwick. On 5 October he wrote to his 'Cosen Greville … If the cause of your refusal be for any wante of partes beseeking that place in the man himself, he is desirous to satisfie you in all objections.' Sir Fulke knew the volatile nature of his kinsman, for he added, 'In the meane tyme yor yeelding at this present to my request can no waie prejudice yor right and I hope yew shall have no cause to seek it violentlie of them.'

In a letter to his fellow alderman and brother-in-law, Richard Quiney, written to him in London in 1598, telling of the town's disasters, Abraham Sturley remarked that

> our countriman Mr. Shakspear is willing to disburse some moneys upon some od yardelande or other att Shotterie or neare about us; he thinketh it a very fitt patterne to move him to deale in the matter of our Tithes. By the instructions u can give him thereof we think it a faire marke for him to shoot att.

Shakespeare was not moved to fire an arrow on this occasion. Quiney took advantage of this burgeoning wealth when he ran short of money during his visit to London. He was there on important Corporation business – to seek to persuade the Privy Council to renegotiate the town's charter and to crave a reduction in the taxes and subsidies that 'the knights in Parliament had just on the grounds of the hardships suffered by the town'. Such was the depth of the depression that the Corporation placed its treasures in pawn with John Combe, a local money-lender. 'Your cousin Sir Combe holds the silver and gold plate,' wrote Sturley to Richard Quiney in 1598. There was one man in the City to whom an impecunious Stratfordian might turn. He wrote 'ffrom the Bell in Carter Lane the 25 October 1598' requesting the considerable loan of £30 from 'my Loveinge good ffrend & contryman Mr. Wm. Shackespere'. 'I am bold to ask of yow, as of a ffrende,' he wrote, 'craveinge yowr helpe with xxx*li* vppon Mr. Bushells and my securytee, or Mr. Myttons with me ...' Richard Myton and Thomas Bushell were agents of Edward Greville, so relations were good at this time. 'Yow shall ffrende me much in helping me out of all the debettes I owe in London,' adds Quiney. 'I thanke god & much quiet in my mynde ... I commit thys to your care & hope of your helpe. I fear I shall nott be backe thys night ffrom the Courts. Haste. The Lord be with you and with us all amen.'[5]

Doubtless the loan was to pay off the officials whom Quiney had dealt with in his pursuit of Stratford's interests. He was to stay in the capital for four months. He cannot have expected too much in the way of expenses from the burgesses he was seeking to represent. It would appear that he got his loan from Shakespeare. The letter was discovered by Edmond Malone in a bundle of papers in a cupboard in the Guildhall at Stratford. Fortunately, this, the only extant letter addressed to Shakespeare, escaped the fate of other documents that came into the critic's possession. It is probably a copy of the one actually sent. Since it mentions named sureties, it was important that a precise record be kept. In fact, Quiney's mission was a success. On 27 January, a warrant was signed by Sir John Fortescue, the Chancellor of the Exchequer, releasing 'the ancient borough' from the payment of taxes on the 'reasonable and conscionable' grounds of the devastating fires.[6] The Exchequer reimbursed Quiney's expenses in London, so Shakespeare would have got his money back. It is gratifying that just six years after his father was named as absenting himself from church 'for feare of processes', the son should be instrumental in the process of securing Stratford's well-being.

Abraham Sturley's fears about the future conduct of Sir Edward Greville were fully justified. After 1598 things worsened as he asserted his supposed privileges with violence. He claimed the right to enclose the riverside common known as the Bancroft and sent his men there to dig ditches and build fences in January, 1600/01. Quiney organised the Stratfordians to destroy the works. A legal action by Greville, in which the great jurist Sir Edward Cocke represented the Corporation, got nowhere. Quiney was defiantly re-elected as Bailiff in September. He worked assiduously against Greville's interest, visiting the Bishop of Worcester with Shakespeare's cousin, Thomas Greene, to enlist his aid in withstanding unjust inroads into the town's liberties. Greville, believing 'we shuld wynne it by the sworde', sent his rowdy followers to make trouble in Stratford taverns.

> Ther came some of them whoe beinge drunke fell to brawelinge in ther hosts howse ... and drew ther daggers uppon the hosts: at a faier tyme the Baileefs being late abroade to see the towne in order and comminge by in yt Hurley Burley came into the howse and commanded the peace to be kept butt colde nott prevayle and in hys endevor to stifle the brawle had hys heade grevously broken by one of hys [Greville's] men whom neither hym self [Greville] punished nor wolde suffer to be punished but with a shewe to turn them awaye and enterteyned agayne.

Quiney did not live out the month. On 31 May 1602, the 'Baily of Stretforde' was buried, the only one to die in office. Greville's triumph was brief. He lost his estates through speculations during the next reign and died in poverty.

During Quiney's ill-fated bailiwick he compiled a list of senior and respected citizens who could vouch for the borough's historic rights. It included the name of John Shakespeare, who, according to an anecdote of his old age, was still to be found in his glover's shop, where Thomas Plume, writing half a century later, claimed Sir John Mennis saw him, 'a merry-cheeked old man – that said – Will was a good honest fellow, but that he durst have cracked a jest with him at any time'. Sir John was only two when John Shakespeare died. Perhaps the anecdote refers to an elder brother or perhaps he heard it from someone else.

If Richard Quiney intended to use John Shakespeare's knowledge, he was disappointed. On 8 September 1601, the old man was buried at Holy Trinity. His widow survived him by seven years. The property we know as 'The Birthplace' passed to his eldest son. William's sister Joan, wife of William Hart, a Stratford hatter, continued to live in the western half until her death in 1646. The eastern half was leased to Lewis Hiccox and became a hostelry, The Swan and Maidenhead, which was much frequented by drovers on market days. It is a curious thought that William Shakespeare owned a pub.

It was probably the same Lewis Hiccox who was the tenant, together with his brother, Thomas, of land at Old Stratford to the east of the borough. On 1 May 1602, William Shakespeare bought four 'yardlands' (107 acres of land and 20 of pasture) from two wealthy Stratfordians, John Combe and his nephew William, for the impressive sum of £320. The transaction was witnessed by five neighbours, including Anthony and John Nash, who lived next door to New Place. William must have been in London at the time, because it was his brother Gilbert who took possession on his behalf.

In the midst of Stratford's troubles, William Shakespeare was regarded as something of a local milch cow. At the time of his son Richard's sojourn in London, Adrian Quiney appears to have written to him suggesting that if he had any surplus funds left from Shakespeare's loan, they might be invested in buying knitted stockings in Evesham to sell in their shop.[6] The poet was now determined to fire a quiver of arrows in the cause of land acquisition. Five months after the Combe purchase, he expanded his holding at New Place by purchasing a garden and cottage on Chapel Lane from the dowager Countess of Warwick.

The confident face of Puritanism was encroaching on Stratford as surely as it was advancing elsewhere. When Abraham Sturley was Bailiff in 1596, he paid four companies of players and 'a show of the City of Norwich', but in 1603 the Corporation, oblivious to Hamlet's strictures against the players' ill-report, banned plays and interludes from its property 'upon payne that whatsoever of the Baylief, Alderman and Burgisses of this boroughe shall gyve on license thereunto shall forfeyte for everie offense 10s'.

The leading Puritan and architect of this ban was Daniel Baker, a High Street mercer who dominated the town's councils for the next forty years. He fulfilled the cliché of his kind, combining a strict public morality with an irrepressible sensuality. A widower, he was presented before the Bawdy Court in 1606 on a charge of sexual incontinence. He failed to appear, but Anne Ward admitted that 'Mr Daniel Baker is the true and undoubted father of the child with which she has been pregnant', saying that he had promised to marry her. She was ordered to make public penance in a white sheet. Baker was excommunicated for non-appearance. He appeared three weeks later and made his denials, but admitted that there was public infamy about the matter. He was ordered to 'purge' himself (make a formal confession before the minister) with six others about whom similar rumours were circulating. When he failed to do so, he was pronounced guilty, but may have escaped public humiliation by paying a fine.

## Honey-Tongued Shakespeare

It is easy to forget that Shakespeare was only thirty-two at Hamnet's death. In London he was a noted figure and the tributes flowing to him mark the start of the enduring cult of Bardolatry. To John Weever, in his *Epigrams in the Oldest Art and Newest Fashion*, published in 1599, he was 'honey-tongued Shakespeare', while Richard Barnfield wrote of his name being in 'Fame's immortal book'. Even more adulatory was Francis Mere's declaration that 'the Muses would speak Shakespeare's fine-filed phrase, if they could speak English'. It is impossible not to be amazed at his phenomenal energy in this period. The organising of his ventures in Stratford – a three-day journey from his professional life in London – may be regarded as a job in itself. He not only wrote the plays, he also acted in them and in those of others. 'The players often mention it as an honour to Shakespeare that in his writing; whatsoever he penned, he never blotted out a line,' said Ben Jonson, although he added, 'My answer hath been, "Would he had blotted a thousand."' The pace of the writing made for a lack of continuity. Mistress Quickly is one of the few characters who appears in all four 'Falstaff' plays, but she is not the same character in all of them. In *Henry IV, Part I*, she is hostess of the Eastcheap Tavern and plays a minor role. She apparently has a husband. In *Part II* she is still the hostess, but Master Quickly has been subsumed. She complains that Falstaff owes her vast sums of money and has welched on his promise to marry her. She has become the mistress of what will be known, decades later, as the malapropism. Her Christian name is revealed to be Dorothy, In the *Merry Wives*, she has decamped to Windsor to become Dr Caius' housekeeper, while in *Henry V* she is betrothed to Corporal Nym but marries Pistol. Later in the play he reveals that she has died 'of malady of France', a euphemism for syphilis. Her Christian name is now Nell.

If imitation be the sincerest form of flattery, then William Shakespeare was indeed flattered. From the mid-1590s, stationers attached his initials to published plays that were clearly not by him. Of course, there were others with the same initials, but the ploy was obvious: to persuade people to buy the volumes under the impression that they were by the popular dramatist, but nowhere on the frontispiece does it actually say so. *Locrine*, a play about the two Trojans who in mythology founded London, was so attributed in 1595, as was *Thomas Lord Cromwell* in 1602.

Like Joseph at the court of Pharaoh, William Shakespeare's success drew his brethren to his side. In Trinity Term 1597, 'Gilbert Shackspere' of St Bride's, haberdasher, stood surety in the Queen's Bench for William Sampson, a well-known Stratford clockmaker. Perhaps William had set up his brother in business in the City. Perhaps he was the supplier of needles, buttons, ribbons and other knick-knacks to the Lord Chamberlain's Men. It may well be that the enterprise did not succeed, for Gilbert was to act for his brother in a number of transactions in Stratford from 1602 onwards. His competence was clearly trusted.

Shakespeare's youngest brother, Edmund, may have joined him around this time. He is later described as a 'player'. If he was an actor, he was not a very successful one, for his name appears on no surviving cast lists, but the word could equally signify a musician.

Little is known of William's other brother, Richard, whose sole impact on the extant records came when he appeared with three other men before the Bawdy Court in 1608 on an unspecified charge. It is unlikely that he would be so little mentioned were he engaged in any trade or profession. Perhaps he was backward, living first with his parents and then his sister, helping with the simple business and household chores.

The troubles associated with Shakespeare's chosen trade never went away. The difficulties suffered by the Lord Chamberlain's Men in relation to the Blackfriars Priory were compounded by the fact that Giles Allen, the landlord of the ground on which stood The Theatre, was becoming increasingly troublesome. On 2 February 1597, James Burbage was buried at St Leonard's church, Shoreditch. The lease of The Theatre passed to his son, Cuthbert, the theatre manager. Allen announced his intention not to renew it and to tear The Theatre down. Cuthbert tried unsuccessfully to renegotiate the lease. Thus when it expired, the Lord Chamberlain's Men were obliged to seek a home in the Curtain Theatre nearby for two years between 1597 and 1599.

A minor poet, Edward Gilpin, used the sad spectacle of this Temple of the Muses standing forlorn and empty as an analogy.

> But see yonder,
> One like the unfrequented Theatre
> Walks in dark silence and solitude.

There were greater troubles in store. Ben Jonson had arrived in the theatrical firmament. His enemies never allowed him to forget that he was the stepson of a master bricklayer and had been apprenticed into that trade. The considerable classical learning that he had acquired at Westminster School was to prove an inhibition in his dramatic career, although he never realised it. Despite writing a handful of sparkling comedies, he never fulfilled his huge potential. Ever fearless, and with a *machismo* on the scale of Christopher Marlowe, he learned to admire William Shakespeare above all others, although his sense of inferiority made him condescending about what he perceived as his friend's lack of classical scholarship. According to his own account, he had served with the Earl of Leicester's expedition to the Low Countries before joining the Admiral's Men as an unsuccessful actor and dramatist. Philip Henslowe had some faith in his abilities, but lack of success tainted him. According to the assiduous Nicholas Rowe, he offered his latest work, *Every Man in His Humour*, to the Lord Chamberlain's Men.

> Mr Johnson [*sic*], who was at that time altogether unknown to the world, had offered one of his plays to the players, in order to have it acted, and the persons into whose hands it was put after having turned it carelessly and superciliously over, were just upon returning it to him with an ill-natured answer, that it would be of no service to their company, when Shakespeare luckily cast his eye upon it, and found something so well in it as to engage him first to read it through, and afterwards to recommend Mr. Johnson and his writings to the public.[7]

Shakespeare acted in the play, which appears to have been first produced in 1598. His name appears among the 'principle comedians' in the 1616 Folio of Jonson's works, together with those of Burbage, Heminges and Condell. That Jonson was 'at that time altogether unknown to the world' is unlikely. He had become notorious in the previous year when the newly reconstituted Earl of Pembroke's Men performed *The Isle of Dogs*, a play he co-authored with Thomas Nashe, at Langley's Swan Theatre. This long-lost play caused outrage in royal circles. The Isle of Dogs is situated at the tip of the Poplar peninsular opposite the royal palace of Placenta. It was where the royal hounds were kept – hence the name. It does not take much imagination to realise that the play was a satire on the royal court. Like her distinguished successor, the Queen was 'not amused'. On 28 July, an order went out informing the Justices of Middlesex and Sussex that

> her Majesty hath given direction that not only no plays shall be used within
> London or about the city, or in any public place during this time of summer,
> but also that those playhouses that are erected and built for such purpose
> shall be plucked down.

The City Fathers must have been delighted. It appeared that, in one swoop, Jonson, Nashe and Pembroke's Men had achieved what they had been plotting unsuccessfully for years: the destruction of the theatres. For innocent parties such as the Lord Chamberlain's Men, the order represented a bleak future. Their friends in high places, such as Hunsdon, must have sought the Queen's ear. As a known lover of the theatre, she may have become more malleable once her initial fury had abated. On 15 August, Hunsdon was present at a meeting of the Privy Council at which *The Isle of Dogs* was condemned as a 'lewd play … containing very seditious and slanderous matter'. It was decided that justice demanded that blame should be accorded to the perpetrators of the outrage rather than the theatre as a whole. It was ordered that the authors and the principal actors in the play should be detained immediately. In advance of the swoop that followed, Nashe fled to Great Yarmouth, but Jonson and two of the leading actors, Gabriel Spencer and Robert Shaa, were incarcerated in the Marshalsea Prison. By 3 October, the rage had cooled sufficiently for them to be released. For Langley, the episode was a disaster. It was ordered that only two companies – the Lord Chamberlain's Men at the Fortune and the Admiral's Men at the Rose – be licensed to perform in London. This effectively finished the Swan as a serious theatrical location, although it staggered on by presenting other forms of entertainment for another two decades. The Privy Council may have taken the opportunity to deal with Langley, who was under suspicion of fencing a valuable Portuguese diamond. Spencer, Shaa and three other actors of Pembroke's Men threw in their lot with Henslowe and were promptly sued for £500 by Langley, who claimed that they had agreed to perform exclusively at the Swan. Since this was no longer possible, this piece of blatant opportunism sheds more light on Langley's character.

Spencer was not with Henslowe for long. The episode may have been the cause for him to hold a deep animosity against Jonson. He had not written the offending lines, merely spoken them in good faith. The two men fought a duel on 22 September 1598. Spencer was a formidable opponent. As well as the dexterity with a sword that he would have possessed as a leading actor, he had a track record of violence. On 3 December 1596, a Coroner's inquest had found that he had killed one James Feake with a rapier at a house in Southwark. On this occasion he did not triumph. 'I have lost one of my company, which hurteth me greatly; that is Gabriel, for he is slain in Hoxton Fields by the hands of Benjamin Jonson bricklayer.' Within months of his release Jonson was back in prison on the capital charge of murder. He was found guilty, but secured his release by requesting 'Benefit of Clergy'. This archaic right was one of the curious anomalies that had escaped the zeal of the Protestant reformers. The appellant was required to recite a verse from the Vulgate, the Latin translation of the Bible, before a representative of the Bishop. If his classical learning proved sufficient, he was deemed to be in Holy Orders and exempt from the full rigours of the law. Ben had good reason to be thankful for his education at Westminster School.

This *Isle of Dogs* affair, together with the loss of The Theatre and the failure of the Blackfriars enterprise must have strengthened the resolve of the sharers in the Lord Chamberlain's Men to acquire their own premises rather than to rent from others. It was decided to move south of the Thames. It was a logical decision. It was beyond the jurisdiction of the City Fathers. Philip Henslowe's Rose Theatre had flourished there for some twelve years. Now it would have a serious rival. Cuthbert Burbage made a gentleman's agreement to secure the leasehold of an extensive plot of land at Maid Lane on Bankside with the owner, Sir Nicholas Brend. He then made a last, futile attempt to renegotiate the lease of The Theatre with Giles Allen. He considered that, although Allen owned the leasehold of the property, the framing timbers of the building had been erected by his father and now belonged to him. On the night of 28 December 1598, he made his move, taking advantage of Allen's absence in the country. A party assembled in Shoreditch consisting of the Burbage brothers; their financial backer, William Smith of Waltham Cross; a skilled master carpenter, Peter Street; and some dozen of his workmen. They had come prepared for trouble. According to a deposition lodged by a still-furious Allen four years later, the Burbage gang

> armed themselves with divers and manye unlawfull and offensive weapons, as namelye, swordes daggers billes axes and such like. And soe armed did then repayre unto the sayd Theater And then and there armed as aforesayd in verye ryotous outrageous and forcyble manner and contraryre to the lawes of your highnes Realme attempted to pull downe the sayd Theater.

According to Allen, 'diver ... servauntes and farmers then goinge aboute in peacable manner' entreated the party to desist from their 'unlawfull enterpryse', but they with

greate violence not onlye then and there resisted them, but also then and
there pulling breaking and throwing downe the sayd Theater in verye out-
ragious violent and riotous sort to the great disturbance and terrefyeing not
onlye of your subjectes sayd servauntes and farmers but of divers others of
your majesties loving subjectes there neere inhabitinge.[8]

The materials were conveyed to Street's warehouse on the Thames near
the Bridewell. Allen pursued a series of legal actions against Street and the
Burbages. None of them got anywhere and finally the Court of Requests
defined him as what would later be known as a vexatious litigant.

It is highly unlikely that William Shakespeare was part of the 'riotous'
assembly that gathered that December night, but he would surely have
been aware of Cuthbert Burbage's intentions. On 21 February following,
he was a party to a formal thirty-one-year leasehold agreement with Sir
Nicholas Brend. The Burbage brothers would jointly own half the value of
the building proposed for the site. The rental would be £14 10s 10d per
annum. To raise the necessary funds for the enterprise they brought in five
other sharers: Shakespeare, John Heminges, Augustine Phillips, Thomas
Pope and Will Kempe, who would each own 10 per cent of the leasehold.
Peter Street's timbers were ferried across the Thames and work began on
the construction of what was to be the Globe Theatre.

Obviously Kempe was sufficiently esteemed within the company to
be offered the chance to participate at the heart of its fortunes, but
it was an opportunity he declined, selling his share to the other four
new sharers. Why he decided to quit is a mystery. He may have stayed
long enough to create the part of the gravedigger in *Hamlet*. It has the
mark of being written for him. Perhaps he simply had a better offer. In
1602, a third company was added to those officially allowed to play in
London. Edward Somerset, the 4th Earl of Worcester, had been moving
up the Royal hierarchy to become the Queen's Master of Horse. Now he
sought to match his elevation with that of his players. When the Earl of
Worcester's Men took over Henslowe's Rose Theatre, Kempe was one of
their company. The arrangement did not last. A year later, the comedian
embarked on his 'Nine Day's Wonder', his famous morris dance over the
100 miles between London and Norwich.

The absence of his principal comedian would have a significant effect
on Shakespeare's dramatic output. He had created a series of parts which
readily identify themselves: Costard, Lancelot Gobbo, Touchstone, Sir
Toby Belch, Falstaff, Dogberry and Bottom.

Kempe's absence almost certainly meant that Shakespeare employed
the ploy familiar to the producers of modern soap operas. If a character
leaves, kill him off. From the epilogue to *Henry IV, Part II*, it would
appear that he had pondered this intention before writing *Henry V*, a
play in which he promises that Falstaff will appear, but may not last
through the action.

One word more, I beseech you. If you be not too much cloyed with fat meat, our humble author will continue the story, with Sir John in it, and make you merry with fair Katharine of France: where, for any thing I know, Falstaff shall die of a sweat, unless already a' be killed with your hard opinions.

Kempe's departure meant that the intention to kill off Falstaff was fulfilled, but not, perhaps, in the way that Shakespeare had intended. Instead, Ancient Pistol was elevated to fill the gap, as is evidenced by the billing on the so-called 'bad quarto' of 1600.

The
Cronicle
Hi tory of *Henry the fift*,
With his battel fought at *Agin Court* in
*France*. Togither with *Auncient*
*Pistoll*

The new Globe Theatre would have been a sight much remarked on as it rose on Bankside. It is possible that *Henry V* was performed there, but it's more likely to have been the last play to be staged by the company at the Curtain, which so achieved lasting glory as the much-quoted 'wooden O'.

For many people, the play still evokes Lawrence Olivier's magnificent patriotic effusion: a film made in the context of the Normandy landings of 1944. This is part of Shakespeare's theme, but, as always, he tempers the martial glory with a sense of the realities of war. Henry's famous 'Once more into the breach, dear friends' is balanced in the same scene by the boy's reaction.

Would I were in an alehouse in London! I would give all my fame for a pot of ale and safety.

The boy realises the martial shortcomings of Falstaff's ragbag former crew in contrast to the King's valour. Bardolph is 'white-livered and red-faced'; Pistol 'hath a killing tongue and a quiet sword'; while Nym 'never broke any man's head but his own, and that was against a post when he was drunk'. In a scene reminiscent of the behaviour of Essex's army in Dieppe in 1591, Bardolph is eventually executed for looting a church.

In *Henry V*, Shakespeare returns to his theme of the inevitable retribution that regicide will bring. In words that echo his father's vow to make a pilgrimage to Jerusalem, the King recounts the spiritual recompense he has sought for the deed and pleads that the inevitable nemesis will not be manifested in the forthcoming battle.

... not to-day, O Lord,
O, not to-day, think not upon the fault
My father made in compassing the crown!

> I Richard's body have interred anew;
> And on it have bestow'd more contrite tears
> Than from it issued forced drops of blood:
> Five hundred poor I have in yearly pay,
> Who twice a-day their wither'd hands hold up
> Toward heaven, to pardon blood; and I have built
> Two chantries, where the sad and solemn priests
> Sing still for Richard's soul. More will I do;
> Though all that I can do is nothing worth,
> Since that my penitence comes after all,
> Imploring pardon.

The divinity of Henry's kingship is juxtaposed with its moral burdens in the scene in which he, incognito, converses with his soldiers in terms that strike into the heart of the issue of personal responsibility against the necessity to obey orders that has been a keynote of twentieth-century moral dilemmas and judicial procedures. When Henry states that the King's cause is just, his soldiers respond in terms evocative of the *Homily Against Disobedience*, but with the irony that it is they who defend the necessity not to question the justice of the cause. Indeed, in terms both immortal and temporal, they see that it is in their interest not to do so. It is the King who puts forward a doctrine of personal responsibility. 'That's more than we know,' says Williams. 'Ay, or more than we should seek after,' adds Bates,

> For we know enough, if we know we are the king's subjects: if his cause be wrong, our obedience to the king wipes the crime of it out of us.

Williams responds with one of the most devastating theological critiques ever written of the moral responsibility borne by those who lead other men to war.

> But if the cause be not good, the king himself hath a heavy reckoning to make, when all those legs and arms and heads, chopped off in battle, shall join together at the latter day and cry all 'We died at such a place'; some swearing, some crying for a surgeon, some upon their wives left poor behind them, some upon the debts they owe, some upon their children rawly left. I am afeard there are few die well that die in a battle; for how can they charitably dispose of any thing, when blood is their argument? Now, if these men do not die well, it will be a black matter for the king that led them to it; whom to disobey were against all proportion of subjection.

Henry puts forward some scholastic and feeble counter-arguments. The party disperses with some acrimony. Left alone, he reflects on the terrifying implications of the soldiers' comments. He has the moral responsibility for 'every fool' in his kingdom.

> Upon the king! let us our lives, our souls,
> Our debts, our careful wives,
> Our children and our sins lay on the king!
> We must bear all. O hard condition,
> Twin-born with greatness, subject to the breath
> Of every fool, whose sense no more can feel
> But his own wringing!

His conclusion recalls the speech of Henry VI at the Battle of Towton.

> What infinite heart's-ease
> Must kings neglect, that private men enjoy!

And all that kings have in return is the shallow pomp and circumstance that Henry calls 'ceremony'.

In the prologue to Act V of *Henry V* the Chorus makes what is possibly the most topical allusion to be found in the Shakespeare canon.

> Were now the General of our gracious Empress –
> As in good time he may – from Ireland coming;
> Bringing rebellion broached on his sword,
> How many would the peaceful city quit
> To welcome him!

The reference is to the campaign of the Earl of Essex in Ireland in the summer of 1599 and it enables the play to be dated to between his departure on 27 March and his return on 28 September. The expedition was not to be the triumph for which the Chorus had hoped. The very appointment of the Earl was part of the dynastic struggle that had intensified at court between his faction and that of the Cecils. To Essex and his supporters, Spain was the natural enemy: the Cecils realised that an accommodation was necessary to bring to an end the lengthy and costly war. In April, 1598, in the Council Chamber, when Essex denounced a prospective peace as dishonourable, William Cecil, Lord Burghley, the Queen's Principal Secretary, replied that he 'breathed forth nothing but war, slaughter and blood'. He pointed to Psalm 55:23 in his psalter. 'Bloodthirsty and deceitful men shall not live out half their days.' The reference was prophetic.

Ireland was a running sore for the English Crown. A full-scale rebellion led by Hugh O'Neill, the 2nd Earl of Tyrone, was draining resources on a massive scale. During a debate in the Council about the appointment of a new Commander-in-Chief there, such was the Queen's exasperation with Essex that she boxed him on the ear. In response he grasped the hilt of his sword: an act that further undermined his diminishing credit at court. Ten days later, an English army in Ireland was routed by O'Neill at the Battle of Yellow Ford. In a ruse to get rid of him, Robert Cecil proposed that Essex be given the command in Ireland. After his advocacy of aggressive policies there, he had little choice but to accept. For both sides, the proposal was a calculated risk. The absence of Essex from court would increase the influence of Robert Cecil (the father had died in August 1598). On the other hand, Essex was to command a force of 16,000 men, the largest English army yet assembled in Ireland. His record as a field commander meant that he was quite capable of achieving a triumph. The lines in *Henry V* were written in this expectation. When he set off on 27 March, accompanied by Shakespeare's old patron, the Earl of Southampton, cheering crowds lined his route for 4 miles. Southampton's seduction of her lady-in-waiting still rankled with the Queen. She had forbidden him the official role as Master of the Horse, so he was riding in a private capacity, but he was effectively so appointed, without the title, by Essex.

'Gracious Empress'? This is not one of Queen Elizabeth's titles. Rather it is a statement of the aspirations of the nation. The four captains in *Henry V* – Fluellen, Gower, Jamy and MacMorris – represent the four nations of the British Isles. In fact, the Scots, traditional allies of the French, would not have fought at Agincourt, although it was Welsh archers who played havoc with the French cavalry. They symbolise the future unity which would be achieved with the anticipated union of crowns after the death of Elizabeth. Beyond that we recall Molyneux's globes. England is forging an empire over the oceans of the world. Hakluyt's *Voyages* speak of the great maritime adventures of the past and call the nation to its destiny on the seas. At the time of writing *Henry V*, moves towards founding the East India Company came to fruition in the following year, Sir Humphrey Gilbert had planted England's flag on Newfoundland sixteen years before and the Virginia Colony would be founded eight years later. The process of acquiring a worldwide empire had begun.

# 13

# A New Theatre, 1599–1602

'The great Globe itself'
— *The Tempest*, Act IV, Scene 1

On 21 September 1599, the Swiss visitor Thomas Platter took a boat with his older brother across the Thames to visit 'the house with the thatched roof': a building better known to posterity as the Globe Theatre, where he saw '*The Tragedy of the first Emperor Julius Caesar*'. Shakespeare's play was probably the first to be produced in the new theatre. Platter does not seem to have understood it very fully, although he found it 'excellent'. He describes the extraneous detail rather than the performance itself. There were some fifteen actors. Because of the raised stage, everyone got a good view, whether they were standing below and paid just a penny, or those who sat, who paid an extra penny and entered through another door. Those who entered through a third door sat on cushioned seats and paid yet another penny. The theatregoer who did this gained a little cachet. It was a place 'where he not only sees everything well, but can also be seen'. During the performance food and drink were carried around among the audience. The actors were 'most expensively and elaborately costumed'. The clothes had belonged to 'eminent lords and knights', who had left them to their serving men. Because it was unseemly for them to wear such apparel, they sold them to the actors for a small sum. It was the finale that Platter enjoyed most. The actors 'danced very marvellously together ... two dressed as men and two as women'. The same happened at another play he saw, possibly at the Curtain Theatre, 'in the suburb of Bishopsgate'. At the end, the actors 'danced very charmingly, in English and Irish fashion'.

The eighteenth-century antiquarian William Oldys claimed to have seen in yet another lost manuscript that the words TOTUS MUNDUS AGIT HISTRIONEM were inscribed over the entrance to the Globe. This quote from the Latin author Petronius is the source of the famous line from *As You like It* – 'All the World's a Stage ...' – although, translated literally, the phrase means 'All the world plays the actor'.

If the opening of the Globe proclaimed a new era for the Lord Chamberlain's Men, it constituted a severe threat to Philip Henslowe, Edward Alleyne and their Rose Theatre nearby, which had become somewhat decrepit. In a bold move, it was decided to move across the river to Shoreditch, the very area where the Lord Chamberlain's Men had been performing not so long before. They contracted Peter Street, the carpenter/architect of the Globe, to build a new theatre – the Fortune – in Golding Lane, north of Cripplegate. His contract still survives. Specific features were to be 'done according to the manner and fashion of the said house called the Globe'.[1] There the Admiral's Men presented plays by Ben Jonson, Thomas Decker and others. It was probably to put the new theatre on the map that Alleyne made a comeback to the stage, finally retiring in 1604.

The writing of *Julius Caesar* represents a new phase in Shakespeare's career. A splendid new theatre was available as the vehicle for his talents. He had completed his great history cycle. The hugely popular Kempe had been the focus of much of his work since the Lord Chamberlain's Men were founded. Now he could give his attention to other issues. Until now, the determining factor of Elizabethan tragedy had been revenge, or the fates. As we have seen, in *Romeo and Juliet*, the last tragedy that Shakespeare had written, some six years before, the lovers are 'star-crossed'. Caesar's downfall – and thereby his tragedy – is brought about by his own foibles and arrogance. In Casca's view, he aspires to overthrow the republic that was established by a forebear of Brutus and make himself king. When Mark Antony offers him the crown, he pushes it aside three times, 'but to my thinking, he was very loath to lay his fingers off it'. Cassius has already observed that Caesar is trying to exalt himself into the future god-like status of the Roman Emperor, although he knows he is a mere man.

> He had a fever when he was in Spain,
> And when the fit was on him, I did mark
> How he did shake. 'Tis true, this god did shake.

This incipient vision of deity leads Caesar to ignore the abundant signs of his imminent doom. He mocks the prophecies of the soothsayer – 'He is a dreamer. Let us leave him.' He ignores his wife's premonitions and those of the augurers. He treats the warning letter of Artemidorus with contempt – 'What is this fellow mad?' Pride and an inflated sense of divine grandeur bring about his downfall.

In contrast, Brutus is brought down by his good qualities – his deep sense of duty and his patriotism, but also the flaws represented by his lack of judgement and mistaken faith in his fellow conspirators: points well caught by Mark Antony in his famous valedictory speech.

> This was the noblest Roman of them all.
> All the conspirators save only he
> Did that they did in envy of great Caesar:
> He only in a general honest thought
> And common good to all made one of them.

With the exception of *King John*, which does not appear to have enjoyed a great deal of success in Shakespeare's lifetime, *Julius Caesar* is the first play to be presented by the Lord Chamberlain's Men that lacks a clown. It does contain one enduring Shakespearean theme: the fear of the ignorant mob is still manifest. Cinna the poet is torn to pieces by the crowd because he has the same name as the conspirator. Yet, whoever controls the mob controls Rome: a point not lost on Mark Antony or, vicariously, the Earl of Essex.

In Ireland, the first act of another tragedy was being played out. The high expectations for the Essex expedition were dashed. Despite some limited success, the rebellion was far from being broached on Essex's sword. His cause with the Queen was not helped by the dedication to him by Sir John Haywood of his chronicle history, *The First Part of the Life and Raigne of King Henrie IIII*. This particular king was considered, at least by Essex's enemies, to bear a close resemblance to the Earl himself. Indeed, the Latin dedication makes this clear.

> Were your name and fame radiant on the brow of our beloved Henry, he would go forth among the people more happily, and more safely as well. For you indeed are a great man, both in the estimation of the present day and also in what we look for from the future.[2]

The extravagant praise brings us once more to the tributes paid by a writer to a person whose patronage he desires. Unfortunately, it achieved the opposite effect, bringing the wrath of the Establishment down on the absent Earl. When the somewhat unworldly Hayward attempted to publish a second edition in April, all 1,500 copies were seized and burnt.[3] On 1 June, an entry in the Stationers' Register recorded an order issued by the Archbishop of Canterbury, John Whitgift, and the Bishop of London, Richard Bancroft, attempting to reassert their control over the publication of printed works. Their main target was political satire, but it was doubtless Hayward's work that inspired the demand that 'noe English historyes be printed excepte they bee allowed by some of her maiesties privie councell'. On 11 July, Hayward was summoned to appear before that body, probably on the instigation of Cecil. The publication had driven the Queen into a state of paranoid fury. She asserted that Hayward was pretending to be the author in order to shield 'some more mischievous person and that he should be racked in order that he might disclose the truth'. She ordered the Solicitor-General, Francis Bacon, to search for passages in the book that might be used to charge Essex with treason. Bacon reported that treason 'surely I find none, but for felony very many'. The felony in question was that Hayward had lifted many of his choicest phrases from Sir Henry Savile's translations of Tacitus. Hayward was spared the rack, but was doomed to spend the rest of the reign in the Tower.[4]

In Ireland, Essex consistently underestimated the power of the rebels. Eventually realising that there was little hope of success, on 8 September he agreed a truce with O'Neil that partitioned Ireland between rebel and royal lands. Despite the fact that the Queen had forbidden him to leave

Ireland without her permission, he sped back to England to plead his case with her. None of the cheering crowds that the Chorus had so optimistically anticipated were there to greet him. Although the truce made sense from certain perspectives, the Queen was furious. 'To trust this traitor upon oath is to trust a devil upon religion,' she said of O'Neill. Essex did not help his cause by forcing his way into the Queen's bedchamber at Nonsuch Palace and confronting her before she was dressed and bewigged. He was relieved of his command and placed under house arrest. Ironically his successor in Ireland, Lord Mountjoy, the father of four children by Essex's sister, Penelope, Lady Rich, achieved great military success through his ruthless scorched earth policy and military panache.

By the end of 1599, another play was adorning the stage at the Globe. Despite his narrow escape from the gallows, Ben Jonson continued to engage in controversy. *Every Man Out of His Humour* was his latest shot in a 'War of the Theatres', fired at the playwrights Thomas Decker and John Marston. Sallies waged back and forth between the rivals. William Shakespeare appears to have been involved in a peripheral and unknown way. There is a reference to a forgotten war of words in the undergraduate play *The Return from Parnassus*.

> Few of the university men pen plaies well, they smell too much of that writer *Ovid*, and that writer *Metamorphoses*, and talk too much of *Proserpina* & *Juppiter*. Why heres our fellow *Shakespeare* puts them all down, I and *Ben Jonson* too. And that *Ben Jonson* is a pestilent fellow, he brought up *Horace* giving the Poets a pill, but our fellow *Shakespeare* hath given him a purge that made him beray his credit.

The 'War' was chiefly played out with the children's companies of the Chapel Royal and St Paul's. Shakespeare alludes to them and, perhaps, to the vitriolic pens of the rival dramatists, in *Hamlet*.

> There is, sir, an aery of children, little eyases, that cry out on the top of question, and are most tyrannically clapp'd for't. These are now the fashion, and so berattle the common stages – so they call them – that many wearing rapiers are afraid of goose quills and dare scarce to come hither.

On 2 September 1600, Richard Burbage, despairing of ever getting a return on the Blackfriars Theatre, had leased it for twenty-one years to Henry Evans, the manager of the Children of the Chapel Royal. It was here that *Cynthia's Revels*, Jonson's latest riposte in the 'War', was produced. In 1600, John Marston contrasted favourably its playgoers with those to be found in the open-air theatres. 'S'Faith, I like the audience that frequenteth there. With much applause a man shall not be choked with the stench of garlic nor be pasted to the balmy jacket of a beer brewer.'[5]

It appears that Henslowe tried to open a second front in the 'War' by attempting to discomfort Shakespeare and the Lord Chamberlain's Men, perhaps in order to undermine the popularity of the newly opened Globe. He commissioned the anti-catholic polemicist Anthony Munday, Michael Drayton, Richard Hathwaye and Robert Wilson to write a play about an issue which simply would not go away, which was presented in November 1599. *Sir John Oldcastle* revives the myths about Henry V's would-be assassin. The Prologue launches the attack with a swipe at the character of Falstaff.

> It is no pampered glutton we present,
> Nor aged Councellor to youthfull sinne,
> But one, whose vertue shone above the rest,
> A valiant martyr and a vertuous peere.

It concludes unequivocally.

> Let faire Truth be grac'te,
> Since forg'd invention former time defa'te.

Shakespeare and the Lord Chamberlain's Men had better things to do than to respond to such provocation, but the furore that the character of Falstaff had aroused in certain influential circles could not be ignored. At some point someone, presumably not Shakespeare, added a piece of ill-suited doggerel to the epilogue to *Henry IV, Part II*.

> For Oldcastle died a martyr and this is not the man.

Shakespeare was working on a grander project which was contained within a much bigger vision: a metamorphosis of the whole idea of dramatic tragedy, a further development of what might well be described as 'Christian Tragedy' – Christian because it portrays redemption (or lack of it) through suffering. The tragic hero is brought down, not so much by external forces, but by flaws in his own nature. Each of Shakespeare's great tragedies begins in the chaos of a world gone mad. This is apparent in *Hamlet*, where the play is nailed early on in the simple line:

> There is something rotten in the state of Denmark.

By the end of the play, this rottenness has disposed of five of the leading characters – and two others, but the suffering has meaning. The corrupt court has been purged.

Of all Shakespeare's plays, *Hamlet* is probably the most problematic in terms of its composition and early stage history. As with a number of the works, there was an earlier play of the same name. The first reference to it occurs in 1589 in Thomas Nashe's preface to Robert Greene's fantasy, *Menaphon*.

English Seneca read by candle-light yields many good sentences, as *Blood is a begger*, and so forth; and if you entreat him fair in a frosty morning, he will afford you whole Hamlets, I should say handfuls of tragical speeches.

Other allusions to plagiarism from Seneca make it likely that Nashe is ascribing the authorship of this proto-*Hamlet* to Thomas Kyd. A further reference to what is probably the same play was made by Philip Henslowe in his diary on 9 June 1594, when he records that the takings for a performance of *Hamlet* at the Newington Butts Theatre were a mere 8s. Despite this apparent lack of popularity, it fastened itself sufficiently in the mind of Thomas Lodge, who, in his pamphlet *Wits Miserie, and the Worlds Madnesse* not only records the only surviving phrase from the play, but also denotes the tone in which it was declaimed. 'Looks as pale as the visard of ye ghost, which cried so miserally [*sic*] at ye theator, like an oisterwife, Hamlet revenge.' There are a number of references to this phrase in the work of other contemporary writers. It obviously became proverbial. It is even possible that the actor who sounded like an oyster wife was William Shakespeare. The Lord Chamberlain's Men were associated with Henslowe's Company at Newington Butts at this time. Years later, Nicholas Rowe sought to discover what parts Shakespeare had played as an actor, but could only pick up one live theatrical tradition.

Tho' I have inquir'd, I could never meet with any further Account of him this way, than that the top of his performance was the Ghost in his own *Hamlet*.

It is possible, but unlikely, that Shakespeare was the author of this play. Had he written it, surely the astute management would have attached his name to it. Yet, even when the play that is undoubtedly his work was published, enigmas remained. The several allusions to the character of Julius Caesar would seem to show that that play was fresh in his mind when he wrote *Hamlet*. 'I did enact Julius Caesar; I was killed i' the Capitol. Brutus killed me,' recalls Polonius. Perhaps the same actor played both parts and we are in the presence of another in-joke.

On 26 July 1602, *Hamlet* was entered on the Stationers' Register as 'latelie Acted by the Lo. Chamberleyne his servantes'. It was published the next year as what has been described as a 'bad quarto' entitled *The Tragivcall Historie of Hamlet Prince of Denmarke. By William Shakespeare. As it hath beene diuese times acted by his Highnesse Servants in the Cittie of London as also in the two Universities of Cambridge and Oxford and elsewhere*. It had not only been played in London, but it had toured in the provinces, so it was a well-established production. The text of this first quarto is another issue. Not only is it only just over half as long as the second quarto, published in 1604, but there are significant differences in the two versions. Even the most famous lines written by Shakespeare vary drastically.

> To be, or not to be, I there's the point,
> To die, to sleepe, is that all? I all.
> No, to sleepe, to dreame, aye mary, there it goes.

Perhaps we are in the presence of lines from the old play of *Hamlet* that Shakespeare was in the process of revising. This thesis is supported by the fact that even the names of some of the characters are different. Polonius is Corambis; Reynaldo, Montano; Osric, 'A Braggart Gentleman'; Francisco, 'A Sentinel'; and then there are 'Guildenstone' and 'Ravenscraft'.

Yet the first quarto has some validity. It contains precise stage directions that do not appear in other versions and an entire scene (usually labeled 4.6) that does not appear elsewhere. Is it a pirated version, dictated inaccurately to the stationer by an actor who played a minor part – or a touring version, cut down for shorter performances? Most likely it is an early draft, a work in progress that will be revised. That the first and second quartos shared the same publisher, Nicholas Ling, tends to strengthen this view. The relationship between the two versions is further revealed on the title page of the second quarto. 'Newly printed and enlarged to almost as much againe as it was, according to the true and perfect coppie.' In other words, this is the completed version: the other one is not negated, but it has been revised from the original manuscript.

None of Shakespeare's plays has so many published variants as *Hamlet*. Collected together, the result is a play that takes over four hours to perform, surely, a time too long for 'the two hours traffic of the stage' to which the playgoer was accustomed.

*Hamlet* is arguably Shakespeare's most Catholic play. The catalyst of the action – the appearance of the Ghost – is entirely dependent on the doctrine of Purgatory. 'I am thy father's spirit,' he tells Hamlet,

> Doom'd for a certain time to walk the night,
> And for the day confin'd to fast in fires,
> Till the foul crimes done in my days of nature
> Are burnt and purg'd away.

Old Hamlet is suffering the torments of Purgatory because he has been murdered without the redemptive benefit of Extreme Unction. The saving grace of the Eucharist has been denied him ('unhouse'led'); he has not prepared himself for death ('disappointed'); he has not been absolved through the confessional ('unanel'd').

> Cut off even in the blossoms of my sin
> Unhouse'led, disappointed, unanel'd:
> No reck'ning made, but sent to my account
> With all my imperfections on my head.

Hamlet is to recall this issue of preparedness for death when he draws his sword, but rejects the chance to kill Claudius while the King is at prayer.

> Now might I do it pat, now he is praying;
> And now I'll do't. And so he goes to heaven;
> And so am I revenged. That would be scann'd:
> A villain kills my father; and for that,
> I, his sole son, do this same villain send
> To heaven.
> O, this is hire and salary, not revenge.

Hamlet has usurped the divine prerogative in claiming God's prerogative of vengeance. He now seeks, with hubris, a role never claimed within the magisterium of the Catholic Church – to judge the passage of the human soul. The irony is that Claudius' prayers are not ascending heavenwards.

> My words fly up, my thoughts remain below.
> Words without thoughts never to heaven go.

Shakespeare makes Claudius a rounded character, not a mere monster of palpable evil. At the start of the play he is an avuncular figure who is concerned about Hamlet's spiritual well-being in relation to his obsessive mood concerning the death of his father.

> To persever
> In obstinate condolement is a course
> Of impious stubbornness 'tis unmanly grief.
> It shows a will most incorrect to heaven,
> A heart unfortified, a mind impatient,
> An understanding simple and unschool'd.

On first seeing the Ghost, Hamlet uses the Catholic formula of intercessory prayer:

> Angels and ministers of grace defend us!

He is left with the question he then posed.

> Be thou a spirit of health or a goblin damn'd.
> Bring with thee airs from heaven or blasts from hell;
> Be thy intents wicked or charitable,
> Thou com'st in such a questionable shape
> That I will speak to thee. I'll call thee Hamlet.
> King, father, royal Dane.

The answer is that the Ghost is both. He is indeed Old Hamlet, but his purpose is not a kingly one, looking to the good of the nation he has sworn to serve in his coronation oath. In the first scene Horatio gives him the benefit of being a benevolent spirit.

> Speak to me.
> If there be any good thing to be done,
> That may to thee do ease and grace to me,
> Speak to me.
> If thou art privy to thy country's fate,
> Which happily foreknowing may avoid,
> O speak.

The Ghost passes by in silence. His purpose is a revenge on his brother and wife that will carry away the entire edifice of the Danish court, taking with it the innocent and the guilty alike. Only half understanding the cataclysms that have occurred, Horatio delineates them in the final scene.

> So shall you hear,
> Of carnal, bloody, and unnatural acts
> Of accidental judgements, casual slaughter;
> Of deaths put on by cunning and forc'd cause:
> And, in this upshot, purposes mistook
> Fall'n on th' inventors heads.

Horatio warns Hamlet of the potential consequence of following the Ghost 'which might deprive your sovereignty of reason / And draw you into madness'. This is why the Ghost must return to the torments of Purgatory. The evil that he self-confessedly did lives after him. He pursues Hamlet relentlessly towards his doom. 'This visitation,' he tells him after the killing of Polonius, 'is but to whet thy almost blunted purpose.' The beautiful speech of Marcellus after the cock crows is something more than the recall of a folk legend about the spirit of Christmas. It is an invocation of the redemption that Christ will bring to the fallen world represented by the Ghost.

> Some say that ever 'gainst that season comes
> Wherein our Saviour's birth is celebrated
> The bird of dawning singeth all night long;
> And then, they say, no spirit dare stir abroad,
> The nights are wholesome, then do no planets strike,
> No fairy takes, nor witch hath power to charm,
> So hallowed and so gracious is that time.

As Horatio has warned, Hamlet is indeed drawn into madness. Every other major character with the exception of the loyal Horatio comments on this. The culmination of this process comes at the funeral of Ophelia – a scene in which the performance of Richard Burbage so impressed one anonymous theatregoer that he wrote of it in a verse elegy. 'Oft have I seen him leap into a grave.' In the final scene, Hamlet acknowledges his own madness, from which he claims recovery, with the implication that he is not culpable for it because he has been led into it by the Devil – or the Ghost.

> Was 't Hamlet wrong'd Laertes? Never Hamlet.
> If Hamlet from himself be ta'en away,
> And when he's not himself does wrong Laertes,
> Then Hamlet does it not. Hamlet denies it.
> Who does it then? His madness. If 't be so,
> Hamlet is of the faction that is wrong'd;
> His madness is poor Hamlet's enemy.

Hamlet is filled with doubt about the task the Ghost has set him.

> Thus the native hue of resolution,
> Is sickled o'er with the pale cast of thought,
> And enterprises of great pith and moment
> With this regard their currents turn away,
> And lose the name of action.

The dreadful knowledge he has gained from the Ghost stultifies him sexually. He has previously paid suit to Ophelia in a way that has convinced her and others of the genuineness of his feelings. He expresses his love in the letter obtained by Polonius.

> O dear Ophelia, I am ill at these numbers. I have not art to reckon my groans: but that I love thee best.

The Ghost's revelation changes his attitude towards women and sexuality – and, in the process, his relation to Ophelia. 'I did love thee once,' he tells her when she seeks to return his letters. 'Indeed, my lord, you made me believe so,' she replies. He tells her that she should not have believed him, 'for virtue cannot inoculate our old stock but we shall relish of it'. Even goodness cannot overcome man's innate fallen nature born of Original Sin. It is a vestige of his love that he urges chastity upon her as her best option in the famous line: 'Get thee to a nunnery'. The now almost traditional interpretation of the line as consigning her to a brothel is immediately belied by the immediate 'Why wouldst thou be a breeder of sinners?' 'O, what a noble mind is here o'er thrown?' concludes Ophelia – and with reason. She has just been subjected to a tirade against women that rises to a crescendo and culminates in a demand for sexual abstinence, not just from Ophelia, but from all mankind.

I say we will have no more marriage: those that are married already, all but one shall live: the rest shall keep as they are. To a nunnery go.

In the play scene, Hamlet appears to revive his affections towards Ophelia, at least sufficiently to deceive the ever-hopeful Polonius, but in fact he subjects her to an onslaught of crude innuendo, interpreted in italics.

| | |
|---|---|
| **Queen:** | Come hither, my dear Hamlet, sit by me. |
| **Hamlet:** | No, good mother, here's metal more attractive. |
| **Polonius:** | [to the King] O ho! Do you mark that? |
| **Hamlet:** | Lady, shall I lie in your lap? |
| | *Shall I have sexual intercourse with you?* |
| **Ophelia:** | No, my lord. |
| **Hamlet:** | I mean, my head upon your lap? |
| **Ophelia:** | Ay, my lord. |
| **Hamlet:** | Do you think I meant country matters? |
| | *A sufficiently well-known double entendre to require no explanation.* |
| **Ophelia:** | I think nothing, my lord. |
| **Hamlet:** | That's a fair thought to lie between maid's legs. |
| | *'No thing' was a crude synonym for the vagina* |

It is shocking (and even more so to an Elizabethan audience) and hugely effective that like crudities are to be uttered by Ophelia as an expression of her own madness.

The catharsis that has driven Hamlet to this psychotic state is his mother's incestuous relationship with Claudius. It is difficult for a modern audience to comprehend how shocking such an affair would be to a contemporary audience. Indeed incest was a catalyst for the Protestant Reformation in England. It was his marriage to his dead brother's wife that Henry VIII attempted to use as a pretext for seeking a Papal annulment of his marriage to Catherine of Aragon. His plea was rejected by the Pope on sound doctrinal grounds – that Catherine's first marriage had never been consummated. In 1560, the Table of Affinity, 'Wherein Whosoever Are Related Are Forbidden by the Church of England to Marry Together', was incorporated into the Book of Common Prayer. Among the unions that are forbidden is that between a woman and her husband's brother (presumably deceased). Whereas to the modern mind, incest is defined by consanguinity, to the Elizabethans it was also defined by marital relationships.

Thus Hamlet's revulsion was not unique, but a generally accepted social view. He expresses it even before the Ghost has informed him of its circumstance.

O most wicked speed, to post,
With such dexterity to incestuous sheets.

Hamlet is deeply disturbed by the highly carnal relationship between his uncle and his mother. In the closet scene, the corpse of Polonius lies virtually forgotten as Hamlet raves against their incestuousness.

> Nay, but to live
> In the rank sweat of an unseamed bed,
> Stew'd in corruption, honeying and making love,
> Over the nasty sty.

At the last, it is Claudius' incest that Hamlet dwells on in his fury of killing, as well as his unshriven state – 'thou incestuous, murd'rous, damned Dane'.

The burden and perceived duty of revenge dulls Hamlet's human sympathy. He is cruel to Ophelia and expresses only a grudging remorse about his killing of Polonius. Despite the fact that Rosencranz and Guildenstern do not know the contents of the letter they carry, he alters it so that it is they who are killed by the King of England rather than himself – and so they too die unshriven: the very condition to which Old Hamlet is condemned.

Death is an unseen character in the play. He stalks the halls of Elsinor like his counterpart in the morality plays. He is to be desired, but feared. Suicide would be a way out of the dilemmas that torment Hamlet, but it is rejected because of 'the dread of something after death'. Before he even knows of the dreadful business the Ghost is to set upon him, he ponders suicide to escape the morbidity that pervades his soul, but cites the moral code delineated in the Councils of the Church with regret.

> O, that this too too solid flesh would melt,
> Thaw and resolve itself into a dew;
> Or that the Everlasting had not fix'd
> His canons 'gainst self-slaughter!

Shakespeare is aware of Catholic Canon Law on the issue of suicide. So would be many educated Englishmen because, somewhat surprisingly, it continued to function in the Church of England until 1604. He shows familiarity with all its nuances in the gravedigger scene and that of the burial of Ophelia, which follows. The 'crowner' (Coroner) has pronounced that because she has not taken her own life, she is entitled to a Christian burial. In the view of both the second gravedigger and the officiating priest, this is because rank ('that great command') has been pulled, but this is not necessarily the case. Ophelia's death might be described as 'accidental' – she falls into the water off a broken branch. Yet she makes no effort to save herself which, as the Second Gravedigger realises, is tantamount to suicide.

Here stands the man; good. If the man go to this water and drown himself, it is … but if the water come to him and drown him, he drowns not himself.

Yet Ophelia did not drown herself 'wittingly'. She is oblivious to her situation. The Coroner could have invoked that condition of Canon Law which mitigated the circumstance when the deceased had been led to self-destruction by the Devil – i.e. when the balance of the mind had been disturbed. The priest asserts his disagreement by restricting the obsequies – there is no Eucharistic celebration that would have constituted a full requiem. The balance is restored by the Queen, who scatters the flowers due to a virgin, as permitted by Canon Law, over the corpse.

The gravedigger scene reveals again one of Shakespeare's favourite dramatic techniques. He creates a world that the characters inhabit which is beyond the immediate action of the play. 'How long hast thou been a grave-maker?' Hamlet asks the Sexton. 'Of all the days i' the year,' he replies. 'I came to't that day that our last king Hamlet overcame Fortinbras.'

| | |
|---|---|
| **Hamlet:** | How long is that since? |
| **Sexton:** | Cannot you tell that? Every fool can tell that: it was the very day that young Hamlet was born. |

We have already seen Cassius challenge Caesar's god-like status by recalling the fever that he had in Spain. Shakespeare had already developed the same technique in *Romeo and Juliet*. The long and apparently rambling speech of the Nurse in Act I, about Juliet's weaning, sets the play in the wider context of the Capulet family and the early loss of virginity in an arranged marriage. The question frequently misattributed to the critic A. C. Bradley – 'How many children had Lady Macbeth?'[6] – while conspicuously absurd, has some credence in the context of Shakespeare's ability to create an entire world in which to set his characters.

Hamlet's irresolution is another aspect of the way in which his character has become stultified as a result of the Ghost's revelations. Ironically, the revenge project is saved by Claudius, who demonstrates greater energy in his cause and becomes the catalyst of his own downfall ('purposes mistook, / Fall'n on th' inventor's heads'). The King is a genuinely tragic character who, like the Macbeth to come, realises that he has made a temporal gain at the price of his immortal soul.

> But, O, what form of prayer
> Can serve my turn? 'Forgive me my foul murder!'
> That cannot be; since I am still possess'd
> Of these effects for which I did the murder –
> My crown, mine own ambition, and my queen.
> May one be pardon'd and retain the offence?

In the real world, Claudius would simply have summoned the contemporary equivalent of 'two men in white coats' and had Hamlet confined to a luxurious asylum. That is not the stuff of drama, however. As Shakespeare has demonstrated in *Richard III* and will demonstrate even more convincingly in *Macbeth*, one gross offence against the moral code is not entire to itself. It leads to others. It is Claudius, by now deeply suspicious of his nephew's motives, who orders Polonius to spy on him, which leads to his inevitable death behind the arras. It is Claudius who plots the denouement which leads to the destruction of the royal house of Denmark.

With the death of Ophelia, *Hamlet* becomes a double-revenge tragedy. Hamlet wishes to kill his uncle and Laertes wishes to kill Hamlet. This leaves us with the question of why we not only sympathise with Hamlet, but identify with him. He is cruel, capricious, revengeful and indecisive. Yet, as Max Beerbohm put it, the part is 'a hoop through which every eminent actor, sooner or later, must jump'. The answer lies in Shakespeare's brilliance as a dramatist. Hamlet is the sole party to the dreadful secret that the Ghost reveals. No one else on stage can grasp the immensity of the revelation, although the suspicions of Claudius slowly change his attitude from avuncular bonhomie to murderous psychopathy. Yet there is one other person that is in on the secret from the beginning: the audience collectively. It follows Hamlet's career through his great soliloquies to that final denouement, at every point perceiving the action from his point of view and, at the last, seeing Hamlet discover himself. He is aware that Claudius has designs to kill him but returns to Elsinor to face his destiny. He expresses 'gaingiving' (foreboding) about the forthcoming fencing contest with Laertes, but when Horatio urges him not to go through with it, he expresses a biblical faith in the divine purpose and a clear indication that he has overcome his fear of death for which he is now prepared. He is not 'disappointed'. He rejects the methods of the classical 'augurers', who predicted the future by observing birds in flight. Instead he seeks Christian absolution ('readiness'), quoting Matthew 10.29.

> We defy augury. There is a special providence in the fall of a sparrow. If it be now, 'tis not to come; if it be not to come, it will be now: if it be not now; yet it will come – the readiness is all.

Another vital process in Hamlet's redemption is his expression of penitence at his treatment of Laertes, who is still set on deception and revenge. At the last each of them finds mutual forgiveness. Hamlet has gone through a form of shriving. His last words, 'The rest is silence', betokens that he has nominated Horatio to recount on his behalf the drama that has led him here. They also recall Psalm 115.

> The dead praise not the Lord, neither any that go down into silence.

Hamlet's benediction is pronounced by Horatio:

Goodnight, sweet prince, and flights of angels sing thee to thy rest,

In the absence of a priest, both the lay absolution and benediction are valid within Canon Law. At the last, the court of Denmark is purged of its mortal sin, but it is carried away in the process. The pattern follows that of the centuries. The flamboyant military leader restores order. One is left with the conclusion that no other work of literature fits Philip Larkin's most famous line so precisely.

Amazingly, the first recorded performance of *Hamlet* was many hundreds of miles from the Globe Theatre. It was at sea on a voyage of exploration commissioned by the newly founded East India Company, in 1607, off the coast of Sierra Leone, aboard a ship called the *Red Dragon*. On 5 September, her Captain, William Keeling, sent Lucas Fernandez, his Portuguese interpreter, 'brother-in-law of the local King, Borea', across to one of the sister ships in the flotilla, 'according to his desier, abord the Hector, whear he brooke fast, and after came abord mee, wher we gave the tragedie of Hamlett'. The little fleet was marooned in gales, so a further Shakespearean production took place on 30 September. Captain William Hawkins of the *Hector* 'dined with me', Keeling recorded, 'wher my companions acted Kinge Richard the Second.' Months later, on 31 March 1608, off the island of Socotra at the mouth of the Red Sea, Captain Keeling invited Captain Hawkins to 'a fishe dinner, and had Hamlet acted abord'. Keeling was one of the first to realise the therapeutic qualities of the Bard, writing that he had put on the Shakespearean productions 'to keepe my people from idlenes and unlawfull games or sleepe'. It may be presumed that he was a regular visitor to the Globe when on shore leave and a purchaser of the quarto editions of the works.[7]

The dark mood that pervades *Hamlet* carries through into what was probably Shakespeare's next play, *Troilus and Cressida*. It is a work fraught with problems. Indeed, the critic F. S. Boas in his *Shakespeare and His Predecessors* defined it as a 'problem play', together with *All's Well That Ends Well* and *Measure for Measure*. It would appear that the playwright is attempting a further literary innovation in *Troilus*. Unlike the other two plays that Boas posits, it has no conclusive outcome. It defies definition as a comedy – although it contains a great deal of venomous bawdy wit – or as a tragedy: there is no conspicuous tragic hero or victim. No character appears to grow in self-knowledge as a result of experience within the play. If there is a tragedy within the play, it is within the common theme of the destruction of values and the basis of human relationships that war inevitably brings. It would appear to have had little success in Shakespeare's lifetime – or for a long while subsequently. Curiously two virtually identical quartos were published in 1609, the one claiming that it had been acted at the Globe; the other that it was 'a new play never stal'd with the stage'. The playwright John Dryden rewrote it later in the century, describing the original as 'a heap of rubbish', although he did acknowledge the excellence of the verse. The play has achieved a greater measure of success in the modern era, perhaps because it attunes with such contemporary themes as sexual explicitness and the futility of war. It serves to remind us that, although not everything that Shakespeare wrote was tinged with genius, very little that he wrote was of no value.

# 14

# End of an Epoch, 1600–04

'For our Solace and Pleasure'
– Royal Charter to the King's Men

## By Reason of Thees Trobles

Although the Earl of Essex may be likened to a Shakespearean tragic hero, it is difficult to categorise the one he most resembles. He certainly possessed the misjudgements of Hamlet and the arrogance of Coriolanus. The role to which he himself aspired, more than any other, was that of Henry Bolingbroke, the overmighty subject who overthrows the monarch and takes the throne himself. After his return from his Irish disaster, he was subjected to an enquiry into his conduct in July 1600 by a panel of statesmen and lawyers. He was cleared of treason but found guilty of misconduct, stripped of most of his offices of profit under the Crown, including his lucrative monopoly of the sweet wine duties, banished from court and kept under house arrest. The latter was rescinded on 26 August, but he had many reasons to feel aggrieved. He was bereft of any opportunity to influence affairs at court, where his enemy Robert Cecil was in the ascendance. The loss of his income was a grievous blow. He was not possessed of vast landed estates, so he was dependent on Crown perquisites to maintain his status and position.

So Essex was disaffected – and the disaffected attract others of their ilk. There is no doubt that he inspired great loyalty, particularly among those who had served with him on the Cadiz expedition. His secretary, Henry Cuffe, was highly influential. He organised secret meetings of Essex's friends at Drury House, the Earl of Southampton's London residence. Those who met there were already closely bonded. 'The first occasion that made me adventure into that course was the affinity betwixt my Lord Essex and me,' said Southampton. 'I being of his blood and marrying his kinswoman – so that for his sake I would have hazarded my life.' Sir Charles Danvers stated that 'what he had done in the business was merely for the love he bore to the Earl of Southampton'. He was a member of a noted Wiltshire family who were subjects of one of the great scandals of the age. In 1593 a servant of Sir Walter Long and his brother Henry, who held a neighbouring estate, was jailed for theft by Sir John Danvers, father of Charles and his brother, Henry. The servant was rescued by Sir Walter Long, whereupon Sir John had him committed to the Fleet Prison.

In revenge the Long brothers killed one of the Danvers' servants. In retaliation, the Danvers brothers killed Henry Long. They sought refuge with the Earl of Southampton before fleeing to France, where they served with distinction in the wars of Henri IV. They were declared outlaws by the Coroner's inquest in Wiltshire, but were eventually pardoned following a plea from the French king. Sir Charles then served with distinction under Essex on the Cadiz raid and in Ireland.

Sir Christopher Blount, Essex's stepfather, the third husband of his mother, Lettys Knollys, and twelve years her junior, was another in the Drury House group. At some point, the conversation turned away from the issue of how the Earl might reingratiate himself into the Queen's favour and into a discussion of the possibility of a coup d'état in which the strategic centres of the royal court or the Tower of London might be seized and Essex installed as regent of the realm. Essex was active in what was becoming an elaborate plot. He was in contact with Lord Mountjoy about the support he might give to the coup by bringing his army from Ireland, with King James VI in Scotland about the succession, and with Sir Thomas Smythe, the Sheriff of London, who had served with him at Cadiz and in Ireland, about the possibility of raising the trained bands in his support. Early in 1601, he began to fortify Essex House, which was not a good idea since it confirmed the suspicions of his enemies that a reckless action was being prepared. When asked what he would do with 'offenders and such as resisted him after he should be possessed of these things', Essex replied that 'he meant to admit them all to honourable trial'. In other words, the Cecil party would share the fate of the favourites of Richard II.

In a curious move, three of Essex's supporters – Sir Charles and Sir Jocelyn Percy and Lord Monteagle, together with three other conspirators, who probably included Essex's Steward, Sir Gilly Meyrick, and Henry Cuffe – spoke with Augustine Phillips and others of the Lord Chamberlain's Men. They were specific about what they required: a performance of 'the play of the deposying and killing of Rychard the second to be played the Saterday next' (7 February). According to Phillips, the actors expressed reluctance, pleading that the play was out of their repertoire. The conspirators, however, made them an offer they could not refuse. They would pay them 40s on top of their normal Saturday take. The actors must have then gone into rapid rehearsal. Whether 'the deposying' meant that the performance included the banned deposition scene is unknown, as is the reason why the conspirators desired the performance. That the play was a favourite of Essex is suggested by the official evidence compiled against him for the enquiry into his conduct in 1600: 'the Erle himself being so often at the playing thereof, and with great applause giving countenance and lyking to the same'. The performance may have been commissioned to boost the commitment of those involved in the coup or it could have been organised in the hope of precipitating riots among the dissatisfied populace. Essex would have remembered the disorders of 1595 and may have been seeking to provoke such an outburst again to give him the pretext of intervening with his preassembled force to restore order. If so, this was another miscalculation. The previous uprisings were caused by rising food prices and resentment against immigrants. No such outburst was ever caused by the mere production of a play. Indeed the performance may have had the opposite effect to that intended by alerting the authorities that something was afoot.

After dining together, a band of the conspirators crossed the river to the Globe, where they were joined by Captain Thomas Lee, a military ne'er-do-well who had long served in Ireland, latterly with Essex. Next day, the Queen sent four of her most senior councillors – Sir Thomas Egerton, Master of the Rolls; Edward Somerset, 4th Earl of Worcester; Sir John Popham, the Lord Chief Justice; and Essex's uncle, William Knollys, Treasurer to the Royal Household – to Essex House, to talk the Earl out of his anticipated attempt, which by then must have been common knowledge. It was a high-powered delegation that was calculated to inspire Essex's confidence. Egerton had interceded in the past with the Queen on his behalf. It was his residence, York House in The Strand, to which Essex had been confined on his return from Ireland. Whether Essex intended to make his move that day is unclear. Certainly the arrival of the delegation precipitated his action. His supporters surrounded the four royal councillors, shouting 'Kill them! Kill them!' Essex had the four men locked in the library. Whether this was to take them hostage, or for their protection, is unclear. Soon after the Sunday sermon had been delivered from St Paul's Cross, he marched off towards Smythe's house in Fenchurch Street with his 300 supporters. It was alleged that he shouted 'England is bought and sold to the Spaniards' as they went up Fleet Street, a reference to Cecil's peace policy. He repeated the sentiment when they arrived at Smythe's house. 'Where is the Sheriff?' he was said to have asked. 'Let him bring muskets and pistols. For I am credibly informed out of Ireland that the Kingdom of England is sold to the Spaniard.' Afterwards several witnesses claimed to have heard Smythe conferring with Essex, suggesting that, if he seized Aldgate and Ludgate, he would bring reinforcements rapidly. In other words, he would only support the plot if it appeared to be succeeding. At some point, Essex must have realised that he was not going to get the support from the City that he had expected. The tension was beginning to tell. He was said to be sweating so much that he requested a clean shirt. The seven gates into the City had been secured by forces loyal to the Crown and Cecil had sent heralds to various points to proclaim him a traitor.

Outflanked in every direction, Essex ordered a retreat to Essex House. Danvers had previously urged him to flee 'to Wales or other parts beyond the seas rather than trust to the city'. He was proved right. A force led by Charles Howard, Earl of Nottingham, surrounded the house and trained their cannons on it. This is the patron of the Admiral's Men, who had commanded the fleet against the Spanish Armada and had been Essex's co-commander on the Cadiz raid. When called on to surrender, Essex climbed on the roof, brandishing his sword. 'I had sooner fly to heaven,' he shouted. In the resulting skirmish, there were casualties on both sides. The Cecil papers reveal payments by the Queen to Reynold Smith, gentleman, 'who lieth bed-rid and had his arm broken at Essex House', and an unnamed man 'that was stricked deaf and became dumb upon his hurts at Essex House'. At just after 10 p.m., Essex surrendered with eighty-five of his adherents. The whole business had lasted just twelve hours. The Queen's reaction was clear. Next day, she told the French ambassador that 'the shameless ingrate had at last revealed what has long been on his mind'.

Despite his arrest, the loyalty of at least one of Essex's followers was unwavering. The renegade of the Irish wars, Captain Lee, escaped arrest at Essex House. Four days later, he plotted to seize the Queen in her chambers and keep her prisoner until she gave Essex an amnesty. He sought to recruit others to his cause and the plot was revealed. He was tried and executed the next day.

The rebellion affected Richard Quiney, in London on Stratford's business. With Thomas Greene, the Town Clerk, he tried to visit Sir Edward Cocke, the Attorney General, to discuss Stratford's problems. He bribed the doorkeeper and a clerk 'that we might have access to their master for his counsel ... butt colde nott have him att Leasure by reason of thees trobles'.[1]

Many must have felt a deep anxiety about the outcome of their parts in the Essex rebellion, including the actors who had performed *Richard II*. Most anxious of all would have been Augustine Phillips, 'servant vnto the L. Chamberlayne'. On 18 February, he was examined before the Privy Council together with 'one of hys players'. Given the penchant of the authorities to prosecute actors who voiced lines of which they disapproved, this was probably either the actor who played Richard or the one who played Bolingbroke. Had it been William Shakespeare, as the author of the play, or as a sharer in the company, he would have been named. It is likely that he had no involvement in the affair, which was a strictly commercial arrangement with the Essex supporters: precisely the line Phillips took under cross-examination.

> Wher thys Examinate and his fellowes were determyned to have played some other play, holding the play of Kyng Richard to have been so old and so long out of use as they should have small or no Companye at yt. But at their request this Examinate and his fellowes were content to play yt the Saterday and had their xls more than their ordynary for yt and so played it accordingly.

The Privy Council did not pursue the issue, either with the actors, or with those who had attended the performance. The exception was Sir Gilly Meyrick, who was charged with treasonous intentions. 'So earnest he was to satisfie his eyes with the sight of the tragedie,' read the indictment, 'which hee thought soon after his Lord should bring from the Stage to the State.' The others involved were indicted and punished according to the parts they were deemed to have played in the rebellion. One of these was poor Henry Cuffe, who had urged Essex not to use force. His fate was cited by the essayist Sir Francis Osborn in his *Advice to a Son*. 'Mingle not your interest with great ones': a sentiment that would have been endorsed by Phillips.

The two leading 'great ones', Essex and Southampton, were brought to trial for high treason on 19 February at Westminster Hall. When they met in the dock, they kissed each other's hands and embraced. The trial was hardly objective. Sir John Popham, who had been imprisoned at Essex House, was one of the seven judges. The jury of twenty-five peers included the Earl of Worcester, who had also been held prisoner, and at least two known enemies of the earls, Lord Cobham and Thomas, Lord Gray, who had feuded with Southampton for years. When Essex asked Popham if he could challenge any of the jury, he was told he could not. Many of the witnesses had been participants in the attempted insurrection. Most of them were not helpful to his case. This was not entirely born of a sense of resentment against the man who had brought them to this pass. They too were on trial for their lives and did not desire to risk their immortal souls through perjury. Essex had been free in blaming others of encouraging him in his disastrous course, so some desire to set the record straight may have come into play.

Each side used religion to denigrate the other. Essex claimed that 'Papists have been hired and suborned to witness against me', while Serjeant Yelverton, in his opening speech for the prosecution, stated that 'the Earl of Essex had none but Papists, recusants and atheists … in the capital rebellion against the whole estate of England'. Nor, despite the fact that the authorities had not pursued the actors, was the commissioning of *Richard II* forgotten. Sir Edward Cocke, who led the case for the Crown, gave his view on the fate of the Queen had the rebellion succeeded.

> I protest vpon my soul and conscience I doe beleeve she should not have long lived after she had been in your power. Note but the precedents of former ages, how long lived Richard the Second after he was surprised in the same manner? The pretence was alike for the removing of certain counsellors, but yet shortly after it cost him his life.

During the trial, Essex sought to undermine his principal enemy, claiming that Cecil had told a fellow member of the Privy Council 'that none in the world but the Infanta of Spain had the right to the crown of England'. Cecil immediately emerged from concealment to deny the accusation and to demand its source. 'Mr Secretary,' Southampton responded, 'if you would have me name the councillor, it was Mr Comptroller.' This was Sir William Knollys, Essex's uncle, who was duly summoned. When he arrived, he declared, 'I remember once in Mr Secretary's company there was a book that treated of such matters, but I never did hear Mr Secretary use any such words ...'

The book in question was *A Conference*. It was another misjudgement on Essex's part to refer to it, since it could only serve as a reminder that its dedication was to him.

Both earls were found guilty as charged. When asked why the death sentence should not be passed, Essex was resigned to his fate. 'I do not speak to save my life, I see that were in vain. I owe God a death which shall be welcome, how soon ever it pleaseth her Majesty.' In contrast, Southampton thought his life worth pleading for. 'Since the law hath cast me down, I do submit myself to death. And yet I will not despair of her Majesty's mercy, for that I know she is merciful, and if she is pleased to extend it, I will with all humility receive it.' The dreadful sentence was passed: the two men should be 'hanged, bowelled and quartered. Your head and quarters to be disposed of at her Majesty's pleasure.' Even then Essex had a reply. 'I think it fit [that] my poor quarters that have done her Majesty such true service in divers parts of the world should be sacrificed and disposed at her Majesty's pleasure.' The two men were returned to the Tower to await their fate.

Eight days later, on 24 February, Shrove Tuesday, the day of feasting before the Lenten fast, the Lord Chamberlain's Men performed at court. The circumstances of this extraordinary event are unknown – not even which play they performed. It was not their business to know that the Earl of Essex was to be executed next morning. If the Queen was present, she would have known. She had signed the death warrant four days before. She had little choice. Had she reprieved him, she would have had to, in all justice, reprieve all the conspirators. She may well have pleaded affairs of state and absented herself. Whether she was there or not, the company must have regarded the performance, which must have been arranged before the rebellion, as a token that no blame was attributed to them for their inadvertent part in it.

Nor did Essex know his fate until the next morning, when the Governor of the Tower advised him to prepare himself for death. His rank ensured that he was spared the sentence ordained by the court. Just before 8 a.m., the executioner 'performed his office ill'. It took three strikes of the axe to sever the head. Ironically the bungler in question was Thomas Derrick, the rapist that Essex had appointed as public executioner. The authorities decreed that the execution should be in private – the only one in the Tower during Elizabeth's reign. Had it taken place on Tower Hill, it could well have led to the very rioting that Essex had sought to provoke. When word spread of the popular hero's suffering, 'the hangman was beaten as he returned thence, so that the Sheriffes of London were called to assist and rescue him from such as would have muthered him'. Ballads lamented his death.

> Renowned Essex, as he past the streets,
> Would vail his bonnet to an oyster wife,
> And with a kind of humble congie gest
> The vulgar sort that did admire his life:
> And now sith he hath spent his livinge breath.[2]

The play of *Richard II* may well have been invoked at the trial of Sir Gilly Meyrick and four other conspirators on 5 March. The Queen ordered Sir Francis Bacon to write the official account of the rebellion. Of Meyrick's trial he wrote:

> So earnest hee was to satisfie his eyes with the sight of that tragedie which hee thought soone after his lord should bring from the stage to the state, but that God turned it vpon their own heads.

Whether this is a quote from the trial or represents Bacon's own verdict is unknown. Certainly his knowledge of Shakespeare's histories was vague. He refers to the wrong play of Richard: nor was Essex ever 'king in possession'.

> The example was remembered of Richard III, who (though he were king in possession, and the rightful inheritors but infants) could never sleep quiet in his bed till they were made away.

Ten men were condemned to death for their part in the rebellion. One of the four who were reprieved was the Earl of Southampton. His plea for the Queen's mercy from the dock was heeded. His sentence was deferred and he was incarcerated in the Tower awaiting her pleasure.

On 4 August, the Queen was at Greenwich examining the rolls from previous reigns with William Lambarde, her Keeper of Records. She picked up a document from the reign of Richard II. 'I am Richard, know ye not that?' she said. 'Such a wicked imagination was determined and attempted by a most unkind Gent, the most adorned creature that ever your Majestie made,' Lambarde replied. 'He that will forget God', answered the Queen in a reference to Essex's alleged atheism, 'will also forget his benefactors. This tragedy was played 40 times in open streets and houses.'[3] The remark is puzzling. Perhaps she was referring to the public playhouses.

## Like a Ripe Apple from a Tree

The Queen was going into a slow decline. On 21 November 1601, she made her last speech to Parliament. Her magnificent oration has a valedictory quality. There is a Shakespearean perspective in her view of the burdens of monarchy.

> To be a King and to wear a crown is a thing more glorious to them that see it, than that appears to them that bear it.

The Lord Chamberlain's Men performed before the Queen on St Stephen's Day and St John's Day (26 and 27 December), but it was but a shadow of previous revels. 'There has been such a small Court this Christmas,' wrote Dudley Carleton on 29 December, 'that the guard were not troubled to keep doors at the plays and pastimes.'[4] The actors appeared before her again on 1 January and on Valentine's Day. Later in the year, she relapsed, complaining of a sore throat as well as aches and pains. She seemed to have lost the will to live. She lay resignedly on cushions in her private apartments, and could not be persuaded to take to her bed. She refused the ministrations of her doctors. The Lord Chamberlain's Men played before her for the last time on 2 February 1603. Some thoughtful courtier must have commissioned them in the hope of stirring her from her deadly lethargy. The ploy did not work. As her condition deteriorated, she lost the power of speech and could only communicate by gestures. After she was persuaded into her bed, John Whitgift, the Archbishop of Canterbury, was summoned. When he spoke of her recovery, she made no response, but when he spoke to her of the joys of Heaven, she squeezed his hand. The issue of the succession remained unresolved to the last. Ironically, the Essex rebellion had given Cecil, his principal enemy, the very power he craved – to be its arbiter. Now he adopted Essex's major project. He had been in secret communication with James VI of Scotland. Not only was the King the Queen's nearest blood relative, he was also male and had progeny. Of the other chief claimants, Arbella Stuart was unmarried. The Infanta was childless and a Catholic. The question of the succession had been live for over half a century. Cecil was happy to forgo any claims to legitimacy the ladies may have had to ensure a stable monarchy. The accession of James would, at a stroke, remove Scotland as England's traditional enemy and further the imperial vision. He claimed to have put the matter to the Queen and that when he mentioned the name of James as her heir, she had squeezed his hand, so giving a putative seal of approval to his plottings. The Elizabethan era came to an end in the early hours of 24 March 1602/03. The diarist John Manningham heard that the Queen's passing was 'mildly like a Lambe, easily like a ripe apple from a tree'. Within eight hours of her death, Cecil had James proclaimed King. She had reigned for forty-five years. Most people, including William Shakespeare, had known no other monarch. There was a huge outpouring of public grief. Her funeral, on 28 April, was a spectacular affair, with a vast procession following her cortège. As was the custom, her effigy lay on her coffin. John Stowe wrote that:

> Westminster was surcharged with multitudes of all sorts of people in their streets, houses, windows, leads and gutters, that came to see the obsequy, and when they beheld her statue lying upon the coffin, there was such a general sighing, groaning and weeping as the like hath not been seen or known in the memory of man, neither doth any history mention any people, time or state to make like lamentation for the death of their sovereign.

Many were the literary outpourings and lamentations on the royal passing. To the fore was Henry Chettle, the workhorse writer and dramatist, who had written so kindly of William Shakespeare in 1592. Now, in his work in prose and verse entitled *England's Mourning Garment*, he upbraded the failure of 'the silver-tongued Melicert' to

> Drop from his honied hand one sable tear,
> To mourn her death that graced his desert
> And to his lays opened her royal ear ...
> Shepherd, remember our Elizabeth,
> And sing her rape, done by that Tarquin, death.

Melicertes, the Greek God of harbours, was a curious pseudonym for an actor, poet and playwright.

The same theme was taken up by the anonymous author of *A Mourneful Dittie, entituled Elizabeths Loss.*

> You Poets all braue *Shakspeare, Johnson, Greene*,
> Bestow your time to write for Englands Queene.
> Lament, lament, lament you English Peeres,
> Lament your losse possest so many yeeres.
> Returne your songs and Sonnets and your sayes:
> To set forth sweet *Elizabeths* praise.

James VI was a known lover of the theatre. In 1589, Queen Elizabeth had sent a company of players to Scotland to entertain him. Little is known of them except that they were led by Lawrence Fletcher and another actor whose surname was Martin. They had probably been recruited in London at the request of the twenty-three-year-old king, who desired to emulate his southern cousin by patronising his own troupe of actors. The cost is likely to have been borne by Elizabeth, who was already paying subsidies to the Scottish court.

The actors played before the King at a 'sumptious banquet' given by the Earl of Arran at Dirleton Castle. 'Divers of the nobility and gentry passed the time right pleasantly with the play of Robin Hood.'⁴ Fletcher and Martin were at the Scottish court in 1595, although their presence produced a predictable reaction among the land's dour Calvinists. Sermons were preached against them. The English ambassador, George Nicholson, reported to Cecil that 'the bellows blowers say that they are sent by England to sow dissension between the King and the Kirk'. The King would not hear of his players being censored and continued to hold them in the highest regard. The actors were in Scotland again between October 1599 and December 1601. On 22 October 1601, Lawrence Fletcher, 'Comedian to his Majesty', was awarded the Freedom of Aberdeen. The Lord Chamberlain's Men must have looked forward to the new reign with a sense of anticipation. They were not to be disappointed.

Three days after the death of Queen Elizabeth, James VI of Scotland received the news that he had become James I of England. On 5 April, he left Edinburgh for London. Cecil had taken every precaution to ensure a trouble-free passage. The ports were closed. A close watch was kept on leading Catholics and other potential dissidents. Lady Arbella Stuart was kept under surveillance at Hardwick Hall. The progress was slow so that the King should arrive in the capital after Elizabeth's funeral. His new subjects flocked to see him, relieved that the succession had sparked neither unrest nor invasion. James was determined to be 'every inch a King'. At Newark, when a cutpurse was caught plying his trade in the crowd, James ordered that 'this silken base theefe' be hanged. This rough justice was tempered with the regal prerogative of mercy. He commanded that all the prisoners in the castle be released. On the estates of the aristocracy and gentry, he indulged himself in the royal pastimes of hunting and feasting. As he entered London, the crowds were so great that 'they covered the beauty of the fields; and so greedy were they to behold the King that they injured and hurt one another'.

The actors' hopes of the new King were fulfilled beyond their expectations. He instructed 'our trusty and welloved councillor', Robert Cecil, to issue letters patent under the Great Seal of England. These provided a royal charter for Shakespeare's company, who were to be known henceforth as the King's Men, under direct royal patronage. The assiduous Cecil missed nothing off the types of performances in which the players had a right to engage. The royal warrant was issued on 17 May, just ten days after the King's arrival in London. Two days later, the formal patent gave licence to

Theise our servauntes, lawrence ffetcher William Shakespeare Richard Burbage Augustyne Phillippes John heninges henrie Condell William Sly Robert Armyn Richard Cowley and the rest of theire Associates freely to use and exercise the Arte and facultie of playinge Comedies Tragedies histories Enterludes moralls pastoralles Stage-plaies, and suche others like as theie have alreadie studied or hereafter shall use or studie aswell for the recreation of our lovinge Subjectes as for our Solace and Pleasure ...

Although it was noted that 'theire nowe usuall howse called the Globe' was their customary base, the patent instructed all justices, mayors, other officers and loving subjects 'to allowe them such former Curtesies as hath bene given to men of theire place and qualitie and alsoe what favour you shall shewe to theise our Servauntes for our sake'. In return for such co-operation, the document instructed, 'wee shall take kindlie at your handes'. The company was now obviated from the necessity to negotiate with difficult officials. The royal warrant would have accompanied them on their tours to be produced triumphantly for the inspection of local Dogberrys.

The nine sharers in the company became 'Grooms of the Chamber', with salaries of 52s 4d per year. Normally these were relatively minor courtiers who performed domestic functions, but in the case of the actors, the position was almost, but not entirely, honorific. A position in the royal household gave them valuable social standing.

Intriguingly, the list of actors on the patent is headed by Lawrence Fletcher, last seen performing before the King in Scotland. James may have expressed a desire to amalgamate his own troupe into the new company – or perhaps the canny actors saw the engagement of Fletcher, who had probably come south with James and already knew him well, as a useful adjunct in the new and breathtaking scheme of things. Either way, he was a popular addition to the company. In his will, probated on 13 May 1605, Augustine Phillips left him 20s in gold.

In an otherwise obsequious account of James's triumphant accession, Gilbert Dugdale, a minor writer, was mildly critical of the King's penchant for distributing honours promiscuously and elevating the actors beyond their station.

> Not only to the indifferent of worth, and the worthy of honour, did he freely deal about these causes; but to the mean, gave grace, as taking to him, the Lord Chamberlain's servants, now the King's Actors.[5]

So the 2nd Baron Hunsdon ceased to be the company's patron, although, as Lord Chamberlain, he had notional oversight over the Grooms of the Chamber. If he felt any offence at the loss of his company, it was not for long. On 8 September, he died, of a combination of congenital syphilis and the toxic effects of the mercury used to treat it. Doubtless there was a full complement of the members of his former company at his funeral in Westminster Abbey. They owed a great deal to this convivial man, noted for his hospitality. Hopefully, there were no comments about 'Winchester Goose' or 'Neapolitan Bone Ache'. 'We have many pocky cases now-a-days,' states the Sexton in *Hamlet*, 'that will scarce survive the lying in.'

The other two companies permitted to play in London also received royal favour. The Admiral's Men, known since the elevation of their patron as the Earl of Nottingham's Men, came under the patronage of Prince Henry, Duke of Rothesay, the eleven-year-old heir to the throne. The Earl of Worcester's Men became the Queen's Servants.

Even before the new King had arrived in London, he was making weighty decisions of State. 'I hear that the Earl of Southampton and Sir Henry Neville were set free at large yesterday from the Tower,' wrote John Massingham in his journal on 10 April. This hasty decision implies that James was in some way a party to the Essex rebellion. This is further confirmed by the rapid advancement of both Southampton and Neville (who was imprisoned and fined because he was aware the plot rather than directly involved in it) and the restoration of the sequestered Danvers estates. Southampton, wrote Sir Francis Bacon, was 'afterward restored in blood, made knight of the garter and one of his majesty's privy council'. By June, he was carrying the Sword of State before the King. He appears unaware of the gravity of the offence for which he had been condemned. When the Queen questioned him about the Essex rebellion, expressing astonishment 'that so many great men did so little for themselves', he replied that their opponents had skilfully manipulated the affair as to make it appear to be a treasonable attack on the Queen's person. That, to Essex's enemies, was precisely what it was. Nor had he curbed his tempestuous nature, adding that, but for this misrepresentation, none of their opponents would 'durst have opposed us'. Lord Gray, a juror at his trial, was standing nearby and fiercely retorted that the daring of the adversaries of Essex was not inferior to that of his friends. Southampton gave his interlocutor the lie direct, and was soon afterwards ordered back to the Tower for infringing the peace of the palace.

Naturally, there was huge public interest in the personality and character of the new monarch. He had literary and intellectual credentials, having three published works to his name. In 1598, he had expounded his views in a brief treatise whose title is self-explanatory: *The True Law of Free Monarchies: or, The Reciprock* [Reciprocal] *and Mutual Duty Betwixt a Free King and His Natural Subjects*. Next year, he returned to the theme in a more expensive way, in *Basilikon Doron* (Greek for 'Royal Gift'), a treatise written to the heir apparent, Prince Henry. Just seven copies were printed in Edinburgh, but the book sold in its thousands when it was published in London on James's accession. It is likely that William Shakespeare bought it. The King was not only his monarch, but his patron and we have seen the duties owed by poets to patrons. In contrast to *A Confession*, James asserts that the monarch claims his authority not from the people, but from God. He even prefaces his work with a sonnet of his own composition to express this theme.

> GOD giues not Kings the stile of Gods in vaine,
> For on his Throne his Scepter doe they swey:
> And as their subjects ought them to obey,
> So Kings should feare and serue their God againe
> If then ye would enjoy a happie raigne,
> Obserue the Statutes of your heauenly King,
> And from his Law, make all your Lawes to spring:
> Since his Lieutenant here ye should remain,
> Reward the iust, be stedfast, true, and plaine,
> Represse the proud, maintayning aye the right,
> Walke alwayes so, as euer in his sight,
> Who guardes the godly, plaguing the prophane:
> And so ye shall in Princely vertues shine,
> Resembling right your mightie King Diuine.

There was a third publication of the King's that Shakespeare undoubtedly perused. This was his *Daemonologie*, a treatise on witchcraft, which he had published in 1597. In 1563, the General Assembly of the Church of Scotland had issued a number of statutes against witchcraft, but little seems to have done about them until the King voyaged to Denmark to bring home his bride, the fifteen-year-old Princess Anne, in 1590. He seems to have been influenced by the strong belief in sorcery that existed in that country. The fleet bringing Anne to Scotland was dispersed by storms. On 23 July 1590, Robert Bowes, the English ambassador in Edinburgh, reported to Lord Burghley that 'it is advertised from Denmark, that the admiral there hathe caused five or six witches to be taken in Coupnahaven, upon suspicion that by their witche craft they had staied the Queen of Scottes voiage into Scotland and sought to have staied likewise the King's returne.' The King took the example of the Danes to heart. On 28 November, the ambassador wrote again. 'The King and Counsaill is occupied with the examinaciouns of sundry witches taken in this contrye, and confessing both great nombers and also strange and odiouse factes done by them.' The account of the North Berwick witch trials, at which the King had personally interrogated the accused, appeared in London as *Newes from Scotland*. It is probably another document acquired by William Shakespeare.

The royal court now had a distinctly Scottish air. A number of his courtiers had accompanied the King southwards: many of these were given positions under the royal favour. Like the King, they spoke in the Scottish dialect, which the Spanish ambassador in the reign of James IV had described as 'as different from English as Aragonese from Castilian'.[6] The Queen had learnt to read and write in Scots and her family was weaned on that language. Before his accession to the English throne, the King had been enthusiastic about its literary potential. In 1585 he had published *The Essays of a Prentise on the Divine Art of Poesie*, which set out the rules for writing poetry in Scots.

Despite the efforts of Cecil to ensure a smooth transition, there were those who were dissatisfied with the new regime. The Bye Plot of May 1603 bore some resemblance to the Essex rebellion in that it was an attempt to seize power by a coup d'état. It was led by Sir George Brooke, youngest son of that Lord Cobham who had been briefly Lord Chamberlain. He was arrested, imprisoned in the Tower and arraigned on 15 June. Under interrogation he revealed that his brother, the 11th Lord Cobham, was involved in another conspiracy, which became known as the Main Plot,[7] which intended to raise 600,000 crowns from the Archduke of Austria, raise a regiment with the money and march on London to place Arbella Stuart on the throne. Cobham intended to return via Jersey to seek the support of the island's Governor, Sir Walter Raleigh. When the plot was revealed, both men were arrested and imprisoned in the Tower. Although it is unlikely that Raleigh knew anything of the plot, it provided a good pretext to get him out of the way. He would oppose the peace treaty with Spain, on which both Cecil and the King were now resolved. As the Essex rebellion had proved, the disaffected were a disparate bunch. John Speed was not far off the mark when he described them as 'pretended gallants, banckrouts and vnruly youths ... setled in pyracie'.

For obvious reasons, the new King desired to be crowned as rapidly as possible to establish his legitimacy as the anointed monarch. The date for his coronation was fixed for 25 July. Unfortunately, in June, plague was recorded in the same poor parish of St Botolph, where it had begun in 1593. It spread through the city and did not begin to abate until mid-September. Some 47,000 people died throughout London. To go ahead with the pageants associated with the coronation would be impossible. The religious ceremony took place as planned. The pomp and circumstance was postponed to an indeterminate date.

Despite the plague, 1603 was a busy time for William Shakespeare and the King's Men. When the theatres reopened in the autumn, he was involved as an actor in Ben Jonson's tragedy *Sejanus: His Fall*. Its playwright must have extolled his work to the company as an exemplar of what a tragedy should be. This formidable classicist was an apostle of Aristotle's 'unities', which he considered that Shakespeare consistently violated. Unfortunately, his play, which was co-authored by 'a second pen' described by Jonson as 'so happy a genius', who was probably George Chapman, was hooted off the stage. The more sophisticated members of the audience, well versed in the classical tradition, seem to have appreciated it, but it was not to the taste of the groundlings. It would be a new experience for Shakespeare, Burbage and the other actors to 'get the bird' (even then an expression). In 1605, one of Jonson's admirers expressed his outrage at the play's treatment in dedicatory lines to the first quarto.

> When in the Globe's fair ring, our world's best stage,
> I viewed the people's beastly rage;
> Best to confound thy grave and learned toil,
> That cost thee so much sweat, and so much oil
> My indignation I could hardly assuage ...[8]

Ben Jonson's penchant for getting into deep trouble was unabated. He had got into a fracas with one of the servants of the hugely influential Earl of Northampton. Subsequently the Earl, whom Ben described as his 'mortal enemy', had him hauled before the Privy Council on charges of 'Popery and Treason' based on the content of *Sejanus*. It was a curious business. Jonson was indeed a Papist, but it was a charge which was leveled at Northampton himself (indeed he died a Catholic). There appears to be little in *Sejanus* – a play set in pre-Christian Rome – to merit such an accusation. Whatever the matter may have been, nothing seems to have come of it.

Around this time, an actor joined the company who was to prove one of its mainstays. John Lowin appears on the cast list of *Sejanus*. He was recruited from the Earl of Worcester's Men, with whom he was playing at the Rose Theatre in 1602. He appears as himself, together with Richard Burbage, Henry Condell and William Sly in the Induction to the King's Men's production of John Marston's *The Malcontent* around 1604. The son of a tanner in Cripplegate, he was baptised on 9 December 1576. Like Robert Armin, he was associated with the Goldsmiths' Company. He was described as a 'brother' when he appeared in the pageant celebrating the election of one of its members as Lord Mayor in 1611. He continued with the King's Men until the theatres closed on the outbreak of civil war in 1642, playing scores of roles in many productions.

On 19 November, the trial of the alleged conspirators in the Bye and Main plots was held in the Great Hall of Winchester Castle. All were found guilty, but only Sir George Brooke was executed – on 5 December – despite pleas to his brother-in-law, Robert Cecil, to intercede. The others, including Raleigh, Cobham and Southampton's antagonist, Lord Gray, were conveyed to the Tower to await the King's verdict on their fate. It would be a long time coming.

The royal household stayed well clear of the City for the rest of the year. In the third week of October, James held court at Wilton House in Wiltshire, the seat of William Herbert, the 3rd Earl of Pembroke and some people's choice as the beautiful youth of the sonnets. Late in November, the King's Men were summoned there 'upon the Councell's warrant'. They departed from Augustine Phillips's house at Mortlake, where they may have been undertaking extra rehearsals; such was the importance of this first appearance before their royal patron. They played at Wilton on 2 December and received the goodly sum of £30 'by way of his majesties reward'.[9]

The royal party felt it safe to move nearer London – to Hampton Court – for their Christmas festivities. The company had clearly pleased with their efforts at Wilton, for between St Stephen's Day and 1 January, they performed four times before the King and twice for Prince Henry under the Gothic roof of Cardinal Wolsey's Great Hall, whose walls were draped – then and now – with tapestries representing the story of Abraham. The distance from London would have meant that the company would have been lodged within the great palace. The arrival of a new audience from Scotland represented a wonderful opportunity to revive old dramas from the repertoire: one of those played before the Prince was 'a play of Robin Goodfellow', almost certainly a memory lapse by the clerk, who should have written '*A Midsummer Night's Dream*'. Again the players delighted, departing with £53. They appeared again at Hampton Court at Candlemas, 2 February. Six days later, Richard Burbage was paid £30 'for the mayntenance and reliefe of himself and the reste of his companie'.[10] Such sums from the royal purse provided a much-needed boost to the company finances while the theatres were closed. The plague must have diminished in the winter months, but the Privy Council maintained the closure orders 'in or neare London by reason of the greate perill that might growe through the extraordinarie concourse and assemblie of people'.

The orders had been lifted by 15 March, when the King made his long-postponed progress through the City. No expense was spared. Indeed the cost was described as 'incomparable'. Three playwrights – Ben Jonson, Thomas Dekker and Thomas Middleton – were commissioned to devise elaborate pageants which were presented at points along the royal route. Seven triumphal archways were designed and erected by the 'Joyner and Architect' Stephen Harrison. Much of the cost of this extravaganza was borne by the City livery companies. Three days before the event, the King, Queen and Prince Henry took up residence in the Tower of London. The royal suite had been lavishly prepared for its guests. 'Such glory in the hangings!' eulogised Gilbert Dugdale. 'Such majesty in the ornaments of the chamber!' It was felt inappropriate that the prisoners still under sentence of death for their parts in the Bye and Main Plots should remain on the premises.

> The Tower was empty of his prisoners; and I beheld the late Sir WALTER RALEIGH, the late Lord COBHAM, the late Lord GREY … with others, conveyed, some to the Marshalsea, others to the Gatehouse, and others to appointed prisons.

Late? Whether Dugdale considered the prisoners to be as good as dead, or whether he anticipated their imminent deaths, is unclear. Certainly Sir Walter was impressively active for a dead man, begetting his son, Carew, who was born in the following year, while still in the Tower.

On the evening before the great progress, a mock battle and grand firework display, commissioned by the Cinque Ports, took place in the Pool of London, opposite the Tower. Next morning, the royal party set off on their triumphal route. Unlike his predecessor, who had a high boredom quotient, the King became impatient at lengthy shows, so much of the content was curtailed. He must have been impressed, nevertheless, by much of what he saw. At Fenchurch Street, there was 'a stately Trophy or Pageant, at the City's Charge, on which stood a shew of workmanship and glory as I never saw the like', raved Dugdale. Naturally, the theme of the Union of Crowns was recurrent. In a somewhat unbeatific show,

> Saint GEORGE and Saint ANDREW met in one combat, and fought for victory; but an old Hermet passing by, in an oration, joined them hand in hand, and so, for ever, hath made them as one heart: to the joy of the King, the delight of the Lords, and the unspeakable comfort of the community.

On one triumphal gate, there was a huge model of the most prominent buildings in London. Another supported a mechanically moving globe of the world. The City's French, Italian and Dutch merchants had commissioned their own lavish pageants: speeches and orations abounded and the air was full of the 'harmonies of drums, trumpets, and music of

all sorts'. Every conduit between the Tower and Westminster was running
with wine with obvious effect.

> Through Ludgate, where the Conduits dealt so plentiously both before and
> after he was passed, as many were shipped to the Isle of Sleep, that had no
> leisure, for snorting to behold the day's Triumph.

The royal troupe of actors played its part. As members of the Household,
each of the nine sharers received four and a half yards of scarlet cloth from
Sir George Home, the Master of the Great Wardrobe with which to have
suits made. This time, the name of William Shakespeare heads the list. Their
function within the festivity is unclear. It would appear that they were not
in the royal procession. Robert Armin gives a clue to where they might
have been. He claimed to have written *Time Triumphant*, the account of
the pageant that was published under Gilbert Dugdale's name. If this were
so, it would explain how the author had seen the elaborate decorations in
the royal apartments of the Tower and the removal of the state prisoners,
although it is less likely that he would describe the actors as 'mean'. Perhaps
he recounted his view of the events of the day to Dugdale, who then wrote it
up. It is likely that the sharers, as Grooms of the Chamber, were called upon
to justify their function and wait upon the King in their scarlet liveries.

The royal extravaganza set the pattern for the reign. The court masque had
been introduced into England from Italy as long before as 1512. It combined
elaborate stage and costume designs with professional actors and musicians.
Members of the Household, including the royal family, participated. Under
James and his successor, Charles, the masque reached its apotheosis. Ben Jonson
reached his zenith as a writer of the genre and his collaborator, Inigo Jones,
became the favoured designer. These entertainments were hugely expensive.
£4,000 was spent on one production in 1608: 3 per cent of the national budget.
Although the King's Men, under the royal patronage, would have been obliged
to participate in some of them, there is no evidence that their chief playwright
was ever involved in their creation. He remained a man of the public theatre,
although, as we shall see, the genre had its influence upon him.

The court had its influence in other ways. The second quarto of *Hamlet*
was published in 1604. Derogatory references to the court of Denmark
were excised – the Queen was Danish – and the passages critical of the
children's companies of actors expunged. She had become the active
patron of the boy-companies.

Yet, the King's approbation of his company of actors was as strong as
ever. Just twenty days after the great extravaganza he caused the Privy
Council to write officially to the Lord Mayor and the Justices of Middlesex
and Surrey requesting them to refrain from interfering with the right of the
players to perform at their 'usual home', the Globe. The same privilege was
requested for the Queen's Servants at the Fortune Theatre and the Prince's
Servants at the Curtain. Doubtless this was a result of personal pleadings
to His Majesty by the actors.[11]

# 15

# The King's Servant, 1603–05

'Unnatural deeds'

*– Macbeth*, Act V, Scene 1

## 'So deere lov'd a neighbor'

By the time of the King's triumphal procession, William Shakespeare was at the only London address where he is known to have dwelt. According to a court deposition of 1612, of which we shall hear more, he had then known Christopher Mountjoy 'for the space of tenne yeres or thereabouts'. So, around 1602, he had taken lodgings in his premises on the corner of Silver Street and Monkswell ('Muggle') Street in St Olave's Ward. It was situated in a crook of the walls of London just a short walk from Cripple Gate. In the court document he is described as 'one Mr Shakespeare that lay in the house'. Why he moved there from Bankside, which was so handy for the Globe, is a mystery. Perhaps he wanted to get away from the noise of the theatres, bear pits, brothels and taverns that dominated the area. For those who prefer a Catholic Shakespeare, the lodgings were ideal. Mountjoy and his wife Marie were Huguenots, French Calvinist refugees. By a charter of 1559, Edward VI granted freedom of worship to foreign Protestants, so members of their household would not be obliged to worship at St Olave's church, just across the street. They attended the French Church in Threadneedle Street. Perhaps it was Jacqueline Field, the wife of the stationer and a fellow member of the congregation, who had recommended them to William Shakespeare, or maybe Mountjoy had provided the company with the headgear for the boys who played the women's parts.

Christopher Mountjoy was a tirer by trade – a craftsman who made tires, elaborate ornamental headdresses of gold and silver wire and pearls and spangles, for upper-crust ladies. He had a successful business. Once, he had even furnished Queen Anne with tires for the handsome sum of £59. His substantial double-garretted premises may be seen on the so-called 'Agas Map' of the City. Behind are what could well be workshops where he worked his craft with his three apprentices who lived on the premises, Stephen Belott, Guido Asture and Ufranke de la Coles.

Despite their ostensible adhesion to the stern moral code of Calvinism, the Mountjoys had what today might be described as an 'open marriage'. Marie Mountjoy had been engaged in an extra-marital affair with a mercer called Henry Wood, who lived just along the City Wall in Swan Alley off Coleman Street. In 1598, he had consulted the astrologer Simon Forman about her, asking 'whether the love she bears will be altered or not'. The situation was, to say the least, *un peu compliqué*. Soon after, Mrs Wood consulted Forman as to whether she should keep a shop with Mrs Mountjoy. He gave her sensible advice. 'They may join, but take heed they trust not out their wares much, or they shall have loss.'[1]

Mountjoy also lived an active and varied sexual life. He was reprimanded by the Elders of the French Church for his womanising – he had two illegitimate children by a servant maid and was eventually excommunicated because of his 'unruly and unregulated life'.

What Shakespeare made of this exotic household, or what he knew of the carnal activities of the Mountjoys, we can only surmise. We may speculate on his domestic arrangements. Clearly he would need more space than a mere bedsit, if only to accommodate the considerable library he must have acquired by this time. Did he eat with the family, or did he fend for himself? He clearly became a familiar part of the household – and a trusted confidant in family matters. The Mountjoys had just one daughter, although another had been buried as an infant in 1596. Mary or Marie Mountjoy cannot have been more than eighteen years old when her parents decided that she was of marriageable age. Their choice fell on their apprentice, Stephen Belott. In material terms such a match made a lot of sense. As refugees, it is probable that they had no relatives in England. Nor did they have a son to whom they could pass the estate. In essence they were proposing to adopt Belott as such. If he were ensconced firmly into the family and the business, its future – and theirs – would be assured. They had frequently remarked that he was 'a very honest fellow' whom Mountjoy regarded with 'great good will and affection'. William Shakespeare, himself the son of a skilled artisan, took an interest in the proceedings around the business, noting that Belott was 'a very good and industrious servant'. He also had the advantage of being French in origin, at least on his mother's side and, like the other apprentices, would have been part of the Huguenot community.

So Mountjoy approached him with a view to his taking on his daughter. She seems to have had little say in the matter, although she must have had a liking for Belott and realised that marriage to a man of her parent's choice was her destiny. Her father offered to conduct the betrothal ceremony – if Belott 'shold seem to be content and well like thereof'. The problem was that he did not 'well like thereof'. Although not averse to the proposed match, he appears to have regarded Mountjoy as something of an exploitative master who was somewhat vague about the terms of the marriage settlement. He must have been coming towards the end of his seven-year apprenticeship when he would be free to go elsewhere and so he held out for terms advantageous to his future position. The Mountjoys were by this time fully committed to the match and were in some state of distress about the apprentice's prevarication. An honest broker between the two parties was needed. There was just such a one on the premises, so Mrs Mountjoy 'did sollicitt and entreat' her lodger 'to move and perswade' Belott of the advantages of the match. William Shakespeare was a man of his time and was happy to be the go-between in the arranged marriage. There followed 'amongeste them selues many conferences about there marriadge' until an agreement was reached. As was the custom, the handfasting ceremony was performed and the relationship consummated before the formal solemnisation was celebrated. Belott had been canny in holding out for a substantial reckoning, but, as a young man, with little direct commercial experience, not quite canny enough. He had not had the agreement drawn up formally so he was reliant on his father-in-law's integrity and William Shakespeare's memory. Both were to prove less than perfect.

The couple were married in November 1604, probably at the French Church. They did not live at the parental home in Silver Street, but in nearby lodgings owned by George Wilkins, who kept an unruly tavern on Cow Cross, Clerkenwell. The host appears to have been as unruly as his tavern. He had been arrested several times for punching prostitutes, harbouring pickpockets and assaulting the constabulary. There is no direct evidence that he kept a brothel, as has been suggested. His court appearances suggest nothing more than that the goings on at the Eastcheap Tavern were not atypical. Yet he was a man of some education who had literary aspirations and connections. Around 1607, he collaborated with two of Henslowe's playwrights, William Rowley and John Daye, in *The Travels of the Three English Brothers*, a dramatisation of the recent adventures in Persia of the three Shirley brothers. Around the same time he wrote a play entitled *The Miseries of Enforced Marriage*, which was based on two notorious murders that had taken place in Yorkshire that year, although he somewhat daringly made it into a comedy. Probably through encountering William Shakespeare through the Mountjoys, he was able to sell it to the King's Men, who later performed it. Another curious piece called *A Yorkshire Tragedy* on the same sensational murders appeared at around the same time. The printer attached the name of William Shakespeare as its author, obviously hoping to sell more copies.

Question marks might be raised by Shakespeare's association with such flawed characters as the Mountjoys and George Wilkins, although Silver Street must have seemed a haven of respectability after life among the stews and common cruelties of Bankside. The point is not how the lodger saw the Mountjoys, but how they saw him. It is clear that they regarded him as a person of mature integrity whom they could entrust with a delicate negotiation which affected the entire future of their family. It is noteworthy that, in the theatrical world in which backbiting and aggression were frequent, no one, after the vicious attack attributed to Robert Greene, seems to have had a bad word to say about William Shakespeare. It is significant that minor writers – those perhaps with most reason to envy him – are to the forefront of the praise. The calligrapher and poet John Davies of Hereford refers to him as 'good Will' and declares that his very presence within it raises the tone of what he regards as a somewhat debased profession.

> And though the *stage* doth staine pure gentle *blood*,
> Yet generous yee are in *minde* and *moode*.

In 1604, Anthony Scoloker, in his *Diaphantus or the Passions of Love*, refers to 'friendly Shakespeare's tragedies'. William Berksted describes him as 'so deere lov'd a neighbor'. In his preface to the *White Devil*, John Webster wrote of 'the right happy and copious industry of M. Shakespeare, M. Decker and M. Heywood'. Jonson recorded that 'the players have often mentioned it as an honour to Shakespeare, that in his writing, whatsoever he penned, he never blotted out a line'. John Aubrey heard from the actor, Beeston, that he was 'very good company and of a very ready pleasant and smooth wit'. Nicholas Rowe heard from the actor Betterton that 'he was in himself a good-natured man, of great sweetness in his manners, and a most agreeable companion'.

Aubrey also heard that Shakespeare 'was not a company keeper'. He 'wouldn't be debauched ... and if invited to, writ, he was in pain'. In other words he demurred from social invitations, which may be an aspect of his 'right happy and copius industry'. Nor is there direct evidence of his involvement with the famous Friday Street Club, which met monthly at the Mermaid Tavern in Cheapside. 'What things have we seen done at the Mermaid!' wrote Francis Beaumont to Ben Jonson.

> Heard words that have been
> So nimble, and so full of subtle flame,
> As if that every one from whence they came
> Had meant to put his whole wit into a jest,
> And had resolved to live a fool, the rest
> Of his dull life.

Yet there clearly was a convivial side to William Shakespeare. He made William Johnson, the landlord of the Mermaid, a trustee of the property he bought in Blackfriars in 1615. 'Many were the wit combats between him and Ben Jonson ...' wrote Thomas Fuller,

> which two I beheld like a spanish great Galleon, and an English man of War; Master Johnson (like the former), was built far higher in Learning, Solid, but slow in his performances. Shake-speare with the English man of War, lesser in bulk, but lighter in sailing, could turn with all sides, tack about and take advantage of all winds, by the quickness of his Wit and Invention.

A few of these exchanges found their way into people's commonplace books. Let one stand as an example of the genre. Mock epitaphs were a cult of the day. 'Here lies Ben Jonson that was once one,' he wrote of himself, asking Shakespeare to complete it. The Bard took up the quill and wrote:

> Who while hee liv'de was a sloe thing,
> And now being dead is Nothinge.

Obviously Ben Jonson's slowness was a laugh in itself. Yet he was a persistent critic of the speed and facility of Shakespeare's writing, which he felt led him into absurdities. 'My answer hath bene,' he responds to the actors who so praised his colleague's facility in writing, 'Would he had blotted out a thousand.' He confesses that the actors regarded this comment as 'malevolent', but he goes on to justify his statement, citing a line from *Julius Caesar*.

> His wit was in his own power; would the rule of it had been so too. Many times he fell into those things, could not escape laughter, as when he said in the person of Caesar, one speaking to him: 'Caesar, thou dost me wrong.' He replied: 'Caesar did never wrong but with just cause;' and such like, which were ridiculous.

It appears that Shakespeare took cognisance of the criticism. The line as it has come down to us reads:

> Know Caesar doth not wrong, nor without cause
> Will he be satisfied.

Jonson is equally scathing in his prologue to *Every Man in His Humour*. He sees *Henry VI* as performed 'with three rusty swords,

> And help of some few foot and half-foot words,
> Fight over York and Lancaster's long jars,
> And in the tiring-house bring wounds to scars.

His own play is exemplary in its pursuit of the classical unities, in contrast to *Henry V*.

> He rather prays you will be pleased to see
> One such to-day, as other plays should be;
> Where neither chorus wafts you o'er the seas,
> Nor creaking throne comes down, the boys to please.

The latter line could refer to *Richard II*, *Henry VI* or *Richard III*, or even all three.

Yet Jonson's criticisms are entirely of a literary nature and are balanced by a deep respect for Shakespeare's personal qualities. 'But he redeemed his vices with his virtues. There was ever more in him to be praised than to be pardoned.' He never subjected Shakespeare to the kind of scabrous attack that was a feature of the War of the Theatres. 'I loved the man and do honour his memory,' he wrote, '(on this side idolatry) as much as any. Hee was, (indeed), honest and of an open and free nature.'

Jonson must have been riled that, although he scrupulously observed the unities, *Julius Caesar* was a far more popular play than his own classical dramas: a point made years later by Leonard Digges in his preface to the edition of Shakespeare's sonnets of 1640.

> Soe have I seene, when Cesar would appeare,
> And on the stage at halfe-sword parley were
> *Brutus* and *Cassius*: oh how the Audience,
> Were ravish'd, with what wonder they went thence,
> When some new day they would not brooke a line,
> Of tedious (though well laboured) *Cateline*;
> *Sejanus* too was irkesome, they priz'de more
> Honest *Iago*, or the jealous Moore.

We have no word of Jonson's view of what was probably the second of Shakespeare's Roman plays, but he must have found it even more infuriating than the first. In *Antony and Cleopatra*, the continuous shifting of scenes across a huge spectrum – Alexandria, Rome, Syria, Messina, Athens and various battlefields around the Empire – negated all that Jonson held to be appropriate to the drama. There are no less than forty separate scenes, more than Shakespeare utilised in any other play. This is another work of uncertain date. It was entered onto the Stationers' Register in May 1608, but was not published until the First Folio of 1623. Nor is there any record of a contemporary performance. This may betoken that it achieved no great stage success in Shakespeare's lifetime. It may be that the sheer diffusion of the action, diverting its focus from the two main protagonists, inhibited dramatic production. Yet it is this very diffusion that epitomises Antony's decline from the decisive character we saw in *Julius Caesar*. It is Shakespeare's achievement that he convinces us that this is the same man, but one whose qualities and abilities are in severe decline. The toll of the years is in part responsible for this, but his obsession with Cleopatra is the main cause. Through her we see 'The triple pillar of the world transform'd into a strumpet's fool'. Antony realises his situation but his tragedy is that he powerless to act against it.

> These strong Egyptian fetters I must break,
> Or lose myself in dotage.

This 'dotage' leads to the misjudgements of the fatal battle of Actium. He compounds his error in even fighting it by obsessively following Cleopatra out of the action when she withdraws in terror of her life.

> Egypt, thou know'st too well,
> My heart was to thy rudder tied by th' strings,
> And thou shouldst tow me after.

The 'dotage' extends beyond the personal. As Antony's famous line – 'I am dying, Egypt' – reveals, these people are the personifications of their nations. Their fate is that of kingdoms and empires, bringing about destruction of dynasties. As Shakespeare put the issue in another context:

> When beggars die there are no comets seen;
> The heavens themselves blaze forth the death of princes.

## Perpetual Peace and Alliance

The accession of James had raised hopes among English Catholics of greater tolerance. The King had been baptised a Catholic, although he had been brought up as a Presbyterian, a denomination he had come to dislike intensely. Anne, his queen, was reputedly a practising Catholic. Before ascending the English throne, he had assured the Earl of Northampton, that he would tolerate 'any that will be quiet and give but an outward obedience to the law'. Removed from the narrow vision and restrictive attitudes of the Kirk, he found the theology of the Church of England deeply appealing, particularly those doctrines that gave him an exalted status as 'the Lord's Anointed'. Thus his main religious contentions when he became King of England were with the Puritan elements in the Church. He had been on the throne but a few months when he was presented with a petition asking that such 'outward badges of Popish errours', as absolution, wedding rings, the term 'priest' and the wearing of the surplice, be banned. He was resolute in his defence of the Episcopal Bench, which the Puritans sought to abolish. 'No Bishop, no King,' he told them. 'When I mean to live under a presebytery, I will go to Scotland again.'

Nevertheless, the Puritans were a force that had to be appeased. One way to do this was to take a firm line against Catholics. Although enforcement of the recusancy laws had been relaxed in the early months of his reign, Parliament, probably under the influence of Cecil, renewed them in the summer of 1604. This dashing of their hopes led a small group of Catholics to begin plotting a desperate deed that would do more harm to the interests of their co-religionists than any other action in the era. They were led by Robert Catesby, a headstrong adventurer who was certainly known to Shakespeare. His father was that Sir William Catesby who had received Edmund Campion at Bushwood House. He was a familiar figure to Stratfordians. 'Yff you can learne where Mr. Robert Catesbie lyeth,' wrote Alderman Daniel Baker, to his 'Uncle Quyne' in London, 'I pray you goe to hym and dessier hym to have a care of mee for hys Father's debt according to hys promise at Rolewright … Hee lyeth about the Strand in a back allie towards Waterside.' Catesby was six feet tall, with a noble, expressive face and strong personal magnetism. He had participated in the abortive Essex rebellion. His fatal combination of charisma and naïvety led him into the Gunpowder Plot of 1605.

From the moment of his accession, the King had realised the necessity to put an end to the seemingly incessant war with Spain, which had dragged on since 1585. In this he enjoyed the thorough support of Cecil, his chief minister. Overtures were made and diplomatic exchanges took place. Teams of negotiators met at Somerset House on 20 May to prepare the ground. In August, two official delegations, one from Spain and one from the Spanish Netherlands, arrived in London. The Spanish delegation, their advisers and retainers were lodged at Somerset House. On 9 August, in their capacity as Grooms of the Chamber, the sharers of the King's Men were called upon to wait upon them and moved into quarters at Somerset House – a like service was performed at Durham House by Queen Anne's Men for the delegation from Flanders. It says much for the King's respect for the actors that he preferred that they attend his distinguished guests rather than his courtly retinue. What they did is uncertain, but they were paid £21 12s for their services. Only Augustine Phillips and John Heminges are mentioned specifically in the Treasurer's accounts, but William Shakespeare must have been among the 'tenne of theire ffellowes' who were in attendance. He who had written so much of history was now present at its making. The actors would be in close proximity to the men in the top echelons of the world's mightiest empire. The leader of the delegations, Juan Fernandez de Velasco y Tovar, Duke of Frias, was Constable of Castile and had been President of the Council of Italy. Juan de Tassis, Count of Villa Mediana, was Head of the Empire's Postal Services. Alessandro Robida was a Senator of Milan. The international nature of the Hapsburg Empire was further emphasised by the delegation from Flanders: Charles de Ligne, Count of Arenberg; Jean Richardot, President of the Privy Council; and Louis Vereyken, Audiencer of Brussels. Shakespeare would have been familiar with all the members of the English delegation: Lord Robert Cecil; Charles Blount, Earl of Devonshire, the lover of Lady Rich, the sister of Robert Devereux and the muse of Sidney's sonnets; the Lord Treasurer, Thomas Sackville, Earl of Dorset, co-author of *Gorbuduc*; Henry Howard, Earl of Northampton, Ben Jonson's 'mortal enemy'; and Charles Howard, Earl of Nottingham, the former patron of the Admiral's Men.

The number of Grooms of the Chamber from the King's Men was now twelve, reflecting an increase in the number of sharers. The new men were Alexander Cooke, a 'principle tragedian' in the cast list of *Sejanus*. Nicholas Tooley, a member of long standing – his name appears in speech prefixes in the First Folio text of *The Taming of the Shrew* – and the new recruit, John Lowin.

The 'Treaty of Perpetual Peace and Alliance' between England and the Hapsburg Empire was signed on 19 August by King James and the Constable of Castile in the chapel at Whitehall Palace. Its terms were not very different from those demanded by Philip II on the eve of the

Armada. England would forbear to interfere with Spanish interests on the Continent and cease harrying Spanish shipping. Pronouncements on commerce between the areas that the two kingdoms regarded as their spheres of influence were couched in sufficient ambiguity to satisfy both parties. Spain recognised that England was a Protestant country and would cease to acknowledge pretenders to her throne. This clause may have further served to stiffen the resolve of Catesby and his colleagues towards desperate acts.

After the signing of the treaty, members of the royal household, including the Grooms of the Chamber, processed to a grand banquet. The Earls of Southampton and Pembroke, both closely connected with the King's Men, acted as Stewards. After the repast, the company divided. The nobility adjourned to a display of bear- and bull-baiting in the courtyard, while the royal family, the distinguished guests and the courtiers attended a ball at which the ten-year-old Prince Henry danced a galliard and the Earl of Southampton escorted the Queen in a dance called a *brando*. His rehabilitation was complete. He had become a great favourite of the Queen, who was still only twenty-eight. She appointed him to her council of advisors and made him the Master of her Game. Without ever becoming estranged, the King and Queen were growing apart. His penchant for the company of male favourites may have been a manifestation of bisexuality, although there is no conclusive evidence for this. Indeed, in *Basilikon Doron*, he had listed sodomy among the crimes that 'ye are bound in conscience never to forgive'. Similarly, there is no evidence that the Queen indulged in extra-marital affairs, although Sir Walter Cope may have had his suspicions. Cope had been Secretary to Lord Burghley and was the trusted confidant of his son, Robert Cecil, who had been created Viscount Cranborne by the grateful King. Southampton had invited the Queen to attend a performance by the King's Men at Drury House. Cope was clearly concerned and wrote 'To the right honorable the Lorde Vycount Cranborne at the Courte'.

> Sir, I have sent and bene all thys morning hunting for players juglers and such kinde of creaturs, but fynde them harde to finde; wherfor, leavinge notes for them to seeke me, Burbage ys come, and sayes ther ys no new playe that the Quene hath not scene, but they have revyved an olde one cawled Loves Labore lost, which for wytt and mirthe he sayes will please her excedingly. And thys ys apointed to be playd to morowe night at my Lord of Sowthamptons, unless yow send a wrytt to remove the Corpus cum causabto your howse in the Strande. Burbage is My messenger ready attending yowre pleasure.
>
> Yours most humbly, Walter Cope.

The Burbage in question was probably Cuthbert, the company's administrator, rather than his brother, Richard, the actor. It is a measure of the seriousness with which Cope regarded the issue that he sent him personally to Cecil, suggesting that he issue a writ to transfer the performance to his own house. Whether this happened or whether the performance took place at all is unknown. Certainly the decision to bring *Love's Labour's Lost* back into the repertory was not a fruitless one. The play was performed before the Queen at court in the following January. This was part of an extended run of court entertainments between All Souls' Day and Shrove Tuesday. The King's continuing delight in his company was amply demonstrated in that of the seventeen performances intended (one was cancelled), eleven were to be presented by 'the Kings Maiesties plaiers': Of these, seven were by Shakespeare: the first, performed on 'Hallamas Day being the first of November', was 'A Play in the Banketinghouse att Whit Hall Called The Moor of Venis'. This first-known performance of *Othello* was recorded by the Clerk to the Master of Revels under its subsequent subtitle. The plot is based on a story called *Il Capitano Moro* ('The Moorish Captain'), one of 110 tales by Giraldi Capitano, aka 'Cinthio', which were published in 1565 under the title *Gli Hecatommi*. There is no known English translation, but Shakespeare was able to access the plot by some means – there is little evidence that he understood Italian. He even retains the name of the story's main female character – Desdemona.

Like Shakespeare's other play with Venice in its title, *Othello* is the story of an outsider. This would have had a profound impact on a contemporary audience. The whole machinery of church and state was geared to achieving uniformity of belief and action. Shakespeare's putative Catholicism would have made him intensely aware of the perils of nonconformity. The only hope for an outsider is to make himself so useful that his services become indispensable – and this is what Othello has done. The news of his marriage to Desdemona coincides with that of the anticipated Turkish invasion of the Venetian territory of Cyprus. When the Duke hears that Brabantio's daughter has eloped without her father's permission, he promises justice.

> Whoe'er he be that in this foul proceeding
> Hath thus beguiled your daughter of herself
> And you of her, the bloody book of law
> You shall yourself read in the bitter letter
> After your own sense, yea, though our proper son
> Stood in your action.

When Othello comes to justify his actions, he wisely stresses Desdemona's delight in his tales of indomitable courage. This is what the Duke, the Senators and even Brabantio most want to hear in terms of the crisis they are facing. It is exactly what Iago has predicted.

> I do know, the state,
> However this may gall him with some cheque,
> Cannot with safety cast him, for he's embark'd
> With such loud reason to the Cyprus wars,

> Which even now stand in act, that, for their souls,
> Another of his fathom they have none,
> To lead their business.

As an outsider, Othello has an uncertain identity. It is not clear how he rose to such a commanding position in the Venetian hierarchy. Indeed it is not entirely certain that Shakespeare knew what a Moor was, although a number of delegations from Morocco were received in London around this time. Moors were not black, as is implicit in the play ('thick lips', 'old black ram', 'sooty bosom'). In complexion they would have differed little from other southern Mediterranean peoples. Shakespeare's other Moorish character, Aaron, is depicted as black in a sketch of *Titus Andronicus* in performance made by Henry Peacham in 1595. Moors were Islamic; Othello is a Christian. He describes the Islamic Turks as 'infidel'. Shakespeare was no stronger on ethnicity than he was on geography.

Just as Othello is a military commander, so is the eponymous play a military play. The Venetians, having gained a bloodless triumph over the Turks, find themselves in the furthest outpost of empire. In the *ennui* of garrison duty, tempers fray and any rumour – however unlikely – becomes believable. Heavy drinking is the order of the hour. 'If I can fasten but one cup upon him,' says Iago of Cassio,

> With that which he hath drunk to-night already,
> He'll be as full of quarrel and offence
> As my young mistress' dog.

With no Turks to fight, the garrison implodes. 'Are we turned Turks,' asks Othello

> ... and to ourselves do that
> Which Heaven hath forbid the Ottomites?

Like *Hamlet*, *Othello* is a revenge tragedy, but with a difference. It is as if, at the denouement, the Prince discovers that King Claudius is innocent of all crimes and it is Horatio who has plotted the whole thing. Shakespeare is fascinated by the concept that there are men who commit evil for its own sake. We met Don John as a lighter version of this theme in *Much Ado* ('Will it serve for any model to build mischief on?'). We will meet it in an even darker form in the character of Edmund in *Lear*. Both Iago and Edmund may seek justifications for their actions, but at heart they are motivated by the force of destructive evil.

A second play received its first-known performance during these extended revels. The clerk recorded that 'Mesur for Mesur' was played on St Stephen's night. It is possible that this production was written with this occasion in mind. The title appears a curious one, but it alludes to

Matthew 7:2: 'With what measure you mete, it shall be measured to you.' The play's underlying theme is one in which Shakespeare knew the King has an interest. It reaches into the very function and nature of monarchy. It is a topic that he has addressed with great seriousness even before his accession to the English throne. We may recognise the role of the Duke Vincentio within the concept of the monarch as a dispenser of natural justice in James's *True Law of Free Monarchies*.

> Where he sees the law doubtsome or rigorous, he may interpret or mitigate the same, lest otherwise *summum jus be summa injuria* [the greatest right be the greatest wrong].

Shakespeare creates the Duke as the ideal of regal justice, perhaps in compliment to James himself. In contrast, the unanointed Angelo, once he grasps the handles of power, becomes tyrannous. It is an issue with which the King had dealt in *Basilikon Doron*.

> For the part of making, and executing of Lawes, consider first the trew difference betwixt a lawfull good King, and an vsurping Tyrant, and yee shall the more easily vnderstand your duetie herein … The one acknowledgeth himselfe ordained for his people, hauing receiued from God a burthen of gouernment, whereof he must be countable: the other thinketh his people ordained for him, a prey to his passions and inordinate appetites, as the fruites of his magnanimitie: And therefore, as their ends are directly contrarie, so are their whole actions, as meanes, whereby they preasse to attaine to their endes. A good King, thinking his highest honour to consist in the due discharge of his calling, emploieth all his studie and paines, to procure and maintaine, by the making and execution of good Lawes, the well-fare and peace of his people … where by the contrarie, an vsurping Tyrant, thinking his greatest honour and felicitie to consist in attaining … to his ambitious pretences, thinketh neuer himselfe sure, but by the dissention and factions among his people, and counterfeiting the Saint while he once creepe in credite, will then (by inuerting all good Lawes to serve onely for his vnrulie priuate affections) frame the common-weale euer to aduance his particular.

'[A] prey to his passions and inordinate appetites', 'unruly private affections' – it is difficult not to think of Angelo as a Puritan, the sect intensely disliked and distrusted by the King. In *Basilicon Doron*, he had warned his son about their false sanctity, calling them the 'verie pests in the Church and Commonwealth, whom no deserts can oblige neither oaths or promises bind, breathing nothing but sedition and calumnies, aspiring without measure, railing without reason, and making their own imagination (without any warrant of the world) the square of their conscience'. We recall, the lascivious and hypocritical Stratford alderman Daniel Baker, although it is unlikely that Shakespeare had such a parochial target in mind.

In *Measure for Measure*, Shakespeare addresses the concerns and aspirations of the monarch and so underlines his royal status. A lesser dramatist would have left it at that, but Shakespeare goes beyond the royal prerogative to dispense law justly as the anointed of God, into the realm of the Natural Law that comes from God, but which can be perceived by all men of good will: that which is 'set down in heaven, but not on earth', as Isabella declares. The play is a dissertation on the nature of morality. Is it absolute, or can it be tempered into what might now be described as 'situational ethics': a system of relativism under which moral rules are not absolutely binding but can be modified according to circumstance? Isabella represents the former, her brother Claudio the latter, although it must be said that the situation in which he finds himself is one in which many would baulk at the demands of an absolutist morality. The great speech in which he expresses his fear of the unknown, 'To die and go we know not where', is reminiscent of Hamlet's 'dread of something after death

> The undiscover'd country from whose bourn
> No traveller returns, puzzles the will
> And makes us rather bear those ills we have
> Than fly to others that we know not of?
> Thus conscience does make cowards of us all;
> And thus the native hue of resolution
> Is sicklied o'er with the pale cast of thought.

As in *Hamlet*, where the casual and flippant attitude of the two gravediggers towards death contrasts with the foibles and anxieties of the Prince, so Claudio's deep worries are juxtaposed with the complete lack of concern about death of the drunken criminal Barnardine. Similarly, the minor peccadillo of Claudio for which he is to receive the ultimate penalty is contrasted with Angelo's abandonment of the interrogation of Froth and Pompey, who are the organisers of a large-scale vice-ring.

Isabella knows 'no pale cast of thought'. Like Hamlet's father's ghost, she knows there is a world of judgement beyond this one. She has made her initial vow of chastity on joining the contemplative order of the Poor Clares. When Claudio pleads with her to accede to Angelo's demand that she fornicate with him so that his life might be spared, she employs a teleological argument:

> Better it were that a brother died at once
> Than that a sister, by redeeming him,
> Should die for ever.

She is citing the Thomist doctrine of double effect. It is always wrong to do a bad act intentionally in order to bring about a good consequence – i.e. if she allows Angelo to take her virginity in order to save Claudio. It is permissible, however, to do a good act knowing that it will bring about bad consequences – i.e. in preserving her chastity although it will lead to the execution of Claudio. Thomas Aquinas cites Matthew 7:17 in defence of this doctrine: 'If the tree be evil, so is the fruit.' He expounds on this as 'If a man pursues a lawful occupation and takes due care, the result being that a person loses his life, he is not guilty of that person's death.' Or, as Isabella puts it,

> Ignominy in ransom and free pardon
> Are of two houses, lawful mercy
> Is nothing kin to foul redemption.

In fact, Isabella's righteous stance is exonerated. Angelo believes that he has fulfilled his desire to take her virginity, but fails to deliver his side of the bargain. Realising that the Duke's return is imminent, he reveals that Claudio's supposed death has been necessary to prevent his own downfall. Here we enter one of Shakespeare's themes, underwritten by King Claudius, that an evil act will solve nothing. It will lead to more and greater evil acts. 'Alack, when once our grace we have forgot,' says Angelo. 'Nothing goes right, we would and we would not.'

*Measure for Measure* is arguably Shakespeare's most theological play. Indeed, together with *Hamlet*, it is arguably his most Catholic play. The Duke not only has the God-given secular power of the monarch, but, in the priestly role he assumes, the God-given power to forgive sins on earth. He can hear confession, give absolution and, finally, respond to the intercessions of Mariana and Isabella. As always, Shakespeare defends his position by carefully setting his Catholic play in the Catholic world, although his sense of geography is lacking. Germanic Vienna is populated by people with Italian names and a pirate languishes and dies in a Viennese jail many miles from the sea. This is the man who made a port out of Milan and gave Bohemia a seacoast. The theme of the mistaken bed-partner was one that weighed with him at this time. It is central to the plot of *All's Well That Ends Well*, a play which seems not to have been too great a success. There is no recorded performance until 1741.

Although only two of his plays were performed against the seven of Shakespeare's, it is likely that the triumph of the extended revels went to Ben Jonson. On Twelfth Night his *Masque of Blackness* was performed. Exotic costumes and sets featuring elaborate mechanical devices were designed by Inigo Jones, who was about to become court architect. The Queen and her ladies appeared, blacked up as Moors (had *Othello* set a fashion?). Such grand shows were not to everyone's taste. 'You cannot imagine a more ugly sight,' wrote Sir Dudley Carleton. The Venetian ambassador found the huge cost of the occasion, which he had heard was 25,000 crowns, the most remarkable thing about it. Such extravagance would contribute to the eventual downfall of the Stuart monarchy, but it had a while to run.

It is not known whether Augustine Phillips performed in this extensive programme of courtly revels. He was presumably in good health in the previous year, when he moved to the grander area of Mortlake. He cannot have been much older than forty. The oldest of his four daughters was but eleven. He made his will on 4 May 1605, 'being at this present, sick and weak in body, but of good and perfect mind and rembrance'. He died within the month. He had been a *tour de force* in the company, as actor, administrator, musician and (probably) dancer. His adhesion to his fellows is demonstrated in the will. In addition to bequests to members of his large extended family, thirteen colleagues are remembered and £5 is left to be divided between the hired men of the company. Henry Condell, Christopher Beeston and William Shakespeare each received a 30s gold piece. Phillips requested to be buried in the chancel of his parish church, St Mary the Virgin, and it was here that his family and friends gathered in late May. Shakespeare and his colleagues must have taken boats upstream from Southwark. Dr John Dee, the physician, alchemist and astrologer much favoured by Queen Elizabeth, may have been in the congregation. His house was opposite the church. He had become much impoverished in the next reign and was forced to sell his possessions to maintain himself.

Another who would have been there was Phillips's 'apprentice' James Sands, who may have had talents as an artist. He could well have been the painter of the so-called 'Sanders' portrait, which appears to have had a long pedigree in his family until its emergence into the public view in the 1970s. Attached to its back is a slip of paper identifying the sitter as William Shakespeare with the dates of his birth and death and the information that the picture was painted in 1603. Tests have shown that the oak panels on which it is painted and the paper are from that era. Art authorities have dismissed it on the grounds that the sitter looks younger than the thirty-eight or thirty-nine years that would have been Shakespeare's age at this time, and also drawn attention to the discrepancies in the physiognomy from the authenticated images of the First Folio and his bust in Stratford church. This is to miss the point. The picture is the work of a talented amateur, not that of an established artist. The age of the sitter is indeterminate. He could well be in his late thirties. In fact the sitter has physical qualities recognisable in the bust – a hint of auburn in the hair which is receding. The family tradition is that it was either painted by James Sanders or his brother, John. It also says that the painter came from Worcester. Diligent research in the city archives might shed more light on the issue.

It is impossible to place a precise date upon the writing of Shakespeare's *Tragedy of Macbeth*. It was surely written after King James's accession in 1603 to take advantage of the prevailing interest in matters Scottish. Shakespeare must have thought that there was much in it to interest King James, whose past interest in witchcraft was well known. There is a strong compliment to his dynastic assumptions. The heirs of Banquo, the founder of the House of Stuart, will rule in Scotland, not those of Macbeth. The witches present the succession of kings who carry 'twofold balls and treble sceptres' (IV.1.20). The first symbolises James's kingship of both Scotland and England. The 'treble sceptres' add Ireland to the equation.

The attempt by Shakespeare to indulge the supposed interests of the King may have misfired. James was greatly relieved to be out of Scotland, with its feuding nobility and fierce sectarianism. When he had left Edinburgh for London in 1603, he promised to return soon. It was to be seventeen years before he did so. There are indications that he regarded with some embarrassment his previous persecution of alleged witches in Scotland. Although witch trials had taken place in England in the past, they had been few and far between. James regarded England as an infinitely more sophisticated society than Scotland. *Macbeth* may have epitomised the primitive society, permeated with superstition, he was trying to put behind him. There is no record of any performance of the play at court, or indeed anywhere, until the astrologer Simon Forman saw a production at the Globe on 20 April 1610. Interestingly, he notes that Macbeth and Banquo rode onto the stage on horseback. He recalls the scene graphically in which Macbeth toasts the absent Banquo at a banquet. The ghost of the murdered man has occupied his chair and is revealed when he turns it round to be seated.

The only extant text of *Macbeth* is that in the First Folio of 1623. There is a lack of continuity that underlines Shakespeare's customary haste in writing and lack of revision. In Act I, Lady Macbeth familiarly declares that her 'breasts have given suck'. In Act III, Macbeth bewails the fact that his heirs will not inherit the throne, but in Act IV Macduff declares that Macbeth has no children. 'How many children had Lady Macbeth?' indeed. The play appears to have been subject to interpolations by other hands, adding anomalous scenes involving the goddess Hecate and two songs taken from Thomas Middleton's play *The Witch*. As it stands, *Macbeth* is by far the shortest of Shakespeare's tragedies. Yet, despite its textual shortcomings, it stands as one of his great works. The theme of the seizure of power by a single criminal act is evocative of Chapter 8 of Machiavelli's *Il Principe* – 'Concerning those who have obtained a Principality by Wickedness'. The argument supports the very course that Macbeth and Claudius in *Hamlet* seek to follow.

> It is to be remarked that, in seizing a state, the usurper ought to examine closely into all those injuries which it is necessary for him to inflict, and to do them all at one stroke so as not to have to repeat them daily; and thus by not unsettling men he will be able to reassure them, and win them to himself by benefits. He who does otherwise, either from timidity or evil advice, is always compelled to keep the knife in his hand; neither can he rely on his subjects, nor can they attach themselves to him, owing to their continued and repeated wrongs. For injuries ought to be done all at one time, so that, being tasted less, they offend less.[2]

Macbeth evokes powerfully Machiavelli's argument.

> If it were done when 'tis done, then 'twere well
> It were done quickly: if the assassination
> Could trammel up the consequence, and catch
> With his surcease success; that but this blow
> Might be the be-all and the end-all here …

In a sense, *Macbeth* is *Hamlet* written from Claudius' point of view: an intense psychological study of the effect that conscience can have on the human psyche. Macbeth must overcome his huge scruples to do the deed that the witches tell him is preordained. Like that of Claudius, his is a crime against the natural order. It is not only treason against the fealties of kinship and kingship. It is an outrage against hospitality. 'He's here in double right,' he says of Duncan.

> First, as I am his kinsman and his subject –
> Strong both against the deed; then as his host,
> Who should against the murderer shut the door,
> Not bear the knife myself.

While Macbeth is inhibited by conscience, it is Lady Macbeth who appears the strong one. 'But screw your courage to the sticking place,' she urges him. Yet it is her guilt that brings her down, not Macbeth's. 'Here's the smell of the blood still; all the perfumes of Arabia will not sweeten this little hand.' she says in the sleepwalking scene. The doctor realises that she is beyond the help of any physician, but needs to reconcile herself to the Almighty.

> Foul whisp'rings are abroad: unnatural deeds
> Do breed unnatural troubles; infected minds
> To their deaf pillows will discharge their secrets.
> More needs she the divine than the physician.
> God, God forgive us all!

Like that of Claudius, and contrary to the view of Machiavelli, Macbeth's crime against nature resolves no issue. It leads him to further crimes, beginning with the murder of Duncan's innocent guards and ending with the massacre of Macduff's household. We are again in the presence of Christian tragedy as Macbeth gains the terrible self-knowledge that the game has not been worth the reckoning. His closing soliloquies are contemplations on the Christ-like theme of 'What shall it profit a man if he gain the whole world yet lose his own soul?' His crimes have placed him beyond a state of salvation and made life appear meaningless, without divine or human comfort.

> To-morrow, and to-morrow, and to-morrow,
> Creeps in this petty pace from day to day
> To the last syllable of recorded time,
> And all our yesterdays have lighted fools
> The way to dusty death. Out, out, brief candle!
> Life's but a walking shadow, a poor player
> That struts and frets his hour upon the stage
> And then is heard no more: it is a tale
> Told by an idiot, full of sound and fury,
> Signifying nothing.

Some have observed a reference to the Gunpowder Plot in the Porter's soliloquy in Act II, Scene 3. 'Faith, here's an equivocator, that could swear in both the scales against either scale; who committed treason enough for God's sake, yet could not equivocate to heaven.' The reference is supposedly to the trial of the Jesuit Henry Garnett, who had embarked on a defence based on the principle of amphibology, which involved rejoining ambiguous answers, which were neither the entire truth nor lies. The formula could be invoked in cases where an entirely truthful answer could place others in jeopardy. Whether these words are indeed evocative of Garnett, or even whether they are those of Shakespeare or of the clown who was extemporising the Porter's scene, is unclear, but they contain their own ambiguity. The Porter's equivocator has indeed committed treason, but it has been 'for God's sake'.

## The Gunpowder Plot
The Gunpowder Plot was the sensation of the age. Although it was conspicuously a Catholic conspiracy, its protagonists were drawn from that class of dissatisfied gentry that had participated in the Essex rebellion. Indeed, several of the plotters had been involved in that fiasco. It was an escapade nurtured in the Stratford neighbourhood. As Robert Catesby gathered his conspirators together, Ambrose Rookwood rented Clopton House to be near his fellow plotters, who were mainly impoverished local Catholic gentry. They whiled away their time 'ryding of great horses and hunting'. On 4 and 5 November, they attended local race meetings to be together when the news came from London. On hearing the worst they fled across country, seizing horses from Fulke Greville's stables at Warwick before making a last stand at Haddington in Worcestershire. Catesby was killed by a bullet in the head. The others were executed with that horror and fortitude the age deemed necessary.

In Stratford the excitement was intense. This was as stirring as the Armada yet closer to home. The armour was again removed from its dusty repository and repaired and replenished. Musters were raised, gunpowder purchased and tactics discussed. On the night of 9 November, the Corporation drank wine at Mrs Quiney's tavern, 'when yt was said that Sir Fulke Greville's house was beseiged'. The horse-stealing incident had grown to a campaign in just three days. An expedition was launched against Clopton House. The local militia was doubtless relieved to find it unoccupied. Goods were seized, including chalices, crucifixes, surplices and other vestments. A further repercussion was a crackdown on those considered to be 'popishly affected', who fulfilled the obligation to attend church, but never received the sacrament. Among those listed were the Sadlers and Susanna Shakespeare. Their names were later struck from the list, so it may be assumed that they conformed.

The clear intent of the Gunpowder Plotters was to assert the rights of Catholics in England. In fact, the reverse was achieved. It was followed rapidly by Parliament's enactment of the Popish Recusants Act 1605, which passed into law in May 1606. It excluded Roman Catholics from the professions of law and medicine and from acting as a guardian or a trustee; and it allowed magistrates to search their houses for arms without a warrant. It also provided a new Oath of Allegiance, which denied the power of the Pope to depose monarchs. It became high treason to obey the authority of Rome rather than that of the King. Those who did not receive 'the sacrament of the Lord's Supper' at least annually in the parish church were to suffer fines of up to £60 or to forfeit two-thirds of their lands. It was probably the King's influence that ensured that certain classes of the aristocracy were exempt from this clause, as were the households of expatriate refugees such as the one where William Shakespeare was living.

# 16

# Ember Days, 1604–11

'The baseless fabric of this vision'
– *The Tempest*, Act IV, Scene 1

There were two routes to London from Stratford and William Shakespeare used both on his three-day journey to the capital. The first took him through Banbury, Bicester and Aylesbury. He may have found literary inspiration at a village on this route. 'The humour of … the constable in *A Midsummer Night's Dream*', says John Aubrey, 'he happened to take at Grendon in Bucks … and there was living that constable about 1642 when I first came to Oxon.'[1] Presumably Aubrey is referring to Dogberry in *Much Ado*. It's a nice story.

The Davenants had thrived in Oxford. On 4 June 1604, John was admitted as a Freeman of the City, with a Bailiff's place on the Council as one of only three local licencees permitted to sell wine. The change of air improved their gynecological prospects. Having had many miscarriages in 1590s, Jennet gave birth to another eight children. A regular participant in the hospitality of their house, where two of the daughters served behind the bar, was William Shakespeare, who was a great favourite. Robert Davenant, the eldest son, who became a clergyman in Wiltshire, recalled that the poet had 'oft showered him with a 100 kisses'. On 3 March 1605/06, William Shakespeare stood as godfather to the second son, either in person or by proxy, at St Martin's church in Oxford. The boy was named in his honour. William Davenant became a poet and playwright, more celebrated in his time than today. According to Aubrey, when in his cups he was wont to hint that the 'god' suffix was extraneous. Doubtless he desired to claim the genetic inheritance of Shakespeare's genius, but the story, although it circulated around Oxford in the seventeenth century, is unlikely. Women do not frequently embark on extra-marital affairs to achieve their twelfth pregnancy and the Davenants were a devoted couple. After Jennet died in 1621, her husband, by then Mayor of Oxford, desired that he be buried 'as nere my wife as the place will give leave where she lyeth'. He achieved his desire just eighteen days later. Nevertheless, the persistence of the scandalous gossip may reflect some memory of a previous liaison between William Shakespeare and Jennet Sheppard. Her dark ladyship cannot be written off entirely.

The two routes to London met at Uxbridge. The way on to the City carried the traveller past London's killing fields at Tyburn. After each Quarterly Sessions at the Law Courts, the condemned – usually some twenty or thirty men and women – were brought there by cart with nooses around their necks. At the place of execution, Thomas Derrick, the hangman, or one of his assistants, hitched the ropes to the huge triangular structure known as Tyburn Tree. It stood in the middle of the roadway, a stark and dreadful symbol of the law. Once all had been attached, the cart was driven away and the condemned died by slow strangulation. Those fortunate enough to have friends present would have them pull on their feet to hasten their passage. The corpses were taken down and buried in the neighbouring cemetery. Nearby stood Tyburn House which was, in the words of Thomas Platter, 'haunted by such monsters that no one can live in it'.

It must be Tyburn Tree that Shakespeare recalls in *Hamlet*. 'What is he,' asks the Gravedigger, 'that builds stronger than either the mason, the shipwright, or the carpenter?' 'The gallows-maker,' replies the Sexton, 'for that frame outlives a thousand tenants.'

Beyond Tyburn, the walls of London appeared. William Shakespeare would enter the City through the gate most convenient for the various places he was to call home – Bishopsgate, Ludgate or Cripplegate.

In September 1604, the King's Men made another foray into Kent. William Shakespeare was probably with them. On 4 October, they played in Dover. The great chalk cliffs were fresh in his memory when he wrote the play he was probably even then contemplating. His description of the cliff that now bears his name has the feel of an eyewitness account.

> How fearful
> And dizzy 'tis, to cast one's eyes so low!
> The crows and choughs that wing the midway air
> Show scarce so gross as beetles: half way down
> Hangs one that gathers samphire, dreadful trade!
> Methinks he seems no bigger than his head:
> The fishermen, that walk upon the beach,
> Appear like mice; and yond tall anchoring bark,
> Diminished to her cock; her cock, a buoy
> Almost too small for sight: the murmuring surge,
> That on the unnumbered idle pebbles chafes,
> Cannot be heard so high. I'll look no more;
> Lest my brain turn, and the deficient sight
> Topple down headlong.

In 1606, Richard Burbage was thirty-eight. It was some five years since he had created the part of the undergraduate Hamlet, who was conveniently aged thirty. Such was the faith of William Shakespeare in the skills of his leading actor that he now determined that he should play an old man.

He was about to play the greatest part ever written. The first recorded performance of *King Lear* was at court at the Whitehall Palace on St Stephen's Day 1606. What the royal party made of this most radical of plays with its great themes of social justice can only be surmised.

> Take physic, pomp,
> Expose thyself to what wretches feel,
> That thou may shake the superflux to them
> And show the heavens more just.
>
> (III.4.33–36)

> So distribution should undo excess,
> And each man have enough.
>
> (IV.1.69–73)

The play was not one of Shakespeare's most popular. The royal performance of 1606 is the only one mentioned specifically as occurring in the playwright's lifetime, although 'kind Lear' was one of Burbage's outstanding roles according to his anonymous elegist in 1619. The play seems to have been revised a great deal in performance. The two quartos of 1608 and 1619 and the First Folio text of 1623 show considerable variations. Like many other Shakespeare plays, *Lear* had a predecessor. *The True Chronicle History of King Leir and His Three Daughters* was acted at the Rose Theatre in 1594 and published in 1605. Shakespeare's version is based on one of his favourite sources, the second edition of Holinshed's *Chronicles of England, Scotlande and Ireland*, published in 1587. The Gloucester subplot he takes from a passage in Sidney's *Arcadia*.

The play is set in a period of ancient British history. Shakespeare follows his usual pattern of placing his play in context. The invocations are to the gods, rather than to the one God. There are no directly Christian references – not even anachronistically. Yet the play is the apotheosis of his concept of Christian tragedy. If texts are to be taken to epitomise its themes, they come surely from St Paul's First Epistle to the Corinthians.

> For the foolishness of God is wiser than men's wisdom, and the weakness of God is stronger than men's strength. (1 Cor. 2:25)
> God chose the foolish things of the world to shame the wise: God chose the weak things of the world to shame the strong. (1 Cor. 2:27)
> Do not deceive yourselves. If any of you think he is wise by the standards of this age, he should become a 'Fool' so that he may become wise. For the wisdom of this world is foolishness in God's eyes. (1 Cor. 3.18)

It is the Fool who sees the foolishness of Lear's action and provides a Chorus of sanity in a world run insane. Presumably the part was played by Robert Armin, who perhaps exercised his well-known capacity to extemporise, so how much of the part is the clown's creation and how much Shakespeare's we can only speculate. After the storm scenes the Fool fades from view – we never discover his fate. He is no longer required. Lear has become his own fool and in the process learnt the wisdom of the foolish. At the terrible nadir of existence, man finds the truth about himself. Until this moment his view of the world is influenced by material circumstance. The lines when he realises that the Bedlam beggar epitomises mankind as it is, without pretence, nail the play. 'Is man no more than this?' he asks.

> Consider him well. Thou owest the worm no silk, the beast no hide, the sheep no wool, the cat no perfume. Ha! here's three on 's are sophisticated! Thou art the thing itself: unaccommodated man is no more but such a poor bare, forked animal as thou art. Off, off, you lendings! come unbutton here.

In his madness Lear finds empathy with man's basic condition. Similarly Gloucester begins to see reality once he is blinded. 'I stumbled when I saw.' The universe appears as unordered as the forces that control it.

> As flies to wanton boys are we to the gods,
> They kill us for their sport.

Yet the process by which the various protagonists gather upon the stormy heath is not morally neutral. Actions have consequences. Lear's situation is the product of his desire for flattery, which Goneril and Reagan are happy to provide. Like Isabella, Cordelia will not abandon principle for expediency. She cannot bestow on her father the love which duty demands she owes her future husband. There is irony in Gloucester's critique that the gods kill men for their sport. 'There was good sport at his making' is as far as he goes in acknowledging his moral duty to Edmund. It is the very product of this 'good sport' that brings about his downfall and thereby his enlightenment. Shakespeare suggests that no sexual act can be morally neutral. Edgar answers his father's cry against the gods when he tells the stricken Edmund,

> The gods are just, and of our pleasant vices
> Make instruments to plague us:
> The dark and vicious place where thee he got
> Cost him his eyes.

Mankind is no longer 'star-crossed' as Edmund expounds, but is responsible for its own destiny, for good or ill. Similarly, Lear's journey through madness enables him to view the universe as a place governed by man's hypocrisy and pretensions. He underlines Gloucester's newfound sense of reality since his blinding. 'A man may see how this world goes with no eyes,' he tells him. This vision, born of his suffering, goes beyond the self-knowledge achieved by Shakespeare's other tragic heroes. He gains a terrifying universal knowledge of the innate corruptibility of man. 'Thou hast seen a farmer's dog bark at a beggar?' he asks Gloucester.

And the creature run from the cur? There thou
mightst behold the great image of authority: a dog's
obeyed in office.
Thou rascal beadle, hold thy bloody hand!
Why dost thou lash that whore? Strip thine own back;
Thou hotly lust'st to use her in that kind
For which thou whipp'st her. The usurer hangs the cozener.
Through tatter'd clothes small vices do appear;
Robes and furr'd gowns hide all. Plate sin with gold,
And the strong lance of justice hurtless breaks:
Arm it in rags, a pigmy's straw does pierce it.

Nowhere else does Shakespeare speak with such a radical voice.

Although there is no direct Christian reference in the play, there is one oblique one. 'I'll speak a prophecy ere I go,' declares the Fool in his valedictory address. He makes a series of pronouncements which are the reverse of what is to be desired. The first of these contrary examples goes to the heart of the religious debate.

When priests are more in word than matter.

The 'word' is the spirit of Puritanism; 'matter' that of Catholicism, with the transubstantiation of the elements in the sacrifice of the mass.

It seems odd to go from Shakespeare's greatest play to what may have been his greatest flop. *Timon of Athens* only appears in the First Folio. It may never have seen the light of a public stage. It is difficult to put a date on it, but thematically it belongs to the era of *King Lear*. It has been suggested that the play constitutes a work in progress rather than a completed work and represents a collaboration between Shakespeare and another dramatist, possibly Thomas Middleton. If indeed it was written around 1607, it shows the growing influence on Shakespeare of the masque tradition – the guests at Timon's banquet are so entertained. There is no evidence that he ever wrote a court masque himself, but a number of masque-like scenes are incorporated in his plays after that date. The play also incorporates a number of bizarre scenes such as the one where Timon seeks his revenge on the Athenians by paying whores to spread VD among them.

Another play whose provenance is not clear appears around this time. Many scholars regard *Pericles* as the product of collaboration between Shakespeare and George Wilkins, the publican/author from Cow Cross, but there is no consensus on the issue. The text as we have it, a corrupt quarto of 1608, appears not to be the final draft. Its absence from the First Folio may indicate that the editors had doubts about its provenance. The Chorus for the play is the medieval poet John Gower, whose elaborate tomb stood, then and now, in the chancel of the church of St Mary Overie, upstream from the Globe.

The play seems to have been well received. Something of its popularity is indicated by the fact that Wilkins followed up its success with a novel on the same theme, entitled *The Pain and Adventures of Pericles, Prince of Tyre*. It is described as 'the true history of Pericles as it was lately presented by John Gower'. Clearly this is an early example of its modern variation: 'the book of the film'.

## Medicus Peritissimus

William Shakespeare must have been in Stratford to give away the bride on the summer day of 5 June 1607, when his daughter Susanna married John Hall at Holy Trinity church. Susanna, 'witty above her sex', was heiress to a fortune. Her dowry was the 105 acres of land in Old Stratford that her father had purchased five years before.[2] She was doubtless pursued by numerous suitors, each carefully vetted by the Shakespeares before the choice fell on Hall. He was a Cambridge graduate born at Carlton, Bedfordshire, in 1575, one of eleven children. He had become a doctor and taken up his practice in Stratford. Shakespeare got on well with him and, given the contemporary inheritance laws, was content to regard him as his heir. Medical references are more closely observed in the plays after the marriage: that most fertile of minds must have been fascinated by Hall's profession. We may be in the presence of another handfasting. 'Elizabeth, daughter of John Hall, gentleman' was baptised on 21 February 1607/08.

Clearly, what we can discern of the character of the man that William Shakespeare decided was a worthy match for his daughter and his own effective heir will shed light on the dramatist's own character. It is known that John's father, William Hall, an astrologer and alchemist, was keen that his bright son should follow him in these arts, which held an esteemed place in Elizabethan society, although Hall had his doubts. The father left his books on these subjects to his servant, Matthew Morris, since John would have 'nothing to do with these things'.

Some have observed John Hall in the character of Cerimon, the aristocratic doctor of *Pericles*.

> 'Tis known I ever
> Have studied physic, through which secret art,
> By turning o'er authorities, I have,
> Together with my practice, made familiar
> To me and to my aid the blest infusions
> That dwell in vegetives, in metals, stones;
> And I can speak of the disturbances
> That nature works and of her cures ...

Hall certainly overturned authorities. 'It seems,' says Dr James Cooke, who edited his casebooks, that he 'had the happiness to lead the way to that practice almost generally used by the most knowing of mixing scorbutics in most remedies; it was then, and I know for some time after, thought so strange, that it was cast as a reproach on him by those most famous in the profession.' Long before such terms were categorised, Hall realised that scurvy was a deficiency disease. His cure, a mixture of scurvy-grass, watercress, brooklime, juniper berries and wormwood, rich in vitamins, cured many sufferers. The eldest son of Mr Underhill of Loxley, aged twelve, bore the excruciating agonies which torment those with this harrowing disease.

> I found him grievously afflicted with the scurvy; on the right side he had a tumor with out discoloration, so that I judged there was a tumor of the liver. He was grown as lean as a skeleton, was melancholy, with black and crusty ulcers appearing on his legs. He had a loathing of meat, a disposition to vomit and an Eratic Fever, his urine was red, as in a burning fever, yet with out thirst or desire to drink.

That this collection of abominations was cured demonstrates Hall's intuitive brilliance. Much of his success was due to psychological insight. Dr Thornborough, the eighty-six-year-old Bishop of Worcester,

> had very unquiet Nights from salt and sharp humours, and Vapors ascending to his Head; and if he did sleep, it was with terror, which happened from the sudden slaughter in one of his Family, which did much to terrify and perplex his spirits and afflicted him grievously with melancholy.

Editha Staughton, aged seventeen, suffered from intense hysteria and depression: 'her courses as yet not having broken forth ... she was very easily angry with her nearest friends, so that she continuously cried out that her Parents would kill her'. The good doctor wisely advised that 'there should be few to trouble her'.

Hall's care was not restricted to the wealthy and influential. The record of one Hudson, a poor man suffering from vertigo, indicates labour among the needy. In 1632, the Corporation paid 4s 7d 'for a portell of sack and a portell of claret given to Thomas Lucy and Sir Robert Lee ... at the Swan, when they came to confer with Mr. Hall about the poor men which were arrested'.

Hall has been described as a Puritan, but there is no direct evidence for this. Indeed it is unlikely that a person with such views would have appealed to the Shakespeares as a son-in-law or to Susanna as a husband. Unlike his father-in-law, he did get involved in the internecine local politics, supporting the Puritan Vicar in his fierce disputes with the Corporation, which was still dominated by the Puritan Daniel Baker. He was forthright in his condemnations. On 14 July 1634, the Clerk recorded that 'Mr. Hall charged some of the company to be forsworne villains.' He was not alone in his distaste for the body civic.

Hall shared something of the intense disillusion with authority of Shakespeare's dark period. His fight against corruption included vigorous opposition to those who purloined money intended for the poor. He paid a £10 fine early in the reign of Charles I, rather than accept a knighthood at a time when the sale of honours was a national scandal. It is apposite again to recall Cerimon, whose medical practice gave him

> More content in cause of true delight
> Than to be thirsty after tottering honour,

> Or tie my treasure up in silken bags,
> To please the fool and death.

Hall's distrust of institutionalised man stemmed from his Christian faith. 'Thou, O Lord,' he prayed on recovery from illness,

> which hast the power of Life and Death ... and drawest from the Gates of Death without art or counsel of man, but only from thy Goodness and Clemency, thou hast saved me from the bitter and deadly Symptoms of a Deadly fever, beyond the expectation of all about me, restoring me as it were from the very jaws of Death to former health.

Whatever his own doctrinal position, Hall was no bigot. He describes an orthodox member of the Church of England, Lady Rainsford, as 'modest, pious and kindly'. He adds 'praised be God' after curing 'Browne, a Romish priest'. The knowledge of his presence would have made Hall an accessory after the fact in any legal proceedings. Browne was probably being harboured by one of the great recusant families like that of the sister-in-law of the Countess of Shrewsbury. Mary Talbot,

> a Catholick, fair, was troubled with the Scurvy, with swelling of the Spleen, livid spots of the Thighs, pain of the Loins and Head, with convulsion and Palsy of the Tongue; her Pulse was small and unequal, her Urine was troubled and thick. The Countess asked me whether there was any hope of life? I answered, Yes, if she would be patient and obedient.

He forbade all drinks except his scurvy cure. 'Afterwards she began to walk, and at last was very well.'

Shakespeare's friend, the poet Michael Drayton, a regular visitor to the Stratford area, was impressed by Hall. In *Poly-Olbion*, his monumental description of the counties of England, the book on Warwickshire opens with a pious and learned doctor, skilled in herbal remedies, who is disillusioned with the ways of man. The picture neatly fits Hall.

> His happy time he spends the works of God to see,
> In those so sundry herbs which there in plenty grow.
> ... who of this world the vileness having seen,
> Retyres from it quite and with a constant mind
> Man's beastliness so loathes, that flying humane kind ...
> Indifferent are to him, his hopes on God that staies ...

Hall's practice covered a wide area. He was probably called in as a specialist when all else had failed. Frantic messengers must have hammered on the door at New Place to summon him to distant bedsides. His dedication is demonstrated during an illness of his own.

About the 57th year of my age, August, 1632 to September, 29, I was much debilitated with an immodest flux of the Haemorrhoids; yet daily was I constrained to go to several places to patients. By riding, a hardness being contracted, the flux was stayed for fourteen days. After I fell into a most cruel torture of my Teeth, and then into a deadly, burning fever, which then raged very much, killing almost all that it did infect.

His devotion was returned by his patients. 'Noble lady,' wrote Lady Eliza Tyrell to her friend Lady Temple,

I have heard lately of your worthy knight's mischance for which I am heartily sorry. And both Mr. Tyrell and myself have purposely sent to inquire of his recovery. Madam, I am very glad to hear that Mr. Hall is the man of whom Sir Thomas Temple hath made choice. In regard, I know by experience that he is most excellent in that art.

William Hall's servant, Matthew Morris, followed the son to Stratford. He married there in 1613 and named two of his children Susanna and John. Perhaps he fulfilled any demand for astrology and alchemy among Hall's patients. Hall's trust in his assistant was shared by his father-in-law. In 1617/18, the poet's house in Blackfriars was conveyed to 'Mathew Morrys' of Stratford and John Greene, Shakespeare's cousin, 'in performance of the confidence and trust reposed in them by William Shakespeare deceased'.

Around 1810, the Stratford historian, Robert Bell Wheler, saw in some old papers that 'Dr. Hall resided in that part of Old Town which is in the parish of Old Stratford.' James Halliwell also saw this document sometime before 1864, but it is now lost. The large early Tudor house now known as Hall's Croft is one of the handful of properties that fulfils the necessary criterion. It is not mentioned in Hall's verbal will made in 1635. If the Halls lived there, they moved after Shakespeare's death, for in 1617 Thomas Greene paid a debt to 'Mr. Hall at Newplace'.

## Blackfriars at Last

Considerable frustration must have been felt by Ben Jonson. His Roman tragedy was a demonstration of how the rules of classical drama should be applied in the contemporary theatre. Yet *Sejanus* was greeted with derision, whereas the plays of William Shakespeare, which blatantly ignored the classical rules, had made him the darling of the stage. Nevertheless, Jonson had much to be pleased about. Several of his comedies were well received, notably *Every Man in His Humour* and *Volpone*. Even more significantly, he had become, together with Inigo Jones (with whom he had a somewhat stormy relationship), the master of the court masque.

Despite this success, there was always something perverse about Ben, a desire to mock convention. Why else would he get involved in writing *Eastward Ho!* in collaboration with John Marston and George Chapman? The play was a rumbustious comedy of contemporary London life of the type that Shakespeare never wrote, but hinted at in scenes like those in the Eastcheap Tavern. It was typical of its genre, but it went too far by satirising the King's penchant for selling off honours to anyone willing to pay to boost the flagging Exchequer. The royal accent was unmistakably mocked. 'I ken the man weel, he's one of my thirty pound knights.' A contemporary note is struck in a scene where an expedition to Virginia is proposed. The colony is described as populated only by 'a few industrious Scots', best friends to England 'when they are out of it'. The insult to the King and his countrymen was compounded by the fact that the play was performed at the Blackfriars Theatre by Her Majesty's own company, the Children of the Queen's Revels – nor had the text been presented to the Master of the Revels for his consideration.

The resulting furore was predictable. Marston followed Nashe's example during the *Isle of Dogs* affair by fleeing to East Anglia. Chapman was arrested and Jonson followed him into voluntary custody. A sentence of mutilation was proposed as fitting for the recalcitrant dramatists. They would have their ears trimmed. Jonson reacted by writing to anyone whose intercession might be influential. The letters were in no way grovelling, but appealed to a sense of humanity and natural justice. He regretted deeply the incident, but argued that he should not be punished without a fair hearing. The strategy worked. The matter was quietly forgotten, although even Ben must have remained chastened for a while. Henry Evans would continue to put on his children's productions at the Blackfriars for a while longer, but the habit of controversy died hard. Nor did George Chapman remain quiet for long. In March 1608, his double bill entitled *The Conspiracy and Tragedy of Charles, Duke of Byron* was performed by the Children of Blackfriars. The action dealt with contemporary events in France. The French ambassador protested to King James about a scene which showed the yet-living French Queen slapping the face of the royal mistress. It appears that the new Master of the Revels, Sir George Buc, had censored the scene but that the management had gone ahead with it anyhow. Another furore ensued. Three of the boy actors were arrested, but Chapman seems to have escaped censure. The King ordered all the playhouses closed, but the royal love of the drama ensured that this was but a temporary measure. A more permanent effect was that the Blackfriars lease was allowed to return to the ownership of the sharers in the King's Men. This may have been at the suggestion of the King, who must have felt that he could trust the discretion of his own company rather than risk further indiscretions from the 'little eyases', with whom his patience must have been wearing thin. This may explain why there was no resistance to the new arrangement from the previously shrill neighbours. On 9 August 1608, a lease was signed on the theatre. It created a syndicate of seven sharers, who each paid £5 14s 4d towards the annual rent of £40: the Burbage brothers, William Shakespeare, John Heminges, Henry Condell and William Sly were from the company. The seventh member, Thomas Evans, may have been the brother of Henry Evans, appointed to maintain his interest. Sly, who had been with the historic company as long before as 1591,[3] died just a week later. Among his bequests was the considerable sum of £40 to the putative Shakespeare portraitist, James Sanders. His share was redistributed among his colleagues.

There is no record of which plays were presented by the King's Men at the Blackfriars Theatre. It is likely that the last of the Roman plays, *Coriolanus*, was among the last to be presented at the Globe before the Blackfriars Theatre opened anew, although there is no record of a public performance of the play prior to the Restoration. Its style more befits the larger arena. It returns to many of the themes explored in *Julius Caesar*. The people's fear that a military dictatorship will destroy their liberties is balanced by the contempt of a great warrior leader for plebeian values.

As a probable eyewitness to the riots during the 'great dearth', Shakespeare appears to have drawn on his memories more than a decade later. *Coriolanus* opens with 'a company of murderous citizens, with staves, clubs and other weapons'. Like the riots of June 1595, these are caused by the resentment of the populace against supposed hoarding in times of acute shortage. 'Let us kill him,' one rioter urges against Caius Martius, 'and we'll have corn at our own price.'

> What authority surfeits on would relieve us. If they would yield us but the superfluity while it were wholesome, we might guess they reliev'd us humanely, but they think we are too dear. The leanness that afflicts us, the object of our misery, is an inventory to particularise their abundance. Let us avenge this with our pikes, lest we become rakes; for the gods know I speak this in hunger for bread, not in thirst for revenge.[4]

In the relationship between Caius Martius and the plebeians, we see again Shakespeare's special talent for creating a world in which the characters have a past and we are parties to an intervention at a particular point in this relationship.

| | |
|---|---|
| **Martius:** | What's the matter, you dissentious rogues |
| | That, rubbing the poor itch of your opinion, |
| | Make yourselves scabs? |
| **First Citizen:** | We have ever your good word. |

The citizens realise that Caius Martius is motivated entirely by his quest for glory and self-aggrandisement. He has no interest in the commonweal. The extraordinary source of his self-belief is revealed in a dialogue between the citizens.

| | |
|---|---|
| **Second Citizen:** | Consider you what services he has done for his country. |
| **First Citizen:** | Very well, and could be content to give him good report for 't but that he pays himself with being proud. |
| **Second Citizen:** | Nay, but speak not maliciously. |

| | |
|---|---|
| **First Citizen:** | I say unto you, what he hath done famously he did it to that end, though soft-conscienc'd men can be content to say it was for his country; he did it to please his mother, and to be partly proud, which he is, even to the attitude of his virtues. |

The character of Volumnia is one of Shakespeare's most incredible creations. Her bellicose qualities are contrasted with the feminine traits of her daughter-in-law, Virgillia. This mother predates Freud's psychoanalytic theories by three centuries and represents their antithesis. She does not desire her son in her bed, but hacked to death on a battlefield.

| | |
|---|---|
| **Volumnia:** | I pray you daughter, sing or express yourself in a more considerable sort. If my son were my husband, I should freelier rejoice in that absence wherein he won honour than in the embracements of his bed where he would show most love … |
| **Virgilia:** | But had he died in the business, madam, how then? |
| **Volumnia:** | Then his good report should have been my son; I therein would have found issue. Hear me profess sincerely: had I a dozen sons, each in my love alike and none less dear than thine and my good Martius, I had rather had eleven die nobly for their country than one voluptuously surfeit out of action … |

Coriolanus is unique among Shakespeare's tragic heroes. He does not bring about his own nemesis. It is his mother who glories in his gory end. The First Citizen proves correct. Caring more for his own aggrandisement and glory than the welfare of his native city, he is only to be diverted by a plea from his mother, on whose opinions he sets ultimate value. He realises that she has sealed his fate.

> O mother, mother!
> What have you done? Behold, the heavens do ope,
> The gods look down, and this unnatural scene
> They laugh at. O my mother, mother! O!
> You have won a happy victory to Rome;
> But, for your son, believe it, O, believe it,
> Most dangerously you have with him prevail'd,
> If not most mortal to him.

Scholars have scrutinised Shakespeare's later plays for evidence of how the acquisition of the Blackfriars Theatre affected the substance and style of his output. Mainly they have scanned in vain. The reason is simple. The main base of the company continued to be the Globe and it was for that theatre that the plays were written. In any case, the players were highly adept at adapting the plays to a variety of settings. The Blackfriars Theatre would not have been so very different from the spaces in which they performed at court, in the private halls of great noblemen and in the guildhalls of local corporations and the courtyards of inns. Yet the Blackfriars Theatre reflected the changing taste of the age. To use the modern term, the theatre, originally firmly based in folk culture, was moving upmarket. Indeed, given the previous local opposition to its very presence, it was necessary for the Blackfriars Theatre to do this to ensure its survival. It was greatly more expensive to attend a show there than the Globe, where the cheapest entrance cost a mere penny. The cost of its most expensive seat – sixpence – was that of the cheapest at the Blackfriars. To occupy the most expensive seat cost the huge sum of half a crown.

Although there is no indication that Shakespeare was ever involved in the production of the elaborate masques so beloved in courtly circles, there is every indication that he tempered his work to the royal taste – the company was, after all, the King's Men. His instincts as a popular dramatist would cause him to bring a taste of these court entertainments into the popular arena. In these closing years of his dramatic output, he embarked on a series of fantasies which incorporated such elements. The first was probably *Cymbeline*, written around 1609. It is set in an ancient Britain whose source is in Holinshed's *Chronicles*, but its tortuous and involved plot represents little of the historic. Simon Forman, the astrologer, saw it, probably at the Globe, in 1611. He seems, literally, to have lost the plot for he concludes his summary with the words, 'And how she was found by Lucius, etc.'

Although the play was categorised as a 'tragedy' in the First Folio, it is better defined as a 'tragicomedy': a genre that Shakespeare had previously explored in plays like *Measure for Measure*. The form is usefully and succinctly defined in John Fletcher's prologue to *The Faithful Shepardess*.

> A tragicomedy is not so called in respect of mirth and killing, but in respect it wants deaths, which is enough to make it no tragedy, yet brings some near it, which is enough to make it a comedy.

In other words, *Cymbeline*, in which allegations of adultery are maliciously levelled against the chaste heroine, is not *Othello* because all is resolved in the somewhat extended denouement. Apart from the unfortunate Cloton, 'it wants deaths'.

Shakespeare achieves his masque-like effect in Act V, Scene 4 when apparitions of the character's family appear before the condemned Posthumous Leonatus. The stage direction is on the grand scale.

> Jupiter descends in thunder and lightening sitting upon an eagle; he throws a thunderbolt ...

Yet Forman makes no mention of this amazing scene. Had he seen it, he surely would have mentioned it. Perhaps it just featured in a royal performance: one of the forty or so unnamed plays performed before the King around 1610. With its somewhat odd setting in Milford Haven, it may even have been commissioned for the investiture of Henry as Prince of Wales in that year.

*The Winter's Tale* forms part of this valedictory cycle of dramas of the twilight years. It contains Shakespeare's best-known stage direction: 'Exit, pursued by a bear.' It is tempting to speculate that the famous Sackerson or his colleague Henry Hunks from the nearby Bear Gardens might have been incorporated into the cast, but this is highly unlikely. These were fearsome animals, capable of killing anyone who strayed into their path, so it would have been irresponsible to have introduced them into the public theatre. Interestingly, Simon Forman, who paid another visit to the Globe Theatre to see the play on 15 May 1611, does not mention this scene in his synopsis, so we have no clue as to how it was played, or even if it was played at all. The play seems to have been popular. It was performed before King James on 5 November 1611. On 14 February 1613, it was one of the plays performed as part of the festivities surrounding the marriage of the Princess Elizabeth to the Elector Palatine. Again, it possesses some of the characteristics of a court masque. Indeed the dance of the twelve satyrs in Act IV may have been lifted directly from Ben Jonson's *Masque of Oberon*, which had been performed at the Whitehall Palace on the previous 1 January. The servant announces the spectacle with the words, 'one three of them, by their own report, hath danc'd before the king'.

The last of Shakespeare's fantasy trilogy is *The Tempest*. Although set in a magical world, as a play it was rooted in real events and widely believed contemporary travellers' tales. The popular imagination was caught by accounts of the remarkable voyage of Admiral Sir George Somers in the summer of 1609. Somers was a celebrated figure who had sailed with Drake and been instrumental in founding the Virginia colony. While conveying settlers and supplies to Jamestown, his flagship the *Sea Venture* was driven onto the coast of Bermuda in a storm on 28 July 1609. The Admiral and his crew remained on the island for ten months. To their relief they discovered that it was more a realm of angels than devils. The very birds that had frightened passing sailors were easy game for hunters. Giant sea turtles provided feasts when they came ashore to nest. Succulent prickly pears grew on the rocky shore. Yet their stay was sorely tried by the presence of huge herds of hogs that had overrun the islands. Presumably they had been introduced by the Portuguese or Spanish seamen who were previous visitors. Even more trying were the mysterious noises that pervaded the air at nights. These were probably the calls of native birds, but Somers and his men concluded that the sounds were made by spirits and demons. Eventually they escaped from the island in two boats they had built from cedar wood. When they arrived at Jamestown, they found that the colony had all but perished. There were only sixty survivors. Somers returned to Bermuda to get further supplies, but died there on 9 November 1610.

It had been assumed back in England that the *Sea Venture* had perished with all hands. The first news that they had survived came in a letter written by William Strachey, a participant in the voyage, to an 'excellent lady' in England. It was critical of the Virginia Company, which attempted to suppress it. Shakespeare could well have seen it. Strachey was a noted theatre buff: a member of the Friday Street Club, a shareholder in the Blackfriars Theatre in 1606, and writer of an ode to Jonson's *Sejanus*.

It was not until September 1610 that the first survivors of the *Sea Venture* arrived home. Their arrival caused a sensation. Five accounts of Somers' voyage were soon published. The first, *A Discovery of the Bermudas, otherwise called the Isle of Divils*, by Sylvestor Johnson, another voyager, appeared as early as October.

Although Shakespeare does not set *The Tempest* in Bermuda, but on an Italian island, he certainly engaged the interest in exotic far-off places that had been aroused by accounts of voyages such as Somers'. Indeed Bermuda is on his mind when Ariel recalls that the site of the shipwreck

> is in the deep nook, where once
> Thou call'dst me up at midnight to fetch dew
> From the still-vex'd Bermoothes, there she's hid ...

Strachey recorded that the castaways fermented cedar 'berries whereof our men seething, straining, and letting stand some three or four days made a kind of pleasant drink'. Shakespeare was intrigued with this, for Caliban reveals that, when he was thirsty, Prospero 'wouldst give me water with berries in't'. The nocturnal disturbances that had troubled the crew of the *Sea Venture* are reflected in the isle's 'noises, sounds and sweet airs'. In a brilliant stroke, Ariel becomes the St Elmo's fire that Strachey had described as hovering around the doomed ship like 'a little round light like a faint star, trembling and streaming along with a sparkling blaze half the height upon the mainmast'.

> I boarded the king's ship; now on the beak,
> Now in the waist, the deck, in every cabin,
> I flamed amazement: sometime I'ld divide,
> And burn in many places; on the topmast,
> The yards and bowsprit, would I flame distinctly,
> Then meet and join. Jove's lightnings, the precursors
> O' the dreadful thunder-claps, more momentary
> And sight-outrunning were not; the fire and cracks
> Of sulphurous roaring the most mighty Neptune
> Seem to besiege and make his bold waves tremble,
> Yea, his dread trident shake.

*The Tempest* is a play about magic. It is the very magic of Prospero that has brought the wrecked ship to the island. Yet this magic is the mere catalyst for the action, the means of creating the fantasy world. Shakespeare does not go into holistic theories of alchemy, astrology or possession. We are no more asked to believe in Prospero's powers outside the context of the play than we are asked to believe in Titania's fairies. Prospero's powers are forces for good. By contrast, Caliban is the reverse of the Rouseauesque 'natural man'. This is a savage about whom there is little that is noble. Prospero claims to have treated him well until he attempted to rape Miranda. Caliban knows no remorse for this act.

> O ho, O ho! would't had been done!
> Thou didst prevent me; I had peopled else
> This isle with Calibans.

Caliban is the product of another travellers' tale. He is the son of the witch Sycorax, who had been banished from the Barbary pirate city of Argier (Algiers) to the island. There she had enslaved the spirits, including Ariel, whom she imprisoned in torment in a split pine. She has died some years before. Although Caliban claims that his sovereignty over the island has been usurped by Prospero, it is clear that his rule was a tyranny over nature.

Sycorax has taught Caliban to worship her god, Setebos. This echoes the account of the peoples of Patagonia written by the Venetian explorer Pigafetta which was translated into English by Richard Eden in his *History of Travel* in 1577. It tells of a race of grotesque giants inhabiting the hinterland. Shakespeare has already used such tales in Othello's account of his travels.

> And of the Cannibals that each other eat,
> The Anthropophagi, and men whose heads
> Do grow beneath their shoulders.

Sir Walter Raleigh, in his *Discoverie of Guiana* in 1596, mentions on hearsay a deformed race inhabiting a region of South America.

The enigmatic Caliban seems to have Bermudan roots. A passage in Strachey's narrative combines human and bovine imagery in a description of a sea turtle. Shakespeare joined the same three elements when he fashioned the features of his wild man, giving him arms like turtle fins and the nickname 'mooncalf' – a term meaning deformed child, but one evoking cattle.

In *The Tempest*, Shakespeare finally fulfilled Ben Jonson's highest aspirations. The play observes the classical unities of time, place and action. Not that he was given much credit for it by Ben, who, in his Induction to *Bartholomew Fair*, refers scathingly to 'a servant monster' and to 'Tales, Tempests and such like drolleries'.

Shakespeare writes some of his greatest lyric poetry in his three fantasy plays. In *Cymbeline*, the language and syntax can be as convoluted and tortured as the plot, but the heights are reached with the exquisite and familiar dirge.

> Fear no more the heat o' the sun,
> Nor the furious winter's rages;
> Thou thy worldly task hast done,
> Home art gone, and ta'en thy wages;
> Golden lads and girls all must,
> As chimney-sweepers, come to dust.

In *The Winter's Tale*, the lightening of the tone in the speeches of both Autolycus and Perdita presages the ultimate happy resolution of another convoluted plot. The flowers of spring anticipate a new beginning with daffodils

> That come before the swallow dares, and take
> The winds of March with beauty; violets dim,
> But sweeter than the lids of Juno's eyes
> Or Cytherea's breath; pale primroses
> That die unmarried, ere they can behold
> Bright Phoebus in his strength--a malady
> Most incident to maids; bold oxlips and
> The crown imperial; lilies of all kinds,
> The flower-de-luce being one! O, these I lack,
> To make you garlands of, and my sweet friend,
> To strew him o'er and o'er!

The two beautiful songs in *The Tempest*, 'Where the Bee Sucks' and 'Full Fathom Five', were set to music by the distinguished lutenist, Richard Johnson. Even the man-beast Caliban has his share of the beautiful lyrics, as he tells the crew of the wonders of the island he calls his own.

> Be not afeard. The isle is full of noises,
> Sounds, and sweet airs, that give delight, and hurt not.
> Sometimes a thousand twangling instruments
> Will hum about mine ears; and sometimes voices,
> That, if I then had wak'd after long sleep,
> Will make me sleep again; and then, in dreaming,
> The clouds methought would open and show riches
> Ready to drop upon me, that, when I wak'd,
> I cried to dream again.

In the sonnets, Shakespeare explored ways of defeating time. He now reveals that even these are ephemeral. The fantasy world of *The Tempest* stands for the fantasy world of the theatre itself, a place for the purveying of dreams. At the end of time, all will dissolve:

> Our revels now are ended. These our actors,
> As I foretold you, were all spirits and

Are melted into air, into thin air:
And, like the baseless fabric of this vision,
The cloud-capp'd towers, the gorgeous palaces,
The solemn temples, the great globe itself,
Ye all which it inherit, shall dissolve
And, like this insubstantial pageant faded,
Leave not a rack behind. We are such stuff
As dreams are made on, and our little life
Is rounded with a sleep.

It was a minor poet, Thomas Campbell, who first suggested, in 1838, that Shakespeare models the character of Prospero upon himself. The graves that at his command 'have wak'd their sleepers' are the galaxy of characters whom the dramatist has returned from history.

                            But this rough magic
I here abjure; and, when I have requir'd
Some heavenly music – which even now I do, –
To work mine end upon their senses that
This airy charm is for, I'll break my staff,
Bury it certain fathoms in the earth,
And, deeper than did ever plummet sound,
I'll drown my book.

Is Shakespeare taking his leave of the stage? It is an appealing thought and one that fits the context. The only snag is that the play was not his last for the company. At least three more followed. Yet clearly retirement to Stratford was at the forefront of his mind. When he was subpoenaed to appear in court in 1612, he was not of London, but of Stratford. He has made his getaway. We may ask why he wanted to leave the metier that had been so long his working life, but we do not know the answer.

# 17

# Retirement, 1612–13

'An Estate equal to his Occasion'
– Nicholas Rowe, 1709

Let us suppose that Shakespeare announces his decision to retire from the stage. *The Tempest* will be his swansong. Consternation ensues. The King's Men are about to lose the greatest name in theatrical history: the one that unscrupulous stationers affix fraudulently to their publications to enhance their sales. He is persuaded to maintain his relationship with the company. He remains a sharer and agrees to assist the rising dramatist John Fletcher. Most of important of all, the company has a continuing association with his name.

John Fletcher was personally symptomatic of the theatre's growing respectability. Born in Rye in 1579, he was far from coming from that artisan background that characterised the origins of Marlowe, Shakespeare and Jonson. His father was a leading Anglican cleric, a Chaplain to the Queen, who had been elevated to the Episcopal Bench, serving briefly as Bishop of London before his death in 1598. The son went up to Benet College, Cambridge, at the age of eleven. He may have been intended for the Church, but by 1606 he was writing for the Children of the Queen's Revels at the Blackfriars Theatre. He became part of the fellowship of the Mermaid Tavern and collaborated with a diverse set of other playwrights. His output was as prolific as Shakespeare's. He wrote, or collaborated in, over fifty plays. His best-known co-operation was with Francis Beaumont. Their most successful work, *The Knight of the Burning Pestle*, was a parody of chivalric values similar to Cervantes' *Don Quixote*. According to Aubrey, Beaumont and Fletcher shared lodgings on Bankside, 'having one wench in the house between them'. The partnership came to an end around 1613 when Beaumont fell chronically ill. Thus Fletcher was free to collaborate with Shakespeare. It was not a great success. Two plays ensued from the partnership – and perhaps a third. *The Two Noble Kinsmen* was adopted from Chaucer's *Knight's Tale* of Palemon and Arcite. Although the quarto edition of 1634 claimed that it had been received with 'great applause', it does not seem to have run for long or been revived very frequently, although there was probably a performance at court in 1619. The quarto is specific about the place of performance: 'presented at the Blackfriars Theatre by the King's Maiesties Servants'. It may be taken as implicit that it did not transfer to the more popular arena of the Globe, although that it was not an entire failure is indicated by a reference to Palemon in Ben Jonson's *Bartholomew Fair*.

The other product of the Shakespeare/Fletcher collaboration appears to have enjoyed even less success and its provenance is distinctly hazy. Although there is no record of a public performance, *Cardenio* won some favour in royal circles. It was acted at court by the King's Men in February, 1613 as part of the celebrations for the marriage of the King's daughter to the Elector Palatine and again on 8 June before the Duke of Savoy's ambassador.

The play's title indicates that it was based on the adventures of the lovelorn Cardenio from the first part of *Don Quixote*. Apparently, no move was made to publish the play until 1653, when a London stationer, Humphrey Moseley, obtained a licence for the publication of *The History of Cardenio* by Fletcher and Shakespeare. It never seems to have appeared. With Oliver Cromwell ruling as Lord Protector, the times were not auspicious for such a venture. No more is heard of it until 1727, when Drury Lane Theatre staged a play called *Double Falsehood, or the Distrest Lovers*. It was described as 'written originally by W. Shakespeare and now revised and adopted by Mr. Theobald'. In his preface to the published edition, Lewis Theobald recognised that the play's sudden reappearance stretched credulity.

> It has long been alledg'd as incredible, that such a Curiosity should be stifled and lost to the World for above a Century. To this my answer is short: that tho' till now it never made its Appearance on the stage, yet one of the Manuscript copies, which I have, is of above sixty years standing, in the handwriting of Mr. *Downes*, the famous Old Prompter; and, as I am credibly informed, was early in the possession of the celebrated Mr. *Betterton*, and by him design'd to have been usher'd into the World. What Accident prevented This Purpose of his I do not pretend to know, or thro' what hands it had successively pass'd.

The story has credibility. John Downes was the historian of the Restoration stage, who worked with Thomas Betterton's King's Company and whose *Roscius Anglicanus* is the seminal history of the contemporary theatre. Theobald's account takes the story nearly back to Moseley's failed attempt of 1653 and Moseley must surely have possessed a manuscript of the play. Whether this was the one transcribed by Downes is uncertain because Theobald claims to possess no less than three such manuscripts, one of which he has obtained from an unnamed nobleman, who has purveyed it to him with a piece of sensational information.

> There is a Tradition ... that it was given by our Author, as a Present of Value, to a Natural Daughter of his, for whose sake he wrote it, in the Time of his Retirement from the Stage.

Natural daughter? This is a new one: a child of the Dark Lady or Jane Davenant? If she existed, her putative father's largesse towards her was not great. The returns from *Cardenio*, if any, must have been decidedly small.

Naturally, scholars have sought traces of Shakespeare's hand in Theobald's production. Michael Wood has found 'idiosyncratic' verse in the text that he believes could have been written by Shakespeare and points out that the song-settings are by Shakespeare's musical collaborator, Richard Johnson.[1] Theobald confessed that his adaptation was not perceived as particularly Shakespearean by the *cognoscenti* who 'have been pleased to urge, that tho' the Play may have some Resemblance of *Shakespeare,* yet the *Colouring*, Diction and *Characters* [conform] to the style and Manner of *Fletcher*'. It is highly likely that the major role in the brief partnership was Fletcher's. The subject matter of *The Two Noble Kinsmen* and *Cardenio* is not particularly Shakespearean and Fletcher was to return to Cervantes as a source in his collaboration with Philip Massinger in the hugely popular *The Custom of the Country*, written for the King's Men in 1620.

## 'Golden Dayes and Spirites'

In 1613, William Shakespeare contributed to a bill for the repair of the highways around Stratford. He had used them more than most. In his autumnal years he was spending more time there, slowly disengaging himself from the metropolis. Perhaps he worked on his collaborations with Fletcher from his study at New Place, sketching out scenes and writing major speeches and songs. The younger dramatist would complete the work.

Thomas Greene, Shakespeare's cousin, the Town Clerk, was living at New Place in 1609 with his wife, Lettice, and two children, aptly named William and Anne. He may have been the minor poet of that name who was criticised, with Shakespeare and Jonson, for failing to compose a funeral elegy to Queen Elizabeth. The accommodation provided by the Shakespeares was generously offered, for Greene wrote that he 'perceyved I might stay another year'. Much Corporation business must have been conducted from the parlour. It was presumably on Greene's behalf that a visiting preacher was entertained there in 1611. He must have delivered one of the three annual endowed sermons at the Guild Chapel. The Corporation paid 20*d* for 'one quart of sack and one quart of clarett wine'. What Greene called his 'golden dayes and spirites' spent in Stratford's service is reflected in his surviving letters, including one to John Marston,[2] the dramatist and lawyer, from his 'Lovinge ffrendes' in Stratford, but the subject is legal not literary. Perhaps Shakespeare had introduced him to the Town Council. Another was written on behalf of the Corporation to Sir William Somerville, praying him to punish Michael Gybson of Knowle for the seduction of Dorothy Field: probably another example of public virtue coinciding with a strain on the rates!

'The latter part of his life was spent,' reported Rowe, 'as all Men of good sense will wish theirs may be, in Ease, Retirement and the Conversation of his Friends. He had the good Fortune to gather an Estate equal to his Occasion, and, in that to his Wish and is said to have spent some Years before his Death at his native *Stratford*.' It is tempting to think that Shakespeare retreated to a kind of rural tranquility after the violent hurly-burly of London life, but this was not the case. 1609 was a notably violent year. William Robyns, a servant of Hornby the blacksmith, was killed in a quarrel over a jug of beer. Another murder took place in the low inner parlour of the Swan in Bridge Street. Lewis Gilbert, a veteran of Essex's disastrous Irish campaign, quarrelled with the host Richard Waterman, his wife and two daughters. When they attempted to eject him, he set his back against the door and resisted. 'He will spoil my father. He will murder my father,' shrieked the daughters. Waterman's brother Thomas was sitting by the fire in the hall. He forced open the parlour door and, seizing Gilbert by the collar, tried to throw him out. Gilbert drew a knife and stabbed him in 'the right side by the navel, from which he died'. Gilbert, of no fixed abode or means of support, fled. The Coroner's jury, meeting over the body of Waterman, found him guilty of wilful murder.

The crime wave kept the courts busy. Richard Barrett of Henley-in-Arden and John Whittle of Bearley were summoned in 1610 to give evidence against James Lord 'in the felonious killing of William Langford'. A capital charge was faced by William Perry in the same year, 'a person suspected of having coined gold'. James Johnson and Nicholas Worrall were 'attached to answer Thomas Townesend for having conspired with one Hugh Browne ... to defraud the plaintiff of divers sums of money at play in a game of cards called Newcutt'. Richard Smyth was attached to answer Henry Collins 'for scandalous words uttered, viz. "Thou art an arrant theife and wast whipped out of the countrie where thou didst dwell for stealinge sheets off a hedge"'. That year, a revision of the charter extended the borough's legal jurisdiction over the church, churchyard and Old Town, 'which last locality is much infested with beggars and vagabonds'.

One who ignored the Corporation's ban on actors was Henry Walker, father of Shakespeare's godson, who as Bailiff in 1608 revived the Guildhall play. There were other breaches of the regulations and they were made more stringent in 1611.

> The sufferance of them is againste the orders heretofore made and againste the examples of other well governed cities and burrowes the Companie heare are contented ... that the penaltie of 10s imposed for breaking the order shall henceforth be £10 ... this to bide until the next common council and from thenceforth for ever, exepted that be their finally revoked and made void.

Adherence to the new regulations depended on the viewpoint of the Bailiff. When Thomas Greene's stepson William Chandler held office in 1618, 3s

4*d* was paid 'to a company that came with a show to the town' and later 5*s* '*per* Master Bailiff's appointment to a company of Players'.

The Stratford registers record the burial on 3 February 1611/12 of 'Gilbert Shakespeare, adolescens'. The last word has been taken to refer to a youthful nephew of William Shakespeare, but from other usages in the same register, it appears that it was the Clerk's term for someone who died unmarried. William's other surviving brother, Richard, was buried at Holy Trinity on 4 February 1612/13.

## London Road

William Shakespeare's move to Stratford did not mean that he gave up his London life entirely: far from it. He was there on 11 May 1612 when he testified in the Court of Requests in a case brought by Stephen Belott against his father-in-law, Christopher Mountjoy. There was something wrong from the start of the marriage. Perhaps the alienation was caused by the formidable and lusty mother rather than the father because the couple moved back into the family home after her death in 1607. Two daughters were baptised at the nearby St Giles church on 23 October 1608 and 17 December 1609. Relations between the two men seem to have deteriorated after that. Stephen claimed that his father-in-law had not paid his £60 dowry. He brought the case to court and William Shakespeare was summoned as a witness. He was not particularly helpful. The record of his testimony is the closest we get to hearing his natural speech. He reckoned that he had known the parties in the dispute for 'the space of ten years or thereabouts'. No, he had never heard Mountjoy 'confess that he had not got any great profit or commodity' out of Belott's service. Yes, he had heard the Mountjoys at 'diverse and sundry times say and report' that Belott was 'a very honest fellow' and, yes, indeed, Mountjoy had suggested that Belott marry his daughter Mary. Yes, Mountjoy had promised to give Belott 'a portion in marriage' but what precisely that was, I cannot remember. Nor can I remember when it was to be paid. Nor do I recall that Mountjoy had promised to leave Belott £200 in his will through his daughter Mary. Yes, Belott was living in Mountjoy's house at the time of the marriage and they had had many conferences among themselves about the marriage which was later consummated and solemnised. More than that I cannot depose. No, I do not know 'what implementes and necessaries of houshould stuff' the defendant gave the plaintiff on his marriage.

The witness stepped down and signed his name 'W. Shakp' in abbreviated form on the deposition. He had told the court nothing that it did not know already. The Recorder adjourned the case until 19 June, when Shakespeare's name again appeared on the list of witnesses. Perhaps he was obliged to attend the court, but he was not called. Others testified that Shakespeare had been a party to the arrangements for the match, but nor could they recall the precise terms of the marriage bond. In exasperation, the Recorder referred the case to 'the Reverend & grave overseers and Elders of the French church in London'. The reputation of both plaintiff and defendant went before them to their place of worship. 'Tous 2 pere & gendre debauchez' was the comment recorded. The grave overseers and Elders considered the case and awarded Belott twenty nobles (£6 13s 4d), well below what he was seeking. A year later, Mountjoy still hadn't paid. The Elders were still unimpressed with his morals. A later entry mentions 'sa vie desreglée & desborde'. His promiscuity led to his eventual excommunication and, thereby, his alienation from the company of his compatriots. The Consistory Court was aware of the kind of company he was keeping. A recently discovered document[3] reveals that on 20 November 1613 'Christopherus Mountjoy de Silverstreet London Marchant Taylor', stood surety in the huge sum of £20 for three countrymen, Jacob Mullet, Abraham Tripple and Jacob Depré, all 'goldworkers' of St Giles. The three men were bound over to appear at the Middlesex Sessions, together with one 'ffrancisca Williams de Whitehapel'. The indictment reveals the eye-catching charge: 'They were all 4 sene in bed together at one tyme.' The man who claimed to have seen them at it, Adam Bowin, 'a tuff tafatamaker' of St Botolph's, Bishopsgate, was also bound over to appear. It is small wonder that the Elders lost patience with Mountjoy.

It is likely that Shakespeare was in London for the most spectacular series of courtly occasions to involve the King's Men. On 14 February 1613, Princess Elizabeth, only surviving daughter of James I, married Friedrich V, the Elector of Palatine in the Chapel Royal. This was a dynastic match. Both bride and groom were sixteen. The Elector was the notional principal power in the Union of Protestant Princes, with which James desired to build an alliance. Lavish celebrations followed: plays, pageants, processions and firework displays. The King's Men put on no less than twenty plays. Eight were by their leading man-of-the-theatre. It is possible that a ninth was requested by royal command. What is indubitably Shakespeare's last work was written at this time. Two days after the wedding, hundreds of people queued to see a play which was cancelled in favour of the 'greater pleasure' of a court masque. The unperformed play may well have been Shakespeare's *Famous History of the Life of King Henry VIII*, or *All is True*. It has all the elements that might be expected from a work written for such an occasion, including a masque and two lavish processions. Its elaborate effects caught the eye of Sir Henry Wotton.

> The King's players had a new play, called *All is True*, representing some principal pieces of the reign of Henry VIII, which was set forth, with many extraordinary circumstances of pomp and majesty, even to the matting of the stage; the Knights of the Order with their Georges and garters, the Guards with their embroidered coats and the like: sufficient in truth to make greatness very familiar.[4]

The fulsome royal tributes that form part of the play also indicate a command performance. Shakespeare finally writes the eulogy to the Virgin

Queen that he had been accused of omitting a decade before. Cranmer greets the newborn Princess Elizabeth with a prophecy.

> This royal infant – heaven still move about her!
> Though in her cradle, yet now promises
> Upon this land a thousand thousand blessings,
> Which time shall bring to ripeness. She shall be –
> But few now living can behold that goodness –
> A pattern to all princes living with her,
> And all that shall succeed. Saba was never
> More covetous of wisdom and fare virtue
> Than this pure soul shall be. All princely graces
> That mould up such a mighty piece as this is,
> With all the virtues that attend the good,
> Shall still be doubled on her. Truth shall nurse her,
> Holy and heavenly thoughts still counsel her;
> She shall be loved and feared. Her own shall bless her:
> Her foes shake like a field of beaten corn,
> And hang their heads with sorrow. Good grows with her;
> In her days every man shall eat in safety
> Under his own vine what he plants, and sing
> The merry songs of peace to all his neighbours.
> God shall be truly known: and those about her
> From her shall read the perfect ways of honour ...

Not surprisingly, England's good fortune extended into the next reign. 'Another heir' will succeed 'as great in admiration as herself'.

> So shall she leave her blessedness to one,
> When heaven shall call her from this cloud of darkness,
> Who from the sacred ashes of her honour
> Shall star-like rise, as great in fame as she was,
> And so stand fix'd: peace, plenty, love, truth, terror,
> That were the servants to this chosen infant,
> Shall then be his, and like a vine grow to him:
> Wherever the bright sun of heaven shall shine,
> His honour and the greatness of his name
> Shall be, and make new nations: he shall flourish,
> And, like a mountain cedar, reach his branches
> To all the plains about him: our children's children
> Shall see this, and bless heaven.

Two decades after these lines were written, Peter Paul Rubens was commissioned to create his great painting to adorn the ceiling of Inigo Jones's new-built Banqueting House in Whitehall Palace. *The Triumph of the House of Stuart* is an allegory of the Union of Crowns in the reign of James

I. Yet the great Flemish artist was not following a new theme. It had been amply explored by the royal players and masqueraders earlier in the reign. Shakespeare's play of *Henry VIII* was a part of this continuing tribute.

Despite such elaborate flattery, it may have been that the royal party, surfeited with the rigours of the celebrations, decided to forgo the play and just view the less demanding masque within it. Clearly preparations were in place for an extravagant spectacle. Sir Henry Wotton was impressed that even the matting at the Globe, which was probably created for the court spectacle, had been painted to resemble the rich carpets adorning the royal palaces.

If William Shakespeare was in London for the royal celebrations, he would have undoubtedly been at the funeral on 25 February of a stalwart of the company, Alexander Cooke, of Hill's Rents within the parish, who was buried at St Saviour's, Southwark.

Shakespeare had further reason to be in town. On 13 March, he bought the Gatehouse to the old Blackfriars Monastery and the adjoining tenement. It was situated next to the King's Wardrobe on a lane leading down to the river at Puddle Wharf. He paid £140 for the property to Henry Walker, described as 'citizen and minstrel of London'. Perhaps he was a musician at the Globe. The considerable sum of £80 was paid in cash. Shakespeare's wealth was not infinite. The residue was on a mortgage, to be paid off in the following year. It is a mystery why he should have wanted to buy this property, the only such purchase he is known to have made in London. It is unlikely to have been a speculative investment. Although he never appears to have lived there, he may have bought it as a future London base. Given the troubles suffered by James Burbage with the neighbours when hé bought the Blackfriars Theatre, it is also possible that Shakespeare bought the property to ensure that it did not fall into the hands of the wrong person. There were enough enemies of the theatre in the City with the money and motivation to buy it up in an attempt to spoil the King's Men's pitch – and Shakespeare still had a vested as well as an emotional interest in the continuing success of the company. Whoever owned the Gatehouse may have controlled the right of public access to the rest of the former monastery, including the theatre.

If Shakespeare was still in London a few days after his purchase, he may have attended the great tournament to mark the tenth anniversary of the King's accession which took place at court on 24 March. It coincided with the continuing celebrations of the royal wedding. The Elector did not take his bride back to Germany until the next month. A week after the tourney, the steward of Francis Manners, the 6th Earl of Rurland recorded the payment of 44s 'to mr Shakspeare in gold about my Lordes impreso' and the same sum 'To Richard Burbadge for paynting & making it'. The work in question was defined by William Camden in 1605.

An imprese, as the Italians call it, is a device in picture with his Motte, or Word, born by noble or learned personages, to notifie some particular conceit of their owne ...

> There is required in an Imprese (that we may reduce them to few heades) a correspondence of the picture, which is as the body, and the Motte, which as the soul giveth it life. That is, the body must be of fair representation, and the word in some different language, wittie, short, and answerable thereunto neither too obscure nor too plaine, and most commended.

Burbage was a talented painter. His familiar self-portrait may be seen to this day at the Dulwich College Gallery. What device he came up with for the occasion, or what verses the poet composed, is unknown, but the task was not easy. As befitted a 6th Earl, Francis Manners bore a complicated coat of arms that had been quartered and re-quartered. Whatever it was, it did not take the eye of Sir Henry Wotton, who was present and complained that 'some were so dark, that their meaning is not to be understood, unless perchance that were their meaning, not to be understood'.[5]

Shakespeare may have lingered in London to oversee the production of *Henry VIII* at the Globe. According to the theatrical historian John Downes, John Lowin took the lead in what was probably the most lavish production ever staged there. His ample figure would fit him well for the part. All the effects from the putative royal performance appear to have been presented. It was a recipe for disaster. The play ran for a few performances before nemesis struck on 29 June 1613. This 'insubstantial pageant' led to the destruction of 'the great Globe itself', leaving 'not a wrack behind'. Sir Henry Wotton recounted the sad story in a letter to his nephew, Sir Edmund Bacon.

> Now, King Henry making a masque at Cardinal Wolsey's house and certain chambers [i.e. cannons] being shot off at his entry, some of the paper, or other stuff, wherewith one of them was stopped, did light on the thatch, where being thought at first but an idle smoke, and their eyes attentive to the show, it kindled inwardly, and ran round like a train, consuming within an hour the whole house to the very ground.
>
> This was the fatal period of that virtuous fabric, wherein nothing did perish but wood and straw, and a few forsaken cloaks, only one man had his breeches set on fire, that would perhaps have broiled him, if he had not by the benefit of a provident wit put it out with bottle ale.

We may presume that Shakespeare was not present during this disaster. He had probably returned to Stratford. Had he been there, the anonymous writer of a mournful ballad about the sad event would surely have mentioned him, as he did his leading colleagues. 'All is true,' he assures the reader, in a reference to the play's subtitle.

> Out run the knights, out run the lords,
> And there was great ado,
> Some lost their hats and some their swords,
> Then out run Burbage too;

The reprobates, though drunk on Monday,
Prayed for the fool and Henry Condye.
Oh sorrow, pitiful sorrow, and yet, all this all is true.
The periwigs and drum-heads fry,
Like to a butter firkin,
A woeful burning did betide
To many a good-butt jerkin:
Then, with swollen eyes, like drunken Flemings;
Distressed stood old stuttering Hemings'
Oh sorrow, pitiful sorrow, and yet, all this is true.

It is unlikely that the King's Men followed up the balladeer's helpful suggestion that, to rebuild the Globe, they should seek

A license to beg for it,
In churches, sans churchwardens' checks
In Surrey and Middlesex.

Within a year, a new and even more splendid theatre had arisen from the ashes of the old, with a tiled roof to prevent a repetition of the disaster. It was paid for by assessing each sharer for £50 or £60 towards the cost. William Shakespeare's name was not among them. England's greatest man of the theatre had made his exit.

Although the destruction of the Globe represented an obvious watershed in the process of Shakespeare's detachment from the stage, it is still apposite to ponder why he chose to go. He was only forty-nine. His colleagues, Burbage, Hemminges and Condell, made no such exit, although the great rival actor Edward Alleyn had long adjourned to the country to become squire of the Manor of Dulwich. It is a sufficient and satisfactory explanation to say that it was Shakespeare's objective to resume his life in Stratford with an elevated social status, having overcome the financial problems that had dogged his father. Yet there may be more to it than that. The spirit of the age was swinging away from his natural metier, the popular theatre, in which his greatest triumphs had been achieved. He does not appear at ease with the new courtly fashion for masques. He may also have been conscious that his literary powers, although still considerable, were failing. *The Tempest* was an undoubted triumph, but his two collaborations with Fletcher achieved, at best, a muted success. It is not clear whether *Henry VIII* represents a further collaboration. The early editors of Shakespeare assumed that the play was written around the time of the other histories, for which Holinshed's *Chronicles* were also a major source. It was only with the discovery of documents relating to the conflagration at the Globe in the mid-nineteenth century that this view was revised. Since then, textual scholars have delineated which scenes might be attributed to Shakespeare and which to Fletcher, but against this it may be argued that *Henry VIII* does not appear in the Folio of Fletcher's works, which includes all his known collaborations. The play appears in the First Folio, from which the editors seem to have excluded his known collaborations, including *Pericles*. It appears that they regarded *Henry VIII* as Shakespeare's work entire.

There may be a further reason why Shakespeare retired from the stage. Perhaps he was beginning to doubt his own powers. In the Mountjoy–Belott court case he forgets the detail. Later when making his will, he cannot recall the Christian names of either his godson or one of his nephews. The hand from which had flowed two plays a year was slowing down and, with it, the virtually automatic approbation that had accompanied his great histories, comedies and tragedies. True, plays like *The Tempest* and *The Winter's Tale* possess great inventiveness and lyrical beauty, but this is not so apparent in other works of his twilight years. If he did indeed write *Henry VIII* in its entirety, then it is almost too obvious to suggest that its epilogue was the last thing he wrote for the stage.

> 'Tis ten to one this play can never please
> All that are here: some come to take their ease,
> And sleep an act or two; but those, we fear,
> We have frighted with our trumpets; so, 'tis clear,
> They'll say 'tis naught: others, to hear the city
> Abused extremely, and to cry 'That's witty!'
> Which we have not done neither: that, I fear,
> All the expected good we're like to hear
> For this play at this time, is only in
> The merciful construction of good women;
> For such a one we show'd 'em: if they smile,
> And say 'twill do, I know, within a while
> All the best men are ours; for 'tis ill hap,
> If they hold when their ladies bid 'em clap.

If Shakespeare wrote such doggerel, he may have realised that his poetic powers were diminishing. If he did not, he may have realised that his potential collaborators were not worthy of his standards. Either way, it may have convinced him it was time to quit. If he wrote anything further during the short years of his retirement, it is lost to the world.

# 18

# Last Will and Testament, 1614–16

'And death once dead'
— William Shakespeare, Sonnet 146

The Shakespeares were disturbed by a distasteful episode during the summer of 1613. On 15 July, Susanna Hall brought a suit for defamation in the Diocesan Court against John Lane the younger of Alveston, who had 'about five weekes past' spread a story that she had 'the runinge of the raynes' (a graphic name for gonorrhoea) and had 'bin naught [fornicated] with Rafe Smith at John Palmer'. Robert Whatcott, probably a servant at New Place, appeared for Mrs Hall. Lane failed to appear and was excommunicated for spreading false report. In 1619 he was presented for 'not receivinge holi communyon according to the canons' and, later that year, for drunkenness.

The incident reveals the close-knit nature of Stratford society. Ralph Smith, one of the Armada volunteers, a haberdasher and hatter, was Hamnet Sadler's nephew. Lane's sister, Margaret, was married to Shakespeare's cousin, John Greene, the Town Clerk's brother. Lane's cousin, Thomas Nash, married Elizabeth Hall in 1626.

## 'Overthrowne and Undone'

On 9 July 1614, Stratford was devastated by another fire, which destroyed fifty-four houses, 'many of them very fair ... besides Barnes, stables, & other howses of Office, together also with great store of Corne, Hay, Straw, Wood & Timber therein', to the value of over £8,000. The 'Brief for the Relief of Sufferers', written in the name of King James I, makes pathetic reading.

> The force of fier was so great (the wind sitting ful upon the Towne) that it dispersed into so many places thereof, whereby the whole Towne was in very great danger to have beene utterly consumed and burnt, by reason whereof, and of two severall Fiers happening ... within these twenty yeares, to the losse of Twenty Thousand Pounds more, not only our saide poore subjects who have now sustained this great losse, are utterly undone and like to perish but also the rest of the Towne is in great hazard to be overthrowne and undone, the Inhabitants there beeing no waies able to relieve their distressed neighbours in this their great want and misery. And whereas the said Towne hath

been a great Market Towne whereunto great recourse of people was made ... now being thus ruinated and decayed, it is in great hazard to bee utterly overthrowne, if either the resort thither may be neglected, or course of travellers diverted, which for want of a speedy reparation may be occasioned. And foreasmuch as our distressed subjects the inhabitants of the said Towne are very ready & willing to the uttermost of their powers to rectifie & new build the said Towne againe, yet finding the performance thereof far beyond their ability, they have made their humble suite unto us, that we would be pleased to provide some convenient measures that the saide Towne may be again rectified and repaired as well for the reliefe of the distressed people ... as also for the restoring and continuing of the sayd market, and have humbly besought us to commend the same good & laudable deed and the charitable furtherance thereof, to the benevolence of all our loving subjects, not doubting but that all good and wel-disposed Christians will for common charity and love to their country and the rather for our Commendation hence of, be ready with all willingness to extend their charitable reliefe towards the comfort of so many distressed people ...

New Place was built of brick and tiles rather than the highly inflammable wattle, daub and thatch, so it escaped the conflagration. Shakespeare possessed the wherewithal to help his distressed neighbours in their want and misery and, hopefully, did so.

The Corporation forbade thatching of houses and ordered existing thatch replaced by tiles and slates. The aldermen again embarked on their fundraising tours, but in 1619 a petition described Stratford as 'the anciente (but now much decayed) Borough'. It was to be 200 years before this decline was reversed.

## John a Combe

Further stress and controversy blew up in 1614 with a plan by a cartel of landowners to enclose the common fields at Welcombe. To the peasant freeholders, who possessed little more than squatters' rights, this meant destitution: to the Corporation, it meant the loss of historic rights and an increased burden of poor relief. The issue was explosive. In the spring of 1607, similar proposals elsewhere in Warwickshire had led to 'tumultuous assemblies' against 'depopulations'. Under Thomas Greene's guidance, resistance was planned. As a tithe holder, William Shakespeare would be inadvertently involved.

The enclosers were men of the new age: Arthur Mainwaring, Steward to the Lord Chancellor; William Combe, the High Sheriff; and his younger brother, Thomas, who had in 1598 denounced his cousins, the Sheldons, for harbouring a Catholic priest. The Combes were a *nouveau riche* family of expanding wealth. 'They say in Stratford that he cannot have less than 20,000 li in his purse,' wrote Leonard Digges of William Combe in 1632, 'increased by honest 8 and 10 in the hundred.'

This distaste for usury affected the posthumous reputation of the Combe brothers' uncle. The wealthiest man in Stratford, he lent money at interest and engaged in regular actions for its recovery. Within four years of his death in 1614, an epitaph was published 'upon John Combe of Stratford-upon-Avon, a notable Usurer, fastened upon a Tombe that he has caused to be built in his life time':

> Ten in the hundred must lie in his grave,
> But a hundred to ten whether God will him have?
> Who then must be interr'd in this Tombe?
> Oh (quoth the Divill) my John a Combe.

Similar verses on an unnamed usurer had been printed previously and mock epitaphs were common. By 1634, it had been attributed to Shakespeare. John Aubrey later added the detail that it had been extemporised in a tavern. In fairness to Combe, he only charged the standard rate of interest. He left £20 to the poor of Stratford and £5 to William Shakespeare. His monument was sculpted by Gheerart Janssen, a young man of Flemish origin who worked near the Globe Theatre. It is probable that Shakespeare commended him to the Combes.

Both sides in the enclosure controversy wooed William Shakespeare. His tithe holdings were important, but not crucial to the project. He was in London on 16 November 1614, a week after the third great fire. Thomas Greene was there too and wrote in his diary:

> At my cosen Shakespeare commying yesterday to towne I went to see him howe he did: he told me that they assurd him they ment to inclose no further than to gospel bushe & so upp straight (leavinge out part of the dyngles to the ffield) to the gate in Clopton hedge & take in Salisburyes peece and that they meene in April to survey the Land & and then to gyve satisfaccion & not before.

Shakespeare's view was clear. 'He and Mr. Hall say they think ther will be nothing done at all': ultimately a correct opinion, but one that was to take a great deal of angst to verify.

Shakespeare protected his position by agreeing compensation with Mainwaring's attorney, William Replingham, for any losses through 'inclosure or decay of tyllage' – a step taken by other titheholders including Thomas Greene and Arthur Caudrey of the Angel, who told William Combe that 'he would never consent without the Towne & that he hadd a house and other things more profitable to him than his Land was & that he rather loose his Land than loose their good willes'. The agreement was witnessed by the Vicar, John Rogers, a vehement opponent of enclosure. That Shakespeare's behaviour was incontrovertible is demonstrated by the lack of any reproach from Greene, who was scathing about others, such as the attorney, Thomas Lucas, who lined his pockets from the dispute.

Even Combe unctuously declared that this rascally lawyer 'could not be an honest man for he had no religion in him'.

The Corporation attempted negotiations with William Combe, sending a delegation 'to present their loves and to desire that he would be pleased to forbeare to inclose & to desire his love as they wil be redy to deserve yt'. Combe was to prefer the potential profits of enclosure to civic affection.

With the breaking of the frost on 19 December, the enclosers acted aggressively to create facts. Combe's men started to dig a lengthy trench. The Corporation wrote to Mainwaring and Shakespeare and sought the support of other landowners. 'I alsoe wrytte of myself,' recorded Greene, 'to me cosen Shakespear the Coppyes of all oathes made then, alsoe a not[e] of the Inconvenyances wold grow by the Inclosure.'

Greene's stepson, William Chandler, and William Walford became tenants at Welcombe, so increasing the number of claimants with whom the enclosers would have to deal. When they attempted to fill in the ditches Combe had them flung to the ground and sat 'laughingly on his horseback & sayd they wer good football players' and 'puritan knaves and underlinges in their colour'. Nor did he ignore attempts at bribery, offering Greene a mare worth £10 'to propound a peace'.

Both sides rushed to law. On 26 January 1614/15, William Chandler wrote 'to my lovinge father Thomas Greene Esquire at his chamber in the Mydle Temple', requesting him to subpoena William Combe and his associates in the Star Chamber. On 28 March the Corporation obtained a restraint order against enclosure at Warwick Assizes. It could only be rescinded if it were justified in open assize. At this point Mainwaring gave up, but for Combe the matter had become a personal vendetta. He beat and imprisoned poor tenants and depopulated the village of Welcombe. He told Arthur Caudrey that 'yf he sowed the said wheat land he would eate yt upp with his sheepe'. Those attempting to fill in the illegal ditches were assaulted and told that

> in the night their corn wilbe eaten and that they will not know against whom to find remedye and tellinge others they shall be compelled and that their ould bones should be fetcht upp twice in a term or such like speeches and by his own and others raylinge and reveilinge hath endeavoured to terrifie the petitioners and others the better to compasse such enclosure ...

A sense of civic duty prevailed. When Combe asked Alderman William Parsons why he opposed enclosure, he replied:

> We are all sworn men for the good of the Borough and to preserve our inheritance. Therefore we would not have it said in the future that we were the men which gave way to the undoing and that all three fires were not so great a loss as the enclosures would be.

Parsons suffered for his probity. A week later he was beaten up by Combe's men.

On 19 April, Lawrence Wheeler and Lewis Hiccox started to plough their land within the intended enclosure. Combe merely railed at them, which encouraged them to return the next day with Anthony Nash, gentleman, Shakepeare's next-door neighbour, who farmed his tithe holding, which implies that the action had Shakespeare's approval. In September, Greene made an enigmatic entry in his diary: 'W. Shakespeare's telling J. Greene that I was not able to beare the encloseinge of Welcombe.' Interpreted literally, this states the obvious. Perhaps Greene meant 'he' rather than 'I'. It is unlikely that Shakespeare was so ill-informed as to imply that his cousin was unable to 'bar' the enclosure, for the forces of legality were mustering against Combe. Sir Henry Rainsford told Greene that the Combes would never succeed and that he intended to sue William Combe for trespass and riot and to seek sureties of £40 against Thomas Combe. Peter Roswell, gentleman, of Welcombe, another freeholder, declared that he intended a similar course and that Sir Edward Greville 'would stick to him'.

On 1 March 1615/16, Combe had another try, his workmen digging out twenty-seven ridges. Next day, William Chandler sent his man, Michael Ward, to fill in the works. He was assaulted by Combe's men, one Stephen Sly shouting that 'if the best in Stratford were to go there to throw the ditch down he would bury his head at the bottom'.

In a petition to the Assizes on 27 March 1616, the Corporation demanded that Combe, 'being of such unbridled disposition ... should be restrained'. Sir Edward Cocke decided not to punish him because he was the High Sheriff, but 'badd him sett his hart at rest he should never enclose nor lay downe his common arable land so long as he [Cocke] served the King'. Despite such leniency, Combe considered himself ill-used and alleged that the Corporation had 'given money to work my Lord [Cocke] and that was no good employment for the town's revenue'.

Combe made new proposals for enclosure, but the Corporation replied that they desired his goodwill, but they would ever oppose enclosure. On 10 April 'Mr. High Sheriff' told John Greene that he was 'out of hope now ever to enclose'. This belated recognition did not soften Combe's belligerency. Instead he launched a war of revenge against the Welcombe tenants. The Bailiff wrote to Combe in December that his conscience was 'blinded as yt seemeth with a desire to make your self Riche by other mens losse', so that he paid no heed to judges, 'nor the mynysters[1] Threatnyngs against Enclosures'. A complaint to the Court of Common Pleas lamented that Combe had not 'laid down meres according to my Lord Hobart's order ... And that he hath decayed 117 ridges of tilling and neglecting the farming thereof contrary to own word and promise made to the judge and justices at the time of their conferences.' Neglect had the same effect as enclosure. 'The grief for decaying is the destruction of our common and the decaying of the tilling is the losse of our tythes with which the poor are free.'

The Bailiff brought a contempt action against Combe in 1617. The warrant was delivered by Richard Hathaway, Anne Shakespeare's nephew. By this time Thomas Greene had moved to Bristol, selling St Mary's House by Holy Trinity Church, to which he had moved in 1609, for £640. Perhaps the absence of his old antagonist encouraged Combe, for in 1618 he brought his campaign into the Borough when his indefatigable workmen began to dig a ditch to enclose Butt Close, next to Clopton Bridge. The Corporation paid its own indeflectable workmen 2s 4d to fill it in.

Combe's reputation was reaching the highest tribunals in the land. In 1619 he received a sharp letter from the Privy Council. He must restore the enclosures and abide by judicial rulings or face the consequences. At last he became alarmed and capitulated. The decision had gone against him in every court and a contempt action was pending. The Corporation, generously and judiciously, decided to cut its losses. On payment of a £4 fine, it granted 'Mr Combe, his pardon for enclosing'.

## 'In perfect Health and Memorie'

On 20 February 1615/16, Judith Shakespeare, aged thirty-one, and perhaps resigned to spinsterhood, was given in marriage to Thomas Quiney, four years her junior and son of that Richard who had been so assiduous in the defence of the Borough's rights. The Quineys were vintners and the marriage may have been long intended and, indeed, long pre-consummated. In 1611, Judith had placed her mark to witness deeds for Elizabeth Quiney and her son Adrian. In the same year Thomas Quiney leased Atwoods, the tavern next door to his mother's house in the High Street.

What looked to be a sound match, linking two leading local families, began disastrously. The bride and groom were excommunicated for marrying in the prohibited season, although this was lifted on payment of a fine. The offence was not serious and may be attributed to the incompetence and greed of the ecclesiastical authorities. Yet Quiney had reason to marry in haste. He was seeking to exchange premises with William Chandler, his brother-in-law, who kept a hostelry called The Cage (formerly the town lock-up), opposite the Market Cross. Judith's marriage portion would help finance the move, which took place in July.

There was a more serious problem. On 26 March, the Consistory Court heard Quiney's confession to carnal copulation (*fassus est se carnalem copulacionem habuisse*) with Margaret Wheeler, daughter of Randle Wheeler, a carrier occasionally employed by the Corporation. This unfortunate young woman had died in childbirth. A sad entry in the parish register on 15 March 1615/16 records her burial with her child. The court ordered Quiney to pay public penance on three consecutive Sundays, dressed in the customary white sheet: a penalty remitted on payment of what was, for this court, the considerable fine of 5s and the performance of private penance before the minister at Bishopton church.[2] The incident did not affect Quiney's standing in the town, for he became a burgess and a constable in 1617 and was Chamberlain in 1621 and 1622. His first accounts were returned as unsatisfactory, but were later ratified. His second accounts carry his elaborate signature and a misquoted couplet from the French poet Saint-Gelais.

> Bien heureux est celui qui devenir sage
> Qui par le mal d'autrui fait son apprentissage.[3]

Quiney's transgressions led his father-in-law to revise his will, changing a draft that had been made in January. He must have been severely ill when he signed this document on the day before the Bawdy Court met at the Vicarage opposite New Place. The three signatures are written with difficulty. Perhaps he was lying in bed and struggled to rise before falling back on the pillow. The signatures are prefaced by the words 'In witness whereof I set my hand and seal'. The word 'seal' has been crossed out. A man of Shakespeare's position and wealth would have possessed a seal ring to endorse legal transactions, so, for whatever reason, it was unavailable.[4] He knew that he was dying for he bestowed the interest on £150 on Judith if she were alive in three years, which assumed that he would not be. Her husband could not touch the capital sum unless he settled lands on her to the same value.

Clustered around the bed were the witnesses. There was Julian Shaw, a wool-dealer who lived two doors away. In 1613, the Corporation, 'much approving his well-deserving in this place, for his honesty, fidelity and good opinion of him', had elected him an alderman. There was Hamnet Sadler, a life-long friend, and two men who were probably Shakespeare's servants, Robert Whatcott and John Robinson.

The will is a lawyer's draft, compiled by Francis Collins, Shakespeare's attorney, or his clerk. The opening statement that the signatory was 'in perfect health and memorie' is a legal convention, as is the religious declaration that follows. Since he died within a month, it is unlikely that he was in perfect health and that his memory may have been failing is demonstrated by his failure to remember the names of two of his legatees. There are no phrases of endearment. It is 'my wife' and 'my daughter', not 'beloved wife' and 'dear daughter'.

Despite the death of Hamnet, the desire to pass the estate to a male heir remained. If not of the name, he should be of the blood. Shakespeare's property was entailed through Susanna to her eldest son. Although she had no sons, at thirty-three there was still hope. Failing this, the estate was to pass through her daughter Elizabeth to her sons. Only if all these contingencies failed was the estate to pass 'to the Right Heires of me the said William Shakespeare for ever'.

Judith was given an ample cash settlement – £100 for her marriage portion and £50 if she renounced her claim to a cottage in Chapel Lane. Perhaps it was intended for her before her marriage was arranged. As a keepsake she received her father's 'broad silver-gilt' bowl.

Other bequests follow. Joan Hart, the poet's sister, received £20, his clothing and the life tenancy of her part of the Henley Street house. The freehold of the whole building passed to the Halls. Joan's three sons were left £20 each, although no one present could recall the name of the youngest. Elizabeth Hall received his plate, while Thomas Russell of Alderminster and Francis Collins were left £5 and 20 marks respectively and asked to act as overseers of the will. The poor of Stratford got £10; William Walker, Shakespeare's godson, £20 in gold, although Shakespeare could not remember his Christian name either. Thomas Combe received Shakespeare's sword, but his aggressive brother, William, was ignored. Some old friends were left 26s 8d (or two angels) each to 'buy them Ringes'. 'My ffellowes John Hemynges, Richard Burbage and Henry Cundell' are the only men of the theatre to receive such bequests. Another recipient was Hamnet Sadler, whose name replaces Richard Tyler's in the second draft. Tyler too had known Shakespeare all his life, but may have been deleted because of suspicions about his character. He was one of five Stratfordians authorised to collect abroad for the victims of the great fire of 1614. An audit in the month that Shakespeare made his second will found 'every one prefferinge his own private benefittes before the general good' and 'exhibitinge to us bills of charges, excedinge theare collections'.

The most famous bequest is to Anne Shakespeare. 'Item I gyve unto my wief my second best bed with the furniture.' This has been interpreted as a posthumous slight: by implication, the best being reserved elsewhere. Yet the bed was probably the marital one, the best being reserved for guests. Others made peculiar provisions for beds. In 1609, the testator in another will drawn up by Francis Collins left his best bedstead to his son. Shakespeare's best bed would not pass to the Dark Lady or some other mysterious paramour, but to his heirs, the Halls.

The only recorded indication of the cause of Shakespeare's death is in another curious note by the Revd John Ward in 1662. 'Shakespeare, Drayton and Ben Jonson had a merry meeting and it seems drank too hard for Shakespeare died of a fever there contracted.' Since Ward's informant was Shakespeare's daughter, Judith, the statement must be taken seriously. If such revelry occurred, it could have been in London. Ben had cause to celebrate in early March when he received royal patronage, with an ample allowance of wine as part of his stipend, in essence becoming the first Poet Laureate. Perhaps Shakespeare's return was through the winds of March over roads that were a quagmire. But perhaps this is too late. Shakespeare was presumably well when he spoke to Thomas Greene in September 1615. By January when he made the first draft of his will, with that perspicacity of pre-industrial man concerning his imminent demise displayed by many of his contemporaries, he must have been aware of his approaching death. He would doubtless have received the ministrations of his son-in-law, Dr Hall. The putative meeting could have been in Stratford. Ben was a great traveller, while Drayton regularly sojourned with his friends, the Rainsfords, at Clifford Chambers. 'I am stopping at a knight's house in Gloucestershire,' he wrote in 1631, 'to which place I yearly used to come in the summer to recreate myself and spend two or three months in the country.' During one of these visits, John Hall treated 'Mr. Drayton, an excellent poet, labouring of a Tertian.' He prescribed syrup of violets with his emetic infusion. 'This given wrought very well both upwards and downwards.'

Shakespeare's death may have been caused by his residence in an unsanitary corner of a pestilent town. Along the length of Chapel Lane ran an open, festering ditch. Many were the complaints about it, the Corporation making futile efforts to clean it up over three centuries. The issue was compounded by the pigs which the inhabitants kept in the streets. Chief offender was the Vicar, John Rogers, who pleaded the necessity of poverty. In 1613, his neighbours petitioned the removal of these sanctified swine, but they crept back under his successor.

'He dyed a papist,' wrote Archdeacon Richard Davies late in the seventeenth century, who, as a member of the Anglican hierarchy, was not a special pleader. It should be noted that he allegedly *died* a Catholic rather than *lived* as one. Such returns are not unparalleled. Catholic priests were still to be found in the area. Many of the local gentry clung to the old faith: the Throckmortons at Coughton, the Ferrers at Baddesley Clinton, the Sheldons at Weston and the Fortescues at Cookhill are but a few of the families who would harbour priests. There was no reason why William Shakespeare should die 'unhouseled, disappointed, unaneled'. William Reynolds, his Catholic friend, lived in Chapel Street and it was to his door in 1603/04 that a 'supposed seminary escaped at Stratford' was seen running, wearing green breeches, high shoes and white stockings. In August 1615, at Clifford Chambers, Reynolds married a Frenchwoman, Frances de Bois, 'of London in Philip Lane'. Perhaps the Shakespeares were present at the wedding. Reynolds was one of those willed money to buy a memorial ring. A ring was a token of a pledge. By law, there was no choice but to be buried in the parish church according to the Prayer Book rite. Was Reynolds's pledge to organise a requiem in the Romish rite conducted by a 'priest in surplice white'?

On 17 April 1616, the funeral cortège of Shakespeare's brother-in-law, William Hart, the hatter, wound past New Place. The poet must have heard the great bell of the Guild Chapel tolling its melancholy tone. On 23 April, the day posterity deemed his birthday, he died. Two days later his funeral procession departed from the courtyard of New Place, crossed the stagnant ditch and passed the gate of the school where he had studied as a boy and the Guildhall where he probably saw his first play. Holy Trinity would have been filled with the names that compose Shakespeare's Stratford: Quiney, Sadler, Greene, Hall, Reynolds, Nash, Shaw, Walker, Hathaway (Anne's nephew, Richard Hathaway, had just been made a churchwarden) and the rest. As the minister intoned the burial service, the body was lowered into its grave at the High Altar: the privilege of a tithe-holder rather than a mark of esteem. Thus the world saw the last of Shakespeare the man. The literary legend would not be confined in the Stratford earth.

# Epilogue

In 1634, an army officer, Lieutenant Hammond, visited Stratford. He recorded the tradition that Shakespeare had extemporised verses on the usurer John Combe. At the church, he admired the 'neat monument of that famous English poet, Mr. William Shakespeare, who was born here'.

The monument had been in place for at least eleven years. In the prefatory poems to the First Folio of 1623, Leonard Digges, a poet with local connections,[1] wrote:

> Shakespeare at length thy pious fellows give
> The world thy works; thy works, by which outlive
> And time dissolves thy *Stratford Monument*
> Here we alive shall view thee still.

According to a sonnet by William Basse, there had been a proposal to reinter the poet's remains in Westminster Abbey, but the erection of the monument may have inhibited any such move. The sculptor was Gheerhart Janssen, of Southwark, who had sculpted the effigy of John Combe two years before. Presumably the poet's London associates oversaw its creation. They may have commissioned and paid for it. The epitaph is more disinterested than one composed for the family, concentrating on Shakespeare as artist, rather than father or husband. It demonstrates a lack of knowledge of Holy Trinity and that Shakespeare was buried in a grave rather than a tomb. It would be difficult indeed to hurry past the monument at the High Altar.

> Stay passenger, Why goest thou by so fast?
> Read if thou canst whom envious death has plast
> Within this tomb. Shakespeare with whome
> Quick Nature dide, whose name doth decke this Tombe
> Far more than cost. Such all yt he hath writt,
> Leaves living art but page to serve his WITT.

Shakespeare, it seems from traces of the original paint, had hazel eyes and auburn hair. The kindest view of the stodgy face is that it is taken from a death mask. The sculptor would have required such an image. The bust was clearly a sufficient likeness to satisfy the family and friends. Perhaps his old company came to see it in 1622, when they attempted to play in the Guildhall. This caused some embarrassment to the Corporation. The regulations forbade plays, yet these actors were under royal patronage. The Chamberlains' Accounts reveal a compromise. The King's Men were paid 6s 'for not playing in the Hall'. Doubtless they got a warmer welcome at New Place.

The inscription on Shakespeare's grave has caused much speculation.

> Good friend for Iesus sake forbeare
> To digg the dvst encloased heare
> Blese be ye man yt spares these stones,
> And cvrst be he yt moves my bones.

The verse is not addressed to the passer-by. Nor is it a prophetic vision of those who seek to exhume the Bard in the hope of proving that the Works are the product of another's hand. The 'good friend' is the sexton, who disinterred bones to make way for newcomers: a practice evoking Hamlet's distaste as he watched the gravediggers dig up poor Yorick's remains. 'Did these bones cost no more in the breeding than to play at loggats with 'em? Mine ache to think on't.' William Hall, who visited Stratford in 1694, declared that Shakespeare wrote the lines to frighten off ignorant clerks and sextons, adding that he 'descends to the meanest of their capacities and disrobes himself of that art which none of his contemporaries had in greater perfection'. Yet it is unlikely that Shakespeare wrote his own epitaph. Few do so for obvious reasons.

No matter who wrote it, the epitaph has served its purpose. Near the bust is the outline of a door which once led into the charnel house where disinterred bones were stored. Such was the fate of the mortal remains of Shakespeare's family. Their bodies were disinterred, their graves occupied by others and their epitaphs wiped out.[2]

In 1616, the year of Shakespeare's death, Ben Jonson became the first author to supervise a folio collection of his works. Perhaps Shakespeare cracked a few jests at Ben's expense while planning to follow suit, discussing the project with the three major shareholders in his old company, who owned the manuscripts. When he knew he was dying did he ask them to continue the task and leave them rings as a reminder of the pledge? Burbage died in 1619, but Hemminges and Condell completed the First Folio, which was published in 1623. In the prefatory epistle they hint at Shakespeare's role in the preparations. 'It had been a thing, we confess, worthy to have wished that the author himself had liv'd to have set forth and overseen his own writings.' Despite their self-confessed shortcomings, their achievement was remarkable. Without them no less than sixteen of the plays would have been lost to posterity and the texts of others would have been less than perfect.

The editors requested various admirers of Shakespeare to append valedictory verses to the volume. Ben Jonson overcame his scruples about his friend's lack of classical learning to pen what was probably the most eloquent and generous tribute ever paid by one poet to another. Its wonder and perspicacity may be summarised in a single line.

He was not for an age but for all time.

Shakespeare's widow, Anne, outlived him by seven years and was buried next to him in Holy Trinity on 8 August 1623. Her Latin epitaph, probably written by her clever daughter, Susanna, translates as 'Oh mother, milk and life thou didst give'. William Shakespeare's desire to create a dynasty, in his blood if not in his name, was not to be. Susanna, described on her tomb as 'witty above her sexe', had no more children. She was buried on 16 July 1649. Her daughter, Elizabeth, married twice, but produced no heirs. The poet's last surviving descendant, she died in 1670. Sadly his daughter Judith bore three sons but none survived to his majority. Shakespeare Quiney died in infancy, while Richard and Thomas Quiney died within weeks of each other in 1633, probably of an epidemic. On 6 February 1662, 'Judith uxor Thomas Quiney gent' was buried at Holy Trinity. In 1680, there died the last person who certainly knew William Shakespeare, his godson, William Walker, whose name he could not recall in his will. Legend could now take the poet where it willed and that it began to do.

# Appendix

# Shakespeare's Library

We may begin to build a picture of the books that Shakespeare possessed in his library from the sources of his plays – only three have no known source. On its shelves might well have been the second edition of Holinshed's *Chronicles* of 1587 (which was a prime source for all his history plays as well as *Macbeth, Cymbeline* and *King Lear*); Edward Hall's *The Union of the Two Noble and Illustre Families of Lancastre and Yorke* of 1550 (*Henry VI, Parts I and II, Henry VIII*); Richard Grafton's *A Chronicle at Large and Meere History of the Affayres of England* of 1569 (*Henry VI, Part II*); John Foxe's *Actes and Monuments* of 1583 (*Henry VI, Part 2, King John, Richard II, Henry VIII*); Robert Fabyon's *New Chronicle of England and France* of 1516 and *The Chronicle of Iohn Hardyng* of 1543. For *Richard II*, Shakespeare drew on the *Cronycles* of the medieval French writer Jean Froissart, which were translated into English by William Middleton in 1523. Thomas More's *History of King Richard the Thirde*, written in 1516, would probably have had its place on the shelves. Shakespeare would have possessed a copy of William Paynter's *The Palace of Pleasure*, of which the most recent version was published in 1582. Some elements of *The Merry Wives of Windsor* may have been taken from another of the stories in the volume. It may have been adapted from a story in *Il Pecorone* ('The Simpleton'), a collection of tales by Ser Giovanni Fiorentino. A version of *Romeo and Juliet* is among the sixty tales in Paynter's volume, as is a translation of *Giletta of Narbona*, from Boccaccio's *Decameron*, the source of *All's Well That Ends Well*. *The Tragical History of Romeus and Juliet*, a narrative poem by Arthur Brooke, first published in 1562, is another source of his play of that name. It is a translation of a novella entitled *Giuleitta e Romeo*, published by Matteo Bandello in 1554.

Plutarch's *Parallel Lives*, from which source material for *Anthony and Cleopatra, Julius Caesar, Timon of Athens, The Winter's Tale* and *Coriolanus* is taken, was translated by Thomas North and published in 1579. The *Timon, or the Misanthrope* of the Greek satirist Lucian was another source for the play of that name. Shakespeare would surely have possessed a copy of Edmund Spenser's hugely popular *The Faerie Queen*, which contains a character called Cordelia, who dies by hanging. The theme of the Gloucester subplot in *Lear* is taken from another hugely popular work, Sidney's *Arcadia*. Book II, Canto X tells the story of King Lear and his daughters. John Higgins's account of the similar themes features in the 1579 edition of *A Mirror for Magistrates*, from which Shakespeare probably also gained his portrait of Owen Glendower in the two parts of *Henry IV*.

Shakespeare was familiar with the doctrines of political statecraft propounded in Niccolo Machiavelli's *The Prince*. The plot of *Othello* is taken from Giovanni Battista Girladi ('Cinthio'), whose *Un Capitano Moro* ('A Moorish Captain') was published in 1565 as part of a collection of 100 tales entitled *Gli Hecotommithi*, modelled on Boccaccio's *Decameron*. This is curious, since there was no translation of the work into English in Shakespeare's lifetime. Cinthio's work was also a secondary source for *Measure for Measure*. The prime source was a work by George Whetstone entitled *The Right and Famous Historye of Promus and Cassandra*, published in 1578. Although he used Paynter's translation of *Il Pecorone* as a probable source for *Merry Wives*, he may well have used an untranslated tale in that volume as a source of *The Merchant of Venice*. The plot for Portia's suitors was the *Gesta Romanorum*, a collection of medieval anecdotes with a moral commentary attached. An English translation was published by Wynkyn de Worde around 1515. In 1577, Richard Robinson, a London printer, published a revised edition of the book under the title *Certain Selected Histories for Christian Recreations*, and the book proved highly popular.

Another untranslated work that Shakespeare may have used as a source for *Cymbeline* was Boccaccio's *Decameron*. Nor was there a translation of *The Prince* – a proscribed work – until 1636. This raises the intriguing issue of whether Shakespeare could understand Italian, although obviously he could have gained his knowledge of the works in question in other ways. He uses Italian phrases in *Love's Labour's Lost*, but these are taken from John Florio's *Second Frutes*, published in 1591. In the same play and elsewhere, he borrows phrases from Florio's Italian dictionary, *A War of Words*. The novellas of the Italian monk Matteo Bandello provided source material for *Twelfth Night*, *Much Ado* and *Romeo and Juliet*. It would appear that not all of them had been translated into English.

Since James I was the patron of his company, it is highly likely that Shakespeare possessed a copy of *Daemonologie*, the King's treatise on witchcraft. Indeed the tract may have had its influence on the writing of *Macbeth*.

Shakespeare was compared to Ovid by Francis Meres. His *Metamorphoses* were translated into English by Arthur Golding in 1567. The tale of Pyramus and Thisbe in *A Midsummer Night's Dream* is taken from Book IV. The story in the same play of the transformation of Bottom the weaver into an ass is from Apuleius's *The Golden Ass*, the only Latin novel to have survived in its entirety.

Ovid is certainly Shakespeare's favourite classical author. His *Venus and Adonis* is based on Book X of the *Metamorphoses*. He uses the text of the story of *Tereus, Proene and Philenela* in the same work as the means whereby the ravished and muted Lavinia reveals her sad story to her father. He takes virtually verbatim Medea's speech in Book VII of the Golding translation for Prospero's invocation in Act V, Scene 1 that concludes with his breaking of his staff. It is on the *Metamorphoses* that Shakespeare bases the Pyramus and Thisbe romp in *A Midsummer Night's Dream*. He also quotes from Ovid's *Heroides* in *The Taming of the Shrew*. It is interesting to note that in 1574 the stationer Thomas Vautrollier had received an exclusive licence to publish the works of Ovid.

Another classical writer whom Shakespeare utilised was the Roman dramatist Plautus. As we saw in Chapter 2, *The Comedy of Errors* was based on his *Menaechmi*. This was not translated into English until 1595, so it is likely to have been one of a number of Latin volumes on his bookshelves.

Shakespeare was familiar with the work of Geoffrey Chaucer. He uses the latter's *Knight's Tale* from *The Canterbury Tales* as the source of the Theseus and Hippolyta plot in *A Midsummer Knight's Dream*. Undoubtedly he drew on the same writer's work for *Troilus and Cressida*. He may also have had access to Chaucer's *Legend of Good Women* as a further source of the Pyramus and Thisbe playlet in the *Dream*. He used another medieval English writer, John Gower, as the source of *Pericles*.

One of the few contemporary writers that Shakespeare used as a direct source was Thomas Lodge, whose pastoral novel, *Rosalynde: Eupheus Golden Legacie*, published in 1590, was the basis of *As You Like It*. Another was the anonymous author of a play called *The Rare Triumphs of Love and Fortune*, published in 1589, which he used in both *Cymbeline* and *The Tempest*. He drew on the works of his own putative antagonist, Robert Greene. The fairies in *A Midsummer Night's Dream* are taken from that author's play *The Scottish History of James IV*, while his popular novel *Pandosto*, written in 1588, provides much of the material for *The Winter's Tale*. He was undoubtedly familiar with George Chapman's masterly translation of Homer's *Iliad*, which started to appear in sequence in 1598. He used it as the backdrop for *Troilus and Cressida*.

Shakespeare's main source for *Twelfth Night* is the prose tale of *Apolonius and Silla* in Barnabe Riche's *Riche his Farewell to Militarie Profession* (1581). The courtier Sir John Harington translated Lodovico Aristio's *Orlando Furioso* into English in 1591. This provided Shakespeare with the projected wedding of Hero and Claudio in *Much Ado* and Don John's schemes to prevent it. Aristio's *I Supposito* was translated by George Gascoigne in 1566. This forms the basis of the plot involving Bianca and her suitors in *The Taming of the Shrew*.

In writing *The Two Gentlemen of Verona*, Shakespeare drew on the Spanish prose romance *Diana Enamorada* by the Portuguese writer Jorge de Montemayor. He most likely based it on an anonymous English play, *The History of Felix and Philiomena*, which may have been based on *Diana*, and which was performed at court at Greenwich Palace by the Queen's Men on 3 January 1585. It is now lost.

In 1596, Lazarus Pyott translated the *Epitome de Cent Histoires Tracgique* by Le Sylvain into English as *The Orator*. One of the tragic stories concerned a Jew who demanded a pound of flesh of a Christian to settle a debt.

In 1612, Thomas Shelton translated Cervantes' *Don Quixote* into English. This was the source of the lost play, *Cardenio*, which Shakespeare wrote in collaboration with John Fletcher.

Shakespeare does not quote a great deal from contemporary literature. He refers to the first known collection of humorous stories and anecdotes in *Much Ado* when a furious Beatrice announces that Benedick had said that she 'was disdainful and that I had my good wit out of the 'Hundred Merry Tales'. This volume was published in London in 1526 by John Rastell, a printer, the brother-in-law of Sir Thomas More. He also quotes from Marlowe's *Hero and Leander* in *As You Like It* – 'Who ever loved who loved not at first sight?' *Tottel's Miscellany*, the publication of which in 1557 was fundamental to the development of the sonnet form, is mentioned in *Merry Wives*.

Shakespeare makes many references to the Bible – 1,200 is a conservative estimate. Forty-two biblical books are referred to: eighteen each from the Old and New Testaments and six from the Apocrypha. The Psalms have the most references. Given their wonderful poetic quality, this is not surprising, but Genesis, Job and St Matthew's Gospel are well represented. Yet it is impossible to say which translation he was most familiar with and presumably possessed. Shakespeare tends to allude to the Bible rather than quote directly from it. A good example of this comes in *Hamlet* (V.2.10). All of the respective translations, up to and including the Authorised Version of 1611, tended to draw from each other. It is a myth that there was no English language translation of the Bible before the Tyndale/Coverdale one of 1526–35. There were indeed many, but Tyndale's was the first to be printed. Apart from this, there were three significant translations before the Authorised Version of 1611–12. The first of these was the Geneva Bible, produced by English Puritan exiles in that city in 1560. It was not published in full in England until 1576. Its tone was highly Calvinistic, not so much in the translation as in the commentary that accompanied it. It proved hugely successful, running through over 100 editions before 1630. It was strongly disapproved of by the Anglican Establishment, which produced its own translation – the so-called Bishops' Bible of 1568. This was appointed to be read in churches and, since church attendance was obligatory, most of the population would have been familiar with its cadences.

The third notable translation was that produced by exiled Catholics. The New Testament was translated at the English seminary at Rheims and published in 1582. It would have been circulated clandestinely, but effectively, in England. In 1589, William Fulke, a Puritan divine, produced an attempted refutation of the Rheims New Testament, setting its complete text and notes alongside that of the Bishops' Bible. This ensured that his book became very popular, running through three further editions.

Although it is frequently asserted that Shakespeare was familiar with the Book of Common Prayer, there are few, if any, allusions to it in his works. He does demonstrate some familiarity with the *Books of Homilies* – collections of discourses appointed to be read in churches – although his experience of them does not appear to have been edifying. 'O most gentle pulpiter!' says Rosalind in *As You Like It*. 'What tedious homily of love have you wearied your parishioners withal and never cried "Have patience, good people"?'

We may presume that Shakespeare possessed copies of those of his works that were published in his lifetime. This would include eighteen quarto editions of his plays, his poems *Venus and Adonis* and *The Rape of Lucrece* and, possibly, other editions like his sonnets and *Love's Martyr or Rosalin's Complaint*, which included his *The Phoenix and the Turtle* and appeared in 1601.

# Notes

## 1. The Background, 1550–69
1. The equivalent of a mayor: a title which was adopted by the Corporation in 1665.

## 2. Childhood and Schooldays, 1564–82
1. *Laneham's Letter describing the Magnificent Pageants presented before Queen Elizabeth at Kenilworth Castle*: Hickman & Hazard, Philadelphia, 1822, pp. 45 and 46.
2. Andrew Gurr: 'Shakespeare's First Poem: Sonnet 145': *Essays in Criticism*, xxi: Oxford University Press, 1971: pp. 221–6.

## 3. Courtship and Marriage, 1582–85
1. For a fuller discussion see James G. McManaway, 'John Shakespeare's "Spiritual Testament"': *Shakespeare Quarterly*, vol. 18, no. 3: Summer 1967.
2. For informative and full discussions of the legal status of marriage in the Elizabethan era, see B. J. and Mary Sokol's *Shakespeare, Law and Marriage* (Cambridge University Press, Cambridge, 2003) and *To Have and to Hold – Marrying and its Documentation in Western Christendom, 400–1600*, ed. Philip L. Reynolds and John Witte, Jr (CUP, New York, 2007).

## 4. The Warwickshire Poacher, *c.* 1586
1. Mark Eccles, *Shakespeare in Warwickshire*: University of Wisconsin Press, 1963: pp. 82, 83.

## 5. The Rise of the Theatre, 1559–96
1. John Northbrooke: *A Treatise Against Dicing, Dancing, Plays and Interludes with other Idle Pastimes*. London, 1577.
2. In 1615, Shakespeare's former colleagues Richard Burbage and John Hemmings were obliged to appear before the Privy Council to answer charges that they had put on theatrical performances during Lent.
3. From the 1613 edition of Stow's *Annales*.
4. Alexandra Halasz: 'Richard Tarlton and the uses of Sixteenth-Century Celebrity': *Shakespeare Studies*, vol. 23: Associated University Press, New Jersey, 1995.
5. Acts of the Privy Council, 29 June 1587. Public Record Office.
6. Cited in *Malone Society Collections* I, p. 173.
7. *Chambers Book of Days*, 1869.
8. Ian Frederick Moulton, '"A Monster Great Deforme": The Unruly Masculinity of Richard III': Shakespeare Quarterly, vol. 47, no. 3: Autumn 1996: pp. 251–68.
9. Mark Eccles: *Christopher Marlowe in London*: Harvard University Press, 1934.
10. Park Honan: *Christopher Marlowe: Poet and Spy*: Oxford University Press, 2005.

11. Bernard Capp: 'Playgoers, Players and Cross-Dressing in Early Modern Theatre: The Bridewell Evidence': *The Seventeenth Century*, 18, 2003: pp. 159–71.

12. Lansdowne MS 60, fol. 47, cited in E. K. Chambers, *The Elizabethan Stage*, vol. 4, Oxford, 1923: p. 305.

13. Quoted by Charles Nicholl: *Evening Standard*: 15 April 2008.

### 6. In London, 1587–92

1. Middlesex Justices in 1596: cited by Schoenbaum, 1987: p. 126.

2. See below.

3. Walter G. Boswell-Stone: *Shakespere's Holinshed: The Chronicle and Historical Plays Compared*: Kessinger Publishing, 1905.

4. Thomas Nashe: *Piers Penniless*: London, 1592.

### 7. An Aspiring Poet, 1593–95

1. It was not until the 1897 that Paul-Louis Simond identified the cause of the disease.

2. For a full and fascinating discussion of the plague years in London, see Graham Twigg: 'Plague in London: Spatial and Temporal Aspects of Morality' in *Epidemic Disease in London*, ed. J. A. I. Champion: London: Centre for Metropolitan History Working Papers Series, no. 1, 1993: pp. 1–17.

3. From *Old Church Lore* by William Andrews: William Andrews & Co., The Hill Press, London, 1891: pp. 152–71.

4. Peter Holmes: 'The Authorship and Early Reception of "A Conference About the Next Succession to the Crown of England"': *Historical Journal*, vol. 23, no. 2, 1980: pp. 415–29.

5. Cited by E. K. Chambers in *William Shakespeare: A Study of Facts and Problems*, vol. 2, Oxford, 1930: pp. 320–1. Hatfield MS, xxxvi.

### 8. Sonnets and a Patron, 1592–94

1. Dulwich College MS II 144.

2. On Drake's West Indian voyage, Thomas Ogle, the steward of the *Talbot*, was 'hanged ... for buggery, committed in the steward's rome with 2 boyes'. Giles Milton: *Big Chief Elizabeth*: Hodder & Stoughton, 2000.

3. Sydney Papers, ed. Collins, ii. 132.

4. Dante entitled his work *La Commedia*. The epithet *Divina* was added by Giavanni Boccaccio. It was not until 1555 that this word appeared in a printed edition.

5. Quoted by Eric Ives in *The Life and Death of Anne Boleyn*: Oxford, 2004.

6. Indeed, in his *England's Heroicall Epistles* of 1597, Drayton inserts an exchange between Henry Howard and the Lady Geraldine.

7. This is an example of the several unrevised texts that are featured in Thorpe's edition of Shakespeare's Sonnets. The original text repeats the phrase 'My sinful earth'. What two-syllable phrase the poet originally wrote is open to speculation.

### 9. The Lord Chamberlain's Men, 1593–94

1. The document was discovered by Arthur Freeman in the Bodleian Library, MS.Don. d.152 f.4v, and transcribed by him in his article 'Marlowe, Kyd, and the Dutch Church Libel', *English Literary Renaissance*, 3, 1973: 44–52.

2. Kyd's letter to Sir John Puckering: BL Harley MS.6849 f.218. It is frequently stated that Kyd was tortured. This may or may not have been the case, but the fact that he was immediately frank and open makes it less likely. The supposition is based on an ambiguous statement Kyd made in his letter to Sir John Puckering.

3. A belief in the separation of Church and State was regarded as treasonable by the Anglican Establishment.

4. William Camden: *Annales Rerum Gestarum Angliae et Hiberniae Regnante Elizabetha*: 'Booke 4': Fisher, London, 1639: p. 65.

5. From the 'Praeludium' to *The Careless Shepherdess*, published 1656.

6. The Revd I. V. Cray: *The Pilgrimage to Parnassus with the Two Parts of the Return from Parnassus*: Oxford: Clarendon Press, 1886: lines 675–8.

7. J. O. Halliwell-Phillips: *Tarlton's Jests and News out of Purgatory*: Shakespeare Society, 1844.

8. C. W. Wallace: 'The First London Theatre: Materials for a History': *[Nebraska] University Studies*, 13, 1913: 278–9, quoted by Schoenbaum.

9. E. K. Chambers: *The Elizabethan Stage*, vol. 4: p. 310.

10. On the night of 28 December, when the Lord Chamberlain's Men gave their last Court performance of the season, an unnamed company performed *The Comedy of Errors* in the hall of Gray's Inn. The performance was such a fiasco that it was dubbed 'the Night of Errors'. It is unlikely that this was Shakespeare's company. They would hardly have committed themselves to another performance on the day that they were to appear before the Queen.

## 10. Troubled Times, 1593–96

1. Thomas Draxe: *The Worldes Resurrection, or the General Calling of the Iewes, A Familiar Commentary upon the Eleventh Chapter of Saint Paul to the Romaines*: London: G. Eld for Robert Boulton and John Wright, 1609.

2. E. G. R. Taylor: *The Writings and Correspondence of the Two Richard Hakluyts*: 2 vols: Hakluyt Society, London, 1935.

3. Francis Consitt: *The London Weavers Company*: vol. 1: Oxford, 1933: pp. 312–16.

4. Quoted by Mikoho Suzuki in 'The London Apprentice Riots of the 1590s and the Fiction of Thomas Delony': *Criticism*, Spring 1996.

## 11. Bankside, 1596–99

1. Calendar of States Papers Domestic, 1547–80, p. 595.

2. James M. Gibson: 'An Early Seventeenth-Century Playhouse in Tonbridge, Kent': essay in *Medieval and Renaissance Drama in England*, vol. 20 ed. S. P. Cerasono: Associated University Presses, Cranbury, New Jersey, 2007: p. 248.

3. Thomas Haywood: *An Apology for Actors*, 1612.

4. See Gabriel Egan: 'John Heminges's Tap House at the Globe': *Theatre Notebook*, vol. 55, 2001: pp. 72–77.

5. See the article by John H. Artington: '*A Drawing of the Great Chamber of Whitehall in 1601*': *Reed Newsletter*, Toronto 1991: p. 6.

6. Quoted by Leslie Hotson, *The First Night of Twelfth Night*: Macmillan, New York, 1954.

## 12. A Man of Wealth, 1594–99

1. Stratford-upon-Avon Corporation: *Minutes and Accounts V*: xix–xx.

2. John Hall, physician, Shakespeare's son-in-law.

3. Quoted by Dr Paul Edmondson in an article in *Around the Globe*, Summer 2010.

4. When things improved, a member of the Shakespeare household sold twenty bushels of malt to Philip Rogers, an apothecary. Rogers failed to pay, so William Shakespeare took out one of his rare lawsuits against him.

5. SBT Records Office. MS. ER27/4.

6. Quoted by Sidney Lee: *William Shakespeare*: p. 295.

7. Nicholas Rowe: *Some Account of the Life &c. of Mr. William Shakespear*: London, 1709: pp. 29–30.

8. Transcribed by C. W. Wallace from numerous documents in the Public Record Office relating to the legal actions between Giles Allen and Cuthbert Burbage, in 'The First London Theatre: Materials for a History': *[Nebraska] University Studies*, 13, 1913.

### 13. A New Theatre, 1599–1602

1. Steve Sohmer: '12 June 1599: Opening Day at Shakespeare's Globe': *Early Modern Literary Studies*, vol. 3, no. 1, 1997: pp. 1–46.
2. *The First and Second Parts of John Hayward's 'The Life and Raigne Of King Henrie IIII'*, ed. John J. Manning: The Royal Historical Society, 1991.
3. A. J. Tipton: '"Lively Patterns ... for Affayres of State": Sir John Hayward's *The Life and Reigne of King Henrie IIII* and the Earl of Essex': *Sixteenth Century Journal*, 23, 2002.
4. *The Cambridge History of English and American Literature: Volume III: Renascence and Reformation*: chap. 15, §12, Sir John Hayward.
5. John Marston: *Jack Drum's Entertainment*: Act V: Scene 1.
6. The misquotation arises from a lecture given by L. C. Knights at the Shakespeare Association in 1932, in which he sought to discredit the school of criticism represented by Bradley. Bradley did, however, ask the question, 'Where was Hamlet at the time of his Father's death?', *Shakespearean Tragedy*, p. 403, Note B.
7. Thomas Rundell: *Narratives of Voyages towards the North-West, in search of a Passage to Cathay and India, 1496–1631*: Hakluyt Society, 1849. The original of Keeling's journal has been lost and it has been suggested that it was a forgery, but it is now generally accepted as genuine. It was accepted as such by E. K. Chambers and reproduced from Rundell's account in his *William Shakespeare: A Study of Facts and Problems*.

### 14. End of an Epoch, 1600–04

1. Mark Eccles: *Shakespeare in Warwickshire*: University of Wisconsin Press, 1961: p. 98.
2. *Poetical Miscellany of the Time of James I*, ed. J. O. Halliwell for the Percy Society, 1845.
3. E. K. Chambers: *William Shakespeare: A Study of Facts and Problems*: vol. 2: Clarendon Press, Oxford (from Lambarde family MS): p. 327.
4. Reg. Com. Scot., 5 May 1589.
5. Gilbert Dugdale: *Time Triumphant*, printed by R. B., London, 1604.
6. Calendar of State Papers, Spain, 1485–1509, vol. 1 (1862), no. 210.
7. It took its name from the French province of Maine.
8. Quoted by Rosalind Miles in *Ben Jonson: His Life and Work*: Routledge & Keegan Paul, London, 1986.
9. PRO – Audit Office – Declared Accounts – Treasurer of the Chamber, Roll 41, Bundle No. 388.
10. Sidney Lee: *A Life of William Shakespeare*: Macmillan & Co., New York, 1916: p. 380.
11. G. F. Warner: Cat. Dulwich MSS: pp. 26–7.

### 15. The King's Servant, 1603–05

1. A. L. Rowse: *The Case Books of Simon Forman: Sex and Society in Shakespeare's Age*: Picador, 1976.
2. *The Prince*: trans. W. T. Marriott, 1908, p. 22: www.gutenberg.org/ebooks/1932

### 16. Ember Days, 1604–11

1. 'William Shakespeare' from *Brief Lives* by John Aubrey: ed. Oliver Lawson Dick: Secker & Warburg, 1949.
2. Mairi Macdonald: 'A New Discovery about Shakespeare's Estate in Old Stratford': *Shakespeare Quarterly*, vol. 45, no. 1, Spring 1994: pp. 87–9, quotes the Archer Papers. SBT. DR 37. Box 113.15. Shakespeare 'gave the said land w[i]th his daughter in marryage to Mr. Hall ...'
3. Sly had appeared in *Three Deadly Sins* around 1587. He appears in the 'Induction' to Marston's *The Malcontent* (c. 1603) as a playgoer.

4. Quoted by Cathy Shrank: 'Civility and the City in Coriolanus': *Shakespeare Quarterly*, 54, Winter 2003: p. 408.

### 17. Retirement, 1612–13
1. Michael Wood: *In Search of Shakespeare*: BBC Worldwide, London, 2003: pp. 201, 315, 330. Treasurer's Accounts in the Bodleian Library. MS A239, leaf 47.
2. Marston and his father had stood as sureties for the admission of Thomas Greene to the Middle Temple in 1595.
3. Charles Nicholl: 'A Naughty House': *London Review of Books*: 24 June 2010.
4. L. P. Smith: *Life and Letters of Sir Henry Wotton*: vol. 2: Oxford, 1907: pp. 32–3.
5. Ibid, p. 17.

### 18. Last Will and Testament, 1614–16
1. John Rogers, the Vicar.
2. The details remained hidden until 1964, when the records of the Stratford Consistory Court were discovered in the Kent County Archives.
3. 'Happy is he who to become wise / By the difficulties of others serves his apprenticeship.'
4. A seal ring was discovered in a field called Mill Close next to Holy Trinity church in March 1810. It was found by a woman called Mrs Martin who was working there. It bore the initials 'W. S.' and was of the Elizabethan period. She sold it to the local historian and lawyer Robert Bell Wheler for 36s. It was presented to the Shakespeare Birthplace Trust by his sister in 1868. The letters on the ring are intertwined with a 'bowen' or true lovers' knot. See http://findingshakespeare.co.uk

### Epilogue
1. He was the stepson of Thomas Russell of Alderminster, who was one of the overseers of Shakespeare's will.
2. The family epitaphs were recorded by Sir William Dugdale in the 1650s and recut in the 1840s.

# Bibliography

Manuscripts
Borough of Stratford-upon-Avon: Accounts of the Chamberlains: Shakespeare
    Birthplace Trust Library (SBT).
Borough of Stratford-upon-Avon: Council Books of the Corporation: SBT.
Wheler, Robert Bell: Wheler Papers: SBT


Articles, Papers & Theses
Nate Eastman: 'The Rumbling Body Politic: Metaphorical Location and
    Metaphorical Government in Coriolanus': *Early Modern Literary Studies*, May
    2007.
Victor Houliston: 'The Hare and the Drum: Robert Person's Writings on the English
    Succession, 1593–6': *Renaissance Studies*, vol. 14, no. 2, 2000.
David McKeen: 'A Memory of Honour: A Study of the House of Cobham in Kent in
    Elizabeth I's Reign': PhD Thesis, University of Birmingham, 1964.
Edward H. Thompson: 'Macbeth, King James and the Witches': paper presented at
    conference on 'Lancashire Witches' at the University of Lancaster: December 1993:
    tesco.net/-eandcthompson/Macbeth.htm


Books
John Aubrey: *Brief Lives*: ed. Oliver Lawson Dick: Secker & Warburg, London, 1949.
E. R. C. Brinkworth: *Shakespeare and the Bawdy Court of Stratford*: Phillimore,
    Chichester, 1973.
Joseph P. Byrne: *Daily Life during the Black Death*: The Greenwood Press, Westport
    CT, 2006.
*The Cambridge History of English and American Literature*: 18 vols: Cambridge
    University Press, 1907–21.
Bernard Capp: *The World of John Taylor, The Water Poet, 1578–1653*: Clarendon
    Press, Oxford, 1994.
E. K. Chambers: *Notes on the History of the Revels Office under the Tudors*: A. H.
    Bullen, London, 1906.
E. K. Chambers: *The Elizabethan Stage*: 4 vols: Clarendon Press, Oxford, 1923.
E. K. Chambers: *William Shakespeare: A Study of Facts and Problems*: 2 vols:
    Oxford University Press, 1930.
Tarnya Cooper: *Searching for Shakespeare*: National Portrait Gallery, London, 2006.
Christopher Devlin: *The Life of Robert Southwell, Poet and Martyr*: Sidgwick &
    Jackson, London, 1967.
Michael Dobson and Stanley Wells (eds): *The Oxford Companion to Shakespeare*:
    Oxford University Press, 2001.
John Downes: *Roscius Anglicanus*: Benjamin Blom, Inc, New York, 1968 (original pub. 1708).

Mark Eccles: *Shakespeare in Warwickshire*: University of Wisconsin Press, 1963.

Alice Fairfax-Lucy: *Charlecote and the Lucys*: Oxford University Press, 1958.

Nicholas Fogg: *Stratford-upon-Avon: Portrait of a Town*: Phillimore, Chichester, 1986.

R. A. Foulkes (ed.): *The Henslowe Papers*: 2 vols: Scolar Press, London, 1977.

Levi Fox (ed.): *Minutes and Accounts of the Corporation of Stratford-upon-Avon and Other Records, Volume 5, 1593–1598*: Dugdale Society, 1990.

E. I. Fripp: *Master Richard Quiney*: Oxford University Press, 1924.

Rocellus Sheridan Guernsey: *Ecclesiastical Law in Hamlet: The Burial of Ophelia*: Bretano Bros, New York, 1885.

Andrew Gurr: *The Shakespearean Playing Companies*: Clarendon Press, Oxford, 1996.

Paul E. J. Hammer: *The Polarisation of Elizabethan Politics: The Political Career of Robert Devereux, 2nd Earl of Essex, 1585–97*: Cambridge University Press, 1999.

*Harvard Concordance to Shakespeare*: Cambridge, Mass., 1973.

Park Honan: *Christopher Marlowe: Poet and Spy*: Oxford University Press, 2005.

J. Leslie Hotson: *The Death of Christopher Marlowe*: The Nonesuch Press, 1925.

C. M. Ingleby, *Shakespeare and the Enclosure of the Common Fields at Welcombe*: 1885.

Joan Lane: *John Hall and his Patients*: SBT, 1996.

Sidney Lee: *A Life of William Shakespeare*: rev. edn: John Lane, London, 1916.

Rosalind Miles: *Ben Jonson: His Life and Work*: Routledge & Kegan Paul, London, 1986.

Allardyce Nicholl: *English Drama: A Modern Viewpoint*: Chambers, London, 1968.

Charles Nicholl: *The Lodger: Shakespeare on Silver Street*: Allen Lane, London, 2007.

Eric Partridge: *Shakespeare's Bawdy*: 2nd edn: Routledge & Kegan Paul, London, 1955.

Tanya Pollard (ed.): *Shakespeare's Theater: A Sourcebook*: Blackwell, Oxford, 2004.

Nicholas Rowe: *Some Account of the Life &c of William Shakespear*: Jacob Tomson, London, 1709.

A. L. Rowse: *Simon Forman, Sex and Society in Shakespeare's Age*: Weidenfeld & Nicholson, London, 1974.

Richard Savage (ed.): *Minutes and Accounts of the Corporation of Stratford-upon-Avon and Other Records, Volume 3, 1577–1586*: Dugdale Society, 1926.

Richard Savage et al. (eds), *Minutes and Accounts of the Corporation of Stratford-upon-Avon and Other Records, Volume 4, 1586–1592*: Dugdale Society, 1929.

S. Schoenbaum: *William Shakespeare: A Documentary Life*: Clarendon Press, Oxford, in association with The Scolar Press, 1976.

William A. Sessions: *Henry Howard, the Poet Earl of Surrey: A Life*: Clarendon Press, Oxford, 1999.

William Shakespeare, *The Complete Works*: ed. Stanley Wells, Gary Taylor, John Jowett and William Montgomery: 2nd edn: Oxford University Press, 2005.

Steve Sohmur: *The Opening Day at Shakespeare's Globe*: Manchester University Press, 1999.

Martin Spevack (ed.): *The Harvard Concordance to Shakespeare*: Belknap Press, 1974.

Revd John Ward: *Diary, 1648–79*: ed. Charles Severn from the original preserved in the Library of the Medical Society of London, 1839.

John S. Wilks: *The Idea of Conscience in Renaissance Tragedy*: Routledge: London and New York, 1990.

# Index